Transgressive Art Films

Transgressive Art Films

Extremity, Ethics, and Controversial Images of Sex and Violence

Oliver Kenny

EDINBURGH
University Press

Edinburgh University Press is one of the leading university presses in the UK. We publish academic books and journals in our selected subject areas across the humanities and social sciences, combining cutting- edge scholarship with high editorial and production values to produce academic works of lasting importance. For more information visit our website: edinburghuniversitypress.com

© Oliver Kenny, 2023, 2025

Kenny, Oliver. 'Beyond Critical Partisanship: Ethical Witnessing and Long Takes of Sexual Violence'. *Studies in European Cinema* 19, no. 2 (2020): 164–78. https://doi.org /10.1080/17411548.2020.1778846. Chapter 5 draws on and revises this article with permission from Taylor and Francis, https://www.tandfonline.com/

Kenny, Oliver. 'Moodysson, Ardenne, Derrida: Reading Genre, Extremity and Controversy through the Art–Pornography of *A Hole in My Heart*'. *Journal of Scandinavian Cinema* 10, no. 1 (2020): 67–83. https://doi.org/10.1386/jsca_00014_1. Chapter 7 is a revised and expanded version of this article with permission from Intellect Books.

Edinburgh University Press Ltd
13 Infirmary Street,
Edinburgh, EH1 1LT

First published in hardback by Edinburgh University Press 2023

Typeset in 12 on 14pt Arno Pro and Myriad Pro
by Cheshire Typesetting Ltd, Cuddington, Cheshire

A CIP record for this book is available from the British Library

ISBN 978 1 4744 8393 3 (hardback)
ISBN 978 1 4744 8394 0 (paperback)
ISBN 978 1 4744 8395 7 (webready PDF)
ISBN 978 1 4744 8396 4 (epub)

The right of Oliver Kenny to be identified as the author of this work has been asserted in accordance with the Copyright, Designs and Patents Act 1988, and the Copyright and Related Rights Regulations 2003 (SI No. 2498).

Contents

Acknowledgements vi
Author's Note viii

Introduction 1
1. Transgression 22
2. Visibility, Proximity, Duration 59
3. Sex, Violence and Sexual Violence 89
4. Trauma 116
5. Witnessing 139
6. Limits 163
7. Genre 183
8. Cinema Art World 208
Conclusion 240

Filmography 243
Bibliography 247
Index 277

Acknowledgements

The early gestation of this research was financially supported by the UK Arts and Humanities Research Council in the form of a Research Preparation Scholarship at the University of Cambridge, and by Queen Mary University of London with a Principal's Studentship for my doctoral research.

The project began life through discussions with Laura McMahon and Emma Wilson who inspired and encouraged me before I even realised I wanted to go into research. Enormous thanks to Libby Saxton and Jenny Chamarette who were the most wonderful doctoral supervisors, from whom I learnt so much, and to whom I owe so much. Thanks to the Institute of Communication Studies (ISTC), and to Mehdi Ghassemi in particular, who gave me the time and space to finish this book.

Thanks to those who graciously provided feedback on this book and related work: Joaquin Montalva Armanet, Laurence Kent, Julian Koch, Michael Portal and Victoria Walden. To Lucy Bolton, Olivier Estèves, Austin Fisher, Maria Flood, James Harvey, Nick Jones, Tina Kendall, Sebastien LeFait and Mathilda Mroz for advice and support over the years. To David Cooke and Craig Lapper for their generous knowledge about the British Board of Film Classification (BBFC).

Thanks to the anonymous reviewers both at the proposal and manuscript stages, who provided excellent feedback that helped to improve the book and its argument. Thanks to all those at and associated with Edinburgh University Press, who have been really helpful and supportive throughout the publication process, including but not limited to Gillian Leslie, Sam Johnson, Grace Balfour-Harle, Barbara Eastman and Susan Tricklebank.

To those whose hospitality and company I've enjoyed many times as part of research and work: Elspeth, Haxie and Rob, James B, Kirsty, Maria, Pierre, Rachel and Patrick, Sarah, Susann and Dan, and especially Florent and Aurélia, Mum, Rachel and Alex, whose welcome has always been so generous.

To my parents, Jane Kenny and Chris Kenny, without whom none of this would ever have happened. To Rachel Kenny, always there through thick and thin, a friend as well as a sibling.

To Magdalena Krysztoforska, whose feedback on this book was invaluable, who has kept me sane throughout the process, and who makes life wonderful for more reasons than I could possibly list here.

Author's Note

A number of texts written in languages other than English that have been consulted in the course of this project are not currently available in English translation. For these works, the translations are my own, and the original reference is provided in the bibliography. For those works available in English translation, the bibliographic reference refers to the translation.

All films are referred to by their English title except for *Baise-moi* which is commonly referred to in English by its original title. The original titles can be found in the filmography at the end of the book.

Two chapters draw on previously published work. Chapter 5 draws on and revises 'Beyond Critical Partisanship: Ethical Witnessing and Long Takes of Sexual Violence'. *Studies in European Cinema* 19, no. 2 (2020): 164–78. Chapter 7 is a revised and expanded version of 'Moodysson, Ardenne, Derrida: Reading Genre, Extremity and Controversy through the Art-Pornography of *A Hole in My Heart*'. *Journal of Scandinavian Cinema* 10, no. 1 (2020): 67–83.

Introduction

Walkouts, fainting, outrage, shock, anger, outcry. From the late 1990s, these became repeated responses to a number of affectively challenging films containing graphic images of sex, violence and sexual violence. *Sombre, Baise-moi, Romance, Irreversible, Twentynine Palms, Trouble Every Day* and *Anatomy of Hell* divided audiences, and created controversy at film festivals, in critical circles and for censors. No other kinds of film in the last twenty-five years have come close to provoking such strong and polarising reactions, across continents, in the specialised and mainstream press, both in the immediate aftermath of their release, and also for years thereafter. They were considered confrontational, aggressive, an attack on the spectator, extreme, but also politically and ethically ambiguous. It was a trend, but not a movement – there was no manifesto or group statement – even as audiences rapidly began grouping them together as a distinct form of cinema based on sensation and extremity. These films have been variously described as 'New French Extremity',[1] 'New European Extremism',[2] 'extreme cinema',[3] 'extreme art cinema',[4] 'new extremism',[5] a '*cinéma du corps*',[6] '*cinéma brut*'[7] and 'extreme realism',[8] as well as 'unwatchable',[9] or films of 'brutal intimacy'.[10] Importantly, despite their graphic scenes of sex and violence, they were not seen only by a handful of dedicated cinephiles on a Tuesday night in a dusty cinema in the Latin quarter, but were given highly promoted premieres at Cannes and double-page spreads in major film magazines, while the filmmakers and stars did the media rounds with all the notable newspapers. This was graphic sex and gory violence being treated as art. Each film was celebrated by some, decried by others, but rarely left its viewers unmoved, given the long, graphic and proximate images of sex, violence and sexual violence. For some, these were welcomely challenging art films, pushing at the boundaries of acceptability and expectation; for others, they were sordid incorporations of gory horror and pornography into the pristine world of arthouse cinema.

As discussion spread well beyond reviews of individual films, it became clear that this was a significant socio-cultural phenomenon. In the media, numerous debates arose about censorship, about the legal frameworks governing sexual and violent imagery, and about depictions of rape and sexual assault. In universities, these films provoked discussions about the ethics and politics of cinema, trigger warnings, and the appropriateness of including particular kinds of images on syllabi. Elsewhere, online communities of cinephiles, horror fans and thrill-seekers latched onto the films, at the same time as certain films were provoking street protests, petition campaigns and changes to classification guidelines. The variety and passion of these debates demonstrated that these films were tapping into broader societal and cultural issues that extended far beyond any one corpus of films. To understand what is at stake with these controversies, it is not enough simply to focus on particular images from individual films. Instead, we require a broader frame that extends from close analysis all the way out to the production, distribution, and exhibition ecosystem of cinema as a whole, which, following Howard Becker, I will call the 'cinema art world'.[11] Given the divergence of opinion, the stylistic differences and varied subject matter, this is no easy task, but we need a coherent theory that brings together all these elements in order to explain and understand how these films become scandalous and controversial amongst all the sexual and violent films made every year. We need an approach that can account for these films on the level of film form, on the level of reception and on the level of theory all at once, because no one scale of analysis can speak to the complexity of these films as a phenomenon. I argue that the stakes of this analysis are unusually high for film-studies research as they pertain not only to my interpretation of the films and their context, but also to the ethical and political implications of engaging in such interpretative work, which itself is part of the discursive construction and framing of these transgressive films. In this book, I present a theory that is attentive to text and context, to the details of a single shot, but also to how that shot might be understood by audiences, festival programmers, distributors, censors and scholars. Why are these films controversial? Why are they described as extreme or as transgressive? What boundaries or limits are they transgressing? What do they and the discourse around them tell us about cinema today?

This project emerges out of an interest in understanding the original corpus listed above, even as my research has led me far beyond it. Commentary on this generation's most scandalous or controversy-prone films tends to coalesce around this small number of films, with an almost universal consensus developing among scholars and audiences that these films are controversial and extreme in some way.[12] They are therefore a natural starting point in the development of a heuristic for identifying and understanding what I shall call 'transgressive art films'. Transgressive art films include images previously considered outside the purview of art cinema, which are recuperated and celebrated as novel and innovative, thereby provoking debate and discussion not only about the individual film, but about the nature of art cinema more broadly. Many films are transgressive in one sense or another, but transgressive art films are those whose transgressions are legitimised by a variety of stakeholders within the cinema art world, such that they become officially transgressive, and celebrated or decried as such, rather than ignored or forgotten. Transgressive art films transgress specific boundaries in specific ways, and are thereby recuperated as legitimately transgressive, and as art, rather than being dismissed. If, following Pierre Bourdieu, we consider art (and art cinema) to be a game with strict but unwritten rules, transgressive art films are allowed to bend and break the rules, which are then recomposed to incorporate and legitimise the infraction.[13] Transgressive art films are a socio-cultural phenomenon that requires exploration and theorisation beyond a limited corpus of films, so that we can understand new films that follow a similar trajectory, and the broader social and cultural frameworks that guide and construct the reception and interpretation of controversial films.

Through close analysis of the images of these controversial films, as well as in-depth examination of their reception discourse, underlying patterns in the images and reception of these 'core' films emerged, which developed into a fully fledged heuristic, allowing for the identification of other films that function in much the same way. Inversely, the heuristic also allows for the particular kinds of controversial film under discussion here to be clearly delineated from other sexual and/or violent films that do not provoke the same scandals. The process of defining and legitimising transgressive art films is complex and involves numerous stakeholders from production through to exhibition, with directors, actors, film festivals, censors, distributors, publicists, exhibitors, interviewers, critics and scholars all contributing to the interpretation and framing of particular imagery. To bring this all together requires a dynamic but coherent framework based upon three pillars: film form, reception and theory.

The first pillar is film form. Through my own close analysis and a meta-analysis of commentary and classification reports on the core seven films, I identified the distinguishing formal features of these films as clustering around three aspects of their depiction of sex, violence and sexual violence: visibility, proximity and duration. The content of the image is certainly important – indeed each of these films combines sex and violence to a degree that is already unusual in art cinema – but an overfocus on diegetic acts misses the crucial point about how such acts are presented. Visibility refers to what can and cannot be seen in an image. This is most obviously relevant in the graphic depiction of aroused genitalia, penetration and ejaculation in sex and rape scenes; the visibility of such acts is normally reserved for pornography, and is therefore censored and restricted in most countries. This is also relevant to gory acts of violence such as cannibalism and battery with a weapon. Proximity refers both to the proximity of the camera to sexual and violent acts, and to the communication of the material, affective dimension of such acts. There are close-ups of vulvas during childbirth, sex and rape, there are close-ups of faces during sex and while being beaten, there are travelling close-ups along skin during sex. During the most shocking and discussed scenes, there are often close-ups, as well as a variety of shots that emphasise touch: of fingertips caressing skin, of vagina on dildo, of penis on anus, of baseball bat on nose, of hands around throats. Commentary on the most violent and sexual sequences also shows an unusual focus on how they drew viewers in and made them 'feel'. Duration refers to the length of shots and sequences, as well as to how long viewers perceived such scenes to be. The shot and scene length in these films is often long, and the pace of the films quite slow, with viewers frequently commenting on how drawn-out sequences feel. In several scenes of sexual violence, minimal editing ensures that viewers experience the temporality of the attack in much the same way as the characters.

Each of these elements is often framed in terms of 'too much': genitals are too visible, the violence feels too close, the rape goes on for too long. And yet, shots of visible sex are often quite brief, affective proximate shots of sex are balanced out by more distanced shots, long takes are longer than average, longer perhaps than is desirable, but relatively short if compared to much self-shot amateur pornography, or narrative films shot in a single take. In other words, they might go a bit beyond rules and conventions about visibility, proximity and duration, but not that much. They are marginally transgressive, but not excessively so. Given that censorship boards and film audiences tend to allow art films a certain room for manoeuvre, sometimes officially, the marginality of this 'too much' is important. These marginal transgressions function precisely as a bending, breaking and remaking of the rules that is particular to transgressive art films, while films whose transgressions are more than just marginal are not recuperated as art. This heuristic, explored in detail in Chapter 2, identifies clear patterns in how individual films have been read, thereby providing a formal account of what links these controversial films, and allowing for the identification of other films that use visibility, proximity and duration in comparable ways. These elements have been evoked separately in relation to individual films, but given the stylistic differences between these core films, scholars have tended to overlook the formal connections that arise if we focus on questions such as 'how visible?', 'how close?' and 'how long?'. Importantly, I am not simply identifying an audiovisual style – certain repeated stylistic choices across the films – but a pattern that matters, a pattern that plays a role in the broader stakes of these films, and this pattern is therefore central to the close analysis in Chapters 2, 3, 4 and 5.

The second pillar is the films' reception, which entails developing a framework for understanding viewer responses. Each of these films has been divisive and polarising, leading to heated debates amongst viewers, and an unusual strength of feeling, both to celebrate and to disparage. Nonetheless, viewers who evaluated a film in polar opposite fashion, would frequently point to exactly the same scenes, and exactly the same kinds of affect in order to justify their views. The reception of films as controversial is closely linked to film form, but is not inherent to it, and so it is important to analyse how and why viewers interpret images in the ways that they do, and how these particular films lend themselves to such oppositional and polarising positions. This is central to integrating reception context into our understanding of the controversies inspired by the filmic text. Much of this book involves moving between the text and the context, both because it is impossible to grasp the impact of a film without understanding how viewers' interpretations are framed prior to their encounter with a filmic text itself, and also because those who have the greatest influence in framing how a film is understood (e.g. festivals, distributors, exhibitors, critics, scholars) actively construct rather than discover a transgressive art film.

Transgressive art films always involve intensely polarised audiences, and divided and contradictory opinions.[14] This is because these films are a challenge to the notion of the art film, they expand and change its definition, and so will always be subject to supporters and detractors. Any film that receives consensus about its artistic or non-artist status is not questioning the boundaries of art cinema. In order to understand the dissensus inspired by transgressive art films, I draw on audience-studies work on sexually violent films by Martin Barker et al. in whose work viewers are categorised as embracers, ambivalents or refusers, and meta-analysis of extreme cinema done by Mattias Frey who distinguishes between two broad kinds of response: the aesthetic embrace and the cynicism criticism.[15] Both of these are very useful in pointing to how the overall value attached to a film by a viewer tends to corollate with their pre-existing views on film art. However, if we are to grasp the full spectrum of responses, and especially how oppositional they are, we have to understand the frameworks according to which viewers are making their decision to embrace, refuse or be ambivalent towards a film.

Borrowing the concept of 'value registers' from sociologist Nathalie Heinich, I argue that we must examine the broad analytical registers underpinning different analyses.[16] Choosing to prioritise the beauty of a film (aesthetic register), or interpreting its meaning and symbolism (hermeneutic register) involves a fundamentally different approach to one that asks what kinds of images are appropriate (ethical register) or one that focuses on the pleasures and sensations of spectatorship (aesthesic register). What is implicit in this 'conflict of value registers'[17] is a position on the art status of the film being analysed: the aesthetic and hermeneutic registers tend to signal that the film is already considered as art, whereas the ethical and aesthesic registers leave the question open. In the context of transgressive art films, which are by definition on the boundary of (high) art and non-art or low art, a conflict of value registers can lead to viewers implicitly disagreeing about the fundamental artistic value of a film, which helps to explain the strength of feeling and irreconcilable disagreements in so much criticism of these films. Put succinctly, transgressive art films provoke polarising analyses and this is best understood by examining their reception through the lens of value registers.

Reception is a useful part of the heuristic for distinguishing the films under analysis from other graphically sexual and violent films. For instance, a variety of horror films (*Saw, Hostel, Martyrs, Livid, Inside*), sexually explicit films (*Shortbus, Q, Sexual Chronicles of a French Family, Leap Year, Diet of Sex, The Daughters of Fire*) and violent East Asian films (*Ichi the Killer, Oldboy, The Isle, Sympathy for Mr Vengeance, Kinatay*) have been compared to transgressive art films because of sex, violence, sexualised violence, or commonalities in style and address. However, none of these created the kinds of polarising controversy and scandal discussed at the beginning. In the case of the East Asian films, this is in part because they are likely othered, orientalised or simply misunderstood in particular ways that dampen the prospects of provoking audiences, as can be seen in the framing of such films along territorial lines by distributors such as Tartan Asia Extreme.[18] Scholars have also noted that extremity is understood differently by East Asian and Western audiences because their understandings of 'good' and 'evil' differ, again suggesting that they are received differently at the most influential film festivals in Europe and North America than they will be in their home countries.[19]

Images of rape and sexual violence offer a clear illustration of how a conflict of value registers underpins oppositional debates about transgressive art films. A viewer prioritising an ethical register might consider how the rape is depicted, how this reflects on the victim and perpetrator, how the viewer themselves is made to feel, and compare this to other images of rape, and writing on rape, in order to judge whether they consider this example to be appropriate. In this case, the emphasis is on the rape, and rape imagery more broadly. By contrast, a viewer prioritising an aesthetic register might consider the colours and the shapes in the scene, might marvel at the cinematography and sound design, might focus on the style and inventiveness of the filmmaker, considering mainly whether the image is impressive or beautiful. In this case, the emphasis is on the film as art, the rape content of the image is secondary, or even irrelevant. The same film can thereby be decried on an ethical level, and marvelled at on an aesthetic level, but such viewers are unable to properly debate or discuss, not simply because they disagree about the film, but because they disagree about the criteria on which the film should be judged. This is particularly relevant for rape imagery because there are commentators who argue that rape imagery is inherently ethically compromised, such that any aesthetic or hermeneutic engagement with it is flawed. Given the complex and heavily disputed image politics of rape, it is unsurprising that rape figures strongly in films that have provoked significant controversy.

This polarised reception is explored in Chapters 3, 4 and 5 leading to two key observations about the films and their reception. Firstly, transgressive art films support contradictory readings and remain wholly ambiguous in their political and ethical perspectives. There is no preferred reading, there is no evidently appropriate value register.[20] I argue that transgressive art films crystallise both the progressive and retrograde potential of sexual, violent and especially sexually violent imagery, providing images that can be read simultaneously as positive and negative, liberatory and exploitative, ethically productive and harmful. They contain the imagery most likely to create a conflict of value registers, a claim that rests as much on a reading of film form as on the films' reception. Secondly, I contend that this means all critical and scholarly analysis of transgressive art films involves ethical and political choices. On the one hand, this is because commentary on these films, explicitly or implicitly, always involves a claim about art, about the film's legitimacy to be treated as film art or not. Critics and scholars do not stand separate from these films' designation as art but actively participate in their recuperation and construction as film art. On the other hand, in the face of sexually violent material, it is not an anodyne choice to prioritise the hermeneutic and especially the aesthetic register. To prioritise an exploration of rape as art over the ethical register, is itself an often unacknowledged ethical and political act. There are significant ethical and political stakes to academic analysis of such imagery, that we as scholars should do more to recognise; film scholarship is part of the ecology of cinema, and it matters what we value and how we choose to value it.

The third pillar is theory. This primarily involves a consideration of transgression in art and cinema. My contention is that we must think more about type and degree of transgression, whilst also focusing on clear and identifiable boundaries. Transgressive art films include numerous elements that are 'almost-transgressive' and a limited number that are 'marginally transgressive'. The main boundaries that I focus on are legal boundaries drawn up by governments and censorship boards, and cultural boundaries about what constitutes art, although these function only as guidelines framing discourse around transgression, rather than as absolute arbiters of artistic limits. Importantly, while the understanding of such boundaries has generally been influenced by sociological theories of transgression, we must separate transgressive acts from artistic transgressions. In this book, I therefore set out the key ideas about both transgressive acts and artistic transgression, and their limitations for talking about transgressive art films. In particular, I argue that Georges Bataille is an important thinker for understanding transgression in cinema, but that his work has often been misappropriated and unhelpfully extrapolated onto artistic transgression without adapting and nuancing it, leading to a conflation of the transgressiveness of depicted acts with the transgressiveness of the images depicting such acts. We must also be more attentive to the different ways in which boundaries are transgressed. In the case of government-mandated boundaries, these can be divided into categories of 'illegal', 'forbidden' and 'restricted', which can apply both to the act of making the image, and to the image itself. Transgressive art films transgress particular boundaries in particular ways, and we require a vocabulary to distinguish these infractions, in order to identify those that matter when it comes to creating controversy. This book's theory of transgression in film provides firstly a means for talking about transgression per se in clear and precise terms, and secondly a means for discerning the important transgressions that underpin the socio-cultural ramifications and impact of the transgressive art film.

If we consider discourse around contemporary cinema and in relation to images more generally, the concept of transgression has generally been superseded by the concept of extremity. In terms of discourse, 'extreme' has come to fulfil the role 'transgression' once played, but specifically in the context of sexual or violent films, the only reliably controversial imagery in twenty-first-century cinema. 'Extreme' is used to signify the crossing of a boundary, to disparage content that is perceived to violate cultural norms, and to recuperate non-art or low-art practices within the realm of (high) art. 'Extreme' is effectively a sub-category of 'transgressive'. Nevertheless, as will be discussed in detail in Chapter 1, given that the way 'extreme' has been used in relation to cinema lacks a rigorous and coherent schema, I propose a careful and specific reassertion of the term 'transgressive' within 'transgressive art film' in order to reinstate clarity about the role that such films play within the cinema ecosystem. Transgressive art films are films that marginally transgress censorship and art-film-convention limits but are nonetheless recuperated and celebrated as art films. This definition is designed to be dynamic and include extreme films, but also to extend beyond them, acknowledging a whole cinema ecology within which the films are constructed and which impacts on their form and reception.

One way in which the almost-transgressive and the marginally transgressive are particularly useful is in providing a coherent framework for understanding the vexed boundary between art and pornography in the context of art films that include pornographic imagery. Images of visible sex remain, in cultural terms, and mostly in legal terms, the domain of pornography, with graphic displays of aroused genitals, penetration and ejaculation generally restricted in some way. Moreover, in both public and official discourse, pornography is considered mutually exclusive from art. At the same time, a cursory look at contemporary pornography shows that it can clearly be artistic, while films like *Romance* and *Anatomy of Hell* are clearly pornographic inasmuch as they show visible sex between actors on the set. While they are separate categories legally and culturally, in practice there is frequent hybridity: art and porn mix but cannot mix. While film-studies work on genre has made great progress in explaining the interactions between film form and reception, little work has considered the specific problems arising when cultural and legal forces prohibit the combination of two complementary genres in an amalgam such as 'art-pornography'. Applying ideas about marginal transgression and polarising reception to poststructuralist readings of genre boundaries, I argue that we can grasp the transgressive and liminal positioning of the transgressive art film, which for a short period, until the rules of art cinema are rewritten, is both art and not-art, pornography and not-pornography. By looking at the films both from the perspective of art cinema and from the perspective of pornography, we are able to better grasp how these films are functioning generically, how this unsettles contemporaneous perceptions of art leading to dispute and disagreement, but ultimately how such films end up being incorporated fully into the realm of art cinema, rather than rejected as pornography.

This three-pronged approach – via form, reception and theory – leads to the conclusion that transgressive art films play a specific and important role in the cinema art world. Transgressive art films are not an inevitable by-product of the cinema art world, but a central plank of its need for newness, innovation and renewal, and as such gain wide-ranging institutional support. Unlike most transgressions in film, which are ignored or dismissed, and play only a marginal role in the cinema art world, films that gain the status of transgressive art film break new ground for film art and allow for the continued renewal and innovation that characterises modern and contemporary art. The legitimisation of particular transgressions over others is always a controversial process, but whether one approves of them or not, transgressive art films are at the forefront of (re)defining what constitutes legitimate film art at any one point. For better or worse, this is why they are some of the most interesting films to analyse from the twenty-first century.

This legitimisation is not decided by any one participant in the cinema art world, but is cumulatively enacted by various agents with the cultural and symbolic capital to influence the interpretation of an individual film text, from funding and production through to exhibition and commentary. For many of those involved in this process, the procedures for recuperating a film as a transgressive art film are frequently framed in terms of 'risk'. Festival programmers, buyers and distributors take the risk by including a film on their programme or in their catalogue that might incur audience backlash, intervention from censors, or even legal prosecution. However, just as scholars and critics do not operate in a hermetically sealed space separate from the evaluation of a film as worthy of discussion, so do these parties not act according to some objective consideration of a film's value. By seeing the film as 'risky', they are recognising that it transgresses certain legal rules or artistic conventions, and by programming or distributing it, they are contributing to the recuperation of those transgressions within the space of art cinema. Seeing the transgressive art film in this way involves a macroscopic view of the whole cinema art world, understood in sociological terms as a complex ecosystem with a variety of stakeholders, all of whom operate within a particular framework, but are also constantly rewriting those rules through the process of applying and enforcing them.[21] At the same time, these rules pertain to the minutiae of individual shots and are inflected through their reception according to a variety of value registers: we can only understand this broad socio-cultural phenomenon by paying attention to all levels of the cinema art world, from close analysis of individual frames, through the discourse constructed around them, up to global distribution and film-festival networks.

*

One of the central problems that arose from this project was the question of definition. The vast body of writing and discussion on artistic controversy has led to a panoply of poorly defined terms to describe films, scandals and moral panics, including 'obscene', 'transgressive', 'pornographic', 'offensive', 'immoral', 'harmful' or 'extreme'. In the twenty-first century, the idea of extremity was quickly attached to the seven core films. Unfortunately, 'extreme' has been used promiscuously by commentators to refer to many elements of controversial films, including diegetic acts, the viewing experience, images, filmmaking, pleasure, indifference, defamiliarisation, corporealities and the films themselves. Although ostensibly designed to frame a range of films, most early accounts of extreme cinema also focused entirely on just one or two films, thus further muddying the waters. As a way of clarifying how these films function, and the role they play in the cinema art world, I chose a new term – transgressive art film – to point to the sociocultural phenomenon as well as its key elements, thus resolving many of the definitional problems that remain in writing on extreme cinema. This term designates the phenomenon of a small number of controversial films recuperated each year by the cinema art world as part of an expansion of the definition of film art, and as such is distinct from most previous theorisations of extreme cinema.

There are some scholars who use the term 'extreme' but do not fit with my suggested heuristic of films that create controversy and polarise audiences. Elena del Río, for instance, proposes to analyse a 'vital ethology of extreme cinemas' but has chapters on David Lynch and Rainer Werner Fassbinder, and her central argument is about readings of violence in society and in film generally, rather than a specific argument about 'extreme' images of sex or violence.[22] In a different fashion, Aaron Kerner and Jonathan Knapp see extremity as an 'affective strategy' linked to body genres, especially pornography.[23] Such a broad affect-focused approach leads them to include *Borat*, *Jackass*, *127 Hours*, internet reaction videos, animated series *Family Guy*, and horror films such as *Hostel*, *Saw* and *Inside* in their analysis, the reception of which shares little with the seven films at the heart of this study. Julien Bétan similarly includes discussion of mondo films, snuff, *The Texas Chainsaw Massacre* and *The Human Centipede*, while somewhat arbitrarily disregarding any discussion of pornography.[24] In these cases, while the authors may touch upon some films discussed in this book, there is no great overlap with the specific ideas of controversy and scandal that underpin my choice of films for this study. Moreover, there is little concerted effort to theorise the extreme, and to reflect on its appropriateness as a term to describe the films under analysis.

Many journalistic accounts follow James Quandt, who defines the 'new French extremity' predominantly in terms of the acts that are made visible: 'gang rapes, bashings and slashings and blindings, hard-ons and vulvas, cannibalism, sadomasochism and incest, fucking and fisting, sluices of cum and gore'.[25] Scholars tend to move away from such a focus on acts given that all of these can be seen in horror, exploitation and pornographic films, and so cannot be considered identifying tropes of extreme cinema. However, in what I would argue is only a subtle shift away from this content-based definition, many scholars have focused on the inclusion of so-called low-art or non-art tropes from horror and pornography as key to the definition of extreme cinema. Simon Hobbs and Alison Taylor focus their definitions of 'extreme art cinema' (Hobbs) or 'new extremism' (Taylor) on 'cultural slippage and hybridisation' or the 'the transgression of genre expectations' between high-art and low-art forms, while Lisa Downing describes such films as 'blur[ring] the boundaries between art film and porno flick'.[26] While this is certainly the case, these definitions are not specific enough about what is being transgressed/slipped/hybridised/blurred, nor about how and to what extent; they can therefore be applied to an unhelpfully large corpus of films. Although these scholarly accounts frame their definitions in terms of genres rather than depicted acts, there is little substantive difference between the inclusion of 'hard-ons and vulvas' in an art film, and a blurring of the line between art and pornography. Adding extra genres, Troy Bordun argues that 'extreme cinema' is 'reorienting and restructuring the notions of genre(s) and spectatorship', notably 'the avant-garde, documentary, melodrama, pornography, and horror', but again this is overly broad and tends moreover towards a reductive account of each of these (super-)genres.[27]

Another common approach is to focus on the nature of the viewing experience, especially the communication of sensation and materiality. This has been done most influentially by Martine Beugnet in her analysis of a 'cinema of sensation', and Tim Palmer in his reading of a '*cinéma du corps*'.[28] In contrast to dismissive accounts such as Quandt's, Beugnet argues against this rejection of sensation from the realm of art film. Her book, which includes discussion of violent images, but is focused more broadly on sensation, pleads for a 'third way' between reading films cerebrally and corporeally, advocating for narrative films that introduce sensation into the viewing experience. Palmer's book is less celebratory than Beugnet's and more descriptive, but similarly focuses on how it feels to watch these films, arguing that they are 'hard to watch' and 'leave[] us stunned, affronted and ultimately wary'.[29] Tanya Horeck and Tina Kendall's collected edition on 'new extremism' similarly focuses on sensation, but also on the ethical potential of such an affective confrontation with the spectator. They suggest that 'new extreme' films are characterised by self-reflexivity, a complex and often contradictory nature, provocation as a mode of address, and the destruction of the passive spectator.[30] Whilst these analyses are complex and thoughtful, in almost all these pieces, there is an evocation of a singular or idealised spectator, who should share their experience of the film with the author, whether that be to criticise, to praise or something else. This is not a problem in and of itself, but focusing on singular readings of the films will always give a partial account, and cannot explain the divisive and polarised reactions of audiences. Moreover, most of this writing involves close analysis of a single film, perhaps two, meaning that their analysis does not lend itself easily to application beyond the subjects of the chapter.

This issue also arises in Asbjørn Grønstad's analysis of 'post-millennial art cinema' and the 'unwatchable', which requires a panoply of invented terms in order to account for different sub-categories of unwatchable film: 'the inwatchable, razorblade gestures, entropic cinema, scopic entelechy, the metapornographic, and slow modes of seeing'.[31] Most of these terms are focused on abstract ideas of spectatorship that do not account for the diversity of readings that these films received from actual viewers, simplifying the complexity of the actual reception. While these definitions hint at the reception of the films, they mostly direct us towards idealised experiences, extrapolated from those of the author, rather than to actual responses from actual viewers. Thus, while these phenomenological and spectatorship-focused accounts will be interesting in terms of close analysis, providing useful data about how scholars interpreted the films, they are only indirectly helpful in thinking through how the films provoke controversy, and how such film form leads to divided audiences. Indeed, most scholarly analyses position themselves explicitly against Quandt, critiquing his normative ideas about what film can and should be, and showing how the films can be read as politically engaged, profound and insightful rather than frivolous, superficial and indulging in shock for shock's sake. In other words, scholars and critics often position themselves in opposition to other commentators, claiming that the others are wrong to be so critical or generous of the films. This, I argue, is the central issue with much of this work, which fails to recognise not only that there are numerous perspectives that audiences can have on a film, but that the deep disagreements that arise from transgressive art films are key to their transgressiveness, and to what makes them so controversial. At stake here is not a debate about who is right about the interpretation of a particular film, but a full understanding of the nature of transgressive filmmaking. A theory of transgressive film that cannot account for multiple contradictory analyses of a film is not worth having, and in order to achieve that, we need to examine a wide variety of scholarly, critical and popular responses to the films.

Two major studies that address this problem are Mattias Frey's *Extreme Cinema* and Martin Barker's work, especially his co-authored BBFC report *Audiences and Receptions of Sexual Violence in Contemporary Cinema*.[32] Frey is one of the few scholars to consider 'extreme cinema' as a cultural phenomenon rather than as a genre or movement, and therefore also provides a more compelling definition of extreme films. Employing a cluster definition to circumscribe his corpus, Frey notes that most of his criteria are not aesthetic, but rather relate to 'institutional, business, functional, artistic, critical, regulatory, and popular discourses'.[33] He is highly critical of many scholars' focus on the film as text, especially on the appeal to an idealised spectator. He argues that in order to understand extreme cinema, we must decentre the viewer from the analysis, and explore the impact of film festivals, distributors, marketing, regulation and filmmaker interviews on the discourse of extremity and extreme cinema. 'Extreme' here is understood as a label, an advertising strategy, a discourse and a genre, a film-industrial term as much as a critical one. Frey is interested in actual audiences as seen through IMDb message boards, fan sites and cinephile fora, as well as through cinema-ticket and DVD sales, streaming revenues, and interviews with distributors and festival organisers. His is in effect a work of current film history giving many of the industrial details that are missed by scholars who work only with the finished text.

This interest in the experiences of actual audiences is also integral to Martin Barker's generally underexamined work on images of sexual violence. In their 2007 BBFC report, Barker and his team interviewed dozens of viewers of sexually violent films – including *Baise-Moi* and *Irreversible* – in order to find out how actual audiences responded to the films. Their most important conclusion was that spectatorial responses do follow certain tendencies but are heterogeneous and stubbornly refuse the kind of idealised responses that are implicitly evoked in many writings on extreme films. Although the BBFC was unhappy about the difficulty of applying these findings to regulation and broadly ignored the report, it is in fact wonderfully revealing of the multiplicity of responses to images of sexual violence. Frey's and Barker et al.'s work addresses the central gaps in much work on transgressive art films: reception by non-professional audiences (i.e. not newspaper critics or academics), and the processes after production and before general release that bring a film to the attention of any one viewer. Nonetheless, Frey's and Barker et al.'s studies are works of film history and of reception studies that actively de-emphasise theory in favour of a focus on factual details and aggregate data, and that ultimately do not attempt to theorise, only to describe the extreme and the transgressive.

What should be clear from this overview is that there is ultimately little consensus about how to talk about controversial images of sex and violence, about how to approach these films, about what it means to describe them as extreme or transgressive, or what other moniker to choose. Although the concept of extremity has gained currency over the last decade with a handful of monographs being published on the subject, each has quite different corpora, and all but one provide little sustained examination of these films as a socio-cultural phenomenon rather than as a generic grouping of stylistically or ethically similar products.[34] Exploring instead the dynamic term 'transgressive art film' situates these films socially and culturally within a global cinema ecosystem, as an integral part of the cinema art world's processes of innovation and renewal.

*

Transgressive Art Films is split into three parts: the first part presents the theory and the main corpus of films; the middle section focuses more on film form and reception; the final three chapters explore theory and the circulation of the films in greater detail. As well as the seven core films, another ten films will be subject to close analysis as part of my argument: *Battle in Heaven, A New Life, The Brown Bunny, Free Will, The Tribe, Holiday, Raw, In My Skin, A Hole in My Heart* and *A Serbian Film*. Including long, proximate and visible shots of sex and violence, as well as provoking controversy and polarising reviews on release, these films are exemplary illustrations of transgressive art films, crystallising the ideas developed in this book. These ideas are not, however, limited in their application to these films and can be applied to other transgressive art films. For instance, other films that could have been analysed are *I Stand Alone, Enter the Void, Taxidermia, The Idiots, Antichrist, Fat Girl, Climax, See the Sea, We Fuck Alone* and so on.

Chapter 1, 'Transgression', considers theories of transgression and extremity as well as the popular and critical discourses around such terms. I argue that terms such as 'transgression' and 'extremity' have tended to be used in vague and promiscuous ways, and that to resolve this and usefully theorise the transgressive art film, it is important to be clear about what boundaries are being crossed, how, to what extent and by whom. In order to do so, this chapter firstly distinguishes between transgressive acts and artistic transgression, summarising the key sociological work that has been done on transgressive acts and on transgression in modern and contemporary fine art, in order to suggest which elements of it are useful for thinking about transgression in cinema. The main lessons to be drawn from this work are that type and degree of transgression matter, as well as the context of the transgression, and the identity of the transgressor. I thus propose that we consider artistic transgressions as involving institutionally recognised marginal transgressions of the limits of that art world's contemporaneous definition of art. This is a very specific form of legitimised transgression, distinct from the most basic idea of transgression as the crossing of a boundary. Secondly, I provide an account of the different ways in which films can transgress legal boundaries and incur censorship, and how these different forms of transgression are received and contained. Separating transgressive films into 'illegal', 'forbidden' and 'restricted', I show how attentiveness to the type and degree of transgression enables a clearer and more coherent understanding of what it means for a film to transgress. Finally, I explain how value registers allow us to understand the transgressions of controversial films that do not transgress any censorship boundaries, as well as their reception. Where many commentators revert to vague claims about transgressing cultural norms or genre expectations, I show through the conflict of value registers how disputes between viewers of transgressive art films remain tied to strong boundaries such as art/non-art, censored/free-to-view, legal/illegal. In sum, this chapter provides a clear framework for what it means for a transgressive art film to transgress, it shows that it is possible to talk clearly and specifically about artistic transgression, and it proposes a way of theorising extremity as a contemporary sub-category of transgression focused on images of sex and violence. It allows us to identify not only what transgression means, but which transgressions matter.

Chapter 2, 'Visibility, Proximity, Duration', explains the heuristic for identifying transgressive art films in terms of film form, exploring how visibility, proximity and duration are used in these films, especially in the most controversial sequences of sex, violence and sexual violence. The corpus for this analysis is the seven core films that both provoked unusual and significant consternation and scandal on their release, and have been included almost universally in critical and scholarly discussions about controversial images of sex and violence, most notably in explorations of extreme cinema. The films in question are *Sombre*, *Romance*, *Baise-moi*, *Irreversible*, *Anatomy of Hell*, *Twentynine Palms* and *Trouble Every Day*. These heuristic elements play a role in the broader cultural stakes of the film, and are not simply evocative of an audiovisual style. I am not simply identifying a pattern, but a pattern that matters for our broader understanding of transgressive art films as a socio-cultural phenomenon. This chapter will show how the theoretical reflections on marginal transgressions in Chapter 1 apply to visibility, proximity and duration, and these conclusions will then form key parts of the close analysis that follows.

Chapter 3, 'Sex, Violence and Sexual Violence', is the first of three chapters focused on the connections between film form and reception. This chapter considers how transgressive art films set up a conflict of value registers. It explores how different film-analytical lenses (here ethical, hermeneutic and aesthetic) lead spectators to hold mutually exclusive views on a film from other spectators. Given that graphic sexual and sexually violent images are at the limit of legal and cultural acceptability, close to the boundary between general release and censorship, banning or even illegality, an otherwise anodyne choice of how to read a film conceptually leads to deeply entrenched oppositional views between intensely supportive and intensely critical interpretative communities. Through close analysis of *Battle in Heaven* and *A New Life*, and the popular, critical and scholarly reactions to these films, this chapter provides more concrete detail to the framework for understanding why transgressive art films elicit controversy and create scandals, and how viewers can agree on so many elements of a film's affective impact, whilst forming entirely contradictory overall opinions on a film. This chapter also begins the exploration of cinema as an art world by reflecting on the ethical stakes of critical and scholarly commentary, arguing that those who undertake aesthetic analyses of sexually violent imagery are taking an often unacknowledged ethical position in relation to the images they examine.

Chapter 4, 'Trauma', continues this combination of close analysis and broader sociological reflection by examining the overlooked conservative sexual and gender politics of two films about rape. Focusing on the narrative framing of trauma and victimhood in *The Brown Bunny* and *Free Will*, I argue that transgressive art films often present deeply contradictory ideas about rape, with these two films being exemplary of this problem. They are both attentive to the deep trauma that can arise from the experience of rape, and use visibility, proximity and duration to communicate this affectively to viewers. In these films, however, the trauma is ultimately presented as that of an onlooker and a rapist, respectively, with the victim's perspective and trauma being elided. Considering issues of the gaze, identification and narrative framing in light of the films' main themes of trauma and grief, I argue that, similar to *Battle in Heaven* and *A New Life*, these films are deeply divisive, provocative and troubling in ways that can be read as both progressive and retrograde. Through close analysis of film form, narrative and audience responses, this chapter demonstrates how the films set up a particularly fraught conflict of value registers that is heightened by their political ambiguity and internal incoherences.

Chapter 5, 'Witnessing', continues the discussion of rape and sexual assault imagery, but takes a wider and more theoretical perspective, considering how films that present rape in long takes crystallise all the supporting and critiquing arguments around rape imagery more broadly. I suggest that rape imagery is always caught between the progressive potential of communicating widely about a frequently hidden and woefully under-discussed aspect of society, and the regressive potential of visualising and spectacularising a crime that leaves little evidence, rarely leads to prosecution let alone conviction, and problematically combines sexual desire and violence. Transgressive art films depicting rape and sexual assault often appear to interpellate a film witness, positioning the film spectator as the witness to the rape, and thus creating an internally incoherent absent witness in the place of an idealised real or diegetic witness, who in most rape cases is not available to corroborate the victim's testimony. If these problems relating to evidence, testimony, visualisation and witnessing are inherent to all images of rape, films like *The Tribe*, *Holiday* and *Irreversible* are perfect examples of all the positive and negative potential of such images, on a theoretical, ethical and political level.

In Chapter 6, 'Limits', I return to a more theoretical consideration of transgression, most notably Bataille's ideas of transgression. Building on the discussion of transgressive acts from Chapter 1, I argue that Bataille's work is of great importance for thinking about transgressive imagery, but that his ideas about transgressive acts are often unhelpfully and misleadingly extrapolated onto transgressive images and artistic transgression. Focusing on transgressive acts in *Raw* and *In My Skin*, and these films' exploration of the violence of patriarchy's imposition of gender norms, I demonstrate that Bataille's ideas are useful for understanding these films' presentation of societal structures and their relation to violence, but that they are insufficient for comprehending how these films are artistically transgressive. This chapter is an attempt to push Bataille's ideas to their limits in terms of their pertinence for understanding the transgressive art film.

Chapter 7, 'Genre', focuses on type and degree of transgression, the almost-transgressive and the marginally transgressive. Having explored this in terms of film form – visibility, proximity and duration – this chapter considers how this theory can be applied to a specific very relevant boundary to transgressive art films: the boundary between art and pornography. Many transgressive art films transgress this boundary, even as it remains an important legal and cultural dividing line between two mutually exclusive genres.

In this chapter, I explore how genre theory is able to shed light on some of the issues provoked by transgressive art films, but is also insufficient to fully explain them. Focusing especially on Jacques Derrida's account of genre, this chapter is an attempt to find a rigorous framework for thinking about genre hybridity and the mixing of low/high art that I have critiqued as unsatisfactory in much commentary on extreme cinema. Using the example of *A Hole in My Heart* and applying ideas about marginal transgression and polarising reception to poststructuralist readings of genre boundaries, I argue that we can grasp the transgressive and liminal positioning of the transgressive art film, which finds itself described and received as both art and not-art, pornography and not-pornography.

Chapter 8, 'Cinema Art World', takes the widest perspective, considering the role that transgressive art films play in the cinema ecosystem as a whole. Moving away from close textual analysis and taking a more sociological approach, this chapter examines the different stages from production, film festivals, distribution, exhibition, reception and intellectualisation, in order to show how the transgressive art film is created by many stakeholders within the cinema art world. I argue that granting a film the status of transgressive art film is about being recognised as having transgressed the right boundaries in the right way. In effect, transgressive art films are those that include imagery and structures that were not previously considered to be part of art cinema, but that are incorporated into the domain of art cinema: they are in that moment both inside and outside art cinema before subsequently becoming part of the canon, and effectively enlarging the limits of film art. This chapter brings together all the ideas about form, reception and theory discussed throughout the book and points to our ethical and political responsibilities as scholars when choosing films on which to focus our attention and research time.

*

This book is a wide-ranging attempt to sketch out a coherent and rigorous framework for understanding some of the most controversial films of the past twenty-five years. The sexual, violent and sexually violent films that I examine under the term 'transgressive art film' are not just a grouping or a genre but a socio-cultural phenomenon. A full account of this phenomenon requires close textual analysis of the films at hand, of how they were received by audiences, critics and scholars, and a theory of artistic transgression, three pillars that underpin all of the book's claims. I began by developing a heuristic around the seven core films, which were considered almost universally to be provocative, challenging and extreme. Using this heuristic to identify other transgressive art films led to the examination of these films as a cultural phenomenon that is informative in relation to scholarship on rape imagery, film ethics, witnessing, genre theory and the broader functioning of the cinema art world. Ultimately, I argue that the stakes of scholarship on these films increases given how it is so implicated in value register conflicts, in framing the reception of these films and in legitimising them within the academy. The subject matter is at times difficult, but I hope that readers will find the analysis useful, as it gets to the heart of how the cinema art world functions, and how new, innovative and non-artistic film elements come to be legitimised as film art.

Notes

1. Quandt, 'Flesh and Blood'; Walon, 'Monstrous Embodiments'; Resmini, 'Reframing the New French Extremity'; Erensoy, 'Rethinking Pornography'.
2. Kendall, 'Reframing Bataille'.
3. Horeck and Kendall, 'The New Extremisms'; Brown, 'Violence in Extreme Cinema'; Frey, *Extreme Cinema*; Kerner and Knapp, *Extreme Cinema*; Bordun, *Genre Trouble and Extreme Cinema*.
4. Kendall, 'Affect and the Ethics of Snuff in Extreme Art Cinema'; Hobbs, *Cultivating Extreme Art Cinema*.
5. Horeck and Kendall, *The New Extremism in Cinema*.
6. Palmer, *Brutal Intimacy*.
7. MacKenzie, 'On Watching and Turning Away'.
8. Williams, 'His Life to Film'.
9. Grønstad, *Screening the Unwatchable*.
10. Palmer, *Brutal Intimacy*.
11. Throughout this book, I will be using Howard Becker's term 'art world' to describe all the constitutive elements 'necessary to the production of the characteristic works which that world ... define[s] as art' (*Art Worlds*, 35). It does not solely designate 'the' art world, meaning the world of fine art, but is applicable to the production and culture of art related to any medium. The 'cinema art world' is therefore all the people, materials and processes relating to cinema from equipment, funding and production through distribution and exhibition, to reception and film education.
12. Films from this turn-of-the-century period such as *The Idiots, Intimacy, The Piano Teacher, Dog Days, Demonlover, In the Cut, Swimming Pool, 9 Songs, Red Road* and *Import/Export* were included in some discussions but were not unanimously subject to analysis as extreme nor always considered highly controversial. This does not exclude them from being considered as transgressive art films, it simply separates them from the core group of prototypical films from which to develop the heuristic.
13. Bourdieu, *The Field of Cultural Production*; Bourdieu, *The Rules of Art*.
14. For a survey of IMDb review statistics supporting this, see Kimber, 'Transgressive Edge Play', 117–18.

15 Barker et al., *Audiences and Receptions*; Frey, *Extreme Cinema*.
16 Heinich, 'The Art of Inflicting Suffering'.
17 Heinich.
18 See Choi and Wada-Marciano, *Horror to the Extreme*.
19 Cagle, 'The Good, the Bad, and the South Korean'.
20 The concept of 'preferred reading' is drawn from Hall, 'Encoding/Decoding'.
21 Bourdieu, *The Rules of Art*, 226.
22 Del Río, *The Grace of Destruction*.
23 Kerner and Knapp, *Extreme Cinema*.
24 Bétan, *Extrême!*
25 Quandt, 'Flesh and Blood'.
26 Hobbs, *Cultivating Extreme Art Cinema*, 13; Taylor, *Troubled Everyday*, 4; Downing, 'French Cinema's New "Sexual Revolution"', 265.
27 Bordun, *Genre Trouble and Extreme Cinema*, 4, 1.
28 Beugnet, *Cinema and Sensation*; Palmer, *Brutal Intimacy*.
29 Palmer, *Brutal Intimacy*, 78.
30 Horeck and Kendall, *The New Extremism in Cinema*, 1–2.
31 Grønstad, *Screening the Unwatchable*, 11.
32 Barker et al., *Audiences and Receptions*; Frey, *Extreme Cinema*. Other useful reception-studies work includes MacKenzie, '*Baise-Moi*'; Hickin, 'Censorship, Reception and the Films of Gaspar Noé'; Kapka, 'Understanding *A Serbian Film*'; Pett, 'A New Media Landscape?'. Other useful audience studies include Barker, '"Typically French"?'; 'Watching Rape'; Selfe, '"Incredibly French"?'; Smith, 'Shock Value'.
33 Frey, *Extreme Cinema*, 8.
34 Frey, *Extreme Cinema*; Kerner and Knapp, *Extreme Cinema*; Bordun, *Genre Trouble and Extreme Cinema*; Taylor, *Troubled Everyday*; Hobbs, *Cultivating Extreme Art Cinema*.

1

Transgression

Transgressive art films have polarised audiences, receiving condemnation and adulation for their affectively challenging imagery and ambiguous political outlook. *Romance, Baise-moi, Trouble Every Day* and *Irreversible* include images of explicit sex and graphic violence, but are also considered to be part of art cinema. They are some of the most controversial films in a generation, and one of the recurrent terms used to describe them is 'extreme'. The focus on extremity has generally served to emphasise the challengingly affective experience of watching these films, treating them as a stylistic grouping, a tendency or a genre. Nonetheless, there has been little sustained theorisation of exactly what 'extremity' might mean in this context, such that the terms 'extreme' and 'transgression' are used vaguely and promiscuously to describe numerous aspects of the films and the experience of viewing them. Indeed, 'transgression' has in recent years been used by humanities scholars to designate a wide range of approaches to bodies and sexualities,[1] and aesthetic style,[2] relating to cinema and many other media. This lack of clarity creates the need for a new term. I propose 'transgressive art film' as a term to grasp the formal, social, cultural, ethical, theoretical and industrial ramifications of these controversial films. As a counterpoint to the imprecise deployment of 'transgression' and 'extreme', a central part of this book's method is the careful and systematic use of such concepts. When using these words I aim to clarify as clearly as possible which boundaries are being crossed, in what ways, to what extent, and by whom or what. This allows for the development of a robust theory of transgression in film, which interconnects with the close formal analysis and the reception analysis, together providing a strong framework for understanding the socio-cultural phenomenon of the transgressive art film.

A cursory glance at the breadth of scholarship on artistic transgression, or indeed at criticisms of such work, will demonstrate that under a 'weak' definition of transgression, just about anything can be considered transgressive. The term 'transgressive' is often applied vaguely to designate something deviant or different, but in an unspecified way, as well as to signal some unspecific form of political, aesthetic or ethical subversion. In other works, its use is often non-specific, being conflated with other terms that pertain to boundaries such as 'marginality', the 'transitory', 'diversity', 'ambivalence', 'blurring', 'confusion', 'experimentation', 'mixing', 'excess', 'non-normativity' and even simply 'difference'. Such 'weak' usages of transgression are applied to any kind of limit, boundary or border that has been crossed in any way, and indeed can become detached from any agent or artwork completely.[3] For instance, in his work on postmodernism in French thought, approvingly quoted by Martine Beugnet in relation to 'the art of transgression', Max Silverman claims that 'modernism thrived on the transgression of boundaries – between order and disorder, between uniformity and heterogeneity, between the public and private spheres – and the confusion of distinct realms'.[4] The borders between these concepts are very unclear, and the subject of transgression is lost. Transgression is effectively thrust into the passive: a boundary is transgressed. But which boundary exactly? And how can we tell? In what ways? To what extent? By whom? This passive conception of transgression is reworked in many scholarly writings on extreme cinema such as in descriptions of a 'blurring of boundaries between auteur and popular', and, more hyperbolically, of a 'muddling of a clear division between spectator and screen'.[5] The concept of transgression is simultaneously over-used and under-discussed. Critics and scholars easily apply it to all sorts of films and images with any number of articles and books describing an oeuvre, a film, a scene, an image or a director as transgressive. However, despite this ubiquity, 'transgression' is often used in quite vague ways, as though it were clear what it means to be transgressive, as though it were clear what is being transgressed. The significant literature on transgression rarely forms a systematic part of discussions about transgression in film.

By contrast, I favour a 'strong' definition of transgression, which is clear about the boundaries and the kind of transgression under discussion. In doing so I distinguish between breaking laws, images of transgressive acts, norm violations, aesthetic innovations and artistic discourse around transgression. It is paramount that film analyses are specific about how they draw on broader theories of transgression, and how they contribute to an understanding of a film as transgressive. The literature on transgression does not, however, solve this problem on its own, as most of the influential work on transgression focuses on real-life transgressive acts rather than artistic transgressions, and when it comes to transgressive works of art, scholarship is predominantly focused on fine art. While insufficient attention has been paid to theories of transgression when talking about films, such theories alone cannot explain what creates controversy in cinema today. We therefore need to look closely at theories of transgression in order to see how they can be better adapted to cinema. This chapter constructs a clear and robust framework for understanding what transgression means in the context of contemporary film, how it relates to work on transgression in other fields, and to extremity, and how it applies to both the microscale of film form and to the macroscale of the cinema art world. This framework is essential for understanding the different elements and mechanisms that come together to make transgressive art films controversial.

This chapter distinguishes between transgressive acts and artistic transgression, summarising key work on transgression in order to suggest which elements of it are useful for thinking about transgression in cinema. I argue that the main lessons to be drawn from this work is that type and degree of transgression matter, as well as the context of the transgression, and the identity of the transgressor. I also examine theories and analyses of extremity in art and cinema, arguing that extremity and transgression are closely connected concepts that have developed slightly divergent discursive valences. Furthermore, I provide an account of the different ways in which films can transgress legal boundaries and incur censorship, and how these different forms of transgression are received and contained. I focus significantly on censorship because it is important in terms of the practical fate of a film (is it banned, cut or restricted?), and because it implicitly shapes how we think about those films (what is important, what is bad/good). Attentiveness to the type of boundaries (e.g. legal boundaries or those dealt with by classification boards), types of illicit imagery (is the film 'illegal', 'forbidden' or 'restricted'?) and degree of transgression (marginal or maximal) enables a clearer and more coherent understanding of what it means for a film to be transgressive. Turning to the question of reception, I explain how the framework of value registers allows us to understand the transgressions of controversial films that do not transgress any censorship boundaries. Where many commentators revert to 'weak' claims about transgressing cultural norms or genre expectations, I show through the conflict of value registers how disputes between viewers of transgressive art films remain tied to 'strong' boundaries such as art/non-art, censored/free-to-view, and legal/illegal. In sum, this chapter provides a framework for what it means for a transgressive art film to transgress, it shows that it is possible to talk clearly and specifically about artistic transgression, and it proposes a way of theorising extremity as a contemporary sub-category of transgression focused on images of sex and violence.

*

'Transgression' and the connected term 'extremity' can refer to a range of physical acts, social conventions, legal regulations, artistic forms, time periods and cultural constraints, and for each of these categories, transgression takes on different forms. At its simplest, transgression entails going across (Latin 'trans', across + 'gradi', to step, walk, go). This is commonly understood as going across a line, a limit or a boundary, sometimes physical (a territory, a space, an area, a body), sometimes abstract (rules, regulations, norms, conventions, laws). The ostensible simplicity of this basic idea of moving from one side of a line to another means that it has been applied by a wide range of thinkers to a broad array of subjects, from legal and social norms, to sporting records, art and culture, ideas and beliefs. Indeed, 'transgression' can end up being used to signal a passage across any number of conceptual boundaries including 'sacred-profane; good-evil; normal-pathological; sane-mad; purity-danger; high-low; centre-periphery and so on'.[6] It is therefore crucial to be attentive to the individual instance of transgression as it relates to specific rules that differ according to context: the transgression of laws, cultural conventions and artistic norms do not operate in the same way.

The most influential ideas about transgression come from sociology, anthropology and political philosophy, as an attempt to grapple with how societies instigate and maintain norms and conventions. In his exhaustive survey of transgression in twentieth-century thought, Chris Jenks traces the concept back especially to Emile Durkheim's theory of social facts, the normal and the pathological, and Alexandre Kojève's re-reading of Hegelian dialectics, which heavily influenced post-war French philosophy, most notably here Georges Bataille.[7] Neither Durkheim nor Bataille wrote extensively on artistic transgression, but they did set the stage for much subsequent thinking about transgressive art, together with other thinkers of norms and control such as Mary Douglas, Mikhail Bakhtin, Howard Becker and Michel Foucault, although most writing on transgression and extremity in cinema ignores them entirely.

In sociology, transgression is considered in relation to the construction, imposition and maintenance of societal norms. For Durkheim, there are what he calls 'social facts' such as legal systems, currencies, and language frameworks, which have no physical form but exert collective structures and restrictions upon a society. In doing so, they distinguish the normal, which adheres to these conventions, from the pathological, which exceeds or threatens them. These norms are external to and predate any individual member of a group, they are general, in that they speak for themselves and appear sustained rather than transitory, and, importantly for our discussion here, they constrain, in that there are punitive consequences for their infringement.[8] Durkheim compares society to a collective organism, asserting that normal social facts, those that typify average behaviour within a society, are analogous to a 'healthy body', while transitory infractions or transgressions, correspond to disease and should be avoided.[9] However, unlike in a body, a society has substantial scope for change and alterations to the broader system, integrating within it that which beforehand may have been considered aberrant.[10] At the same time, that which is not integrated and remains a crime 'serves as a negative reinforcement for the collective sentiments; crime creates outrage, punishment gives rise to expiation, the normal has its boundaries once more confirmed'.[11] The examples of Galileo Galilei and Charles Darwin serve to elucidate this distinction: while Galileo's transgressions brought the full force of the Catholic Church down upon him, Darwin's discoveries arose within a society more inclined to integrate than expel them.[12]

Anthropologist Mary Douglas reiterates these ideas in terms of the transgressor as polluter:

> the polluter becomes a doubly wicked object of reprobation, first because he crosses the line and second because he endangers others. ... When [a society] is attacked from within by wanton individuals, they can be punished and the structure publicly reaffirmed.[13]

In this reading, like in Durkheim, transgressive acts are those that question prevailing societal structures and conventions, and thus cannot simply be dismissed as individual caprice. Either they must be expelled as disease or pollutant, or conventions must alter to incorporate them within a new set of norms, that exclude a slightly different set of beliefs and behaviours.[14] For these thinkers, specificity and context dependence were essential for fully comprehending the idea of disease or pollutant:

> a fact can be termed pathological only in relation to a given species. The conditions of health and sickness cannot be defined *in abstracto* or absolutely. ... The habit, far too widespread, must be abandoned of judging an institution, a practice or a moral maxim as if they were good or bad in or by themselves for all social types without distinction.[15]

Similarly, in the ensuing discussion of artistic transgression, it will be of central importance not to speak of transgression *in abstracto* but to link it to boundaries between specific concepts or the infringements of clearly identifiable laws.

Later work in sociology also emphasised the importance not only of providing context for the transgressive act, but of thinking about the identity of the transgressor in whether a particular act comes to be connoted as transgressive or not. As Howard Becker notes about the designation of behaviour as deviant,

> the same behaviour may be an infraction of the rules at one time and not at another; may be an infraction when committed by one person, but not when committed by another, some rules are broken with impunity, others are not. In short, whether a given act is deviant or not depends in part on the nature of the act (that is, whether or not it violates some rule) and in part on what other people do about it.[16]

For instance, those in positions of power, or from a privileged class, may be able to redefine their acts in ways that oppressed minorities cannot: sexual assault becomes 'wandering hands', murder becomes justified self-defence, theft becomes an unfortunate indiscretion. Miles Evers points to a comparable dynamic within norm violations at a geopolitical level between states. Separating norm transgressions into four types (rejection, adaptation, inclusion and exclusion), he argues that it is paramount to consider the identity of the transgressor (an insider or an outsider), and the purported aim of the transgression (to contest or change regulatory norms, to undermine the insider/outsider distinction, or to redefine those considered to be insiders).[17] Each of these types of transgressions is perceived differently by those involved depending on which state is transgressing, and which boundaries are being transgressed, over and above the exact legality of the action: the illegal NATO bombing of Yugoslavia was broadly acknowledged to be legitimate, the illegal invasion of Iraq by US/UK forces provoked greater consternation but little action from other states, while the illegal Russian invasion of Ukraine became a full-blown global crisis. Studies of deviance and geopolitics offer two perspectives on transgression amongst many potential examples that reinforce how important the context of a transgression is. Even as the stakeholders change starkly, the underlying importance of precisely identifying the boundary being transgressed, as well as the power and societal role of those involved remains clear. In terms of artistic transgressions, this means we need to be attentive to the cultural and symbolic capital of the filmmakers, as well as, for instance, the extent to which a film is presented at festivals and in marketing as an auteur film, which elevates the director to the status of artist, and thereby changes their potential to act and have their actions recognised within the system.

In both these examples, defining an act as deviant/transgressive involves firstly the transformation of an atypical act into an infraction: if an act's deviance is simply ignored, it becomes unusual rather than transgressive.

Secondly, it entails a recognition that deviance is about the relation of the act to structures of power rather than about anything inherent to the act: designations of transgressiveness change according to time, place, the identity of the transgressor and the specific context of the act.[18] Taking a wider view, this also points to the fact that transgression in the abstract can never be seen as political, even as scholarly work in literature and film has a tendency to conflate transgression with political action.[19] Specific transgressions can be political (such as assassinations or civil disobedience), but there is nothing inherently political, progressive or revolutionary about crossing a boundary per se. Indeed, artistic transgressions have to be institutionally recognised as transgressing the right boundaries in order to attain the status of 'transgressive art' or risk being marginalised and ignored. Transgression understood so far is part of the process of maintenance and evolution of boundaries set up by a system. To transgress is to highlight the boundary, and is an action that can be punished as an infraction, that can lead to the boundary changing, or that can be ignored entirely. This understanding of transgressive acts is also relevant to artistic transgression, which can be understood as a necessary part of an art world, ensuring innovation and renewal. These transgressions ultimately play a normative rather than revolutionary function.

*

In their different ways, Durkheim, Douglas, Becker and Evers all point to the importance of transgression in the constitution of boundaries, and show, implicitly if not explicitly, that studying instances of transgression can teach us a lot about the nature of a particular boundary, especially through its negative reinforcement via the punishment of infractions.[20] However, in each of these accounts, transgression remains a relatively binary concept: a line is either crossed or not crossed, transgressions that are noticed are either punished or incorporated. The work of Georges Bataille and Mikhail Bakhtin points us towards two other ways of approaching transgression that reframe the meaning and value of transgression within society: the idea of 'limited transgressions', which are transgressions of a limited nature and only of certain rules, and the idea that these limited transgressions are required in order to maintain the smooth functioning of society. Following later Durkheim, Bataille considers society to be constituted of complementary profane and sacred worlds: 'The profane world is the world of taboos. The sacred world depends on limited acts of transgression. It is the world of celebrations, sovereign rulers and God.'[21] Bataille argued that for society to function, prohibitions restricting the profane (or in Durkheim's terms, the normal) must be sporadically transgressed in order to unproductively expend accrued energy and wealth. On an individual level, the experience of going beyond the constraints that structure society is also of paramount importance: 'without the extreme limit, life is only a long deception, a series of defeats without combat followed by impotent retreat – it is degradation' because 'the act whereby being – existence – is bestowed upon us is an unbearable surpassing of being, an act no less unbearable than that of dying'.[22] Being especially interested in prohibitions related to sex and death, Bataille described these interdictions as 'taboos' to argue that transgression 'does not deny the taboo, but transcends and completes it', with transgression being both integral to the functioning of society (by completing taboos) and a transcendent act for the individual.[23] In this reading, rather than being an aberration, transgression is necessary both on the level of the individual and of society. Indeed, for Bataille, it is dangerous for a society if such release is repressed, as it leads to forms of violence that are destructive rather than constructive. In drawing this distinction between different forms of boundary infraction, Bataille is arguing for a distinction between certain limited forms of transgression that support and sustain societal norms, and other kinds of transgression such as the destructive violence of war, or what he describes as 'evil' acts: transgression is 'organised and limited . . . evil is not transgression, it is transgression condemned'.[24] This account of transgression emphasises that the degree of transgression is important. Not only should we consider whether or not a boundary has been crossed, but also the extent to which it has been crossed. Limited and unlimited transgressions are not of the same order.[25]

If we consider a specific example of acts of limited transgression – the carnival – we can see the regulatory function of transgression in action, as well as appreciating the limited political potential of such acts. As Bakhtin notes, 'during carnival time life is subject only to its laws, that is, the laws of its own freedom', a space is provided where standard taboos and regulations are temporarily suspended.[26] Most notably this applied to drinking and debauchery, sexually provocative behaviour in public, mocking the Church and the ruler, occupying the streets and selling your wares, and not going to work.[27] Traditional hierarchies are set aside, overturned, undermined and equalised. People associate freely with all others regardless of social status. Obscenity and profanity reign, and the body's corporeality is released from its repression with gluttony, lust, greed and sloth all acceptable for the period of the carnival. Afterwards, however, hierarchies are reasserted, social status reaffirmed, taboos around sex and bodies reimposed, with the desires for transgression and hedonistic release having been purged for the year. In this sense, the carnival functions far more as a safety valve against the build-up of any serious political contestation than as a challenge to the system: 'there is no a priori revolutionary vector to carnival and transgression',[28] because it is a codified period of limited transgression. The fact that these transgressions are permitted distinguishes them from transgressions that challenge the structures of society: as Terry Eagleton points out,

> carnival, after all, is a licensed affair in every sense, a permissible rupture of hegemony, a contained popular blow-off as disturbing and relatively ineffectual as a revolutionary work of art. As Shakespeare's Olivia remarks, there is no slander in an allowed fool.[29]

For Bataille, this is not a critique of transgression, but rather is an illustration of transgression's normative function: there must be a taboo in order for there to be transgression, and there are many taboos that should be broken in limited and codified ways, in order to reassert the value and power of that taboo. Temporarily permitted transgressions allow for acceptance of the rules for the majority of the time. Eagleton's comment linking carnival to art is also instructive in emphasising the limited political potential of art, however revolutionary, as well as reminding us to be attentive to the elements of transgressive acts that can be brought to bear on artistic transgressions.

As Michel Foucault explained in a tribute to Bataille after his death, transgression for Bataille was neither ethically productive nor revolutionary, neither inherently positive nor negative: 'Transgression is neither violence in a divided world (in an ethical world) nor a victory over limits (in a dialectical or revolutionary world).'[30] Rather, it is an affirmation both of the limit itself and the innate limitlessness that the transgression of a limit opens up, a key to understanding rather than overturning society:

> Transgression contains nothing negative, but affirms limited being – affirms the limitlessness into which it leaps as it opens this zone to existence for the first time. But, correspondingly, this affirmation contains nothing positive: no content can bind it, since by definition, no limit can restrict it. . . . The limit and transgression depend on each other for whatever density of being they possess: a limit could not exist if it were absolutely uncrossable and, reciprocally, transgression would be pointless if it merely crossed a limit composed of illusions and shadows.[31]

For Foucault, transgression is how we make sense of a world without a God: once we remove the possibility of an infinite being, the world is finite. Where an infinite world is limited by an infinite Godhead ('the limit of the Limitless'), a finite world paradoxically knows no real limits, and this finite lack of limits is affirmed in the possible transgression of any limit ('the limitless reign of the Limit').[32] Specifically in relation to sexuality and eroticism, 'sexuality achieves nothing beyond itself, no prolongation, except in the frenzy which disrupts it'.[33] Transgression in this reading is a particularly secular preoccupation, whereby the flaunting of the limit is a means of coming to terms with the limitlessness of a godless world. The unproductive expenditure of sex, violence and controlled destruction are the transgressions which allow for self-affirmation and serve to bind society together in the face of meaninglessness. While Foucault's idea of transgression here is very broad, it does helpfully pinpoint the non-political character of transgression as a concept.

Bataille built up his ideas around limited transgressions and codified forms of nonproductive expenditure into a theory of general economy. In *The Accursed Share*, Bataille draws on Marcel Mauss's analysis of the potlatch to argue for the economic necessity of excessive nonproductive expenditure: 'the problem posed is that of the expenditure of the surplus. We need to give away, lose or destroy.'[34] The limited infraction of prohibitions is integral to the psychological containment of the individual, and also the maintenance of the broader economic system, which he argues cannot function on rationality, profit and productivity alone. Members of a society produce more than the system needs for its own survival, and must therefore engage in nonproductive expenditure – useless consumption – to avoid catastrophic expenditures such as war.[35] If not, 'we will be suffering the desire for expenditure rather than living it in positive ecstasies (that can be sexual, artistic or of other kinds)', and this desire is ultimately destructive both for the individual and society.[36] Simply put, societies function based on a complex array of rules and regulations, that inevitably open up the space for their transgression. Depending on the context, transgressive acts can be punished in order to reaffirm the rule (most obviously in crimes such as murder), integrated into a new system with slightly altered rules (as with the legalisation of homosexuality), or allowed temporarily in specific moments (in the case of carnival and erotic transgressions). Bataille's ideas about transgressive acts are specific, and make distinctions between different kinds of transgression, as well as how they impact on the individual and on society at large. Transgressive acts are not, however, the same as transgressive representations, and it is therefore important when turning to artistic transgressions to situate any claims carefully in relation to this work on transgressive acts.[37]

*

A sociological framing can still be maintained when shifting our focus to transgressive imagery by examining how sociologists of art have considered artistic transgression. This involves considering art worlds as games with loosely codified rules that transgressive artworks are able to bend and even reshape. Like in Bataille's work on transgressive acts, limited transgressions playing an important normative role within an art world, but substantial transgressions are marginalised or punished. The key aspect of artistic transgression that plays little role in discussions of transgressive acts is 'the new', which relates especially to questions of form, an aspect mostly absent from discussions of transgressive acts. Novelty, innovation and renewal are highly prized in all forms of modern and contemporary art, and have become ineluctably intertwined with notions of transgression, such that, unlike transgressive acts, artistic transgression is put on a pedestal and considered to be at the forefront of contemporary art. Just as transgressive acts are codified and used by state apparatuses such as the police, courts and prisons to negatively reinforce the rules, artistic transgressions are regulated by professional art commentators, critics and scholars, who use a variety of defences to legitimise transgressive art. Such defences also provide a useful insight into what constitutes artistic transgression.

Despite the fact that Bataille is often appealed to in work on sexual representation, his ideas about transgression rarely address the representation rather than the act of transgression. There is one point in his book on the paintings at Lascaux, where he does suggest that art can be a form of transgression, because art belongs to the realm of play and the carnivalesque rather than of work:

> An art independent of the impulses that engender the feast is unimaginable. In one respect, play is the transgression of the law of work: art, play and transgression come not singly, but every time joined in defiance of the principles presiding over the disciplined regularity of work. ... Transgression has always adopted marvellous forms of expression: poetry and music, dance, tragedy, or painting.[38]

Nonetheless, Bataille is here describing the artistic process as an act that evokes the realm of the sacred, rather than examining transgressive art: art as a transgressive act, rather than transgression in art. In Bataille's reading, if transgression can be applied to artistic expression, it is to all artworks for their limited transgression of the law of rationality and productivity which governs the realm of work. If we wish to examine transgression in art, or the sub-category of transgressive art, we must look beyond Bataille.

It is almost an aphorism in the humanities to point out that yesterday's transgressions are today's banalities. Representations that are transgressive in one era, frequently become unexceptional in the next, and indeed unexceptional images can be re-evaluated in transgressive terms years later. Although the nudity of *Emmanuelle* caused quite a stir on its release in 1974, and in the UK was cut to reduce the sexual explicitness, it barely raises an eyebrow today. At the same time, its rape scene was originally only subject to cuts to reduce sexual detail, despite framing the rape as a positive experience for the protagonist. By the time of its re-release in 1991, discourse had changed and most of the original cuts to erotic material were reversed but the rape scene was thought wholly unacceptable and cut entirely. Finally in 2007, all cuts to sexual content were reversed and the rape scene was considered so dated that it was now acceptable for uncut release.[39] The transgressiveness of different elements of the film (sexual explicitness, attitudes towards rape) increased and decreased depending on cultural context. This being said, the transgressiveness of a film is generally assessed based on the moment at which it was released; first-year film students still learn about the scandal surrounding *The Kiss* from 1896, or about Mae West's provocative sexual innuendos, even as contemporary recreations of these constitute the height of banality. Novelty is an important facet of artistic transgression.

While transgression is always associated with newness, the inverse is also true: newness in art has long been associated with transgression. Scholars such as Chris Jenks locate this broad shift in thinking with the onset of modernity:

> what Baudelaire proposed with his concept of 'modernity' was both ontological and epistemological. That is, he saw it as a new object for artistic address but also a new quality, experience and understanding of modern being. So, modern art becomes preoccupied with newness, with breaking rules, with stepping outside of constraint and convention.[40]

Focusing on the figure of Van Gogh, Nathalie Heinich offers a comparable analysis:

> this progressive normalisation of the notion of the avant garde and the imperative of singularity marks the triumph of originality ... originality goes together with the transgression of the canon, the acceptance and even valorisation of abnormality, such that the exceptional [*le hors-norme*] tends to become the norm.[41]

In other words, in contrast to pre-modern Western notions of art focused on the skilful replication of agreed-upon aesthetic standards, modernity recast the notion of art as unavoidably entangled with newness, innovation and originality. The exception *qua* transgression of canonical standards became the heart of the new definition of art. Contemporary art then takes this one step further by transgressing the very definitions of art, and not only those aesthetic choices established by tradition: 'the nature of contemporary art is to transgress the frontier, established by tradition and common sense, between art and nonart'.[42] In his study of the new, Boris Groys reformulates this idea from the perspective of newness, reaffirming the importance of including the idea of accepted transgressions within this analysis: 'innovation accordingly means a strategy that links a positive to a negative continuation of the tradition in such a way as to formulate both the continuity and also the break with the greatest possible clarity and intensity'.[43] In art, the new is inevitably transgressive.

This connection between artistic transgression and newness is integral to fully understanding transgressive imagery. What links all transgressive art is the status of novelty and innovation: not just novelty or innovation per se, but the status of the new, the official perception of an artwork being new. In part, this is because artistic transgression is always in fact accepted artistic transgression. Anybody can transgress or indeed ignore artistic conventions, but not every dissension from these rules will be accepted as an innovation instead of an aberration. However innovative an artwork may actually be, accepted artistic transgression is always novel in one sense, because it is the first time that such transgressions have been institutionally accepted, and made visible to a broader public. As Anthony Julius notes, 'transgressive art is an art of the subversive exception made the rule'.[44] It is the making of the rule which is novel, thus constantly marking accepted transgressions with the stamp of innovation. A good transgressive-art-film example of this is *Irreversible*, which was considered stylistically innovative and original by critics, but which undertook a mainstreaming of aesthetic innovations director Gaspar Noé had been inspired by from less-well-known works of visual art.[45] Within the context of narrative film and/or films on general release in cinemas, *Irreversible* was stylistically innovative and received valorisation as such, but as with any artistic development, the innovations did not come out of nowhere and can be seen in other works that did not achieve mainstream success. A transgression accepted as innovative must carefully identify its links with the norm, whilst at the same time signalling how it breaks with tradition, which is a fine tightrope to walk. Laura Kipnis sums this up well when she suggests that, 'as the avant-garde knew, transgression is no simple thing: it's a precisely calculated intellectual endeavour. It means knowing the culture inside out . . . To commit sacrilege, you have to have studied the religion'.[46] Accepted artistic transgressions are examples of how to successfully play the game of art; they demonstrate a keen awareness of the conventions and limits to be played with and of how they must be breached in such a way that these infractions are recognised rather than rejected; successful transgression involves 'breaching the limits without being declared off-side'.[47]

Art which is accepted institutionally (by curators, critics, scholars, buyers, owners) includes transgressions that are connoted as original or innovative, whereas transgressions that do not attain institutional recognition are relegated to various artistic backwaters (forgotten works, artistic obscurity, low art). Moreover, by (re)making the rule, the boundaries codifying what counts as transgression change and therefore future transgressive work will necessarily need to cross different limits, which demands innovation as previously transgressive forms will no longer be considered as transgressive. Given that most artistic conventions are inherently contingent and, unlike transgressive acts such as murder or rape, are not anchored in a concrete reality, artistic boundaries can be transgressed and rewritten constantly, allowing for the valorisation and normalisation of transgression, without the punishment that comes with the transgression of taboo acts. In cinema as in fine art, 'the rules of the game are being played for in the playing of the game'.[48] In a manner analogous to Durkheim's social facts, an art world creates a set of rules that predate the individual, appear general rather than transitory, and constrain in the sense that there are consequences to their infringement. However, unlike with social facts, which create a separation between the normal and the pathological, the rules of an art world are designed to be constantly broken and made anew; it is just that those who are accepted as having legitimately broken the rules are very few in number.

Just as social facts must be imposed and maintained through the institutionalised use of violence and force, so do art worlds require their own institutions of legitimisation. If a transgressive work of art is understood to have legitimately broken the rules of an art world, this means that previously it was not legitimate art, but has now been recuperated within the domain of art. While transgression may be a key component of contemporary art, and transgressive art may be a commonly vaunted sub-category of art, mechanisms must exist by which repudiative practices are legitimised and attributed with the status of 'art'. As Leslie Graves notes, transgressive art may be important to an art world, but broadly speaking, that world's main aim is to produce non-transgressive works of value: 'on any reasonable construal of the motivations of the art world, it evinces a great deal of concern with issues of status, reputation, survival, and the desire to provoke admiration and acclaim, not just to shock and outrage'.[49] Art worlds, whether cinema or fine art, have therefore developed a range of discursive tactics for justifying the artistic status of transgressive works that by definition break the rules for art at that moment.

Anthony Julius identifies three main tendencies in the legitimising discourse: the 'estrangement' defence, the 'canonic' defence and the 'formalist' defence.[50] The first defends an attempt to shock the viewer into seeing the truth by destabilising interpretations of conventional images; the second highlights the connections to earlier now-canonical art, positioning the new work as a successor to established formerly transgressive artworks; the third argues that art is about aesthetics, that it functions in its own realm distinct from the rest of the world. Together, these provide justifications for accepting within the realm of art that which does not conform to the current expectations of art.[51] While Julius, Graves and Heinich are discussing contemporary fine art, which has its own set of institutions and conventions distinct from cinema, this basic approach to artistic transgression is just as applicable to film.

In moving the discussion from transgressive acts to artistic transgression, the focus of the analysis has shifted, most notably with the emphasis on newness, innovation and originality, which are not particularly salient features of theories of transgressive acts. Moreover, while acts can be transgressive in relation to numerous boundaries instantiated in specific laws, such as between normal–pathological, sacred–profane, insider–outsider, to repeat only those mentioned in this chapter, artistic transgressions relate almost exclusively to distinctions between art and not-art. Within this distinction there are certainly many nuanced elements – does 'art' mean art cinema, films on general release or all films? Is it pertinent to distinguish high art from low art? Can pornography be art/istic? Who is or should be eligible to make these distinctions? – but one way or another, the borders erected pertain to definitions of art and artistry. Nonetheless, there remain numerous connections to theories of transgression, including analogies to social facts, the importance of limited and codified forms of transgression, and the centrality of transgression to the continuity of the society or art world that would otherwise stagnate and stultify. As we move to a concrete discussion of the cinema art world and the institutional limits to which films are subject, this offers a clear basis for how to understand what constitutes transgression in cinema.

*

Today 'extreme' has come to fulfil the role once occupied by 'transgressive' in the context of sexual or violent films, the only reliably controversial imagery in twenty-first-century cinema. It is used to signify the crossing of a boundary (often official), to disparage content that is perceived to violate cultural norms, and to recuperate non-art or low-art practices (especially those related to pornography) within the realm of (high) art.[52] 'Extreme' covers much of the same ground as 'transgressive', but in the specific context of sexual and violent images; extremity is effectively a sub-category of transgression.[53] In the context of visual media, 'extreme' is intimately linked to the transgression of legal and cultural boundaries, it is used both to denigrate and recuperate films, and it is intimately linked to perceptions of art and artistry. Nonetheless it lacks the historic attachment to novelty and originality that 'transgressive' has gained, and so remains connoted most especially with spectacular, morally problematic, low-cultural objects, some of which may be critically feted.

The little theory that explicitly engages with the concept of extremity tends to focus on what Paul Ardenne has analysed as the *extremus/exter* function of extremity. Looking at the etymology of 'extreme', there are two meanings: the Latin *extremus* means 'to the utmost extent' (outermost inside area) and is also the superlative of *exter*, which means 'on the outer side', 'outward' and 'external'.[54] In dictionary terms, 'extreme' can signify both inside and outside a limit. Ardenne utilises this linguistic tension to separate 'extreme' into two constituent parts: *extremus* and *exter*.[55] Elements of an artwork that push up against but do not transgress a boundary constitute *extremus*. Elements that marginally transgress a boundary and occupy the space just beyond a boundary constitute *exter*.

In Ardenne's book, which opens with a long discussion of a piece of performance art involving a game of Russian roulette,[56] and in other scholarship on the sociology of extreme behaviour, the border being marginally transgressed is that between life and death. Most of this writing predates 9/11 and does not enter into discussions of political extremism; it is mostly interested in extreme sports, risk-taking, and life-threatening performance art. This work draws implicitly on Bataille's contention that 'at the elusive extreme limit of my being, I am already dead' and on Georg Simmel who posited that death 'limits, that is, it gives form to life . . . continually colouring all of life's contents'.[57] For instance, Patrick Baudry argues that the modern body is an extreme body in a state of ambiguity, in that dangerous activities allow a person to experience the extremes of life and the potential for death, while Helga Peskoller explains that extreme activities such as high-altitude rock climbing trouble the boundary between the order of life, and the disorder of death.[58] In other words, these activities are pushing up against the limit of life (*extremus*) and, in putting that life at significant risk, marginally transgressing it (*exter*). Bataille's work on transgression remains key here as this marginal transgression of the border with death is in the Bataillean sense of incorporating death into life in acts of violent and/or sexual transgression.

Ardenne applies this idea of the just-inside/just-outside the border to other artistic images of sex and violence, distinguishing these examples of 'art' from the 'maximalist' spectacles of pornography or hardcore horror. Many elements of pornography that transgress, strive towards maximalism: porn performers' bodies are as visible as possible, sparse narratives make sex as uninterrupted as possible, noisy orgasms show sex is as pleasurable as possible.[59] Ardenne argues that like artworks that remain carefully within limits, maximalist spectacles fail to shock us. In effect, this reformulates the idea of accepted and rejected transgressions, and incorporates the estrangement defence in order to argue that the extreme spectacle has the 'power to unsettle, [the] capacity to violate intimacy, to break through our defences, to alarm us, *really*'.[60] In other words, he argues that the maximalist spectacles of horror and pornography go 'too far', while normative spectacles don't go far enough; it is only that which remains close to the boundary – the extreme spectacle – that has an impact on the spectator. In thinking about transgressive filmmaking, this more detailed examination of Batailléan limited transgressions is instructive, most notably because it demands that we focus not only on the elements that are marginally transgressive but also those that are almost transgressive.

Thinking about the degree of transgression is important because many justifications of artistic transgressions are predicated upon different judgements of the part and the whole. While some images may be judged in and of themselves (e.g. sexualised images of children, or images of animal cruelty), other images, especially sexually explicit images, are considered in the context of the film more broadly. Most legal jurisdictions effectively have rules about pornography that can be marginally broken, if a work is considered artistic; in the UK, for instance, an 'image may, by virtue of being part of that narrative, be found not to be pornographic, even though it might have been found to be pornographic if taken by itself'.[61] Moreover, in tandem with such exceptions for art, it is not uncommon to see official definitions of pornography that rely on broad descriptions of filmic effects rather than on precise descriptions of particular images. In the UK, pornography is a film 'whose primary purpose is sexual arousal or stimulation', with the understanding of 'purpose', 'primary' and 'sexual arousal' all being left open to interpretation, while in Germany an image is pornographic if sex is placed in the foreground of an image.[62] Under such circumstances, an uncut five-minute close-up of penetration and ejaculation might disqualify a film from claiming that its 'primary purpose' is artistic, but shorter shots of penetration, and many non-sex scenes that advance the narrative (such as in *9 Songs* or *Romance*) allow for a claim that the film is not primarily about arousal. In other words, smaller transgressions (in this context, less visibility, proximity, duration) are still transgressive by showing aroused genitals (normally the exclusive purview of pornography) but avoid being ruled 'offside' and censored.

Degree is also important in terms of the non-transgressive elements of a film, in terms of the inside of a boundary. The almost-transgressive helps us to think about how close non-transgressive images in a film might be to crossing a border or limit. In order to understand not just which images/films can be considered transgressive, but also those that spark controversy and scandal, we have to take into account the visual context of the transgressive image. Where a single image or short sequence is transgressive, but the rest of the film poses no regulatory questions whatsoever, the chances of that film being considered controversial diminish. However, if that sequence is long or detailed, or if there are numerous elements of a film that push up against the prescribed limits of representation, then it is more likely that the film as a whole will create controversy, or at least concern the censor. For example, in *Born in Flames*, there is a very brief shot of two hands placing a condom on an erect penis. While it is politically radical, this film contains no other images of sex and violence that might concern censorship boards and so this image actually went unnoticed and the film elicited no scandal relating to its sexual imagery.[63] When sexual imagery becomes more detailed and the sexual scenes become longer, there are more likely to be censorship questions posed as the broader context of the film, and not just a single image, pushes up against the limits of representation. Consider the popular interest in the 'racy' scenes of *Monster's Ball*, *Basic Instinct* and *Blue Valentine*, which although never strictly transgressive, include long scenes of sex and are as detailed as possible without featuring explicit shots of sex or genitalia.[64] Full-blown controversy only seems to arise when these two elements are combined: many images of sex and violence that test censorship limits without actually transgressing them, and some images that do transgress those limits but not enough or in significant enough number to revoke the film's status as art.

For many transgressive art films, these marginal transgressions involve explicit sexual imagery, or imagery that combines eroticism and violence, and are thus transgressive according to contemporary censorship regulation, as well as including numerous almost-transgressive images of sex and/or violence that become the dominant structural elements of the film. In practice such films are often criticised for their episodic narrative structure or emphasis on spectacle over narrative. While this clear separation of spectacle as 'effect', and narrative as means of interpretation is unhelpfully reductive, we can recognise the unusual centrality of sex and violence to the structure of texts described as extreme, anchoring the action and shaping the narrative, even as the extent of violence and spectacle is frequently exaggerated by mainstream critics ignorant of the margins of mainstream representation.[65] Reading transgressions through the lens of extremity encourages us to be more attentive to the degree of those transgressions, and to the proximity of the mostly non-transgressive elements to identifiable limits of representation. In this context, the overall length of scenes, visibility of body parts, and perceived proximity to violence are as important as the few brief images that clearly constitute an infraction to the overall status of a film as a transgressive art film.

*

Using a strong definition of transgression in relation to cinema immediately focuses attention on a small number of potential boundaries, namely those related to censorship, which are clearly set out in laws and classification guidelines. Censorship is not, however, a singular concept. Films can be censored for many reasons and in many ways. Transgressive art films are transgressive in particular ways, and so it is useful to think through the different ways in which censorship and transgression are connected. As will be discussed in Chapter 2, particular engagements with visibility, proximity and duration are the stylistic elements that signal that we are dealing with a transgressive art film, and the reasons why these provoke controversy are linked to the transgression of censorship rules, present in most countries, pertaining to pornography and eroticised sexual violence. Throughout the book, I will refer to 'forbidden' and 'restricted' images to contextualise and give details about what is transgressive about transgressive art films, so it is important to explain what these terms mean. Laws and classification guidelines are not the only arbiters of what constitutes transgression or extremity, but they are an important context for how audiences conceptualise the artistic boundaries that a film can transgress. As such, it is important to examine how boundaries are conceived of by censorship boards if we are to understand audience reactions to transgressive art films.

Although the exact rules vary according to time period and legislation, transgressions eliciting censorship fall into three broad categories: illegal, forbidden and restricted.[66] Illegal transgressions can pertain to images both as acts of recording and as representations, while forbidden and restricted transgressions relate only to images as representations. Illegal images transgress laws. Forbidden images may transgress laws but mainly transgress classification guidelines, and therefore may not be distributed or exhibited.

Restricted images transgress classification guidelines, and may only be distributed and exhibited under certain conditions. For the sake of consistency, my examples are almost entirely drawn from UK laws and classification decisions, but this taxonomy of censorship is written to be applicable to a wide range of censorship regimes, whatever the exact content of those laws, or the precise classification rules in place.

The illegal category includes acts and representations. In this context an image that is also an illegal act is one where a recording is made of a crime and the recording is considered complicit in the crime: depending on the jurisdiction, examples might include animal cruelty undertaken specifically for the camera, child-abuse imagery, non-consensual explicit images, and drug-production manuals. If any part of the production, distribution, exhibition or possession of child-abuse imagery constitutes an illegal act, then the image is as much part of the crime as the abuse itself. If voyeuristic images taken without consent such as 'upskirting', or nude images taken via hidden cameras, are illegal, these would also constitute an illegal act, as the act of procuring the image is the crime, rather than anything inherent to the image: the consent of the subject distinguishes between a legal and an illegal image. Images that incite illegal activity can also be considered illegal acts even if no crime is committed in the process of making the film: instruction manuals for drug cultivation can fall into this category. Historically, this would also have included certain forms of blasphemy. I describe these as illegal, rather than forbidden, when legislation has been passed specifically prohibiting them, whereas forbidden images are censored based on classification guidelines that are written by a classification body. Even within this category, the consequences are wildly varied, with complicity in a serious crime such as murder or child abuse generally leading to long prison sentences, whereas production of a drug manual may just lead to the film being refused classification but no further action.[67]

Illegal representation describes situations where the acts being filmed are legal, but the images of those acts are illegal. Manuals for producing illegal drugs are not a problem because of what they show (drug production can be seen in many mainstream films), but because they constitute incitement to commit a drugs offence (producing or distributing an illegal substance). However, in illegal representations, it is the image itself that is illegal. In the UK this arises from obscenity laws, and laws proscribing 'extreme pornography' as could be seen in the 2012 obscenity trial of Michael Peacock for making hardcore BDSM videos, and the 2011 prosecution of Kevin Webster for making photographs of play-acted eroticised murder.[68] In these cases, legal sexual acts such as fisting or urolagnia (as in the Peacock case) or play-acting murder (as in the Webster case) produced illegal images. Even if both men were ultimately acquitted, the prosecutions pursued based on this and other UK legislation makes clear that there are many situations in which representation can be the problem and not the acts per se, which if not filmed can be perfectly legal.[69]

This legislation was notable for criminalising the representation of otherwise legal acts, but also for the vague use of the term 'extreme' and of dubious scholarship on harm to justify the decision.[70] Moreover, the term 'extreme' became used to distinguish these illegal images from restricted pornographic images: while pornography is restricted (see below), 'extreme pornography' is illegal. Extreme pornography transgresses a boundary that pornography alone does not. Moreover, to emphasise the links between artistic transgression and extremity, even though these images were amateur or at least relatively unprofessional productions, there was nonetheless recurrent evocation of their non-artistic nature to exclude any suggestion of their recuperation as acceptable. In a House of Lords debate on the proposed legislation, one peer specifically referred to 'this extremely nasty pornography that in no circumstances can be counted as art'.[71] 'Extreme' here is used to signify that a boundary has been crossed (although prior to the law being passed it was often unclear exactly which boundary discussants were referring to), necessitating intervention, and also broadly to denigrate images that offend. Conceptually, UK discourse around extreme pornography and illegal images is then closely connected to the understanding of transgression at play in the transgressive art film.

The vast majority of films deemed to have officially transgressed by breaking regulations set out by the government or censorship body involve images that are legal to produce and own, but that subsequently have restrictions imposed upon their distribution and public exhibition. The restrictions are entirely related to the content of the images themselves rather than the process or act of making them: this is the territory of artistic transgression rather than transgressive acts. Films or images that may not be distributed or exhibited in any way I describe here as forbidden: the production, simple existence and ownership of the material is not illegal, but its distribution may be. In countries that require classification to distribute films, this makes distribution illegal, while in countries such as the US, where there is no legally mandated censorship board, such censorship is *de facto* rather than *de jure*, as distribution becomes very difficult without the classification, even as there is ultimately no legally enforced censorship of forbidden images. In some cases the entire film may be forbidden,[72] while in others cuts may be acceptable to secure classification, in effect making certain images from the film forbidden.[73] The only direct consequences of forbidden images for the filmmakers is that their films, or certain images from the films, are censored. The issue is not taken any further, unlike in the case of illegal acts and representations where prosecution is a possibility.

Like with illegal transgressions, in the case of films either being censored for forbidden images or where there is popular discussion about whether censorship should be enacted (such as for films discussed in this book like *Irreversible*), there is a tendency to use the term 'extreme' to describe the film or its content. In the BBFC's annual reports, 'extreme' is an infrequently used word, but when it does occur, it returns repeatedly to describe controversial and scandal-provoking films that were subjected to censorship, as well as others that just managed to avoid it. 'Transgressive' does not feature at all in these reports. To give just a few examples, *Baise-moi* is said to contain 'extreme sexual imagery',[74] *Irreversible* to depict 'extreme physical aggression',[75] *In My Skin* to show 'extremes of gory self-mutilation'[76] and *The Human Centipede II* and *The Bunny Game* to include 'extreme violence against women'.[77] Each of these films was close to the boundary of censorship in some way: two were released uncut but created controversy (*Irreversible* and *In My Skin*), one initially had some images cut but was later released uncut (*Baise-moi*), one was initially refused classification outright but was eventually released with some images cut (*The Human Centipede II*) and one was refused classification entirely (*The Bunny Game*). The word 'extreme' signals the transgression in some way of the board's rules, even if those transgressions were not ultimately sanctioned.

Films that fail to walk the delicate line and keep their transgressions minor and/or infrequent find themselves censored. Films such as *The Bunny Game* or *Grotesque* feature too many and too-detailed images and sequences that transgress the boundaries relating to sexual violence, and too few features that pull the narrative away from these transgressive images. As such, they are ruled 'off-side' and do not end up causing particular popular controversy, but are instead relegated to obscurity. On the other side of this line, torture films such as *Saw* and *Hostel*, despite being considered graphic in popular discourse, contain only brief images of physical violence, using cinematography, editing and sound to accentuate the horror and increase the terror. The *Saw* series is notable for featuring almost no nudity at all, while *Hostel* keeps the sex and violence resolutely separate.[78] In these examples, *Saw* and *Hostel* push up against, but do not transgress, censorship limits because non-sexual violence is effectively unrestricted in most countries,[79] while *The Bunny Game* and *Grotesque* went far beyond the BBFC's limits. In relation to the 'forbidden' category, degree of guideline transgressions and non-transgressions is integral to understanding perceptions of their artistic transgressions. Films perceived to be close to the limits in one way or another are often described as extreme, but it is only those that include many almost-transgressions and some marginal transgressions that appear to provoke major controversies, as did *Baise-moi* and *Irreversible*. The exact rules will vary according to jurisdiction, and censorship boards will exert varied influence on their country's film culture, so the precise classification decisions about these films is different from country to country. Nonetheless, what this close discussion of UK censorship shows us is that looking in greater detail at type and degree of transgression provides a framework for distinguishing transgressive art films from other sexual or violent films, as well as for seeing what makes their transgressions so controversial.

Since the legalisation of pornography, 'restricted' has referred most specifically to the restrictions placed on work that is considered pornographic, although it could theoretically apply to any restricted images. There is nothing illegal about the images produced, but censorship bodies stipulate that they may only be viewed by certain persons, generally adults, under certain circumstances. These restrictions may include the requirement of a licence to sell the material, particular tax arrangements, restrictions on how the material may be sold or packaged, or on when such material may be screened. This does not refer to age classifications, which only apply to children. Rather, it designates restrictions applied to adults, who are allowed to view this material, but not as freely or as easily as non-restricted material. The rules distinguishing restricted and forbidden sexual images have changed over time; for instance, in the mid-twentieth century, many countries restricted access to 'softcore' pornography (nudity and simulated sex acts, but no visible genitals or intercourse), while forbidding 'hardcore' pornography (explicit images of sex, sex performed on set by the actors). Today softcore images generally have no specific restrictions on them, while hardcore pornography is restricted.[80] When discussing transgressive art films, this boundary between the restricted and the free-to-distribute is of particular importance.

In a different way, restricted imagery, mostly synonymous with hardcore pornography at the current moment, which transgresses the limits on material permitted for general release, has also become associated with extremity. In rejecting a claim from certain porn producers for their work to be reclassified as non-restricted after the apparent relaxation of rules around explicit sex in the early 2000s, the BBFC's appeals committee described the pornographic material as 'explicit and extreme' and therefore unsuitable for unrestricted distribution.[81] Although the use of 'extreme' here denotes pornography rather than extreme cinema, 'extreme' appears to replace 'transgressive' in signalling that the limits of general-release sexual explicitness have been transgressed. Many recent controversial films transgress this limit by including explicit sex and find themselves denigrated or praised as extreme in the process. According to Emma Pett, 'extreme' seems therefore to signal an 'awkward' liminal cultural position, designating a disturbance of traditional boundaries between the pornographic and the non-pornographic.[82] Transgressive art films transgress the boundary separating the unrestricted from the restricted enough to trouble commentators and classifiers, but not quite enough to be actually restricted or forbidden.

Bringing together the forbidden and restricted categories, we might say that content described as extreme is frequently associated with pornography *qua* sexually explicit material, but also with spectacles of violence that have increasingly been described as pornographic.[83] While the idea of transgressive representation has become associated with (high) art, extremity is associated with its non-art corollary, pornography. Extremity and transgression are therefore both still intimately linked to questions of art, artistry and artistic status, even as the connotations of one can be partially seen as the inverse of the other. Over time, the transgressions of sexually explicit imagery can change type, for instance, historically in the UK, any depiction of aroused genitals, penetration or ejaculation was forbidden prior to the late 1990s, but since the late 1990s has only been restricted (most countries have followed a similar trend, just at different points in time). Transgressive art films and other sexually explicit films[84] of the 2000s and 2010s transgressed this boundary by including such images but without ultimately being categorised as pornography. The point here is that explicit sexual imagery and certain kinds of sexually violent imagery, both of which are common in transgressive art films, transgress definable boundaries laid out by national censorship regimes.

What this detailed description of laws and guidelines surrounding images serves to show is, firstly, that reflecting on the type and degree of transgression is necessary if we are to have a full understanding of how images transgress today and of how films end up being controversial. Secondly, it demonstrates that all of these transgression types are tightly bound up with discourse around extremity. Finally, it shows that just like transgression, extremity is also intimately tied up with ideas about art, and blurrings of the boundary between art and non-art, although the emphasis with extremity is more on the non-art (or pornographic) side of the boundary than with transgression, which is more discursively anchored in the realm of high art.

This close examination of censorship and transgression demonstrates how the framework of the transgressive art film functions in relation to several different boundaries, and how it operates coherently across different elements of discourse around extremity.

*

This chapter has laid out in detail the theory pillar of the framework underpinning the transgressive art film as a socio-cultural phenomenon, but the cinematic examples so far have mostly been linked to film form. In this final section, I therefore turn to the reception pillar in order to make clear the links between this theoretical idea of transgression and how transgressive art films are received. The focus nonetheless remains on the boundaries of art/non-art and censored/free-to-distribute.

When it comes to artistic transgressions, official boundaries are only part of the story, although they do function as a guideline for outrage. While it is common to hear moralistic arguments about controversial films like *Irreversible* or *Baise-moi* as 'sick' or 'depraved', even the unhappiest critics only rarely call for the films to be censored; they simply deplore them as a sign of an unhealthy society. Deciphering the exact societal conventions that make a film 'depraved' in the eyes of a tabloid journalist can partially be explained with reference to legal boundaries, but while the idea of the almost-transgressive is helpful here, it is not the full story. Moreover, it does not explain why the boundaries have been drawn in the places they have. In the twenty-first century, the kinds of films most likely to create controversy are those that include the confluence of eroticism and violence, or sexually explicit scenes as part of the diegesis. Concretely this means rape and sexual violence that is considered eroticised in some way, violent sex, images of menstrual blood, sexualised murder and/or cannibalism, and any scenes featuring explicit sexual acts between the actors. In these cases, however, trying to conceive of particular boundaries that might be transgressed by these images leads us into the vagaries of weak definitions of transgression. It is best to turn to audience reception as the final part of the puzzle, as controversies ultimately involve audiences vocally reacting to a film, most often being divided into opposing groups of defenders and critics. Viewers approach films through particular lenses and come to the cinema with particular preconceptions about what constitutes art, what kinds of images are appropriate for particular genres and narratives, and what kinds of acts should or should not be depicted on screen.

In the case of most films, these differences of approach are relatively inconsequential. Individual viewers prioritise different aspects of the film in their analyses such as focusing on aesthetics over political ideology, or on the film experience over the behaviour of the director on set, and these different prioritisations can exist alongside each other without any problems. In the case of films that are potentially transgressive of the aforementioned legal boundaries however, a viewer's approach to a film, and to whether its transgressions should be permitted, become central to deciding if a film is restricted or on general release, forbidden or available. I argue that transgressive art films include ambiguous imagery that not only allows for, but encourages, viewers to analyse the film in multiple ways (e.g. ethically rather than aesthetically) and these distinctions lead to some viewers regarding a film as worthy of art, while others decry the very same images as non-art, or inappropriate for artistic expression. The audiences of such films are therefore deeply divided, and what is more, these divisions are mutually exclusive, such that supporters actively dispute the validity of detractors' opinions, in ways that rarely arise in discussions of non-extreme films, where it is possible to accept a different approach to the film taken by another viewer. Considering a transgressive art film to be one that sets up these mutually exclusive viewing positions provides another means of describing a film's transgressions whilst maintaining a strong definition of transgression.

Cultural-studies work on reception based on Stuart Hall's idea of encoding/decoding has often focused on the idea that a text has a preferred reading encoded into it, and that audience responses to it are either 'dominant', 'negotiated' or 'oppositional'.[85] However, this presupposes that there is a clear ideological reading encoded into the text that is then engaged with by the reader or viewer, which may be the case for heavily ideologically imprinted texts such as news programmes, but is much harder to pinpoint in art films. Work on actual audience responses continually shows that individual spectator reactions are complex and rarely conform neatly to the categories proposed by scholars, being analogous to 'wrestling with a jellyfish; it squirms in so many different directions simultaneously that it seems impossible to control'.[86] Coming to terms with all these audience positions involves moving beyond basic comprehension of the meaning of the text, however complex that may be, and considering pre-existing interpretative schemas. In the case of transgressive imagery, the interpretative frameworks that count most are those pertaining to art and to ethics.

A useful concept for analysing these frameworks is Nathalie Heinich's concept of value registers. She argues that we must see transgressive art as moving 'the disagreement upstream toward the question of whether or not the litigious work of art appeals to morals, art, or symbolism'.[87] In other words, the impossibility of common ground between denigrators and embracers lies not in a conflict about surface elements of a film (narrative, cinematography, style), but in a conflict of value registers, which viewers bring to bear on the film. Prior to any specific discussion of an artwork or a film, viewers are always prioritising a paradigm through which to view a work, a value register that then provides a framework for analysing all aspects of the work and the experience of viewing it: 'value registers are the frameworks that enable participants to agree on which criteria are relevant in appreciating an object'.[88] To choose one value register over another is to reject *a priori* the lens through which another person is viewing art, images or a film as a whole. Choosing to prioritise the beauty of the film (aesthetic register), or interpreting the meaning and symbolism of the film (hermeneutic register) involves a fundamentally different approach to the film than one that begins with questions about what kinds of images are appropriate (ethical register) or one that focuses on the pleasures and sensations of spectatorship (aesthesic register).[89] As such, even when particular descriptions or physiological effects are shared by viewers (shock, arousal, discomfort), they are analysed through incompatible lenses: such viewers are unable 'to agree not only on the qualities of the object, but, at a higher level, on its axiological nature – indicating that there is conflict over which evaluations are relevant in analyzing the object'.[90] Many discussions about transgressive art films return to questions of ethics, but if a viewer is using a hermeneutic register to address ethics, they will always be talking at cross-purposes to a viewer who is using an ethical register for their analysis.

In the case of many non-transgressive films, the use of different registers can simply be shrugged off as an unremarkable difference of approach: the material stakes of choosing an analytical paradigm for *Shrek* or *Amélie* are negligible. In the case of transgressive art films and artworks, however, the registers are mutually exclusive because the choice to prioritise one register signals a rejection of another register. The value register chosen for a transgressive art film can signal whether that film should be cut, whether distribution should be allowed, whether it should spark a moral panic, and in the most extreme cases, whether a filmmaker should be prosecuted.[91] If we take the example of an explicit sex scene, the aesthesic register, focusing on the sensations elicited in the spectator might lead to it being considered to be pornography as it is a vehicle for arousal. Using the ethical register might also lead to a categorisation as pornography, because of a value of immorality attached to images of naked bodies.[92] By contrast a hermeneutic register might focus on the symbolism of the actors and their interactions, seeing a connection with a canonical painting or an ancient Greek myth, thereby classifying it as art. An aesthetic register might lead to a recognition of its beautiful depiction of bodies, sensuality and passion, that elevates it to art. In these examples, each of these registers is leading to an evaluation of the scene's value as art and, implicitly or explicitly, arguing that it should be restricted (pornography) or freely available (art). Defences against prosecution for obscenity precisely recognised this and tended to revolve around emphasising the hermeneutic or aesthetic register, with literature experts mobilised to defend *Fanny Hill* (Cleland, 1749) or *Lady Chatterley's Lover* (Lawrence, 1928) as genuine words of art, and with pornography experts fulfilling the same role in prosecutions for extreme pornography.[93] In these cases, the aesthetic or hermeneutic paradigm is not a disinterested choice, because it amounts to defending the artwork or film against those who wish to censor it. The choice of paradigm involves shades of grey if far from the limits of representation, but at those limits the same choice involves picking a side.

This example of defences of erotic works of art demonstrates the connection between value registers and perceptions about the nature of art, especially the acceptability of challenging affect in a work of art. The answer to the question 'is arousal a legitimate effect of an art film?' can lead to a viewer's analysis being placed on one side of an untranscendable boundary between art/not-art, art/porn, acceptable/not acceptable, free to distribute/censored, legal/illegal. Despite the increase in interest in the affective dimensions of art and film, for many critics there remains something unsavoury about films that address the body directly, and that invite identification with bodies on screen, notably in the genres of horror, melodrama and pornography.[94] If a viewer maintains a view of art in the Kantian tradition where aesthetic appreciation is disinterested and distanced, cerebral rather than affective, then any evocation of arousal is likely to lead the viewer to discount its artistic qualities before or without any significant engagement with the film itself. If instead, a viewer concurs with scholars of affect and welcomes a film's impact on the body, seeing it as an alternative form of engagement with audiovisual media that expands and undermines the hegemony of the visual,[95] or at the very least does not consider the affect of pornography or horror to preclude a film from being art, then that viewer is far more likely to be open to including graphic images of sex and violence within the domain of art. In other words, a viewer's pre-existing openness to affectively challenging images, and their broad convictions about what constitutes film art, can pre-determine the value judgement they are likely to make of a film. In terms of value registers, the hermeneutic and aesthetic registers tend to be adopted by those who embrace a film as art (exploring or ignoring the challenging affect), while the aesthesic and ethical registers tend to be part of analyses that reject the artistic value of the work (seeing the affect as unartistic or unethical).[96] Notably, these different approaches to a film involve reacting to the same experience – being viscerally moved by a film – but interpreting it differently because of the interpretative schemas that frame the viewer's encounter with the actual images.

Mattias Frey's distinction between the 'aesthetic embrace' and the 'cynicism criticism' as responses to extreme cinema, discussed earlier, captures this idea by linking a reaction to the film (embrace or criticise) to a kind of interpretative schema (aesthetic or cynical).[97] The aesthetic embrace covers those who embrace extreme films as challenging works of art. This is common amongst academic scholarship and involves a recuperation of the film's transgressions, often using the defences of transgressive art mentioned previously. The films are given a positive evaluation, with praise being given to their shocking, challenging nature, and with criticisms of the film often rejected or ignored. In this reading, the films are high art and therefore are seen to have an aesthetic, ethical or political vision of their own, which also entails a positive reading of the filmmaker's words and claims. In terms of my discussion, this involves a broad view of art that includes many kinds of affective response in the viewer, and either an aesthetic or hermeneutic value register: 'canonic' or 'formalist' defences of art evoke the aesthetic register, while an appreciation of the filmmaker's vision and an exploration of the film's meaning mobilise a hermeneutic register.

On the other side of Frey's viewer-response schema, there is the cynicism criticism, which encompasses rejections of these films, either as low-art spectacle or not as art at all. This view is more common in journalistic criticism and involves a dismissal of any profundity in the work, treating it as a superficial attempt to shock the spectator, as a spectacle designed to appeal to bodily affect rather than to the intellect. Such criticisms often involve an implicit rejection of body genres, and emphasise connections with pornography and body horror. In this reading, transgressive art films are a cynical attempt to exploit graphic images of sex and violence to shock the spectator, and have little or no artistic value. Furthermore, the films are often criticised as morally repugnant or at the very least amoral and nihilistic, especially in relation to their misogynistic treatment of women and rape, but also in terms of homophobia, racism and transphobia. This approach involves a more exclusive concept of art, that rejects challenging affect from its realm, and mostly employs the aesthesic and ethical registers: it prioritises the sensations of the film (as problematic), or focuses on the ethical nature of the images over and above any symbolic or aesthetic value they may have.

Importantly, as Frey notes, emphasising reactions to the filmmaker's claims about their film: 'although the two critical paradigms maintain opposing evaluations, they hinge upon structural similarities. Whereas the aesthetic embrace accepts the auteur's words but reads textually against the grain, the cynicism critic takes representation at face value and doubts the artist's sincerity'.[98] While this binary approach to interpretative paradigms requires nuancing, it usefully highlights how these opposing claims are ultimately based upon the same data, despite their quite different conclusions. The conflictual reception of transgressive art films always involves this talking at cross-purposes; disagreement on the level of values (what should we think about these images) is inevitable and intractable, because there is no agreement 'upstream' about the interpretative framework and criteria being used to answer that question. Frey is ultimately critical of both these camps for their blinkered approach to the films – the embracers blindly accepting 'even the most exploitative representations and amoral scenarios' and the cynics actively 'dumbing-down' the films in a haze of nostalgia for the transgressions of yesteryear – arguing that we should move beyond this false dichotomy for a more rigorous analysis that incorporates both perspectives.[99] He proposes that we situate embracers' claims as discursive aspirations within particular material contexts, and be sceptical both of those who wholeheartedly embrace aesthetic readings, and those who reject any reading of these films as artistic. While Frey sees these perspectives as ultimately reconcilable because each position is being selective and blinkered to serve its own critical ends, I suggest that we should instead see these oppositions between different readings of a transgressive art film as integral to what makes them controversial.

Value registers also bring the discussion back to the boundaries of art/non-art, acceptable/forbidden, freely distributable/restricted. While an exploration of value registers is in part a means of dealing with situations where it is difficult to see what boundaries a film may have transgressed, and therefore might tempt us to use a weak definition of transgression, discussion of value registers is important because it brings us back to specific boundaries even if they are not actually crossed in any legal or institutional sense of the word (i.e. the film has been released uncut). As noted previously, while the difference between freely distributable films and those that are restricted or forbidden is very clear in terms of its consequences, the terms used to characterise films on either side of the boundary are subject to significant interpretation, and are highly influenced by value register. In many jurisdictions, there are exceptions to pornographic images if they are 'artistic' or not meant primarily to arouse, while forbidden images of sexual violence are mainly those that are 'eroticised'. In the first case, this is directly related to a viewer's willingness to accept affective imagery as artistic rather than banishing it to the realm of pornography. In the second case of 'eroticisation', while it is often framed as clear by classification boards, working out what is erotic is always complex and open to interpretation, especially in relation to nudity: what forms of nudity are erotic? Do aroused genitals always lead to eroticisation, even in a rape scene? Does removing brief shots of buttocks in sex or rape scenes make a scene any less erotic?[100] Moreover, the nude has long been a part of high-art painting and sculpture, with sexually explicit Japanese *Shunga* drawings or Jeff Koons's explicit *Made in Heaven* series displayed in many major museums and galleries. An aesthetic or hermeneutic register is capable then of not only ignoring the aesthesic elements of an explicit artwork, but of actively celebrating them, just as an ethical register could allow a viewer to praise eroticisation (perhaps for eroticising non-normative bodies and expanding the visual field) or to denigrate it (perhaps for being inappropriate in public). Regardless of the actual film in question, questions of art and eroticisation, despite being central to deciding on the official transgressiveness of a film, are highly dependent on the viewer's conceptions of art and the value register they bring to bear on it. These underlying divisions become even more important in the context of rape imagery, where identification is a particularly thorny issue. How do we distinguish between rape imagery that revels in the pain and suffering of the victim, and that which seeks to enlighten its audience to the horror of rape? Is there necessarily any clear difference between two such images? There is little in such images that unequivocally cues a particular ethical response, and so a viewer's analysis of the image is likely to be heavily based on previous convictions about representation and its effects, and the value register they prioritise in their interpretation. It might be difficult to ascertain what specific boundaries films like *In My Skin* or *Holiday* transgress or almost-transgress, but a reflection on value registers shows how their evaluation by viewers, critics, scholars or censors can always be brought back to boundaries related to art and censorship.

Thinking through the reception of transgressive art films in this way provides a coherent way of conceptualising the irresolvable disagreements in audience responses to the films. It is important to reflect upon value registers rather than simply on values, as this not only gives an insight into the variety of views that arise in relation to particular films, but is at the heart of the controversy and insurmountable disagreements we see in the reception of transgressive art films. It allows for the discussion to remain focused on the same boundaries that are pertinent to the close analysis of film form –

those related to art and censorship – whilst also being dynamic enough to account for appreciable differences in the precise concerns and interpretations of audiences. Chapters 3, 4 and 5 examine how this theoretical exposition of transgressive art film reception translates into actual responses to individual films. In order to grasp the broader socio-cultural implications of transgressive art films, it is not enough to identify the almost- and marginally transgressive elements in the film form, it also entails a close examination of the splintering and divergent effect the film produces in its reception. With transgressive art films, these divergences occur not only on the level of value, but more profoundly on the level of value register.

*

The understanding of transgression outlined here in terms of artistic transgressions, marginal transgressions, extremity, art, censorship and value registers is central to the argument of this book. Transgressive acts and artistic transgressions are quite distinct and must be addressed in different ways. Nonetheless, key elements of sociological theories of transgressive acts, such as limited transgressions and transgression as normative, are helpful for theorising artistic transgression. Artistic transgression is mainly about recuperating and legitimising non-art practices within the domain of art, although it is important to acknowledge that the limits of art are heavily influenced by censorship rules. In order to grasp how a film is transgressive, it is important to be specific about the type of transgression, as well as the degree. Illicit transgressions of censorship rules can be separated into illegal, forbidden and restricted, with each category involving different kinds of transgression, and different consequences. In the past few decades, there has been a lexical shift in describing such infractions, with 'extreme' becoming a central term for designating films or images that go 'too far'. Analysing discourse around extremity in films, suggests that it is a sub-category of transgression, often used pejoratively and in the context of sexual, violent and sexually violent material. Understanding how transgressive art films are received by audiences involves thinking about the value register they apply to the film. The framework used to approach a film correlates substantially with viewer evaluations of scenes, and overall films, and helps to explain the polarised reception of these controversial films. All these ideas are present throughout the book and provide a framework for understanding transgressive art films, at the microscale of film form up to the macroscale of the cinema art world.

Notes

1. See Braziel and LeBesco, *Bodies out of Bounds*; Donnan and Magowan, *Transgressive Sex*; Dean, 'The Erotics of Transgression'; Hallam, *Screening the Marquis de Sade*; Papenburg and Zarzycka, *Carnal Aesthetics*; Aldana Reyes, *Body Gothic*; Dumas, *Genre et Transgression*; Gwynne, *Transgression in Anglo-American Cinema*; Richardson, *Transgressive Bodies*; Chappell and Young, *Bad Girls and Transgressive Women*; Birks, *Limit Cinema*.
2. See Dierkes-Thrun, *Salomé's Modernity*; Foley et al., *Transgression and Its Limits*; Jorgensen and Karlsen, *Transgression in Games and Play*; Mortensen and Jorgensen, *The Paradox of Transgression in Games*; Kang, *Transgression and the Aesthetics of Evil*.
3. See, for instance, Gournelos and Gunkel (*Transgression 2.0*) on transgression and remixing, pornography, pirates, spam emails, rioting and live news broadcasts, or Foley et al. on 'transgression in cinema, photography, art, law, music, philosophy, technology, and both classical and contemporary literature and drama . . . sexuality, violence, and the figuration of the human body . . . demotic speech, gender issues, and antihumanist music' ('Introduction', xi).
4. Beugnet, *Cinema and Sensation*, 34; Silverman, *Facing Postmodernity*, 3.
5. Taylor, *Troubled Everyday*, 4.
6. Jenks, *Transgression*, 2.
7. Jenks, *Transgression*.
8. Durkheim, *The Rules of Sociological Method*, 20–28; see also Jenks, *Transgression*, 23–25.
9. Durkheim, *The Rules of Sociological Method*, 52–66.
10. See Lukes, 'Introduction', xxiii–xxvi for a brief summary of critiques of this position, especially relating to its normativism. See Jenks about how in later years Durkheim moves away from this 'mechanically explicit concern with the specification of the natural unequivocal moral order of society in terms of generalities, their constraining influence and thus their causal significance' (*Transgression*, 25).
11. Jenks, *Transgression*, 25.
12. Jenks, 34.
13. Douglas, *Purity and Danger*, 165–66.
14. See Jenks (*Transgression*, 37ff.) and Ogien ('Les limites du tolérable', 52) for discussions of how Talcott Parson's social theory includes a comparable idea of transgression, with social bonds affirmed through forms of repression and socialisation reminiscent of Freudian psychoanalysis.
15. Durkheim, *The Rules of Sociological Method*, 56.
16. Becker, *Outsiders*, 14.
17. Evers, 'On Transgression'.
18. See Ogien, 'Les limites du tolérable'.
19. See any number of publications on the transgressive poetry of X, the literary transgressions of Y or the transgressive aesthetics of Z. In many of these cases, non-normative might have been a better word as it involves non-normative bodies, sexualities, gender presentations, formal structures or even genre adherence.
20. Even when, as is the case with Durkheim, their writing does not specifically make use of the word 'transgression'.

21 Bataille, *Erotism*, 67–68.
22 Bataille, *The Bataille Reader*, 69–70 ['The Torment']; Bataille, 226 [*Madame Edwarda*].
23 Bataille, *Erotism*, 63.
24 Bataille, 127.
25 Bataille, 65–66.
26 Bakhtin, *Rabelais and His World*, 7.
27 Some of this is maintained in modern-day carnivals, or in *braderies*, such as the one in Lille, where rules about bar-closing times and selling goods in the street are partially suspended resulting in all-night parties and huge semi-impromptu flea markets across the city centre. Nonetheless, rules about drunkenness remain strictly enforced and those related to selling alcohol are actually reinforced. Bakhtin's comments pertain to ancient, medieval and renaissance carnivals, a tradition that has mostly been lost in the modern era; these modern iterations he would describe as 'empty frivolity and vulgar bohemian individualism' (*Problems of Dostoevsky's Poetics*, 160).
28 Stallybrass and White, *The Politics and Poetics of Transgression*, 16.
29 Eagleton, *Literary Theory*, 148; see also Bataille, *The Accursed Share*, 2: 90–93.
30 Foucault, 'Preface to Transgression', 35.
31 Foucault, 34–35.
32 Foucault, 32; see Richardson (*Georges Bataille*, 6) for a discussion of the differences between Foucault's and Bataille's readings of transgression.
33 Foucault, 'Preface to Transgression', 30.
34 Bataille, *The Accursed Share*, 1:69; Mauss, *The Gift*, 6ff.
35 Bataille, *The Accursed Share*, 1:23.
36 Lübecker, *The Feel-Bad Film*, 132.
37 These lines can be blurred when directors commit crimes (such as Roman Polanski), or abuse their actors on set (think of *Last Tango in Paris*). Artistic transgressions can also lead to legal sanctions when an artist's transgressions are political in nature (e.g. Pussy Riot). On performance art that seeks to blur these boundaries, see Ardenne, *Extrême*.
38 Bataille, *Lascaux*, 38. Bataille does make a number of observations about transgression in *Literature and Evil*; see the chapter on Emily Brontë and in *The Accursed Share*, 2:105–107, 3:411–26 but these do not pertain to transgressive art, or even to transgression in art. They are more involved with questions of sovereignty, or with the experience of reading literature and the role of imagination.
39 See BBFC, '*Emmanuelle*'.
40 Jenks, *Transgression*, 84.
41 Heinich, *Le triple jeu*, 23. See Graves ('Transgressive Traditions', 43ff.) for a discussion of how Theodor Adorno on de Sade, Noël Carroll on Jarry, and Page du Bois on Sappho have all discussed the long-standing tradition of art subverting its own practices. Heinich also discusses this further in other publications ('De la transgression en art contemporain'; *Le paradigme de l'art contemporain*).
42 Heinich, 'The Art of Inflicting Suffering', 207.
43 Groys, *On the New*, 103.
44 Julius, *Transgressions*, 12.
45 Palmer, 'Style and Sensation', 32n1; Palmer, *Brutal Intimacy*, 59, 84–87; Palmer, *Irreversible*, 79–80.
46 Kipnis, *Bound and Gagged*, 164.

47 Heinich, *Le triple jeu*, 56; see also Becker, *Art Worlds*, 129.
48 Bourdieu, *The Rules of Art*, 226.
49 Graves, 'Transgressive Traditions', 45.
50 Julius, *Transgressions*, 26. These correspond more or less to descriptions of what constitutes art in the philosophy of art: for instance, in a film context, Shyon Baumann describes certain Hollywood films as art 'because they succeed on one or more levels, concerning their aesthetic characteristics, their relationship to other films, their communicative dimension, or their place within a recognized oeuvre' (*Hollywood Highbrow*, 6.).
51 See Heinich (*Le paradigme de l'art contemporain*, 5–16) for concrete examples of how this is done in the fine art world.
52 For comparable discussions in relation to 'torture porn' and 'extreme porn' see Jones, *Torture Porn*; 'Extreme Porn'.
53 For a discussion of this from a sociological perspective, see Baudry, *Le corps extrême*; 'La logique de l'extrême'. In this sense, I disagree with Hemmens and Williams (*Autour de l'extrême littéraire*) and Bétan (*Extrême!*) who seek an easy separation of extremity from transgression.
54 Lockwood and Smith, *Chambers/Murray Latin-English Dictionary*, 257.
55 Ardenne, *Extrême*, 19.
56 Serge III Oldenbourg's *Solo pour la mort* (1964).
57 Bataille, *The Bataille Reader*, 75 ['The Torment']; Simmel, 'The Metaphysics of Death', 74.
58 Baudry, *Le corps extrême*, 53; Peskoller, *Extrem*, 75.
59 Ardenne, *Extrême*, 211–12; Williams, *Screening Sex*, 5. See also Sargeant, 'Filth and Sexual Excess', 11; Paasonen, *Carnal Resonance*, 3.
60 Ardenne, *Extrême*, 95–96.
61 Criminal Justice and Immigration Act, section 63, paragraph 5. Similar provisions existed in previous legislation designed to censor films and literature, and indeed the same broad idea is applied in many countries. If restrictions on pornography exist, but films such as *Romance*, *Baise-moi*, *Anatomy of Hell*, *Antichrist*, *9 Songs* and so on were screened without restrictions, this means that films considered broadly to be artistic are given greater leeway in sexual representation than identical depictions in a film considered pornographic would be.
62 BBFC, 'Guidelines 2019', 12. See also Chapter 2, footnote 6.
63 See, for instance, BBFC, '*Born in Flames*'.
64 The same can be said for the sex scenes between Adèle and Emma in *Blue is the Warmest Colour*. Although the film is well known for its many erotic but non-explicit sex scenes, there is in fact a very brief inclusion of an erect penis in the early sex scene between Adèle and Thomas, distinguishing it from the other films just mentioned.
65 On exaggeration by critics and scholars, see Jones, *Torture Porn*, 185. On sex and violence as structuring elements, see also Durand and Mandel, 'Introduction'; Coulthard and Birks, 'Horrible Sex'.
66 Historically, blasphemy has blurred the illegal-act, illegal-representation and forbidden-representation categories I propose here, given that in the UK, for instance, (1) oral blasphemy has in itself been a crime that could be prosecuted, (2) most prosecutions of blasphemy dating back to the nineteenth century were for publications, while oral blasphemy was effectively decriminalised from the early twentieth century onwards and

(3) most films considered blasphemous or offensive to religions in the twentieth century have been refused classification but not prosecuted. However, given my focus on the present day, where blasphemy is no longer of particular relevance, and no longer on the statute books in most European countries, I will not address this in any further detail here.

67 See, for instance, BBFC, 'High-Yield Hydroponic Systems'; BBFC, 'Introduction to Indoor Growing'; BBFC, 'Mushroom Growing Made Easy'; BBFC, 'The Hash Man'.
68 For more details see Attwood and Smith, 'Extreme Concern'; Jackman, 'The Following Content Is Not Acceptable'; Smith, 'Breathing New Life into Old Fears'.
69 In the UK, this is slightly complicated by rulings from the so-called Spanner trials in the early 1990s when the House of Lords ruled that it was not possible to consent to certain sexual practices between adults (namely those including significant violence).
70 On the logical inconsistencies and intellectual dishonesty of 'harm', the other key element to these debates, as used to promote the criminalisation of 'extreme pornography' see Attwood and Smith, 'Extreme Concern', 177; Petley, Film and Video Censorship; 'The Censor and the State in Britain'.
71 In Hansard, HL Debate, 21 April 2008, c1358.
72 Examples from the UK include the pornographic films Lost in the Hood and My Daughter's a Cocksucker, and the non-pornographic films Grotesque, The Bunny Game and Murder-Set-Pieces.
73 Examples from the UK include I Spit On Your Grave, The Human Centipede II, A Serbian Film and Baise-moi.
74 BBFC, 'Annual Report 2001', 54.
75 BBFC, 'Annual Report 2002', 34.
76 BBFC, 'Annual Report 2004', 60.
77 BBFC, 'Annual Report 2011', 5. See also Bumfights – Cause for Concern – Volume 1, apparently 'so extreme and exploitative that it was rejected outright' (BBFC, 'Annual Report 2003', 70) and a description of Hostel, never censored but subject to significant media discussion, considered to contain 'extreme violence and gore' (BBFC, 'Annual Report 2006', 76).
78 Hostel: Part II is a slight exception to this with a scene of a naked torturer getting aroused as she slits her victim's throat. The transgressive nature of this image seems confirmed by the controversy it created with the film being explicitly mentioned in the House of Lords as part of a debate about 'extreme pornography' (in Hansard, HL Debate, 8 October 2007, c117–18).
79 Although countries such as Germany, Ukraine, Spain, Malaysia, Thailand and Australia did choose to ban or censor some of the films in the Saw and Hostel series.
80 It is interesting to note that on porn tube websites, 'softcore' is sometimes used today together with 'female-friendly' as a signifier of gentler pornography, even when including hardcore shots of penetration, ejaculation and so on.
81 BBFC, 'Annual Report 2005', 82.
82 Pett, 'A New Media Landscape?', 92–94.
83 See Petley, 'Cannibal Holocaust and the Pornography of Death'; Tait, 'Pornographies of Violence?'; Hester, Beyond Explicit for a detailed discussion of this.
84 Such as 9 Songs, The Pornographer, Ken Park, The Life of Jesus, Q, Raspberry Reich, Shortbus, Stranger by the Lake, I Want Your Love, The Wayward Cloud, The Story of

    Richard O., The Night, The Daughters of Fire (see Davis, 'The View from the Shortbus'; Kenny, 'Breaking Conventions?').
85 Hall, 'Encoding/Decoding'.
86 Lewis, *The Ideological Octopus*, 115.
87 Heinich, 'The Art of Inflicting Suffering', 219.
88 Heinich, 210–11.
89 In developing an all-encompassing sociology of values, including discussions of architecture, bull-fighting, popular music and performance art, Heinich identifies a total of twelve value registers: 'aesthetic (referring to art or beauty), ethical (referring to morality, or consideration for others), aesthesic (referring to pleasurable feelings or sensations), hermeneutic (meaning or signification), reputational (renown or honor), authenticity (referring to integrity or purity), economic (monetary value), civic (referring to general public interest), domestic (referring to familiarity or close relations), functional (referring to utility or convenience), legal (referring to legality or conformity to rules), and epistemic (referring to knowledge and truth)' (212). Examining discourse around transgressive art films demonstrates that only the hermeneutic, aesthetic, aesthesic and ethical registers are of significant relevance here.
90 Heinich, 211.
91 Consider the attempted prosecutions of the makers of *Cannibal Holocaust*, and of a festival organiser who screened *A Serbian Film* (Pape, 'So Scandalous a Prosecutor Took Notice').
92 See endnote 96.
93 Clarissa Smith, for instance, a Professor in Media, has acted as an expert witness in numerous trials for extreme pornography.
94 Williams, 'Film Bodies'.
95 cf. Marks, *The Skin of the Film*; Sobchack, *Carnal Thoughts*; Barker, *The Tactile Eye*.
96 While this is a common tendency, this dichotomy is not inherent to the registers. For instance, a reading that focused on the treatment of performers on set, the depiction of non-normative bodies, and the sexual ideology of the representations could be using an ethical register to analyse the film, but with a more progressive political outlook.
97 Frey, *Extreme Cinema*, 30–45.
98 Frey, 44.
99 Frey, 38, 40–41.
100 See Kenny ('British Film Censorship in the Twenty-First Century') for a detailed discussion of the BBFC's approach to these questions.

2

Visibility, Proximity, Duration

First released in 2000, *Baise-moi* provoked scandal and outrage across the world. A campaign by religious groups in France led initially to it being banned, until street protests by filmmakers forced ministers to rewrite the classification rules in order to reinstate it. Censorship boards in the UK, Australia, New Zealand and Canada stepped in to cut the film, with filmmakers publicly protesting the film's censorship by the Ontario Film Review Board. Critics complained loudly about the film's inclusion of shots of penetration during the rape scene, described in an audience study as 'the most graphic rape scene I've seen', and 'like watching an *actual* rape'.[1] Over the period of a few years, films like *Romance* and *Irreversible* similarly courted controversy for their explicit scenes of sex and violence, and how uncomfortably visceral their images were. The length of the unedited rape scene in *Irreversible*, and the close-up shots of genitals and childbirth in *Romance* were the subject of many shocked and distressed reviews.

How visible? How close? How long? These are the key questions we must ask to identify the formal qualities associated with transgressive art films, especially their depictions of sex, violence and sexual violence. In this chapter I will develop a heuristic for pinpointing and understanding the kinds of images at the centre of the controversies around transgressive art films. Not just stylistic elements, nor signifiers of genre adherence, the particular engagements of transgressive art films with visibility, proximity and duration are directly linked to their propensity for provocation, and their susceptibility to being censored. It is not simply a pattern, but a pattern that matters. Together with the analysis of reception and theory, it sheds light on what links individual transgressive art films to one another, as well as explaining why controversies revolve around these particular stylistic choices and subject matter. The corpus for this analysis is the seven films that provoked unusual and significant consternation on their release, and have been included almost universally in critical and scholarly discussions about controversial or extreme images of sex and violence: *Sombre, Romance,*

Baise-moi, Irreversible, Anatomy of Hell, Twentynine Palms and *Trouble Every Day*. The analysis of these films is drawn from the substantial scholarly writing on them, from journalistic reviews, popular discussions and my own close readings. While visibility, proximity and duration are frequently mentioned separately in reviews of individual films, the development of an overarching heuristic employing these three concepts to understand an array of controversial films is my original intervention. The analysis here is both textual and discursive, including detailed consideration of scenes from transgressive art films, as well as careful examination of how critics and scholars discuss these films, how they frame their arguments, and the theoretical issues that arise from this work. In connection with key theoretical terms from the previous chapter – the almost-transgressive and the marginally transgressive – I will also show how these films dedicate substantial screen time to images that push up against, test or almost-transgress clearly definable boundaries, with only a limited number of images marginally transgressing those boundaries.

In relation to visibility, I explore especially how penetration, genital contact, erections and ejaculation are obscured or made visible in scenes of sex and rape. Considering proximity, I examine the use of close-ups and extreme close-ups, haptic imagery, the evocation of disgust and arousal, and the use of shock and surprise. Finally, in terms of duration, I investigate the tendency to privilege the long take and long scene when depicting sex and violence. Much of the analysis revolves around the fraught issue of images of sexual violence. This chapter demonstrates the problematically central role of sexual violence in transforming uncomfortable images, which cinema is ultimately full of, into the full-blown controversies that led to innumerable walk-outs and faintings,[2] that saw some journalists engaging in open warfare within individual publications,[3] some reaching for decidedly extreme vocabulary to denounce these films, and others hailing the works as masterpieces. Reflecting on the role of criticism and scholarship in recuperating sexually violent imagery, this also raises questions about how such transgressions become valorised by scholars, thereby furthering the legitimisation of graphic scenes of sexual violence. Paying careful attention to scenes that emphasise visibility, proximity and duration is important as this is the precise locus of the transgression. At the same time, we must recognise that such analysis forms part of the cinema ecosystem, and therefore plays an important role in elevating a film to the status of transgressive art film.

*

Visibility is the most evident illustration of transgression in film, primarily because it is the most tangible and easily describable transgression, and the main focus of censorship. For many commentators, it is also the most striking feature of transgressive art films: visible erections, penetration, ejaculation; menstrual blood, childbirth; graphic beatings, cutting, wounds; explicit scenes of sexual assault and rape. While sex and violence are common to art cinema, it is highly unusual for the detail of such acts to be made visible to the camera: visible penetration belongs generally to pornography, while graphic images of violence find their home standardly in horror or exploitation films. The visibility of sex and violence immediately brings us up against two boundaries: between (high) art cinema on the one side, and non-art (pornography) or low-art (horror/exploitation) on the other. In order to frame the detailed discussion of the core films, a brief explanation of how these two boundaries relate to visibility is useful. The issue of art/not-porn versus non-art/porn is dealt with explicitly by censorship and classification boards, and is often couched in terms of what can or cannot be seen in the image. The question of high art versus low art is the domain of critics and scholars, and relates to visibility when films are denigrated for emphasising spectacle over narrative. Visible sexual acts, and spectacularised sex and violence are therefore the most obvious kinds of images that transgressive art films bring controversially into the realm of art cinema.

In the simplest terms, censors examine what is visible in film images, and decide whether they can be made visible to the public. The censor holds the power to make images visible, by allowing or refusing permission for images to be screened, by obscuring or forbidding images, or banning a film in its entirety: the material is removed from, or made available to, the visible realm. Censors commonly classify films according to what is visible on the screen, or to the words that are spoken. The visibility of certain objects or acts denotes pornography (e.g. erect penises, penetration), the use of certain swear words will restrict its exhibition to adults. For instance, at the time of release of most transgressive art films in the UK, the BBFC defined a 'sex work', as material containing 'clear images of real sex'; these are passed at 'R18' (available only in licensed sex shops).[4] These 'clear images' are compared to the 'simulated' images which may pass at '18', a distinction violated by the explicit images of many transgressive art films.[5] These descriptions highlight that simulation/reality and visibility are important in the board's distinction between pornographic and non-pornographic films. The exact rules do of course differ across countries, but today a distinction between visible sex in restricted hardcore pornography, and simulated or non-explicit sex in films on general release is quite standard.[6] Given this standard association of visible sex with pornography, the visibility of sex or body parts has raised particular concerns in scenes of sexual violence, where it has been considered to eroticise the scene. For instance, the graphic shot of penetration during the rape scene in *Baise-moi* was removed in several countries for its potentially 'titillating' nature,[7] while in the UK numerous edits were required of the rape-centred film *I Spit on your Grave* predominantly in order to remove shots of the victim's breasts and the naked buttocks of both victim and rapists.[8] In each of these cases, a simple connection is made between visibility and pornography, between visibility in the image and the kinds of visibility afforded to that image in the world.

This denigration of visibility has been reiterated in many forms, mostly related to the idea that in transgressive art films, sex and violence are transformed into titillating spectacle, where the making visible of spectacle is contrasted unfavourably with narrative. A repeated criticism of transgressive art films is that they focus on spectacles of sex and violence to the detriment of narrative, with the implicit claim that this leads the spectacles to be tawdry, dirty and unsavoury.[9] Indeed, *Irreversible*'s rape and murder sequences were frequently described as pornographic as a result of flesh being visible, with one critic going as far as to argue that the camera 'leers' at Monica Bellucci (who plays the rape victim) during the rape sequence because her dress is somewhat revealing, despite the fact that the camera is mostly static.[10] For such critics, visibility is associated with low art, gory horror and pornography, and their analyses have much in common with critics of pornography and 'pornification', who often couch their concerns in terms of excess visibility. Dominique Baqué, for instance, describes as pornographic that which 'makes flesh visible in all its crudeness', while Michela Marzano describes the erotic (which she separates from the pornographic) as that which 'forces the spectator to engage with a register other than solely the visible'.[11] In other words, for scholars seeking to separate art films from supposedly low- or non-art bodily spectacles, the visible, or indeed the too-visible, is a key fault-line for distinguishing the two. Before we even begin to analyse the detail of the images, visibility can be considered central to divisions between art cinema on the one hand, and non-art or low-art cinema on the other. Transgressive art films include 'clear' images of sex, and long spectacles of sex, violence and sexual violence, thereby risking being tarnished as unartistic for transgressing the boundaries of acceptable visibility.

Despite many conservative critics' exaggerated claims about the extent of visibility in transgressive art films, however, there are actually relatively few explicit images, and the clarity of those images is often limited. Many images can be considered almost-transgressive, but there are only a few marginally transgressive images in each film. As such, these infractions are broadly tolerated as limited transgressions, allowing the films to escape being designated as pornography, even as some of their images may be considered pornographic.

In *Trouble Every Day*, we see this in two scenes of sexual violence. In one sequence, the male protagonist (Shane) seduces a hotel maid in a locker room, but the consensual gropings quickly transform into screams of pain as the man sinks his teeth into the woman's vulva, rising with a blood-smeared face to penetrate her whilst he licks and bites her face. In another, the female protagonist (Coré) sucks a man's blood during intercourse after a series of extreme close-ups that graze his expectant aroused body. Each scene features an unusually graphic sexual image: Shane's mouth up against the maid's vulva, and Coré inserting her lover's penis into her vagina. At the same time, transgressive art films often use genital prostheses for the sex scenes, and so it remains unclear what took place on set in terms of penetration or genital contact. For the purposes of most censorship boards, the details of actions on set are not of primary importance, only what is seen on screen. Both these images are nonetheless shrouded in darkness, as are many of the later shots, such that it is difficult to make out exactly what is being inserted, licked or bitten. Extreme close-ups dissociate parts of the body from the whole without making it clear what is being shown, and in the case of the close-ups of Coré's attack even make it unclear which direction is up and down, as the camera rotates. Whilst sexual and sexually violent content is made visible, it is only very brief, and the darkness makes it very difficult to see in any case. These scenes are disturbing for many reasons, not least the proximate cinematography, and the blurring of the nature of the acts (as it is unclear when a consensual sexual partner's moans of pleasure become a victim's screams of pain), but in terms of visibility, the transgression of the limit between general release and pornography is only marginal. Even if *Trouble Every Day* is unusually erotically charged and explicit in terms of mainstream depictions of sex and violence, most of the sex and violence remains obscured or outside the frame, and much of the film is taken up by images that are not of sex or violence: walking around Paris, shots of hotel corridors, a day in the laboratory.

Trouble Every Day therefore troubles the boundaries of visibility – of what we can see, what we can understand, what we consider should be shown – but it pulls back from significant foregrounding of any one controversial image, such that whole scenes, and indeed the whole film, communicates a sense of unease and disquiet, drifting shockingly but briefly into gory eroticised violence, only to draw back into something else. Commenting on the oral attack on the woman's vulva during which the film cuts to a shot of her head at the moment Shane bites, Laura McMahon sums up the potency of this play with boundaries as opposed to a more visible display of sexual violence, writing that the film 'refus[es] to display the horror of the event up close . . . It is precisely in its engagement with the abyssal real of this kiss that the film finds itself eschewing representation.'[12] We see this engagement/eschewal schema in another scene when Shane runs into the bathroom when having sex with his wife in order to masturbate furiously for fear he will kill her in a cannibalistic rage: the flight of the ejaculate is visible from a position behind Shane but his erect penis remains just outside the frame. A man graphically masturbating to ejaculation would ordinarily be considered pornographic, but here it is only partially shown.

We frequently see this dynamic in transgressive art films: clear images of penetration, aroused genitals and ejaculation. However, in general the explicitness is brief, or only takes up a small part of the frame, or it is only just visible because of dark lighting, or we see the aftermath but not the sex itself. Sex is central to many sequences, and explicit sexual imagery is part of many scenes, but it is not foregrounded. For example, in *Anatomy of Hell* brief close-ups make a vulva and vaginal penetration visible on a few occasions, but aroused genitals are mostly hidden from view. In *Romance*, the protagonist clearly places her partner Paul's penis in her mouth, but it is hidden mostly by her hand and he quickly stops her and pulls up his underwear. In another sequence, with new lover Paolo, his erect penis is visible at the bottom of the frame for some time, but mostly to put on a condom, and later when he goes to penetrate her, but the penetration is obscured by his leg, and most of the scene is dominated by head shots of them talking. In a fantasy porn sequence at the end of *Romance*, multiple women are visible from afar being penetrated by numerous men, while others stand around masturbating, but there are no close-ups. This finishes with a very brief shot of ejaculation, which cuts to gel being squeezed onto the protagonist's belly for an ultrasound scan. In an early scene in *Irreversible*, set in a BDSM club, there are glimpses of sex and masturbation in side rooms as the point-of-view camera roams from side to side, while in the central rape scene, there is a brief glimpse of a detumescing penis.[13] In *Baise-moi*, almost all of these are included: a brief close-up of penetration during a rape scene, brief shots of penetration taken from afar (from a high surveillance-type angle of the rape, and from the other side of the room in a sex scene, which are also barely visible because of the low lighting), and a shot of ejaculate wiped on one of the character's skin by a penis post-sex.

Taken separately, each of these images can be considered pornographic in the sense that it shows aroused genitals, penetration or ejaculation. However, in the context of an art film whose other scenes do not show visible sex, most censors were willing to grant these images an artistic exemption, transforming them into accepted transgressions. At the same time, these transgressions occur in the context of often long, almost-transgressive sequences, rather than arising suddenly in the midst of otherwise innocuous images. A brief shot of a rope being pulled across a vulva in *Romance* is part of a long sequence of a woman being tied up and gagged in an erotic BDSM scenario; the fantasy porn sequence follows a scene where numerous medical students insert their fingers into her vagina, a procedure that is overtly sexualised by the voice-over. The characters in *Anatomy of Hell* spend much of their time naked and discussing the details of sex and bodies. The detumescing penis in *Irreversible* is shown after what is often acknowledged as the most gruelling rape scene in cinema history, and precedes the violent mutilation of the woman's face. Each film as a whole pushes up against the limits of acceptable representation in terms of graphic sexual display, and then includes a few brief transgressions of those limits.

These limited transgressions can be usefully contrasted with the maximalist depictions of horror pornography pastiche *Re-Penetrator*, which, like *Trouble Every Day*, depicts bloody cunnilingus and murder during penetrative sex. In *Re-Penetrator*, a female corpse is brought to life by a male doctor, with whom she has copious sex before eating him alive. The sexual acts between doctor and zombie are filmed in great detail and last for most of the film (there are no other narrative elements – even the position changes are edited out). From the beginning, both characters are covered in blood, and extra blood is regularly added to the scene. Fellatio, manual stimulation, vaginal penetration and cunnilingus are all shown in lengthy close-ups, emphasising the unambiguous nature of the actors' interactions. When the doctor is eaten in the final scene, we see his intestines ripped out, limbs thrown across the room, and his now-flaccid penis beaten violently. *Re-Penetrator* attempts to make every sexual and violent act maximally visible, with heavy-metal music added to amplify the intensity of the thrusting.

To understand how the transgressions of *Trouble Every Day* are controversial, while *Re-Penetrator*'s are banal, it is important to consider the degree and type of visibility in a film: brief shots of barely visible penetration are considered quite differently from long takes of clearly visible penetration. The limited transgressions of *Trouble Every Day*'s explicit sex enable it to be contextualised against the norms of art cinema, while *Re-Penetrator*'s maximalist visibility is framed against the norms of heterosexual pornography. Critics of transgressive art films often claim that they are 'showing extreme and graphic physical violence', or that there are 'rivers of viscera and spumes of sperm ... fucking and fisting, sluices of cum and gore'.[14] The details of these hyperbolic descriptions are more pertinent to horror pornography or hardcore horror, than to anything you might likely see in your local cinema, but the very hyperbole shows how provocative these brief excursions outside art cinema can be. At the same time, the shocking impact of *Trouble Every Day* derives from its constant pushing at the limits of acceptable visibility as well as its brief inclusion of transgressive visibility. Transgressive art films are not maximalist, but rather include images that are mostly not transgressive, often almost-transgressive and sometimes marginally transgressive.

Understandably, these transgressively visible and shocking images are a core part of many viewers' overall reactions to the films. Broadly speaking, discussions around visibility divide into the critical and the embracing.[15] Critics focus mainly on the issues of censorship and pornography discussed so far, but embracers argue just as much about the positive value of visibility, extolling the virtue of including explicit sex and violence in art films. Embracing accounts tend to fall into two broad categories: those that mobilise the estrangement defence of transgressive art, arguing that transgressive or extreme imagery shocks viewers into looking differently at the world;[16] and those that see such films as expanding the visible world, as extending the bounds of what members of a society are able to see and imagine. As the negative view of visibility in relation to censorship or pornography is more straightforward and has also been explored in some detail in the previous chapter's discussion of censorship, this section on visibility will focus on how these same elements have been recuperated, and framed as positive ethico-political interventions.

Visibility is raised most by embracers of transgressive art films in terms of positive recuperations of the shock of graphic sex and the discomfort of graphic sexual violence, with an appeal to an idealised spectator. Unexpected, transgressive visibility 'alienate[s] us from our preconceptions, by making the familiar strange and the unquestioned problematic' and is thereby challenging to our sensibilities and disturbs the frameworks by which we come to analyse the world.[17] In this reading, the shocking visibility of diegetic acts or events makes visible the structures and frameworks of violence, power and domination that many of us do not see or have become problematically accustomed to. Such a reading of *Baise-moi*, for instance, considers the unseen structuring violence of patriarchy to be made visible in the barrage of physical male violence that overwhelms the opening twenty minutes of the film, including the explicit shots of rape. *Baise-moi* follows Manu and Nadine, who at the beginning of the film are physically and verbally abused by people, mainly men but also women, leading to them killing a brother and a housemate, respectively. Prior to this, Manu and a friend are kidnapped and raped in a warehouse in a now infamously violent and visible sequence, which includes shots of penetration during rape, and led to censorship in many countries. Many of the men who inflict the assaults remain nameless, history-less and their assaults unexplained. That this is about systemic domination rather than individual eruptions of physical violence is further highlighted in the cross-cutting between the verbal abuse of Manu by her brother, and of Nadine by her (female) housemate; just because Nadine's housemate is a woman does not mean she escapes being part of patriarchal violence. Nadine's and Manu's acts of murder are their first violent responses to the systemic violence that surrounds them, and the film's visualisation of physical acts of violence stands as a shocking proxy for otherwise less visible apparatuses of power and coercion. This contention about the making visible of structural violence effectively draws upon a distinction between physical acts of aggression, conflict and brutality, and the violence that sustains the status quo, the invisible forces of control, power and enforcement that underpin societal relations, and that inflict symbolic and systemic violence on particular groups. The visible acts of violence that viewers can see are symptomatic of the broader structural violence they cannot. In this reading, the making visible of the details of these acts is interpreted as an ethical intervention that makes visible the structural violence.

In commentary on these core transgressive art films, those who appreciate the films often turn to this idea of visibility as an ethical intervention in their interpretations of the most controversial transgressively visible images. For viewers of films such as *Baise-moi*, this was often understood in terms of 'reality'. Martin Barker et al.'s study into sexual violence, which questioned viewers about *Baise-moi*, noted frequent references to the film's authenticity or realism, terms which were often linked to the visibility of penetration in the rape scene. In this scene we see the lead rapist's erection on several occasions and two clear shots of penetration, one in close-up and one in medium-long shot. As one of the study's respondents says, 'it's like watching an *actual* rape, that's what's so disturbing seeing it, he's actually having sex with her . . .' and another says 'although its consensual, its still real [*sic*]'.[18] For these and many other viewers, the visibility of the sex and violence is integral to the ethical impact of this scene because it emphasises the intrusive, penetrative, invasive aspects of rape. It makes concrete and visible what happens when a person is raped. Indeed, numerous respondents in this study criticised the BBFC's decision to cut the penetration shots from the UK release because these visible shots are 'a sign of a will to intrude on the[ ] [women's] bodies' and 'a way of possessing them'; the cutting of this scene was 'regretted since it reduces that awareness of the women's "possession" by men'.[19] The visibility of penetration is integral to making visible aspects of rape (physical penetration) that are not normally visible in film. Even more compelling for this interpretation is the fact that respondents who criticised the film because visible penetration is a 'marker of pornography' and a sign of the 'will to arousal', agreed that the visible penetration in this scene had nothing to do with arousal.[20] As another of Barker et al.'s respondents asks: 'you do know that rape in the real world often has penetration, right?'[21] Implicitly, these respondents are acknowledging the links between the visibility of penetration, and the making visible of the invasive violence of rape, because they cannot link these images of penetration to arousal as they ordinarily would. This visible depiction of the details of rape is interpreted as revealing an alternative non-pornographic way of looking at a close-up image of penetration.

Visibility is read in this ethico-political way by many scholars in relation to transgressive art films. To give a brief selection of these analyses, *Romance*'s and *Anatomy of Hell*'s explicit sexual imagery and *Romance*'s rape scene are seen to evoke the phallocentric domination that underpins sex, womanhood and gender relations.[22] In *Irreversible*, the visibility of the rapist's penis and of the victim's battered face are read as leading the viewer to a wider cultural point about the lack of attention and empathy given to wounded female bodies.[23] Clear shots of Katia urinating in *Twentynine Palms* are seen as speaking to a desublimation of the quotidian; and through a slightly more complex logic, *Trouble Every Day*'s shocking images of sexualised cannibalism are seen to evoke the links between infection, science and colonialism.[24] Beyond the core films mostly discussed here, the graphic and sexualised violence of *Antichrist* has been connected to the violence of structures of gender, sexuality, heteronormativity and bodily autonomy,[25] while *Fat Girl*'s long scenes of coerced sex, and the closing scene of stranger rape, have been understood as different sides of Breillat's controversial comparison of male seduction and rape, both read as forms of patriarchal violence.[26] *In My Skin*'s graphic self-mutilation is seen as revealing the normative constraints of capitalism and patriarchy.[27] In terms of links between bodies and nations, *Battle in Heaven*'s scenes of explicit sex are read as evocative of a biopolitics of race and gender in Mexico,[28] while *A Serbian Film*'s litany of sexual violence is read as symptomatic of the Serbian national, economic and social situation.[29] Each of these readings is premised, in one way or another, on the ethical and political valorisation of the unusual visibility of sex, sexual violence and violence in these films, as well as the figure of the idealised spectator. Such interpretations serve to recuperate the kinds of marginally transgressive images that are considered problematic and ethically dubious by censors and those critical of the films.

The other approving approach to visibility operates a similar form of recuperation but frames it in terms of expansion. Challenging imagery, or what Asbjørn Grønstad calls 'unwatchable' imagery, 'transcends the threshold of the visible world' in the sense that going beyond the limits of the visible expands the outer limits of conventional images and enables an (idealised) viewer to look at the world in ways not previously possible.[30] Images that are difficult to watch are often far beyond the viewer's lived experience, expanding viewers' ideas about a subject, and also the total sum of images available to all viewers. In Grønstad's reading, this is a positive ethical move, and this ethical approval of unwatchability was evoked by several viewers in Barker et al.'s study in relation to the images of rape in *Irreversible*:

> [Ross]: 'I want the film to provoke this reaction in me' . . . [David] 'the longer it went on, the more uncomfortable I was with it. But I don't think that was a bad thing, I think that was a *really* good thing.'[31]

Ross and David compare what is and what should be, suggesting effectively that transgression is necessary for this film to remain ethically acceptable. For these viewers, *Irreversible* is at the limits of what should be made visible, and yet the transgression of that line is still seen as a good thing.[32] In this reading, the limit of the watchable has ethical resonance: in pushing viewers to the limits of what they are willing to watch, a film asks questions about the difference between what is visible and what should be visible, thereby forcing a reflection on the ethics of particular images, but also on the ethics of their choice to watch and continue watching. Transgressive visibility here is seen to perform the classic transgressive move of pushing back the limits of the acceptable by marginally transgressing them.

This idea can also be reframed as a 'normalisation' in that the explicit aim is to bring the currently transgressive, abnormal or, in Durkheim's terms, pathological into the realm of the standard, normal or generally accepted. It shows a desire for affective images to be taken more seriously and for strongly affective imagery to be a standard part of art cinema. Thomas Morsch and Martine Beugnet frame their affective readings precisely in this comparative manner, calling for an expanded idea of cinema and the role of affect within it. For them, the expansions of the visible world can be seen not as a '*loss* of aesthetic distance and the capacity to judge, rather . . . a *gain* in corporeality and somatic intensity' that is 'no longer simply destructive but also a "sensual and sensitive extension of our selves".'[33] Attention is focused on phenomenological interpretations: rather than reading the violent or sexual images as shocking or unwatchable, they are considered to be intensely affective, communicating via the body, pulling away but not detaching themselves entirely from the narrative-centred concerns of most mainstream cinema. The visibility of bodies, bodily fluids, and violent and sexual acts is important here as an appeal to the non-visual senses. Visibility is necessary to achieve this.

Such a valorisation of bodily affect and somatic intensity can also be seen in accounts of transgressive art films that praise them for recuperating images that have been co-opted by pornography, and for giving such images new meaning beyond the limited realm of arousal and masturbation. In contradistinction to the predominantly masculine gaze of heterosexual pornography, 'such acts reveal alternative, non-pornographic ways of being sexual' by displacing, fragmenting, relativising and undermining conventional pornographic modes of spectatorship.[34] In this way the touch of tongue on clitoris, the pulse of an erect penis, the moisture of an aroused vagina, and the corporeal reaction in the spectator they might provoke are recuperated from the non-art realm of pornography, and normalised as legitimate film-art imagery. This line of argument has been widely used in relation to the films of Catherine Breillat, but has also been applied to broader corpora of films.[35]

The importance of visibility for the censor as well as audiences is underlined by the overwhelming focus on these scenes by viewers of the films. As Barker et al. demonstrated, a viewer's evaluation of scenes that are transgressively visible is generally analogous to their overall feelings about the whole film.[36] Moreover, as I have shown, the issue of visibility comes to dominate interpretations of these scenes, not only in relation to what should or should not be shown, but as a more abstract ethico-political schema. Whether to denigrate as part of a criticism of spectacle, or to praise as part of a revealing of hidden societal structures and an expansion of the visible world, the visible as a concept runs through many often-contradictory interpretations of the visibility of sex and violence in transgressive art films. Most viewers agree that explicit sexual imagery has affective, if not overtly arousing, effects, and that shots of penetration or graphic images of sexual violence are transgressive of established limits. What they ultimately disagree on is how to evaluate and interpret such visibility, whether to forbid it (censorship), to restrict it (as pornography) or to recuperate it within the domain of the art film. This demonstrates the importance of considering visibility to identify transgressive art films on a formal level, to understand how they are read by audiences, critics and scholars, and how this fits into larger legal and cultural frameworks such as those related to censorship.

*

Proximity is the second formal concept paramount to transgressive art films, their transgressions and the discourse around them. In transgressive art films, the power of the close-up and extreme close-up to evoke sensation is frequently exploited, especially in disturbing or erotic situations, contributing to their reputation for being provocative and affectively challenging. Close-ups of vulvas (in the context of menstruation, childbirth, sex and rape), of skin, hair, hands and feet, of brutal bodily violence inflicted on faces, and other body parts, are used repeatedly. *Anatomy of Hell*, *Romance* and *Trouble Every Day* feature close-ups of skin, limbs, genitals and intertwined bodies during sex. *Baise-moi*, *Irreversible*, *Trouble Every Day*, *Sombre* and *Twentynine Palms* contain close-ups of sexual and non-sexual violence. In proximate, visible detail we see bodies being touched; genital penetration; heads being crushed; blood, penises and labia being sucked. Beyond the visual close-up, transgressive art films also use aural close-ups and disorienting cinematography to overwhelm viewers. Critics and scholars often describe the discomfort of watching sex and violence in these films, the way the films get under one's skin, how the images feel 'too close'. Close-ups are an important part of many scholarly analyses of transgressive art films,[37] and have been frequently associated with the evocation of materiality.[38]

While close-ups do often increase the visibility of violent and sexual acts, this section is interested in how they evoke the sense of proximity to the diegetic acts in ways that trouble the limits of watchability and of mainstream representation. While proximity is less obviously linked to censorship rules, which focus almost exclusively on visibility, we shall see that together with duration, it also plays an important role in allowing the transgressions of these films to be accepted as artful rather than being rejected. Once again, we will see that proximity, whether in terms of close-up imagery or the evocation of materiality and sensation in other ways, only briefly and marginally goes 'too far' in these films, with most images being unexceptionally distanced from diegetic events. The sustained communication of bodily affect, especially in the context of sexual and violent scenes is nonetheless unusual and received as intense and daunting by many viewers. This combination of unusually intense affective images with shockingly proximate shots of sex and violence is another of the hallmarks of transgressive art films.

Romance and *Anatomy of Hell* are good examples of the shocking and sensuous use of close-ups, especially in their sex sequences. *Romance* follows

Marie's adventures with and reflections on sex with husband Paul, stranger Paolo and colleague Robert, as well as her subsequent pregnancy. In a scene in which Marie is tied up by Robert for the first time, we are given visual and aural close-ups of the detailed manoeuvres: the rubbing of the rope is audible, each knot is shown in close-up emphasising each small element making up the whole of 'a BDSM scene'. A close-up shot of Marie's pubic hair draws viewers towards her genitals, the image and sound of the rope being pulled tight across them very clear as the rope rubs along her genitals, accentuating the sensual intricacies of sexual submission. In several sex scenes, the close-ups are central: for instance, when Marie has sex with Paolo (as he penetrates Marie, the camera slowly zooms in onto their heads, and then during sex, pans slowly across to their lower halves and back towards their heads, a camera movement repeated when Paolo climaxes); and when Marie and Robert kiss for the first time (the camera focuses on his eyes flicking down to her lips, the camera runs up and down Marie's arm, then a close-up on Marie with Robert's face slowly moving into the frame). In a later scene, we are given a close-up shot of a baby and associated viscera emerging from Marie's vagina, the stretching of such a small hole made visible, the pain of labour emphasised by the cut to a shot of Marie's house exploding. These close-up shots (and close-up audio) emphasise the materiality of skin, rope and amniotic fluid, bringing viewers close to what is happening through the camera's proximity to the acts.

In *Anatomy of Hell* there is a similar approach to sex that confrontationally foregrounds bodily sensation. *Anatomy of Hell* depicts four nights during which an unnamed woman pays an unnamed gay man to 'watch her where she is unwatchable'. The woman is mostly naked, conversationally and physically exploring her body, ultimately including sex with the man. The camera regularly surveys the woman's naked body in close-up, the implements that are placed in her or ooze out of her, the texture and viscosity of these implements and secretions, the man touching them. At one point the man leans down to look at the woman's vulva, and a close-up of her genitals suddenly fills the frame as a stone dildo is expelled from her vagina. The dark bushy pubic hair and the visceral close-up of the oozing vulva stand in stark contrast to the pristine, hairless genitals of the conventional, maximally visible, porn performer. In another scene, the man reaches inside the woman's vagina and brings out a clear jelly-like substance on his fingers – natural vaginal lubricants, also seen in *Romance* – which he touches uncertainly and rubs into his hair. In two other scenes, the texture, taste and materiality of menstrual blood are emphasised, partially through close-ups but also in longer shots that highlight touch. In one, the woman takes her used tampon, dips it in a glass of water, inviting the man to drink. The man clearly wishes to avoid this watery mix of menstrual blood and vaginal secretions, which evokes his disgust and revulsion, but he eventually drinks it, admitting there was little to be concerned about. In a later scene, the man penetrates the woman vaginally, engaging in wild thrusting which pushes them over the edge of the bed as he climaxes. The camera cuts to a side-shot close-up of his bloodied penis leaving her vagina as blood spurts out into a pool on the bedsheets. We see a longer shot of him massaging his bloodied penis, sitting on the blood-spattered bedsheets while the woman stands, facing away from the camera, a thick line of blood dripping down the back of her thigh. The materiality of blood is emphasised here in the spurting motion, the trickle down her leg, and the way he touches himself and the blood, feeling its viscosity and texture both against his penis and against his hand. Sex, here, is not a metaphor, it is a material thing evoked through the focus on bodily fluids, the touch of genitals and the caress of skin.

From Hugo Münsterberg to Béla Balázs the close-up was a focus of early cinema theory heralded as transcending the theatre stage, widening our vision of life and allowing greater emotional engagement with the characters through images of their faces.[39] Contemporary scholars, especially those interested in haptics and film phenomenology, have continued in this vein, exploring the close-up's ability to emphasise the non-visual or extra-visual elements of the body, and somatic experience more generally.[40] The extreme close-up can go further, reducing 'our understanding of the image ... to an awareness of texture, of light and shade, the abstract rather than the concrete'.[41] Moreover, scholars have also pointed to the capacity of the close-up to alter spatial and temporal perspectives. As Gilles Deleuze puts it: 'the close-up does *not* tear away its object from a set of which it would form part, of which it would be a part, but on the contrary *it abstracts it from all spatio-temporal co-ordinates*'.[42] For Mary Ann Doane, by disrupting 'perspectival realism' and undermining the viewer's ability to sense depth, the close-up becomes heavily associated with the image as superficial and two-dimensional, extracted from spatial anchoring points.[43] This spatio-temporal disruption can be seen as producing 'an intense phenomenological experience of presence'.[44] Most of these accounts look upon the close-up positively, using renowned arthouse films or artists' film and video as their examples, more or less explicitly contrasting their examples of the subversive close-up to the longer, wider shots privileged by classical Hollywood cinema.

Accounts of transgressive art films that emphasise the positive qualities of proximity, often draw on Laura Marks's formulation of 'haptic vision', which is heavily tied to the close-up's capacity for drawing the viewer into a contemplation of the image itself, rather than into the narrative of which that image forms a part.[45] In this context, a viewer is encouraged to 'dissolve his or her subjectivity in the close and bodily contact with the image'.[46] In other words, these images evoke a sense of presence, which is read as touching the viewer, dissolving the boundary between viewing subject and viewed object, and 'repudiating the marginalization of the visceral body in traditional aesthetics'.[47] Martine Beugnet, for instance, argues that the close-up cuts out so much contextual information that viewers must think carefully in order to understand the unfamiliar material. Unable to grasp contextual signifiers of meaning, viewers are forced to focus on what is in front of them to find meaning, and their conclusions might be quite different from those to which the context might have led us:

> in contrast with the body caught in action in medium or long shot, filming in close-up makes it possible to evoke a body that is temporarily freed from its function as social, cultural and even gender signifier, ... it dis-locates the object of the gaze, fragments it and carves it out of its surroundings.[48]

As a result, the images in Breillat's films can be read as challenges to the clichés of pornography. For instance, the images of vulvas in *Romance* and *Anatomy of Hell* create an 'effect of extreme defamiliarisation' in the context of a familiar image from heterosexual pornography, which 'enforces a self-conscious interrogation of what exactly it is the female body is cloistered for supposedly containing'.[49] As with the images of menstruation and childbirth, the female genitalia are rendered banal rather than endowed with metaphysical significance. Scholars consider them to evoke the presence of female corporeality generally overlooked in pornographic representation, as well as to reclaim the visceral depiction of sex for arthouse cinema, and for a female gaze.[50] In this reading, fragmentation is a good thing; it challenges dominant modes of perception.

Proximate presence is not only evoked through the close-up. Marks points to the capacity of a 'haptic work' to 'resolve into figuration only gradually' or to 'evade[ ] a distanced view, instead pulling the viewer in close', which can be achieved through close-ups, but also other techniques that evoke texture and sensation.[51] The key distinction between haptic and optical visuality is not precise film form, but a forcing of the viewer 'to contemplate the image itself instead of being pulled into narrative' in moments where 'figure and ground commingle'.[52] This way of conceiving of presence, evocative of proximity, but not predicated on the close-up, can be seen in writing on many transgressive art films, but is most noticeable in analyses of *Sombre*.

Sombre follows Jean, a travelling puppeteer who performs for children, and also kills prostitutes. He meets Claire, a virgin, who is fascinated by him, and with whom he has a sexual tryst. People, objects and acts are often obscured from view in *Sombre* because of low lighting, out-of-focus images, or objects blocking our view. In the first murder scene the image is dark from the start, with Jean visible in medium close-up. The camera follows him as he stands up, but his face is blurred; the camera stops moving as it focuses on the back of his neck. Cutting to a two-shot of him and a woman, his hands just visible on her face, the camera moves so that a blurred shot of Jean's neck blocks our view of the woman. Another cut reveals her to be naked, which was not clear before. The scene develops with a similar dark blurred aesthetic, faces and body parts obscured by the other person. As the sexual manoeuvres turn violent and he stuffs his fingers into her mouth, the image goes black for a moment and only the noise tells viewers that she is being hurt. A blurred close-up shows the woman's flailing limbs. The scene ends with a blurred close-up on Jean's hands, and a very dark shot of him standing in the corner of the room, his hand twitching. It is frequently difficult to see what is going on, and so viewers are likely drawn squinting towards the screen, trying to decipher what they are seeing.

Many scholars read these dark, shaky, blurry out-of-focus shots as affectively impacting the viewer rather than encouraging them to interpret narrative. These analyses often describe *Sombre*'s images in terms of sensation, materiality, viscerality and somatic intensity. Marcus Stiglegger, for instance describes how the 'grainy and often deliberately blurred' images are like 'a flood of impressions poured over the viewer', accentuated by 'a grumbling drone that eats into the viscera'.[53] Referring to a scene in *Sombre* where the protagonist's presence is signalled only by the reactions of those watching him, Morsch argues that 'through the shot of the human face, the image gives expression to a power, an intensity, a feeling that eludes direct recording' suggesting that it is precisely in not making the man visible that the affective intensity of his presence is increased.[54] Similarly, Jenny Chamarette reads many of Grandrieux's images as 'exceeding the boundaries of representation'.[55] During *Irreversible*, a comparable effect is created through slanted, swinging and rotating frames, fast-moving overhead tracking shots, and plunges through walls, ceilings and floors, accompanied by a bass drone at the beginning that ebbs and flows, and a disconcerting red-lit environment. These readings suggesting an embodied communication, and the evocation of sensation, consider viewers to be drawn into the images on a bodily level, a feeling of proximity established not through the close-up, but by a sense of being enveloped or touched by the images.

This evocation of presence is, however, not always so well received. Much like the critiques related to excess visibility, bodily sensation is often contrasted unfavourably with the intellectualism of high art. Quandt's original attack on 'New French Extremity' lays this out clearly, criticising the

> growing vogue for shock tactics in French cinema . . . [as] images and subjects once the provenance of splatter films, exploitation flicks, and porn . . . proliferate in the high-art environs of a national cinema whose provocations have historically been formal, political, or philosophical

emphasising the unwelcome supposed encroachment of low art into arthouse filmmaking.[56] The acceptance of certain transgressions is clearly demonstrated here: while formal and political provocations are to be feted, the bodily transgressions of pornography and horror are 'too much' and should not, in Quandt's eyes, be accepted. This reading fits with broader perceptions of the differences between artistic and pornographic depictions of sex, where excessive corporeality and an extreme focus on the bodiliness of bodies is what characterises pornography, in contradistinction to the suggestiveness and indirectness of eroticism. Visceral evocations of bodily presence are rejected as evoking the animality of sexuality, as reducing sex to bodies, and even as destroying the viewer's very sense of humanity, whilst eroticism is read as intellectual, spiritual and a transcendent exercise for the mind.[57] Where embracing scholars welcome the expansion of the realm of art's engagement with viewers, refusers reject 'an apparent lack of proper aesthetic distance, a sense of over-involvement in sensation and emotion'.[58] For refusers, the close-ups enable an unwelcome invasion of excessive bodily sensation, which is either morally compromising or artistically flawed. Once again, embracers and refusers tend to agree on the invasive, shocking and proximate sensations communicated to viewers by these films, but disagree on how such affect should be judged.

The fragmentation of the body in the close-up, read positively by Doane, Marks, Beugnet and others, can also be read negatively in line with feminist film theory's critique of the fetishistic fragmentation of the (female) body. As Laura Mulvey notes in relation to the films of Josef von Sternberg,

> the beauty of the woman as object and the screen space coalesce; she is no longer the bearer of guilt but a perfect product, whose body, stylised and fragmented by close-ups, is the content of the film and the direct recipient of the spectator's look.[59]

The fragmentary close-up here delimits the woman, reducing her to her beauty, and encouraging the viewer's sexual investment in the woman as object of desire, rather than as a viewing subject herself. A similar criticism is often made of heterosexual pornography, in which the woman's body is transformed 'into a desubjectivized multitude of partial objects ... while the men working on it are also desubjectivized, instrumentalized, reduced to workers serving these different partial objects'.[60] It is perhaps unsurprising to see highly critical approaches to close-ups of sex given that close-ups of genitalia and penetration have been typical of (heterosexual) pornographic content since the deeply misogynistic beginnings of the genre.[61] As such, close-ups of genitals in *Anatomy of Hell*, *Romance*, *Trouble Every Day* and of bodies engaged in sex in *Twentynine Palms* were quickly denigrated as pornographic, or at least as voyeuristic and sensationalist. Put succinctly, the issues of sensation and of bodily fragmentation in transgressive art films are divisive, and a viewer's conclusions about such depictions depend on their preconceptions about the use of close-ups in relation to filming bodies and sex.

Just as noted in the discussion of visibility, the issues of presence and erotic fragmentation become extremely problematic in the context of rape imagery. This is partially because the viscerality of brutal images of rape and sexual violence are often subordinated to politics or philosophy, 'reinforc[ing] the hierarchy of masculine imagination over feminine body'.[62] One example of this is the somewhat tortured scholarly debates about identification during rape scenes, with many analyses of transgressive art films discussing whether the spectator is themselves 'raped', whether identification tends towards the victim, the perpetrator or a mix of the two, whether the images resist easy identification, or appeal to identification with the material elements of the scene.[63] Central to many accounts of identification are readings of rape scenes as evoking forms of touch, shock, viscerality, arousal, disgust and corporeality through proximity, whether these be focused on presence, fragmentation or a mixture of the two. As Tanya Horeck has noted in relation to televised rape trials, the socio-sexual context of viewing and the discourse that surrounds such viewing can transform the spectacle of rape into a kind of spectator sport,[64] an analysis that can be extrapolated especially to the framing of transgressive art films as 'ordeal cinema',[65] where watching a brutal rape scene is seen as an achievement. Thinking back to the conflict of value registers within transgressive films, discussed in Chapter 1, we should see numerous parallels here with this analysis of proximity, especially in rape imagery. Given that embracers effectively employ an aesthetic register, accepting the films as art and then considering what the proximity might mean, and refusers employ an ethical register, rejecting the close-up images of sex (and violence) as pornographic, the difference between a viewer's preconceived ideas about proximity plays a substantial role in their ultimate judgement of the film. In the context of rape imagery, the kind of identification evoked by this proximity becomes a particularly heated one, given the ethical stakes of a film encouraging identification with the victim, rapist, witness, camera or something else. This partially explains why proximate imagery of sexual violence is so controversial, and why it therefore appears so frequently in transgressive art films.

What this section has shown is the importance of proximity, both in terms of close-ups and the evocation of sensation, in transgressive art films and commentary on them. This is nonetheless the first account that brings together all these different elements of proximity and identifies them as a hallmark of these core transgressive art films. While the almost-transgressive and marginally transgressive elements are less easily identifiable with proximity given the lack of clear parameters against which such transgressions might be judged, the descriptions here and the wealth of phenomenological readings of the films attest to the unusually affective experience of watching these films, while viewers also speak repeatedly of the visceral shock of the explicit close-ups.

*

The third part of the heuristic for identifying and understanding transgressive art films is duration. The long take and the long scene are frequently occurring stylistic devices in transgressive art films and are often paired with a film's most shocking, explicit or violent material. Moreover, these are often the most discussed and critically divisive of scenes in films that already contain numerous images of violence and sexualised violence. Extended duration features in sex scenes in *Romance* and *Trouble Every Day*, rape scenes in *Irreversible* and *Twentynine Palms*, and scenes of murder in *Irreversible* and *Sombre*. Moreover, the length of the scenes is frequently emphasised by a lack of other changes in cinematography, mise-en-scène and sound. In the rape scenes in *Irreversible* and *Twentynine Palms*, the camera remains static for long periods; in *Sombre*, scenes are frequently devoid of dialogue for long periods; in *Anatomy of Hell* the characters remain alone for long periods; in most of the films, non-diegetic music is rare. Just as with visibility and proximity, the impact of these long sequences is often linked to realism, but also to the ordeal of watching disturbing acts for such a long time with little to no distractions. Critical and scholarly work on these films refers repeatedly to long sequences and long takes while regularly discussing the ethical and political consequences of sex and/or violence seen in protracted duration.[66] Duration becomes a touchpoint for oppositional readings of the film, with audiences interpreting it both negatively as spectacular, voyeuristic and akin to pornography, but also positively as aiding reflection, productively challenging the viewer and realistically brutal. This final section considers the specific qualities of duration in transgressive art films, exploring why their long takes and long scenes are considered especially realistic and brutal, and how this formal choice divides opinion.

Twentynine Palms follows David and Katia as they wander in their SUV around the Californian desert. Katia is Russian, David is American, and they communicate in rudimentary French while engaging in angry sex and arguments. The pace is slow, there are many long takes of empty landscapes, and outside the sex scenes there is relatively little action. Towards the end of the film, three men force their Hummer off the road and drag them from the car. Katia is stripped, while David is beaten in the face with a baseball bat before being anally raped. The other attackers look on and force Katia to watch before driving away. From the point at which the couple's car is rammed from behind on the empty road, the rape sequence constantly emphasises the duration of the actions depicted. As the Hummer is being pushed, David shouts, his screams so long he has to take a breath to continue. As the cars come to a halt, the action does not immediately progress: there are a few seconds of suspense, during which nothing happens, before the attackers jump out of the car. This long scene is made up of two long takes before and after the rape, and during the rape the rhythmic grunting of the rapist forms a sound bridge across close-ups of Katia, David and the rapist.[67] As the attackers drive off, we are left with a static 105-second-long shot of Katia and David lying prone in the sand. Before, during and after the attack, the passing of time is emphasised, and the moment-by-moment development of the attack highlighted. As with other long takes and long scenes discussed here, there is little to distract from the physicality of the rape and the beating David receives, both of which Katia is powerless to prevent. The rapists are strangers, their motivation entirely unknown, the long take at the end is static for the whole shot, there are no sounds other than the characters' screams and groans, and the film ends very soon afterwards with David murdering Katia before committing suicide. Not only are the characters' motivations obscure but it is hard to see what socio-political meaning can be drawn from this surprising and unexplained entrance of sexualised violence into the narrative.

A comparable description can be given for *Irreversible*, which is ostensibly filmed in a series of long takes in reverse chronological order. Much like in *Twentynine Palms*, spectators have no idea about the motivations of the characters, at least not until later in the film when earlier events are revealed. The combination of duration and brutal violence is clear from the beginning of the film. The second scene follows two men into an underground gay BDSM club in a long take where the camera dizzyingly swings and swoops around as one of the protagonists, Pierre, abuses and harasses the club's patrons until a culminating scene where he is attacked and nearly raped. His attacker is then pummelled to death with a fire extinguisher, all in the same take, the final attack in close-up. The length of the takes becomes especially clear in the central rape scene, when the camera follows another of the protagonists, Alex, into a tunnel and there remains static on the floor for nearly ten minutes as she is raped by a stranger, and then almost beaten to death. In each of these films, the duration of the violent scenes approximates the duration of the diegetic acts.

Although transgressive art films do feature a much longer average shot length than in mainstream narrative films, this average is nonetheless much shorter than the average shot length of pornographic films.[68] Moreover, when placed in comparison with the exceedingly long takes of *Russian Ark* or *Victoria*, even the ten-minute-plus single takes in *Irreversible* seem relatively short.[69] I say this to once again counter the tendency in critical writing about violence to exaggerate the extent to which a particular element of the films, in this case scene length, is unusual or aberrant. From *Straw Dogs* to *Last Tango in Paris*, *Last House on the Left*, *I Spit on Your Grave* and *The Accused*, rape has often been shown in long, challenging sequences. To understand transgressive art films, we have to consider the detail of the long take and its reception, as well as the inclusion of visibility and proximity, which feature much less in other lengthy depictions of rape.

For those who embrace transgressive art films, the importance of the long take or long scene lies especially in an evocation of 'reality'. Interpretations of the long rape scene as 'realistic' were immediately pushed by the director of *Irreversible*, Gaspar Noé, in interviews marketing the release of the film. He contended that the 'real time' aspect to the rape scene makes it especially difficult to watch: 'I thought the time was realistic. . . . I don't think there are many rapes that are less than five minutes.'[70] For Noé, the scene communicates a sense of authenticity because there is no evidence of temporal manipulation; the length of the scene within the narrative is no different from the length of the scene that we watch, and this idea runs through several transgressive art films' unprecedented bringing together of duration with explicitness and/or rape.[71] It is important then to think carefully through what 'realistic' might mean here, especially given the many pitfalls that discussions of reality can create.

André Bazin's work is the most useful for thinking about the links between duration and realism. For Bazin, realism relates to the ontology of the photographic image and the lack of human intervention in the process of mechanically imprinting the reflections of light on celluloid.[72] As a result, film as a medium has a privileged relation to reality for Bazin. He draws a distinction between long takes and montage based on their relation to spatial reality. The long take preserves 'the spatial unity of an event', which is particularly important given that 'certain situations can only be said to exist cinematographically to the extent that their spatial unity is established'.[73] Moreover, for Bazin cinema can also produce temporal realism, especially with one-shot sequences, which 'refus[e] to break up the action, to analyze the dramatic field in time' and are 'far superior to anything that could be achieved by the classical "cut"'.[74] In *Nanook of the North*, durational unity achieved by the long take is particularly emphasised in the hunt sequence, where 'the length of the hunt is the very substance of the image, its true object' because we see 'the actual length of the waiting period'.[75] Bazin's realism sets the scene for contemporary perceptions of realism and the long take, as well as theoretical discussions of them. Nonetheless, to understand them in the context of transgressive art films, we must go beyond Bazin and consider more thoroughly questions of process.

What do spectators take away from the experience of viewing extremity in extended duration? What impact does a scene's duration or slower editing pace have on the spectator? The emphasis placed on the process of time passing in transgressive art films echoes Stanley Keeling's thinking on duration, which he splits into 'unitary' and 'processive'. Unitary duration is oriented towards reductive descriptions of the time elapsed between two points in history, while processive duration denotes the moment-by-moment playing out of the time between those two points. Processive duration takes account of the experience of the duration, of the chronology of events within the period, of the development of someone or something. Keeling gives the following example:

> We may think of a man now dead when we think of his existence *as a whole*, a single duration limited, say, by his birth and his death: a unity so constituted. Or, again, we also think of his existence *processively*, as it was lived through in time by him. But the one, though it has the same 'content' as the other, is not the same in the respect that the latter is further determination of the former. The man's life *as a unitary whole* limited by his birth and death *is unalterably* what it is. But that *same* life was *also* processive, *ever altering*, from birth to death.[76]

For Keeling, these two types of duration are applicable to any period of time because every time period includes stages and processive development as well as a unitary existence as 'this period of time'. When watching a film, long scenes and long takes can point towards processive duration by showing what constitutes the unitary whole of an event. Anything that draws our attention beyond the fact that something is happening to the passing of time during that event, highlights processive duration. Transgressive art films draw particular attention to processive duration by removing aspects of a film that can distract our attention away from the passing of time. Camera movements, dialogue, changes in the depicted acts, changes in focus, zooms and extra-diegetic music can all draw our attention away from the passing of time. If, however, these are kept to a minimum, processive duration can be emphasised and this is precisely what happens in many long scenes of sex and violence in transgressive art films.

That long takes in transgressive art films encourage viewers to consider processive duration is highlighted in an audience comment made about the aforementioned rape scene in *Irreversible*:

> I must admit that I have a somewhat sadistic streak in me and was initially aroused by the first thirty seconds of the rape. But then it just kept going. And going. By the end I just wanted it to stop. I wasn't turned on, just horrified that I'd felt that way.[77]

This comment demonstrates, firstly, that this viewer was aware of the process of the rape, as he highlights stages in it ('the first thirty seconds', 'the end') rather than only referring to the whole; secondly, that the length of the scene is noticeable, indeed palpable ('it just kept going . . . and going'); and finally that he is aware of the processive development of his own reactions to the scene, which pass through at least three stages: arousal, not arousal, horror. This viewer is aware of the scene's temporal stages, the process of rape, the length of uncomfortable time that has passed, and his feeling of horror or arousal at that moment. The evocation of processive duration is possible in any film but is emphasised in transgressive art films by a lack of distracting devices.

The duration of certain key scenes in transgressive art films is central to the impact the overall films have on viewers. In Barker et al.'s study, the more a person embraced *Irreversible*, the more likely they were to read the intolerable length of the rape scene as a good thing, emphasising the spectator's helplessness and throwing their voyeurism back at them.[78] Many approving scholarly accounts of *Irreversible* have reproduced this idea, arguing that it leads to identification with the rape victim[79] and that time becomes palpably material.⁸⁰ This fits in with broader thinking about the ethical potential of duration in relation to slow cinema. As Grønstad argues about long takes in slow cinema, 'while duration as a temporal mode and experiential frame might not necessarily be ethical in and of itself, it nevertheless provides a condition of possibility for intrinsically ethical acts'.⁸¹ Read in this way, the length of rape scenes in *Twentynine Palms* and *Irreversible* can undermine the voyeuristic pleasure so often associated with cinematic violence, challenging viewers to sympathise with the victim, but also to reflect more deeply on their position as a spectator, and potentially the excessive use of insufficiently shocking depictions of sexual violence in cinema. While most scholarly accounts that pursue this interpretation invoke an idealised spectator, this reading is very much supported by Barker et al.'s audience analysis.

The connotations of the long take also contribute to divisions between embracers and detractors of transgressive art films. In critical accounts, the absence of montage is often compared to pornography, while in positive responses, the long take is more likely to be interpreted as part of an arthouse style. Most evocatively, Leslie Felperin argues that the long-take rape scene in *Irreversible* puts 'one in mind of porn films' through its 'unedited, detached monotony',⁸² and David Edelstein considers both the murder and the rape scenes to present 'brutality so extreme that it borders on pornography'.⁸³ In this case, the lack of editing is seen to communicate a sense of reality, but more like in amateur pornography in which long takes are common for technical reasons (self-filmed, very low budgets), and for which the unedited shots emphasise the unstaged nature of the diegetic acts. By contrast, embracing accounts of the film see the long take as part of an artistic lineage that highlights its artistic qualities, with Eugenie Brinkema comparing the camera work in *Irreversible* to Alfred Hitchcock's *Rope*, with its 'serpentine movements and insistence on avoiding cuts',⁸⁴ and Tim Palmer drawing comparisons with Michael Snow's films *La région centrale* and *Back and Forth*.⁸⁵ Again, we see the unresolvably opposing viewpoints arising from different interpretations of the same element, here the long take, which is either objectifying and disturbingly erotic, or stylistically masterful, depending on the cultural reference point.

Another dividing line between positive and negative views of the films based on duration is the affective power of these scenes. As Barker et al. note, what appears to underpin the evaluation of the use of duration is once again the viewer's convictions about the value of bodily reactions to art: 'the main prerequisite for embracing this film [*Irreversible*] is about being *willing* to be "made to feel". This is not a film you can have a non-reaction to.'⁸⁶ Viewers who appreciate the film's corporeal potential are more likely to read these films as a positive evocation of some aspect of the rape, while those who denigrate an appeal to bodily sensations are more likely to associate it with pornography or gory horror. A viewer's experience of sexual violence must also be taken into account. As Schlesinger et al.'s study of audience reactions to *The Accused* demonstrates, respondents who had themselves been raped were less likely to see any ethical value in the graphic depiction of rape scenes than those without experience of sexual violence.[87]

Long takes and long scenes in transgressive art films often means the evocation of processive duration and of a kind of temporal realism. They encourage viewers to focus on the mechanics of the filmed acts, the progress of sex or violence, the development of their feelings towards the images. Some viewers read this positively as disrupting a supposed lack of attention to details on the part of the mainstream viewer, and by allowing for ethical reflection. By others, this is seen negatively as spectacularising sex and violence, and as recalling the focus on the mechanics of bodily interactions in pornography. Like proximity, there are no strong boundaries against which to judge transgressions of such duration, but these long takes are often framed by viewers in terms of 'too much', the unwatchable, the unbearable or indeed the obscene, concepts closely connoted with the transgression of personal limits on what should be made visible. The evocation of processive duration in the context of sex, violence and sexual violence therefore plays a key role in identifying and understanding transgressive art films.

*

What this analysis shows is that there is a pattern of formal elements that can be identified across transgressive art films, and that these elements each lend themselves to a multitude of competing interpretations. The multifaceted appeal to contradictory artistic, political, ethical and aesthetic evaluations is precisely what makes transgressive art films provocative, and what elicits controversy when they are screened. It is not an interesting facet of a single film but is instead a central part of the socio-cultural phenomenon of the transgressive art film.

In other words, transgressive art films appear to find numerous wedge issues that divide audiences into taking mutually exclusive positions, before then dividing them again, at times by enabling the defences of transgression, but then undermining the justification for those defences (a facet explored further in subsequent chapters). The close analysis here of *Sombre*, *Romance*, *Baise-moi*, *Irreversible*, *Anatomy of Hell*, *Twentynine Palms* and *Trouble Every Day*, as well as public, critical and scholarly interpretations of these films, has demonstrated that they can be formally linked through a consideration of their approaches to visibility, proximity and duration. In the context of sex and violence (especially rape and sexual violence), visibility, proximity and duration become central dividing lines between interpretations of the films as art or pornography, as ethically productive or morally bankrupt, as corporeally challenging or viscerally reprehensible. By examining all positions on the films, we can understand that the controversial nature of these films is heavily linked to their ability to polarise critical opinion through particular formal choices, that tap into central boundaries dividing high-art films from non-art or low-art films. In doing so, we move away from vague descriptions of the extremity of images, and from talking vaguely about transgressions of arthouse conventions, towards a consideration of more clear-cut boundaries, of actual audience responses and of the specificities of discussions around rape imagery.

This is a pattern that matters. This analysis is not just about identifying certain stylistic commonalities, but about highlighting formal elements, that play an important role in the stakes of the films. These formal aspects are intimately connected with the reception of the films, as well as with broader theories of transgression. As such, they will form a central part of the close analyses of the films in the next part of the book. Having developed a heuristic that is pertinent to the seven core transgressive art films, which are almost universally acknowledged to be controversial and extreme, this framework can be applied it to a range of other films from that period as well as afterwards.

Notes

1 Quoted in Barker et al., *Audiences and Receptions*, 88.
2 See BBC, 'Cannes Film Sickens Audience'; Romney, 'Le Sex and Violence'; Smith, 'Claire Denis'; Saunders, 'Box-Office Gross' on violent physical reactions from audience members.
3 See for instance the high-profile debates about *Irreversible* in *Sight and Sound* in the UK, and *Positif* in France: Kermode and James, 'Horror Movie'; Valens, '*Irréversible*'; Rouyer, '*Irréversible*'.
4 BBFC, 'Guidelines 2014–15', 23; emphasis added.
5 BBFC, 23.
6 To give some other examples, France's legal code similarly specifies that pornography relates to 'unsimulated' sexual acts, Australia's board of film classification designates it as 'material which shows actual sexual intercourse', and Germany's Bundesgerichtshof emphasises visibility by specifying that in pornography, sex is blatant and in the foreground of an image.
7 BBFC, 'Education – Case Studies – Baise-Moi'. Although in 2013 this decision was overturned to allow for an uncut release.

8. BBFC, 'BBFC Cuts A Serbian Film and Remake of I Spit on Your Grave'.
9. For a few examples see Tesson, 'Souverain poncif'; Holden, 'Erotic Horror'; Baumgarten, 'Trouble Every Day'; Joyard, 'Sexe'; Burr, 'Breillat's Graphic "Anatomy"'; Levy, 'Twentynine Palms'; Walker, 'No Real Bite'; Butterworth, 'Twentynine Palms'; Levit, 'The Race Is Not to the Swift'.
10. Edelstein, 'Irreversible Errors'; on *Irreversible* as pornographic, see also Felperin, 'Reviews: *Irreversible*'; Paris, 'Irreversible'.
11. Baqué, *Mauvais genres*, 44; Marzano, *La pornographie*, 97.
12. McMahon, *Cinema and Contact*, 133–34; see also Nancy, 'Icon Fury', 3.
13. In *Battle in Heaven* (see Chapter 3) there is a shot of the actor's actual detumescing penis, while in *Irreversible* it was added in post-production.
14. Lugan, 'Mangeuses d'hommes'; Quandt, 'Flesh and Blood'.
15. For more details about embracing and criticising, see discussion of this in Chapter 1.
16. Julius, *Transgressions*.
17. Julius, 25–27.
18. Barker et al., *Audiences and Receptions*, 88, 71; see also 70–72.
19. Barker et al., 5, 91.
20. Barker et al., 40.
21. Barker et al., 71. For more on this aspect see MacKenzie ('*Baise-Moi*'); Brown ('Violence in Extreme Cinema').
22. Wilson, 'Deforming Femininity'; Brinkema, 'Celluloid Is Sticky'; Grønstad, 'Abject Desire'; Gorton, 'The Point of View of Shame'; Belot, 'Embracing Sexual Difference'; Mtshali and Fahs, 'Catherine Breillat's *Romance* and *Anatomy of Hell*'.
23. Brinkema, 'Irréversible'.
24. Coulthard and Birks, 'Horrible Sex', 84–85; Taylor, 'Infection, Postcolonialism and Somatechnics'.
25. Downing, 'On the Fantasy of Childlessness'; Zolkos, 'Violent Affects'; Chiesa, 'Of Bastard Man and Evil Woman'; Grodal, '*Antichrist*, Explicit Sex, Anxiety, and Care'.
26. Horeck, 'Shame and the Sisters'; Keesey, 'Split Identification'.
27. Azalbert, 'Le corps défendant'; Tarr, 'Mutilating and Mutilated Bodies'; Palmer, *Brutal Intimacy*, 84–85.
28. Lahr-Vivaz, *Mexican Melodrama*; Ordóñez, 'Carlos Reygadas' *Battle in Heaven*'.
29. Featherstone and Johnson, '"Ovo Je Srbija"'; Featherstone, 'Coito Ergo Sum'; Kendall, 'Affect and the Ethics of Snuff in Extreme Art Cinema'; Herron, 'Victim Sells'; Jackson, 'Euro-Snuff'.
30. Grønstad, *Screening the Unwatchable*, 10. This draws on Kaja Silverman's reading of Jacques Lacan (*The Threshold of the Visible World*, 2, 11).
31. Barker et al., *Audiences and Receptions*, 179–80.
32. On how this has been problematically framed as the 'rape' of the spectator, see Wheatley, 'Contested Interactions'.
33. Morsch, 'Der Körperdiskurs des Films', 10; Beugnet, 'La forme et l'informe', 68; citing Vivian Sobchack.
34. Grønstad, *Screening the Unwatchable*, 82; Downing, 'French Cinema's New "Sexual Revolution"', 278.
35. On Breillat see Wilson, 'Deforming Femininity'; Coulthard, 'Desublimating Desire'; Gorton, 'The Point of View of Shame'; Bordun, *Genre Trouble and Extreme Cinema*; more

generally see Downing, 'French Cinema's New "Sexual Revolution"'; Davis, 'The View from the Shortbus'; Grønstad, *Screening the Unwatchable*.
36 See Barker et al., *Audiences and Receptions*.
37 See Brinkema, 'Celluloid Is Sticky', 150; Palmer, 'Under Your Skin', 176; Young, *The Scene of Violence*; Belot, 'Embracing Sexual Difference'; Coulthard, 'Uncanny Horrors', 179–80; Larsson, 'Close Your Eyes and Tell Me What You See', 149; Wheatley, 'Naked Women, Slaughtered Animals', 95; Chamarette, *Phenomenology and the Future of Film*, 198; Wilson, 'Catherine Breillat and Gustave Courbet'; Coulthard and Birks, 'Horrible Sex'; Young, 'Visage/Con'; Bordun, *Genre Trouble and Extreme Cinema*.
38 See Beugnet, *Cinema and Sensation*; Scholz and Surma, 'Exceeding the Limits of Representation'; Grønstad, *Screening the Unwatchable*, 23; Horeck and Kendall, *The New Extremism in Cinema*, 5; Kendall, 'Reframing Bataille', 51; McMahon, *Cinema and Contact*; Dooley, 'Haptic Visions'; Walton, *Cinema's Baroque Flesh*, 111–25; Taylor, *Troubled Everyday*, 18–21.
39 Münsterberg, 'The Photoplay'; Balázs, 'The Face of Man'; 'The Close-Up'.
40 E.g. Sobchack, *The Address of the Eye*; *Carnal Thoughts*; Marks, *The Skin of the Film*; *Touch*; Barker, *The Tactile Eye*; McMahon, *Cinema and Contact*.
41 Lury, 'Closeup', 104.
42 Deleuze, *Cinema 1*, 95–96.
43 Doane, 'The Close-Up', 91.
44 Doane, 94.
45 Marks, *The Skin of the Film*, 163.
46 Marks, *Touch*, 13.
47 Grønstad, *Screening the Unwatchable*, 118; see also Grønstad, 'Abject Desire', 167; Beugnet, *Cinema and Sensation*, 89–90.
48 Beugnet, 'Close-up Vision', 30; Beugnet, *Cinema and Sensation*, 90.
49 Beugnet, *Cinema and Sensation*, 71. For a discussion of these close-ups, their art-historical heritage and links to Gustave Courbet, see Wilson, 'Catherine Breillat and Gustave Courbet'.
50 On Breillat and the female gaze, see Wilson, 'Deforming Femininity'; Phillips, 'Catherine Breillat's *Romance*'.
51 Marks, *The Skin of the Film*, 163.
52 Marks, 163, 183.
53 Stiglegger, 'Haptische Bilder', 48.
54 Morsch, *Medienästhetik des Films*, 299.
55 Chamarette, *Phenomenology and the Future of Film*, 191.
56 Quandt, 'Flesh and Blood'. This nostalgic disdain is also ahistorical, omitting to note the profligate images of sex and sexuality in 1950s, 1960s and 1970s art cinema, both in the films and in the marketing strategies (see Lev, *American Films of the '70s*; Frey, *Extreme Cinema*, 41–45).
57 E.g. Baudry, *La pornographie et ses images*; Baqué, *Mauvais genres*; Bayon, *Le cinéma obscène*; Marzano, *La pornographie*; Bernas, *La photographie et le sensible*; Jean, 'Le Porno et la grâce'. For further discussion, see Kenny 'Eroticism, Pornography, Love'.
58 Williams, 'Film Bodies', 5.
59 Mulvey, 'Visual Pleasure and Narrative Cinema', 841.
60 Žižek, *The Plague of Fantasies*, 180.

61 Williams, *Hard Core*, 80–81.
62 Russell, *Rape in Art Cinema*, 6.
63 On *Irreversible* see Wilson, 'How Does the Use'; Nicodemo, 'Cinematography and Sensorial Assault'; Keesey, 'Split Identification'; MacKenzie, 'On Watching and Turning Away'; on *Baise-moi* see Archer, '*Baise-Moi*'; on *Twentynine Palms* see Coulthard, 'Uncanny Horrors'; on bodily perception and identification with the material body see Beugnet, *Cinema and Sensation*; Morsch, *Medienästhetik des Films*; Oxen, 'Das Sensorische Bild'. For comprehensive explorations of these problems related to identification and rape scenes see Projansky, *Watching Rape*; Horeck, *Public Rape*; Young, *The Scene of Violence*.
64 Horeck, *Public Rape*, 89–90.
65 Kuhn and Westwell, *Oxford Dictionary of Film Studies*, 152.
66 See Tesson, 'Souverain poncif', 81–82; Felperin, 'Reviews: *Irreversible*'; Brinkema, '*Irréversible*'; Quandt, 'Flesh and Blood'; Downing, '*Baise-Moi*'; Williams, 'Hard-Core Art Film'; von Brincken, 'Das Leid an Der Zeit'; Young, *The Scene of Violence*; Barker, '"Typically French"?', 158; Horeck, 'Shame and the Sisters'; Keesey, 'Split Identification'; Grønstad, 'On the Unwatchable'; Brown, 'Violence in Extreme Cinema'; Kendall, 'Reframing Bataille'.
67 This combination of duration with a metronymic beat during sex or rape scenes is used in several transgressive art films: see also *Battle in Heaven*, *The Tribe* and *Free Will*.
68 Frey, *Extreme Cinema*, 168–69.
69 *Russian Ark* and *Victoria* have average shot lengths of 96 and 138 minutes, respectively.
70 Quoted in Keesey, 'Split Identification', 96.
71 On duration and the unprecedented see Williams, 'Hard-Core Art Film'; Horeck, 'Shame and the Sisters'.
72 Bazin, *What Is Cinema?*, 1:9–16.
73 Bazin, 1:50, 1:52.
74 Bazin, 1:34.
75 Bazin, 1:27.
76 Keeling, *Time and Duration*, 6.
77 Quoted in Barker et al., *Audiences and Receptions*, 161.
78 Barker et al., 8.
79 Scott, 'Bearing Witness to the Unbearable'; Brinkema, '*Irréversible*'.
80 Von Brincken, 'Das Leid an Der Zeit'; Nicodemo, 'Cinematography and Sensorial Assault'.
81 Grønstad, 'Slow Cinema and the Ethics of Duration', 274.
82 Felperin, 'Reviews: *Irreversible*'.
83 Edelstein, 'Irreversible Errors'. On *Irreversible* as a 'virtual porn-snuff film', see Paris, 'Irreversible'. On 'art-house crypto-porn', see Gingrich, 'Irreversible'.
84 Brinkema, 'Rape and the Rectum', 40.
85 Palmer, 'Style and Sensation', 30; *Irreversible*, 81. Palmer also draws avant-garde connections between Gaspar Noé and Hollis Frampton, Paul Sharits and Tony Conrad.
86 Barker et al., *Audiences and Receptions*, 151.
87 Schlesinger et al., *Women Viewing Violence*; see also Horeck, *Public Rape*; Young, *The Scene of Violence*.

3

Sex, Violence and Sexual Violence

Romance has received high praise for its explicit exploration of sexuality and female desire, being described as 'exemplary art ... about the integrity of sex to human identity, and how this is represented on screen'.[1] Other critics were much less impressed, deploring the pompousness, the pseudo-philosophical posturing and the 'unapologetic scenes of masturbation, oral sex, intercourse and intricate bondage', claiming audiences who chose to see it were deluded.[2] A similar kind of disagreement played out with *Sombre*, with some praising its affective imagery and its exploration of the 'darkness of humanity',[3] while others have condemned the copious images of sexual violence and eroticised murder, calling its depiction of sexual desire repugnant.[4] Images of sex, violence and sexual violence have provoked drastically different responses from audiences, and been central to the passionate debates taking place around these films. If we are to grasp what provokes the controversies and virulent arguments about transgressive art films, we have to explore the formal details of the images, as well as how they are received and interpreted by viewers. This chapter will focus on close analysis of the film form and reception of *Battle in Heaven* and *A New Life*, films which are not part of the original corpus of seven transgressive art films, the starting point of this book's exploration of controversial films, but which exhibit the same characteristics, and fit within the heuristic of transgressive art films presented throughout this book.

The main focus of the analysis is on how the images of sex and sexual violence (in particular their proximity, duration and visibility) were interpreted by the public, critics and scholars, and why these particular depictions provoked controversy. This analysis considers not only the value a viewer might attach to a film – good, bad, ethical, immoral and so on – but also the conceptual framework, or value register,[5] which orients and guides their analysis. The four value registers relevant to film are: aesthetic, hermeneutic, ethical and aesthesic, which relate to whether the conceptual framing prioritised by the viewer is based on beauty, meaning, ethics or feelings, respectively.

Given that it is not always possible to link the transgressions of transgressive films directly to a particular limit or boundary, value registers provide an indirect way of approaching clear boundaries – especially the limits of censorship and art – rather than trying to identify non-specific cultural limits or norms that a film may have transgressed. A viewer's prioritisation of value register, as well as their preconceptions about what constitutes art, cues the values they are likely to attach to a film, and in the context of censorship boundaries and disturbing imagery, such values are integral to categorising a film as worthy of public display (art) or requiring censorship (pornography, or images that are illegal, dangerous, immoral). Guiding questions for this chapter are: what is it about *Battle in Heaven*'s sexual imagery, and the sexual violence of *A New Life* that provoked such critical controversy? Why were they not simply ignored by the film establishment? How did critics and scholars participate in the framing of these films, and how should this be evaluated ethically? What do the answers to these questions tell us about the transgressive art film?

This chapter begins with an analysis of *Battle in Heaven* and its depiction of sex, considering the film in relation to the three formal elements of the transgressive art film heuristic: visibility, proximity and duration. *Battle in Heaven* is an excellent illustration of the controversial role of sexual affect in arthouse film, and how this can be usefully read in terms of a conflict of value registers. Criticisms of sex as 'shock value' and 'meaningless provocation' tend to use an ethical or aesthesic register, criticising sexual imagery, and locating the film implicitly outside the realm of film art, while a hermeneutic register is mostly used by viewers to position the sexual imagery and affect as part of the film's socio-political critique. Moving beyond more binary analyses of embracing versus rejecting (proposed by Frey and Barker et al.), this analysis helps to understand why viewers come to such different conclusions about films like *Battle in Heaven*, and also why these differences of opinion create such conflict and controversy. The conflict of value registers is explored further through the images of sexual and sexualised violence in *A New Life*. Here analysis of the critical and scholarly reactions demonstrates how the virulent backlash to the film, both positive and negative, was based on mutually exclusive ideas about film art, and about images of sexual violence. Commentary on *A New Life* makes greater use of the aesthetic value register, which raises numerous problematic questions in the context of rape imagery. Together the analyses of these two films provide a means for considering how transgressive art films can be understood, and importantly how they have been understood. Rather than my specific account of how to interpret the films, this chapter is about the affordances of transgressive art films, the analytical frameworks brought to bear on them, and how we should rethink and reframe work on controversial films that does not account for the plurality of opinions, and the contradictions in their overall reception. Moreover, it is a reflection on the ethical and political stakes of scholarly engagement with these ideas, considering what it means to choose to engage with films using certain registers and not others. In this way, the close analysis of form and reception is explicitly linked to broader elements of the cinema art world, such as the role of scholarly criticism in constructing transgressive art films.

*

Battle in Heaven depicts the tribulations of chauffeur, Marcos, who is embroiled in an extramarital sexual relationship with his employer's daughter, Ana, and has undertaken the botched kidnapping of a friend's baby, who died before any ransom could be extracted. In the violent final act, Marcos murders Ana with a knife and then appears to perform a sacrificial pilgrimage, crawling with a bag on his head through the streets up to the city's basilica. The film reiterates the long takes, slow pans and sexual tension of Reygadas's previous film, *Japón*, but places visible sexual acts at the forefront, by beginning and ending with close-ups of oral sex between the two protagonists, and by including several long scenes of erotic imagery and visible sex. The film opens with a close-up of a man's face, glasses on, blinking slightly against a grey background. The camera tracks down, revealing a large man, Marcos, with pronounced breasts and a rotund belly, and then a mass of oscillating dreadlocks in front of his crotch. As a single violin note sounds, the camera circles round and zooms in towards his penis. Cutting to a position behind the man, obscuring the dreadlocked person, the camera tracks left and zooms in to reveal a woman with her eyes closed, rocking back and forth with the man's penis in her mouth. The camera zooms in on her eyes, capturing a tear and then goes black. A similar, more smiling scene, in which the characters profess their love for each other, closes the film. In this final scene, the fellatio is much more visible, but the whole scene is just twenty-eight seconds long, part of which is a shot of Marcos's face. It is hard to know how to understand these scenes: are they dream, fantasy, allegory, gratuitous erotica or shock material? Like other transgressive art films, these descriptors are difficult to disentangle, with all of them being true to a certain degree, and in the context of explicit sexual content, this led to divided audiences and fierce debates.

Following its release at the Cannes Film Festival in 2005 (and with rumours already circulating about its explicitness), *Battle in Heaven* created outrage for its graphic sex scenes.[6] Not only does the film begin and end with explicit images of fellatio, but it also includes two lengthy scenes of explicit sex, one of masturbation, and several sequences set in a brothel where Ana works. Moreover, two of the sexual protagonists, Marcos and his wife, Berta, are short, middle-aged and obese, far from the young lithe physiques that dominate mainstream sex scenes. Regardless of one's feelings about the sex scenes in *Battle in Heaven*, they had a substantial impact on the critical and scholarly reception of the film, are integral to its framing as transgressive, and sex is far from incidental to the narrative. As such, a focused analysis of the sex scenes in *Battle in Heaven* is essential to any full understanding of the film's transgressions, reception, ethics and political outlook.

At the same time, numerous images of the Mexican flag being raised and taken down in Mexico City's main square situate the film as a reflection on nationhood and identity. As a film so overtly invested in national identity and local socio-political dynamics, *Battle in Heaven* has predominantly been addressed through the lenses of Mexican or Latin American cinema history, especially the golden-age melodrama, and of broader Mexican symbolism.[7] More specifically, and particularly because the film eschews psychological explorations of the characters and their motivations, the protagonists are frequently read in metonymic terms, as representative of a two-class system that correlates heavily with race: Marcos is the disenfranchised, lower-class, precariously employed, darker-skinned Mexican, and Ana is the dominant-class, property-owning, white Mexican.[8] The film has also been compared to the metaphysical cogitations of Bresson, Dreyer, Rossellini and Tarkovsky because of the slow-paced narrative and extensive use of long takes and wide angles,[9] as well as being discussed in terms of its Christian spirituality, because of its frequent references to biblical imagery, crucifixes, churches and pilgrimage.[10] Given this book's aim is to understand what leads to controversy rather than to analyse specific films, I do not provide a competing reading of the film, but situate these readings within and in relation to the controversy that it sparked, most notably because of *Battle in Heaven*'s explicit sexual content. I am interested in how these readings speak to questions of visibility, proximity and duration, even if the authors do not necessarily frame their analysis explicitly in these terms, and in showing how all this fits formally, and on the level of reception, with the analysis provided in the preceding two chapters.

The visibility of the sex acts in *Battle in Heaven* makes clear the 'authenticity' of the sex acts, however acted out or simulated their exact movements and expressions may have been, and whatever prostheses may have been used to create the final effect in some scenes.[11] At the same time, like in *Romance*, *Anatomy of Hell* and *Baise-moi* discussed in Chapter 2, as well as in *The Idiots*, *Taxidermia*, *Antichrist* or *Holiday*, these moments of explicitness occupy only a small amount of screen time and in the case of vaginal penetration, take up only a small portion of the frame. Even though ostensible genital contact between the actors in the opening/closing scenes is not hidden, explicit images of mouth–penis contact remain very brief, mostly blocked by Ana's head, or Marcos's buttocks. The boundary with hardcore pornography is therefore transgressed, but only marginally, and only for a very short period, with the vast majority, even of the sex scenes, remaining in the realm of softcore erotica, feasibly involving simulated penetration, had it not been for the overt signifiers of actual penetration being present in other shots.

These scenes include a great number of proximate images, including close-ups and extreme close-ups, but unlike what might be expected from hardcore pornography, these tend to focus on skin, hair, hands and feet. Rather than clearly framing the body part, they are often disorienting by being so zoomed in that it is unclear exactly what is being shown. Close shots like this are used on several occasions with extreme close-ups of a kiss, of Marcos's and Berta's intertwined bodies, or with Ana's dreadlocks, both in the fellatio and the later intercourse scenes, when the matted locks and attached beads are not immediately recognisable, especially when moving swiftly in and out of the frame as they do in the intercourse sequence. In another scene, this time between Marcos and Berta, just prior to sex, there are several close-ups of Marcos's hands running through Berta's thick hair, and during the sex, the camera runs up and down their bodies as penetration occurs, g(r)azing at/along the textures of their bodies, and moving in close onto their naked skin.[12] Like in *Trouble Every Day*, *Anatomy of Hell* and *Sombre*, this emphasises the materiality of the encounter, eliding contextual information that might initially serve to orient understanding of the scene, although a substantial part of the scene is nonetheless made up of shots that frame at least their heads and torsos, if not their whole bodies. Although less shocking in its execution than in *Romance*, *Anatomy of Hell* or *Baise-moi*, there is also a sudden close-up of Ana's vulva, again, however in a different context to that of conventional hardcore pornography. Rather than a maximalist open-legged gaping to show its depths, or 'proof' of orgasm/penetration (vaginal fluids or semen), it is shown from above, Ana's legs together and straight as she lies next to Marcos after sex (instead the 'evidence' of penetration and orgasm comes from Marcos's erect but slowly detumescing penis, which we see from above as Ana dismounts him). It therefore only marginally transgresses rules on the explicit display of eroticised genitals, by showing a close-up of genitalia in a sexual context but only from one position and only for a brief moment. *Battle in Heaven* does not shy away from the graphic depiction of the genitals and intercourse, and emphasises the materiality and texture of bodies when doing so, but in general does not focus on sexual display.

Aside from the fellatio scenes, the intercourse scene between Marcos and Ana is one of the film's most commented scenes, not only for its frank depiction of functional sex, but also because of the central long take, which is bookended by sex, but dominated by the banalities of life in the surrounding apartments. The sequence begins with a close-up of a furry brown mass, rocking in front of the camera; breathy noises enter, and a hand reaches up to adjust what turns out to be Ana's hair as she removes her headband. We discover it is Ana and Marcos having sex, Ana straddling Marcos, who lies flat on the bed, his face impassioned; he leans up to touch and kiss her breasts. The image returns to the angle of the first shot, but further from the couple thus showing Ana's smiling face as she jokingly tells Marcos to stop grabbing her breasts: 'calm down, Marcos'. A 206-second shot begins at the side of the bed showing Marcos, now unmoving, hands by his sides, while Ana thrusts vigorously, the bed shaking and squeaking. Without cutting, the camera dollies back, exits through the window, and moves upwards, the sounds of copulation receding, being overtaken by noises from surrounding buildings as the camera pans slowly anti-clockwise – capturing children playing in a yard, high-rise buildings in the distance, curtained windows in a building opposite, a radio in a window, a dripping tap, cracks in the paint – before returning through the window, the couple entwined post-coitally, Ana unmoving on Marcos's chest. A shot from the ceiling shows Ana dismounting to lie next to Marcos, whose detumescent penis is then the only movement in the frame as it slowly droops. They hold hands. There are close-ups of Marcos's face, Ana's crotch, their hands, the soles of their feet. Ana gets up to grab a robe, telling Marcos to leave; Marcos remains unmoving for this entire time. This whole sequence is devoid of extra-diegetic music, emphasising the processive duration of the sex and the other banal events in the world outside the bedroom.

Battle in Heaven therefore shares numerous aspects with the core transgressive art films. Like *Irreversible* and *Twentynine Palms*, shots and whole scenes in *Battle in Heaven* are often very long, and the longest shots are reserved for the most shocking sequences, in this case of sex. The rhythmic knocking of the bed against the wall (Marcos/Ana), or flesh slapping against flesh (Marcos/Berta), gives a metronomic reminder of the passing of time, of the length of the shot, and of the material encounter of flesh in each successive thrust. Even more so than the opening sequence, the images of sex between Marcos and Ana show the interlinking of duration with proximity and visibility in this scene: the camera is close to Ana's head and skin at the beginning, but then moves far away as it exits by the window; the unbroken rhythm of their thrusting underscoring the duration of the scene (six minutes). Marcos's penis detumescing against his skin, and the close-up of Ana's crotch highlight the practical, material aspects of intercourse. Not only is there an emphasis on the passing of time as can be seen in many other examples of 'slow cinema', but the duration combined with the lack of other information from the sound or images emphasises the material details of the depicted actions. Sex is presented as process, not just as a single act.

As with other examples of transgressive art films, the story is told through the messy, erotic and ultimately violent display of bodies, intimate but brutally so, tied to a narrative, but frequently distanced from it, interested in spectacle and sensation, but never slipping into abstraction.[13] It is in part for this reason that scholars have been drawn to the film, seeing in the explicit sexual images a complex socio-political critique, even as many critics dismissed the film's sex scenes as pointless shock tactics.[14] It should be clear from this description that just as with the core films discussed in the previous chapter, the transgressions and almost-transgressions of *Battle in Heaven* are most productively read through the lens of visibility, proximity and duration, especially its most controversial sequences. It includes some visible sex, but this is brief and infrequent, an emphasis on haptic visuality with some shocking close-ups, and several long scenes of sex with little distraction from the actions of the protagonists.

Having established the formal credentials of *Battle in Heaven* as a transgressive art film, we can now turn to its reception, examined in terms of value register, in order to grasp how these formal elements provoked controversy amongst audiences. While the claim of gratuity or shock is often levelled pejoratively at films like *Battle in Heaven*, in order to discredit its artistry and indeed to discredit it as art, it would be naïve to suggest that these played no role in their inclusion in this film. As Mattias Frey has observed, sex and shock have long been used to sell arthouse films, regardless of the purported sincerity of the filmmakers,[15] and the choice of Ana's beautiful naked body post-coitus as the DVD cover image, cropped notably from Marcos's less conventionally beautiful body lying next to her in that scene, attests precisely to this.[16] The placement of fellatio as the opening shot of the film, not least because it plays no obvious narrative role, and involves the eroticisation of a body normally sidelined by cinema, can reasonably be understood as an attempt to shock audiences, inserting pornographic spectacle into an arthouse film in a way that confuses viewers, destabilises their expectations, and is openly transgressive of the boundary between porn and not-porn.[17] Moreover, considering the film's major themes, we can see it as an explicit reworking of tired gender tropes from the history of literature, cinema and narrative pornography: the rich woman who seeks out sex work as a result of boredom, the rich (white) woman who seduces her servant (of colour), the promiscuous woman who will sleep with anyone, the taciturn underling enamoured with his confident employer, the middle-aged man distracted from his wife by the beauty of youth and so on. Read in this way, the sexual explicitness could be little more than a way of rejuvenating and providing novel scandal to otherwise tired and well-worn narrative tropes. This critique can be made through an aesthetic register to argue that the film's lack of originality is a sign of being a less impressive work of art, but it is normally made by those who use an ethical register in order to argue that these kinds of outdated tropes should not be part of contemporary cinema.

At the same time, a recuperative reading of these shock tactics using a hermeneutic register suggests *Battle in Heaven* can be seen as a critical reflection on these issues of gender, race, class and bodies. The film's shock has been read by scholars such as Elena Lahr-Vivaz and Samanta Ordóñez as an affective appeal to the (idealised) spectator to look again at the meanings attached to particular bodies, as an attempt to startle the spectator into a reconsideration of the acts, bodies and situations shown on screen, and their own implication within processes of looking, naming and conceptualising.[18] The sex scenes are shocking in their viscerality, and disrupt normative perceptions by using erotically charged images of non-normative bodies. This can first be seen when obese Marcos and Berta have sex, a scene that is shot with sensuous, caressing camerawork, which eroticises their stomach rolls, their sweaty skin and inexpressive faces. Later we see Ana take great pleasure in her sex with Marcos, thus subverting common representational tropes of only the young and attractive engaging in good filmic sex. The close-ups and caressing long shots draw attention to these characters' touch and penetration, and encourage viewers to see these bodies as tender, arousing and sexual even though mainstream images tend to elide them from view, attributing sexuality and arousal more commonly to thin, white people. Viewers might be encouraged to reconsider what bodies can count as sexual, arousing and beautiful in cinema, confronted with the physical, affective power of these marginalised bodies, which in itself has been read as a form of 'critical corporeality'.[19]

This hermeneutic register allows for a much more detailed analysis of the film's affect, down to the postures and movements of the characters. As

Ordóñez argues, Marcos's body is tasked with signifying the racialised precarity of workers in neoliberal Mexico, especially in contrast to the poor-but-happy image projected in the melodramas of Mexico's golden age of cinema: the 'opening scene juxtaposes the corporeal rigidity and moral deficiency of Marcos's brown male figure, with a sensuous and emotionally layered image of Ana, a phenotypically white Mexican woman'.[20] In the Ana–Marcos sex scene, Lahr-Vivaz suggests that the wider relevance of the power relations in the bedroom are highlighted by leaving it and, through the 360-degree single-take revolving shot, involve the rest of the community in this comment, suggesting that the choice of Marcos as the film's protagonist was a matter of chance, with his story being representative of many other Mexicans.[21] In these readings, the provocative affect of the sex scenes makes explicit the socio-economic groups the two characters represent, and asks viewers to look again at how they view the social and political context of contemporary Mexico. Using the estrangement defence,[22] the socio-political critique is made through the shock of the sex scenes rather than despite it: it is precisely through a visceral provocation of the viewer that a rethinking of how to look at poor indigenous or wealthy white Mexicans comes about. As Tiago De Luca puts it, the controversial sexual encounters 'contribute to the production of a new social order and, in so doing, expose the establishment and its mechanisms of exclusion while upsetting the dominant cultural codes and revealing these same codes as partial, historical and contextual'.[23] As discussed in Chapter 2, these interpretations are based on the premise that the making visible of bodies makes visible social and cultural structures of domination and oppression. Here, it is the racialised differences between the bodies and their postures that point to racialised power structures and colonial systems of oppression, with the spectator's affective reaction to one seen as potentially analogous to an ethical encounter with the other.

Those who criticise the explicit sex in *Battle in Heaven* tend to employ the ethical register, asking whether it is right to include such images in a non-pornographic film, before or without considering the particularities of those images, thereby disregarding the complex context of the images, and dismissing the explicit sex as little more than a marketing stunt. By contrast, embracers of the film prioritise its artistic status, and only secondarily interpret the sex scenes as a political or ethical manoeuvre that uses the affective capacities of cinema to address viewers. The decision made by a viewer about how to approach the film is therefore integral to their overall reaction to the film's transgressions: prioritise judgement about the pornographic nature of the sex or focus on the sexual/gender politics of the narrative, and you will likely be critical of the use of explicit imagery; prioritise the film as a serious artistic endeavour, and you will likely find positive value in the film's use of shocking imagery, embracing the sex scenes as part of a broader political or ethical project, directed at an idealised spectator. The inclusion of explicit sex in this film renders these positions mutually exclusive, given the cultural dynamics that control the porn/not-porn boundary, and leads to unresolvable disagreements between spectators, and a controversial reception for the film. *Battle in Heaven* is therefore an excellent illustration of how long, proximate scenes of visible sex can create a conflict of value registers, whereby certain viewers reject the film as outside art cinema, and others, ultimately more successfully, recuperate it within the domain of art cinema.

Like with other transgressive art films, this conflict of value registers is further complicated by the lack of coherence between the film's different themes and narrative strands. While many scholars have sought to find recuperative analyses of the film's shocking imagery, there is a notable lack of clear political message, a lack of obvious reason behind the provocations, a lack of any sense of truth or underlying knowledge that has been exposed by the affective experience. *Battle in Heaven* (as well as *A New Life*) lacks a coalescing storyline to distract our attention from the materiality of the events taking place: exactly why Ana is working in a brothel, why she was at the airport, why she sleeps with Marcos, what drives Marcos to kill Ana in the film's climactic scene, are all unclear.[24] As Euhna Choi has pointed out, much commentary on the film 'attempt[s] to resolve a series of polarities'[25] between politics and philosophy, universalism and national specificity, provocation and sincerity, ethical and exploitative. Just as Nikolaj Lübecker suggests that *Twentynine Palms* is uncomfortable and 'feel-bad' partially because the three narrative strands he identifies – metaphysical, political, physical – do not 'organically combine', so does *Battle in Heaven* leave its narrative strands irreconcilable into a chain of cause and effect, afloat, 'contradictory, incoherent and averse to didacticism'.[26] It may be common for arthouse cinema to provide de-psychologised characters, or to demand that viewers make the effort to piece together a fragmented storyline, but it is unusual to do this in the context of graphic violence and explicit sex, and it is unusual within narrative cinema for such affectively overwhelming images to be left unresolved from beginning to end. Ultimately, the bodies of *Battle in Heaven* both bring together the film's different elements, and at the same time disrupt and interfere with them, much as we saw with *Romance*, *Baise-moi* and *Twentynine Palms* in Chapter 2.

The contradictions of the film and the incompleteness of any standard recuperative analysis of its transgressions are further made clear in thinking about the production ethics. There is a sense of exploitation in the use of 'non-professional' actors who are asked to perform visible sexual acts for the camera; not least because the actor who plays Marcos was an employee of the director's family, and the actors were not given any context to the scenes when acting them out,[27] thus placing the director and the actor in the sort of coercive power relationship that the film critiques. As Ordóñez points out, there is an uncomfortable sense that the filmmaker (a wealthy white man) was enacting the problematic power relations at the same time as criticising them.[28] However, we must not exaggerate the impact of this ethical issue on the viewing experience, given that this production element was generally absent from journalistic criticism of the film.[29] Nonetheless, as the exposure of political realities related to class and race are key to many readings of this film, it is pertinent to include the director's apparent extra-filmic actions in relation to them in any examination of the overall ethics of the film. Reygadas addresses this directly, seeing criticisms of the production conditions as coming from a paternalistic attitude that considers the actors to have little or no agency in decisions about their working conditions, especially as these concerns seem to relate mostly to the indigenous actors in *Japón* and to Marcos in *Battle in Heaven* rather than to the more self-assured Ana.[30] Nevertheless, these issues related to power relations built around class and race should not be shrugged off, not least because they are the focal point of the film itself. This may not be the most uncomfortable ethical issue with a transgressive art film, but it does point to these political ambiguities not only within the film, but here within the production processes, in relation to the very issue that the filmmakers and the film seek to reflect upon.

As with so many transgressive art films, the images are challenging to watch, without it being clear how to interpret them. The choice of value register as well as pre-existing ideas about the value of affect in cinema guide viewers into irreconcilable positions of embrace or rejection, of approval or disapproval, of acceptance or dismissal. Given the inclusion of explicit sexual imagery and its unavoidable questions of artistry, censorship and ethics, transgressive art films like *Battle in Heaven* force a taking-of-sides, and make those sides multiple, ambiguous and contradictory. In *Battle in Heaven*, societal power structures are literalised in affectively challenging images of sex, but in ways that remain provocative and ethically problematic in terms of the use of sexually explicit imagery, the power dynamics within the production process, and the chauvinistic sexual and gender tropes. What this analysis has shown is how the formal elements of visibility, proximity and duration connect to the reception elements of value registers in a transgressive art film. It provides an example of how to read a film together with the film's context, as well as other interpretations and its reception, in order to see how an individual film fits within the broader phenomenon of transgressive art films.

The gravity and degree of these ethical concerns become even more provocative and controversial when sexual violence is part of the mix, as in *A New Life*, where these problems arise within the images themselves and led to a much more vociferous critical and scholarly reaction than in the case of *Battle in Heaven*.

*

Philippe Grandrieux's films, most notably, *Sombre* and *A New Life*, have attracted adulatory attention from scholars because of their attention to sensation, materiality and the body[31] as well as specifically to sound.[32] While many images, ideas, characters and narrative elements are obscured or unclear in these films, there remain numerous conventional parts in the films. They are thus frequently considered to open up but not destroy the conventions of narrative cinema.[33] Although some scholars try to distance Grandrieux from what they consider the less profound spectacular provocations of Noé or Breillat,[34] his films have consistently been discussed together with the other transgressive art films explored in Chapter 2.[35] Although I begin by considering the film form, this section is focused on the film's reception, as there is a particular wealth of criticism and scholarship on this film, that helps to illustrate the conflicts of value register. It is also one of the films that mobilised the aesthetic register in scholarly literature the most, and as such is a useful example for exploring the ethical stakes of scholarly engagement with transgressive art films.

A New Life is a telling case of how to think transgressive art film form and reception through the lens of ethics, not only because the critical reception was so virulent and so divided (no one, it appeared, was unmoved by *A New Life*), but also because these divisions hinged largely on the critic's or scholar's approach to the film's ethics. Whilst *Sombre* had received a certain grudging respect, the sexual violence of *A New Life* received a swift backlash from audiences and the press, grounded predominantly in complaints about the exploitative nature of the images of sex trafficking and forced sex work.[36] In reaction, a group of critics and scholars quickly organised an edited collection precisely to provide a positive perspective on the film.[37] Broadly speaking, the negative, mainly journalistic, critiques focused on ethical readings of the film, dismissing its aesthetics as aestheticising suffering;[38] the positive critiques focused on aesthetic analyses, particularly of the film's evocation of affect, dismissing ethics as an inappropriate lens through which to understand the images.³⁹ These positions were rapidly entrenched with both sides rejecting the other's ideas out of hand and vociferously defending their own approach.⁴⁰ Even as the unresolvable conflict of value registers is emblematic of the reception of transgressive films, *A New Life* pushes the ethical conflicts and contradictory politics of transgressive art films to an extreme.

A film about people trafficking, sexual slavery and brothels set ostensibly somewhere in Eastern Europe, *A New Life* follows Seymour (an American seeking sex), Mélania (a trafficked sex worker) and Boyan (a people trafficker). Seymour seeks to buy Mélania from Boyan, after purchasing her services as a sex worker. One of the key reasons for considering *A New Life* within the context of transgressive art films is its emphasis on bodies in states of excess, most notably the numerous scenes of sexual and sexualised violence against women, as well as the camera's erotic interest in the victims of that violence. This combination of sex/eroticism and violence is central to the confrontational experience of transgressive art films, and to the vociferous critiques films like *A New Life* received upon release. There are three long scenes of sexual violence, which I will examine in detail, as well as several scenes of violent male domination of women. A scene of forced haircutting evokes gender-based violence towards war victims, and the cutting, undertaken with a knife and recorded with a very close microphone, got under the skin of many viewers.⁴¹ In another scene, again evoking war violence as well as slavery, a group of half-naked women are lined up and inspected like horses, with a man examining their teeth before deciding who to buy. Finally, the brothel where much of the narrative takes place, populated by sex-trafficked women, is depicted much like a strip club, with lingering close-ups on the women's bodies, camera positions mostly conflated with the male customers' gaze, and a soft-focus effect commonly used for erotic or sex sequences in romance films. *A New Life* includes explicit sexual imagery, most notably a shot of a masturbating client as well as proximate shots of violence, a plethora of haptic and affective imagery, and numerous long scenes including long takes, all in the context of sex, sexual violence and violence.

As with other transgressive art films, *A New Life* has been read ethically in multiple unresolvable ways. Firstly, there is the lens of exploitation, reading the film as allowing a putatively male gaze to revel in the eroticism of female bodies with little regard for anything beyond their sexual appeal. This reading uses the ethical register, questioning the ethical value of depicting women in such sexually violent ways, before or instead of considering the artistic quality of the images. This was the register often adopted by journalists on the film's release, shocked by the graphic scenes of abuse.[42] Secondly, there is the lens of ethical recuperation, the mobilisation of the estrangement defence, whereby the film shocks an idealised viewer into reassessing how they look at the violence of forced sex work. This interpretation uses either the hermeneutic or aesthetic register: the film is first and foremost understood as an art film, a work of art in the broadest sense, a worthy text for scholarly examination and understanding, and only subsequently does the question of ethics arise. This reading, adopted especially by academic scholars, acknowledges the film's ethical problems but finds ways of embracing them, considering them as just another part of the film that requires explaining and understanding. Finally, there is the aesthetic lens, which not only uses the aesthetic register but entirely rejects the validity of any other approach to the film. While the first two positions approach the film in similar ways, choosing to prioritise one register over another, scholars using the aesthetic lens sideline any reflection on ethics from the domain of film criticism. In what follows, I will take a closer look at these three approaches to *A New Life*, focusing on the depictions of sexual violence. This will demonstrate the ethical conflicts of transgressive art films discussed theoretically in Chapter 1, showing how they arise specifically as a result of the long, proximate and visible images of sexual violence, and how *A New Life*, like other transgressive art films, includes a number of internal ethical incoherences that add to its ambiguous and opaque political outlook.

If we look at *A New Life* as a whole and analyse it via the ethical register, prioritising an analysis of the film's depiction of sex, desire and gender politics, a deeply troubling picture emerges. Mélania is placed in an unambiguous position of spectacle object both diegetically for the lustful Seymour and for the film spectator. In this position of sexual object, Mélania is abused by various men in several long sequences: from a long, forced haircutting sequence, to two scenes of sexual violence, to a hellish orgy-like sequence. The viewer's gaze is never aligned with hers, but often with Seymour's or Boyan's, and frequently falls upon beautifully filmed images of her, often in close-up, fragmenting her body into breasts, hands and legs. For instance, in the first scene in which we see Mélania on stage, the shots are only of details of her body: first her breast, then her hand, followed by her shoes and her legs, then her midriff, Seymour's face in her breasts, and a shot of her bare back. Moreover, the raised stage right next to the seats suggests a version of a strip club where men leer at women for sale, a point emphasised by reverse shots of Seymour as he watches, and the clear gender divide between the scantily clad women higher up on stage, and the fully clothed men drinking in the anonymising darkness below. The problematic beautifying of Mélania and her position as sex slave is made even more incongruous and troubling given that designer Karl Lagerfeld dressed Anna Mouglalis (Mélania), despite her character being as far from the world of high fashion as possible.[43] Finally, the objectification of Mélania, even if she is fully clothed and given an individual identity denied to all other women in the film, is encouraged by the close-up images of the naked bodies of the pole-dancers on stage, whose faces are often hidden by darkness or outside the frame, and whom we see for many minutes before Mélania makes her entrance. These women are made into sensuous, lithe, beautiful dancers, their plump and youthful features a marvel for greedy male eyes while the languid, fluid shots of Mélania's meeting with Seymour, apart from suggesting a romantic rather than a financial relationship, emphasise Mélania's beauty and attractive body.

Materiality, viscerality, sensation – indeed – but it is not an anodyne choice to expose these in such a violent, misogynistic context. Still using an ethical register, such an aestheticisation of squalor and ignominy tends to legitimise the atrocious conditions Mélania experiences, and undermines any political attempt to raise awareness, incite pity or bring about change in her situation. This reaches a peak in an oft-commented, aesthetically astonishing sequence of Mélania dancing with her captor, Boyan. The image is filled with the sweeps of her body as fast-motion shots of her spinning send her into a blur of colour, overwhelming the screen with a panoply of forms. Visually stunning, this is nonetheless an image of a slave, who has been raped and viciously beaten already in the film, being manipulated by her owner. Olivier Joyard captures the disturbing contradictions of this depiction in a general remark about transgressive art films: 'it's unbelievable but it's like this: rape is a trashy, chic experience, a trendy aesthetic loop-the-loop, the dark horizon of modernity'.[44] For me personally, this context made it a deeply uncomfortable scene to watch, torn between disgust at the situation, and admiration for the virtuosity of the images. This same feeling pervades much of the film. In a later scene shot with a thermal-imaging camera, and intercut with more images of dancing, a naked Mélania screams, writhing and crawling around amongst a crowd of older men. This scene finishes with thermal images of a seemingly fatigued Mélania creeping around on her knees, before collapsing on her back, the camera at various points getting close-ups of her vulva and her breasts. Was she part of an orgy? Was she raped? Has she been beaten? With the thermal imaging and many post-production distortions added to the shots, there is no clear answer to these questions, but the context of a brothel where the women are sex-trafficked, beaten and raped is essential to any full understanding of these images, however artistically innovative they may be. Most scholars, however, ignore this context entirely in their descriptions of these and other sequences, demonstrating how easily the violence of Mélania's situation is forgotten in the face of a beautiful image. It is worth pointing out that the scenes of dancing and the thermal orgy could easily form part of a different narrative based on consent and mutual pleasure. The artistic qualities of these images would not be weakened by a different narrative context, and it is therefore a specific ethical choice to place them within the context of rape, sexual violence, sex trafficking and slavery. Read through the gaze, the lens of exploitation and the ethical register, *A New Life* is a distinctly troubling, cruel and misogynistic film, that revels in the artistic pleasures and potential of the female body, regardless of how exploitative the images might be.

At the same time, using the hermeneutic register, and therefore prioritising an interpretation of the film's meaning, it is possible to recuperate these exploitative, troubling images as part of a progressive ethical agenda, by reading them as provoking an idealised spectator to rethink their understandings of sex trafficking, sexual violence and sex slavery. This interpretation involves seeing the film as using the affectively disturbing images of violence as a means to communicate the horror, not only of what Mélania is subjected to, but of the structures that enable such violence. In *A New Life*, this is clearest in three scenes of sexual violence.

In the first, Seymour treats Mélania like a ragdoll: unable to gain an erection from her semi-consensual stimulation, and only able to perform when he begins violently physically controlling her. She begins by trying to reassure him, attempting intimacy by helping him take off his clothes, placing his hand on her breast to encourage him to enjoy her body, and initiates fellatio. When this does not work, she is at a loss and looks fearful at the potential consequences of her failure to arouse and placate the client. Suddenly Seymour pushes her onto the bed, flips her onto her front, as if to avoid her gaze, and penetrates her vigorously, ejaculating after just a few thrusts; she is impassive throughout. Afterwards she gets up to wash herself while he lies on the bed. 'OK?', she asks to confirm that her contractual obligations have been met; 'Yeah OK', he replies, and she leaves to service another client. In this second scene of sexual violence, which runs directly on from the first, an unknown Frenchman takes sexual pleasure in terrifying Mélania with threats of violence. He quickly controls her with commands about which clothes to remove, whilst creating a deep sense of unease by saying little else. He grabs at her face, stretching out the skin as though examining a fabric before slapping her several times across the face. The rest of his words are shouted orders, forcing her into particular positions, coming close to her with the now constant threat of violence, running his hands along her thigh before slapping and punching her repeatedly in the face as she scrambles to get away, finally hiding in the corner in the foetal position. The Frenchman disregards her as she gets her clothes and leaves; he masturbates on the couch, now ignoring her presence entirely, the camera focusing on his naked self-pleasuring, but with the image heavily blurred. Finally, in the climactic sequence, which finishes with the roaring upturned face which adorns the DVD cover and was used in advertising, Seymour seems about to engage in consensual pleasurable sex with a dancer, when in medium close-up, he pins her front-down on a table and rapes her. She whimpers in pain as the camera swings to the side. Seymour repeatedly shouts 'shut up' while grabbing her hair with both hands. He then starts punching her back, the sound of which is loud and brutal. Suddenly she is on her back, still being raped in medium close-up. He pushes her head away after climaxing and walks away. The camera stays focused on her face.

Given the length of these scenes, the constant proximity to the violent acts, the affectively charged cinematography, and the lack of dialogue or other contextualising information, these are difficult scenes to watch. There is no prettification of what Mélania is forced to do: it is brutal, violent, frightening, painful, and completely out of her control. Within the logic of the film, there can be no relations between men and women that are not based on control, coercion and the infliction of pain. There is no sense that these are sex scenes, even if they begin somewhat sexily; they are about violence and power. Not only do we see the physical violence that is meted out towards the forced sex workers, but we are given an insight into the structural power that these Western men hold over their Eastern-European prey. In the first scene, a clear distinction is made between sex and rape, as Seymour's pleasure is found in the violence and power of rape, not in the eroticism of sex. In the second scene, we see even more clearly that the Frenchman's (erotic) pleasure at the brothel derives from violent domination and control. In the final scene, the sound of Seymour's fists on the woman's back are used to emphasise the violence of the encounter, and his screams of 'shut up' are piercing, making visible the power structures of the rape and of the brothel. These scenes can be read as explorations of the brutality and dehumanisation of sex trafficking and rape. The lengthy affectively charged scenes demonstrate what it means to be violently abused at the hands of a man to whom your consent means nothing, and whom you cannot refuse. In this reading, the affect of the camerawork challenges viewers to see and feel more closely the physical mechanisms of control and violation at work in sex trafficking and rape.

Although most viewers will clearly associate the people traffickers and male sex tourists with the perpetration of immoral acts, the film is not interested in attributing specific ethical responsibility to characters. As such, like the reading of affect in *Battle in Heaven*, one of the key ethical aspects of *A New Life* can be seen as its attempt to bring spectators into a kind of affective material contact with the disturbing structures of violence that operate within a human sex-trafficking market. To make visible structures of oppression through the visibility in the images of physical oppression and violence. For Beugnet, films like *A New Life* 'destabilise normal patterns of perception', aggressively demanding that viewers look more closely and look again at how they interpret the images they are confronted with, but without ever (re)stabilising them.[45] There is no clear political message to be attached to any potential awareness that may be elicited about sex work, sex trafficking or rape. However, this is something of a dubious ethical position that can easily slip into a callous apolitical appreciation of a rape scene's 'intensity': 'the ethical consequences of this are grave and horrifying – *La Vie nouvelle* threatens the dissolution of those boundaries of ethical acceptability to present a new world of terrifying possibility and vertiginous (in)humanity'.[46] Read as such, *A New Life* demands a radical form of ethical questioning that arises from the encounter with the challenging and deeply problematic images and offers no clear political or moral schema by which to move beyond the film. It is an ethical challenge to the spectator, provoking them to reconsider how they look at the world, but as I have earlier critiqued, such readings are premised on an idealised spectator, with little data available to ascertain the extent to which this was a common interpretation amongst actual audiences.

This is, in a nutshell, the recuperative embracing analysis made of the sexual violence in *A New Life*, reading the disturbing and violent imagery as a reflection on structures of violence and what it means to experience such domination and control. For some scholars, the ethical force of these images comes precisely from the destabilising and problematic nature of these images which force the viewer to seek stability and thereby reflect on what has troubled them in these images. In this reading, scholars suggest that viewers should consider the experience of watching *A New Life* as operating at 'the limits of knowability', where 'the possibility of uncertainty, dissensus and the limits of what can be grasped filmically' reign over the certainty and consensus of essences or truths.[47] It is the way that 'the inchoate hubbub' and the lack of 'customary coherence' unsettle us and demand that we both rethink the images and cogitate on them long after the film ends, that renders the films so powerful but also so problematic.[48] Although this analysis is deeply concerned with ethics, it is quite different from the first approach via the ethical register, because it accepts the film as worthy of artistic status before reflecting on how its images should be evaluated ethically. In this way, although ostensibly sharing a methodological approach with the ethical register – 'ethics' – the criteria for judging the film's images are fundamentally different when using the hermeneutic register, hence the irresolvable conflict between such positions.

Other variants of this embrace of uncertainty and trouble try to reframe the film as indirectly accessing something absolute or essential that cannot be approached directly. Working once again with the interpretative scheme 'visible violence makes [concept] visible', scholars have proposed as this concept: 'a pure corporeality, a primal fear, the existential';[49] Eastern Europe's 'political unconscious';[50] a 'pure image' or an 'originary condition of visuality';[51] 'the most crucial, dimension of human reality;'[52] and even the Holocaust.[53] According to such readings, challenging images in *A New Life* reveal something fundamental about Eastern Europe, violence, the slave trade or sex work (although the essentialism of these interpretations poses its own problems, by trying to control and pin down a film that seems resolutely to eschew 'truths'). However we might feel about these sometimes tenuous symptomatic readings, not least their reliance on the figure of an idealised spectator, my point here is that all these kinds of aesthetic embrace accept that there are troubling aspects to the film, but prioritise its status as art and then recuperate the morally problematic images as ethically progressive as part of an estrangement defence.

A third approach to *A New Life* involves an exploration of the aesthetic qualities of the film, while rejecting or at least not addressing any ethical concerns. This may be a standard aesthetic approach to transgressive art, the 'formal defence' in Julius's terms, but it becomes particularly controversial and provocative in the context of eroticised sexual violence. While the haircutting sequence is unpleasant and frequently discussed, the sexual violence and eroticised physical abuse are sidelined in accounts that prioritise Grandrieux's innovative approach to sound and materiality. For instance, in his article which focuses heavily on Mélania's dancing body and 'the Dionysiac confusion of a crowd that is saturated by music and noise', the two consecutive long scenes of rape and sadistic violence discussed above are described by Adrian Martin as follows:

> The two scenes of Mélania's prostitution, one placed directly after the other in Grandrieux's cinema of cruelty, provide an inventory of bodily postures figuring fright, uncertainty, panic and stress, a primal, physical language of animals under threat: Seymour's instant post-coital blues,

> Mélania's vulnerable nakedness, and the icy upper-body stress of the French client, who finally withdraws into himself and away from the Other in order to masturbate in a fuzzy, atomised blur.[54]

Asked to think of 'an inventory of bodily postures' and 'vulnerable nakedness', we would not realise that the two scenes are terrifying abusive experiences for Mélania. Martin also spends much time analysing the dance sequence mentioned above, seeing it as a brief moment of almost transcendent escape: 'in this fury of defiguration, a miracle is performed . . . She is freed at last', a deeply uncomfortable claim given her enslavement.[55] Martin is not alone in this approach to *A New Life*: Greg Hainge makes a similarly dubious claim, suggesting that Mélania's situation 'enables her in the end to transcend not only her social but also ontological condition'.[56] Elsewhere, Nicole Brenez's many contributors conspicuously avoid any serious discussion of the final rape scene and Hainge declares that 'morality simply has no place here', aligning themselves with Grandrieux's own explanation that morality in these films is akin to the morality of actions in a dream.[57] This is not specific to *A New Life*: Hainge also pursues a comparable reading of *In My Skin*, where he rejects any readings of the film as social commentary, arguing that the violence of the film 'can be found not in the scenes of literal violence to which we are witness but, rather, in the abnegation of the wound that defines our relation to the cinematic sign'.[58] Like Martin's claims about *A New Life*, these conclusions claim that violence is not to be found in literal violence, even as an acceptance of this would in no way have undermined Hainge's broader points about the other forms of violence. This refusal of even the most literal interpretations of transgressive art film images is a repeated phenomenon in accounts employing the aesthetic register. Brenez notably argues that the brutality and misogyny of the film should be normalised so that 'instead of constituting a scandalous and transgressive object, [it] should appear as an ordinary film'.[59] Following this aesthetic reading, art films ultimately fall outside of the domain of ethics, and as such, ethical readings of the film are not only misjudged but entirely unreasonable. While the recuperative lens tries to combine the aesthetic and ethical analyses (whilst still prioritising a hermeneutic register and therefore coming to the opposite conclusion to the ethics-first approach), this aesthetics-only approach is entirely irreconcilable with the ethics-first approach. There is a fundamental conflict of value registers.

Nonetheless, this aesthetics-only approach has always already involved ethical reflection, and the taking of a specific position on film ethics. As with Martin's suggestions about Mélania's freedom, these attempts to avoid any

Sex, Violence and Sexual Violence **109**

consideration of ethics have led to some intellectually acrobatic conclusions: Hainge argues that we should

> see Mélania not simply as the victim of Boyan ... but as his creation, for it is through these acts of apparent horror that her transformation and will to power are able to take place. [...*A New Life* should be read] as a utopia, as an envisioning of the possibility of life within the real as it stands.⁶⁰

Again, the complete domination of, and brutal physical violence against, a woman are read as utopian empowerment, whilst also arguing that the processes of her empowerment should not be subject to ethical discussion, a claim he takes even further in a later publication:

> this is, I believe, the challenge laid down to us by the film: to accept that the treatment that Mélania undergoes is necessary in order for her new life to appear, to enable her to live life not as an imposter ... but, rather, intensively.⁶¹

Her enslavement, rape and abuse is necessary? These assertions of the irrelevance of ethical concerns in relation to *A New Life* conform to Dominique Russell's description of a standard discourse around rape in art cinema:

> When on-screen rape, often casual and unacknowledged, causes controversy ... that controversy is more often than not doused by evocations of art and a higher purpose – a stepping away from the complicated questions of the entanglements of rape and seduction, and the basic, but no less complex issue of 'what does it matter who is speaking?' – back into a myth of the misunderstood artist. This reinforces the hierarchy of masculine imagination over feminine body.⁶²

Hainge's and Martin's analyses precisely reiterate this hierarchy, treating rape and sexual violence as just another tool in the artist's repertoire, akin to camera angle or soundtrack.

While Hainge might claim to be reading the film 'outside of our habitual moral and psychological frameworks', he is in fact following a time-worn moral and psychological framework that refuses to take sexual violence seriously, and ridicules critiques of such images because they pay insufficient attention to (male) artistry.⁶³ It is also a framework which strives at all costs to read sexualised violence against women as violent sex, or as revealing a violence at the heart of sexuality. Hainge describes the scene with the Frenchman, in which Mélania being slapped and punched in the face operates as erotic foreplay for a client, as showing the unconsummated, open-ended Deluzian force that 'perdures', arguing that 'there is here no possibility of containing or interpreting what we are presented with according to a world and principles that we would already know in advance'.[64] One has to wonder at the blinkered lens required to claim that the images of sexualised violence, which Hainge describes in graphic detail, are impossible to read through any pre-existing theories. As Joan Hawkins asks, who is allowed to determine when sexual violence is a metaphor or not?[65] Why do they get to argue that ethical approaches to these images are invalid? While these pro-Grandrieux critics are laudably looking beyond the basic content of these images, and justifiably criticising journalistic accounts that refused to recognise the aesthetic innovativeness of the images, this anti-ethics position conforms to a long and problematic history of artists and critics conspiring in the visual domination of the female body, and in the delegitimising of critiques of sexual violence. Despite their best efforts to extract Grandrieux from ethics, that decision is a specifically ethical one.

I am clearly critical of this aesthetics-only approach to sexual violence, not least because of its unacknowledged ethical positioning. Whether one chooses the ethical, hermeneutic or aesthetic register for one's analysis, in the context of sexual violence, and graphic sexual or violent imagery more generally, it always involves an ethical choice, regardless of whether one acknowledges it or not. This choice is not arbitrary or random, it may be a choice that is justified by the traditions of the discipline, but it is clearly a choice, the ethical and political nature of which often goes unacknowledged. In terms of the ethics of transgressive art films, this (meta-)analysis shows how the depiction of sex, violence and sexual violence in these films cues mutually exclusive positions that hinge on the viewer's approach to film art and the subsequent choice of value register. What distinguishes Brenez, Hainge and Martin from other critical or recuperative commentators is not just their attitude towards Grandrieux, but a broader view of art that sees it as a domain separate from ethics. What distinguishes Beugnet, Chamarette, Goddard, Stiglegger, Morsch and others using the hermeneutic register, from those who reject the film out of hand, is a prioritisation of the film's artistic endeavours over straightforward ethical concerns; by perceiving of the film as artistic first and foremost, they can recuperate the ethically troubling elements as part of an estrangement defence or similar, which would not be mobilised if the film fell into the category of not-art. Those who critique the film as immoral, like Rosenbaum, Joyard and Azoury, use an ethical lens, seeing its artistic status as secondary to the question of whether such images should be made and shown.

In other words, we can see that within approaches to *A New Life*, there are at least three ways of looking at the images, each of which is effectively incompatible with the others. As an exploitative sensual enjoyment of abusive power dynamics and bodily control that worryingly eroticises slavery, rape and people trafficking. As an affective appeal to an idealised spectator to see and feel rape and sex trafficking in ways they had not considered before. And as a disinterested aesthetic experience, unencumbered by moral concerns. On the one hand, different lenses are more appropriate for certain scenes than others, with the early scenes where Boyan chooses Mélania and cuts her hair demonstrating the violence of her situation, and later scenes of dancing tending more towards sensual excess and eroticisation. On the other hand, there are numerous scenes, most notably the final rape scene, but also the sex-work sequences and the shots of her walking between the clients' rooms, which can readily be understood as operating in each of these ways: Mélania is eroticised and consistently positioned as the object of the camera's gaze, whilst her situation is also shown as unpleasant, demeaning and exploitative, and filmed in innovative and virtuosic ways. The affectively charged images oscillate between these different viewing positions, without ever clearly settling on one or the other. As Chamarette suggests, we cannot dismiss audience anger at the aestheticised spectacles of sexual violence, nor the dehumanising presentation of so many characters, but in doing so we must also not dismiss readings which foreground sensation and materiality over ethics.[66] In order to understand the controversy of transgressive art films like A New Life, we have to grasp all of these positions, and the interpretative frameworks that lead viewers to them.

A New Life is a prime example of the conflict of value registers seen in transgressive art films, of the unresolved and unresolvable contradictions in critical approaches to these films. Brenez, Hainge, Martin et al. reject any approach based on visual ethics, showing certain interpretations of the film are entirely incompatible, and that critics and scholars can be unhelpfully partisan in their dismissal of other ways of approaching the film. While this prioritisation of one aspect of a film over another is part of any critical or scholarly examination of a film, graphic images of sex and violence occupy a specifically controversial space in the cultural imaginary at the limits of the acceptable or legal, whereby to prioritise one aspect over another means the rejection of other prioritisations, rather than their acceptance as alternative feasible approaches. It is precisely this rejection of other readings that leads to mutually exclusive positions and critical controversy.

*

Although *Battle in Heaven* and *A New Life* are ostensibly quite different films, their use of visibility, proximity and duration, as well as the divisiveness of the spectator's ethical encounter with their images, demonstrate that they can both be connected to the core transgressive art films. By affectively challenging the viewer, there is already a conflict of value registers being set up in terms of a prioritisation of ethics, hermeneutics or aesthetics. In the context of sexual and sexually violent imagery, this conflict is linked to mutually exclusive category choices such as art/pornography, acceptable/unacceptable, freely distributed/available under licence, uncensored/censored, which raises the stakes of any individual analysis and often leads to controversy. Transgressive art films render these fraught decisions even more difficult through their internal incoherences, ambiguous narratives and contradictory political projects, which undermine simple attempts to dismiss them, but also to recuperate them as coherently progressive films. Examining the detail of these films' form and their reception reveals how these infractions come to be legitimised by audiences, how particular uses of visibility, proximity and duration lead to controversy, and how the reception of the films is best framed by a consideration of value registers. This sets the stage for the more focused reflections on depictions of sexual violence, trauma and witnessing that form the heart of the next two chapters. I have also laid out here details of the ethical and political stakes of critical and scholarly engagement with sexual, violent and sexually violent imagery, in order to demonstrate the interconnection between the three main pillars of analysis in this book: form, reception and theory. Film form is never separate from the broader machinations of the cinema art world, and professional critics and scholars play a central role in framing and giving value to formal readings, the stakes of which are especially high in the case of transgressive art films given the controversial nature of the images involved, and the fact that they entail the legitimisation of imagery within the art world that previously had not attained artistic status.

Notes

1 Di Mattia, 'The Devious Conflict'.
2 Turan, 'Uneasy Bedfellows'; see also French, 'Romance'.
3 Chamarette, *Phenomenology and the Future of Film*, 228.
4 Rosenbaum, 'Problèmes d'accès', 62.
5 Heinich, 'The Art of Inflicting Suffering'.
6 See Romney, 'Battle in Heaven'; Hoberman, 'Carlos Reygadas'; Szurmuk, 'Batalla En El Cielo'; Woodend, 'Not Your Usual Sex Movie'.
7 Tompkins, *Experimental Latin American Cinema*; Lehnen, 'Sex, Silence and Social

Disintegration'; Benmiloud, 'Batalla en el cielo'; Lahr-Vivaz, *Mexican Melodrama*; Ordóñez, 'Carlos Reygadas' *Battle in Heaven*'.

8   Saporosi, 'Corporeidad, distanciamientos y el concepto de praxis'; Lehnen, 'Sex, Silence and Social Disintegration', 4; Ordóñez, 'Carlos Reygadas' *Battle in Heaven*'; Paz, 'Las leyes del deseo', 1069–70; Choi, 'Plural Perspectivism'. 'Though numerically inferior, white creoles are [Mexico's] phenotypical ideal ... institutionalized by a colonial caste system that placed the European at the pinnacle and the Indian [indigenous Mexican] at the bottom' (Charles Ramírez Berg in De Luca, *Realism of the Senses in World Cinema*, 85).
9   Tompkins, *Experimental Latin American Cinema*, 173; De Luca, *Realism of the Senses in World Cinema*.
10 Citko, 'Transcendent Images and *Semina Verbi*'.
11 Firobri, 'Anapola Mushkadiz'.
12 On gazing/grazing, see Marks, *The Skin of the Film*.
13 Cf. Palmer, *Brutal Intimacy*; Beugnet, *Cinema and Sensation*.
14 See Booth, 'It's a Fight'; Johnson, '"Battle in Heaven"'; Reichert, 'Head Trip'.
15 Frey, *Extreme Cinema*, 5–6.
16 Sexualised images of female characters on DVD covers is common with transgressive art films: see the naked woman on the *Anatomy of Hell* and *Romance* covers, and the woman in her underwear for the *Baise-moi* cover. Note nonetheless the softening of images' transgressiveness: for *Battle in Heaven*, Ana's hair is lengthened to cover her breasts; for *Romance* the film's title is place across her nipples; and for *Anatomy of Hell*, her nipple is covered over with a camisole in some countries. For an in-depth discussion of this in relation to *My Mother*, see Kendall, 'Reframing Bataille'.
17 See Frodon, 'À l'horizon des corps'; Bonnaud, 'Review: Battle in Heaven'. The same can be said of *Bad Luck Banging or Loony Porn*, which opens with an amateur porn video filmed by the protagonist, but is otherwise a stylistically varied arthouse reflection on gender and sexual politics.
18 See Lahr-Vivaz, *Mexican Melodrama*, 126–36; Ordóñez, 'Carlos Reygadas' *Battle in Heaven*', 85–86.
19 Saporosi, 'Corporeidad, distanciamientos y el concepto de praxis'; see also Tompkins, *Experimental Latin American Cinema*, 174.
20 Ordóñez, 'Carlos Reygadas' *Battle in Heaven*', 84.
21 Lahr-Vivaz, *Mexican Melodrama*, 130.
22 Julius, *Transgressions*. See Chapter 1 for more detail on the defences of transgressive art.
23 De Luca, *Realism of the Senses in World Cinema*, 91.
24 See also De Luca, 80–85; Badt, 'No Slave to Realism', 23.
25 Choi, 'Plural Perspectivism', 49.
26 Lübecker, *The Feel-Bad Film*, 118; De Luca, *Realism of the Senses in World Cinema*, 32; see also De Luca, 'Carnal Spirituality'.
27 BBC, 'Director Defends Explicit Movie'; Ordóñez, 'Carlos Reygadas' *Battle in Heaven*', 92; Higgins, '"I Am the Only Normal Director"'.
28 Ordóñez, 'Carlos Reygadas' *Battle in Heaven*', 92.
29 With the exception of Smith, 'Battle in Heaven'; F, 'Love Their Movies'.
30 See also Granados, '¿Quién diablos es Carlos Reygadas?'; De Luca, *Realism of the Senses in World Cinema*, 90.
31 Rondeau, '*Sombre*, la surface et la chair'; Philippe, '*La Vie Nouvelle* de Philippe Grandrieux';

Martin, 'Dance Girl Dance'; Brenez, *La Vie Nouvelle, Nouvelle Vision*; Hainge, 'Le Corps Concret'; Guest, 'Darkness Visible'; Morsch, *Medienästhetik des Films*; Stiglegger, 'Haptische Bilder'; Bonino, 'La Caméra Haptique de Philippe Grandrieux'; Watkins, 'Robert Bresson's Heirs'; Costa Júnior, 'Apesar Da Noite'; Oxen, 'Das Sensorische Bild'.
32. Lucca, 'Internal Affair'; Hainge, *Philippe Grandrieux*.
33. Martin, 'Dance Girl Dance'; 'A Magic Identification with Forms'; Prédal, *Le jeune cinéma français*; Beugnet, *Cinema and Sensation*; Bradburn, 'Nothing Is True'; Chamarette, *Phenomenology and the Future of Film*; Petrenko, 'Philippe Grandrieux's Transversal Cinema'.
34. Guest, 'Darkness Visible'.
35. Quandt, 'Flesh and Blood'; Beugnet, *Cinema and Sensation*; Hainge, 'Le Corps Concret'; Horeck and Kendall, *The New Extremism in Cinema*; Coulthard and Birks, 'Desublimating Monstrous Desire'.
36. See Chamarette, 'Shadows of Being in *Sombre*', 70–73, 80n5.
37. Brenez, *La Vie Nouvelle, Nouvelle Vision*.
38. For details see Hainge, 'L'Invention Du Troisième Peuple'; Guest, 'Darkness Visible'.
39. Prédal, *Le jeune cinéma français*, 79; Brenez, *La Vie Nouvelle, Nouvelle Vision*; Hainge, 'Le Corps Concret'; 'L'Invention Du Troisième Peuple'; *Philippe Grandrieux*.
40. Notable exceptions to this are Beugnet, *Cinema and Sensation*; Chamarette, *Phenomenology and the Future of Film*.
41. For a phenomenological reading of the haircutting scene, see Chamarette, *Phenomenology and the Future of Film*, 198.
42. E.g. Azoury, 'Grandrieux sans manières'; Elley, 'A New Life'; Stanners, 'New Life'; Quandt, 'Flesh and Blood'.
43. Azoury, 'Grandrieux sans manières'.
44. Joyard, 'Sexe', 11.
45. Beugnet, *Cinema and Sensation*, 31.
46. Chamarette, *Phenomenology and the Future of Film*, 208.
47. Chamarette, 188.
48. Beugnet, 'Evil and the Senses', 183.
49. Stiglegger, 'Haptische Bilder', 52.
50. Goddard, 'Eastern Extreme', 88.
51. Morsch, *Medienästhetik des Films*, 297–98.
52. Grandrieux quoted in Beugnet, 'Evil and the Senses', 176.
53. De Lastens, 'D'une histoire naturelle du mal'; Ladegaard, 'Spatial Affects'; for further examples related to the Holocaust, including statements by Grandrieux himself, see Hainge, 'L'Invention Du Troisième Peuple', 231–32.
54. Martin, 'Dance Girl Dance'.
55. Martin.
56. Hainge, *Philippe Grandrieux*, 114.
57. Brenez, *La Vie Nouvelle, Nouvelle Vision*; Hainge, 'Le Corps Concret', 20; Grandrieux, Au commencement était la nuit; see also Hainge, *Philippe Grandrieux*, 108–47.
58. Hainge, 'A Full Face Bright Red Money Shot', 575.
59. Brenez, 'Entrée (en matière)', 14.
60. Hainge, 'L'Invention Du Troisième Peuple', 234–36.
61. Hainge, *Philippe Grandrieux*, 127.

62 Russell, *Rape in Art Cinema*, 6.
63 Hainge, *Philippe Grandrieux*, 116. Indeed, Hainge's unquestioning deference to Grandrieux's artistic vision, to the details of his script and to his reading of the film tends at times towards the hagiographic.
64 Hainge, 122.
65 Hawkins, *Cutting Edge*, 196.
66 Chamarette, 'Shadows of Being in *Sombre*', 80. While her comments pertain specifically to *Sombre*, they are just as relevant to *A New Life*.

4
Trauma

Transgressive art films often have problematic and ambiguous outlooks on the politics of rape: *Irreversible* weaves homophobia and transphobia into its rape-centred narrative, and *Twentynine Palms* frames rape as potentially shameful for the victim. *Fat Girl* had its final rape scene cut from its UK release on the grounds it encouraged a paedophilic gaze,[1] and *A New Life* sparked outrage for its aestheticisation of sexualised suffering. These films also seem to elicit a tendency in commentary to read the rape imagery not so much in terms of an attack on the victim, but as an assault on the spectator, reframing victimhood and trauma away from the diegetic victim and onto the spectator.[2] In this chapter, I think through the ethical and political implications of the framing of sexual assault in transgressive art films, focusing in particular on narratives of trauma and victimhood, with close analysis of *Free Will* and *The Brown Bunny*. Following a rapist, and an onlooker to a rape, these two films notably reframe the trauma of being a rape victim, as the trauma of perpetrating or assisting in rape.

Transgressive art films are almost obsessed with communicating the reality of rape to the fullest extent possible through cinematic representation using explicit images of penetration, long scenes showing the processes of violence, and proximate images evoking the material acts being inflicted on the victim. The transgressive potential of the rape scene is substantial and, as such, it is unsurprising to find so much of it in films that overall create controversy. As Robin Wood astutely pointed out with *Irreversible*, reading reviews of transgressive art films, one could sometimes conclude that they were composed only of rape and sexual assault, given the lack of attention shown to the rest of the films' narratives.[3] This book is nonetheless about controversy and therefore the analysis here necessarily focuses on the scenes of sexual assault and their role within the broader narrative of the films. This chapter digs further into the framing of rape in *The Brown Bunny* and *Free Will*, providing readings of their approaches to trauma, approaches that are structurally relevant to any number of transgressive art films, even as the precise narrative details pertain only to the film in question.

This examination of the portrayal of onlookers and perpetrators demonstrates the contradictory narrative and interpretative framings that are made possible through explicit depictions of sexual assault. I use the term 'onlooker' to signify someone who partakes in a rape by watching and condoning the actions. This is different from a 'witness' who provides testimony of a rape, although complex questions of complicity and responsibility mean that there is no clear distinction between the two. Close analysis of *The Brown Bunny* and *Free Will* reveals the insurmountable disagreements that can easily arise based on the value register through which a viewer might choose to analyse a film, and how these become even more controversial in the context of rape imagery. The difficulty of watching transgressive art films often leads to claims that they attack the spectator and that the experience of watching them is traumatic. I explore this trauma in detail here, thinking firstly about the most ethically positive reading we could ascribe to these films, by examining how their use of shocking and difficult imagery can be read as a productive exploration of grief (*The Brown Bunny*) and the perpetration of rape (*Free Will*). I also propose a more critical reading of the representation of rape, arguing that these films' framings of onlooker and perpetrator responsibility disturbingly reframe the trauma of being raped as the trauma of being a rapist or onlooker. This chapter therefore provides multiple readings of two films' portrayal of rape and trauma, pointing to the ambiguous sexual politics of transgressive art films, and situating all this within broader scholarship on rape imagery.

*

The Brown Bunny follows a depressed Bud Clay, a motorcycle racer, driving across America, reminiscing about his ex-girlfriend, Daisy, and having brief inconsequential encounters along the way. Like *Twentynine Palms*, *The Brown Bunny* revels for much of its running time in quotidian banalities – driving along the highway, long shots of motorcycle racing, petrol stations, brief conversations with strangers – before exploding into its drawn-out but spectacular and provocative conclusion.[4] The final sequence includes visible fellatio performed on Bud by Daisy, and flashbacks to Bud watching Daisy be gang-raped while drunk, after which she will die choking on her own vomit, as Bud abandons her. As well as the visibility of oral penetration, *The Brown Bunny* corresponds to other transgressive art films in its reliance on long-take sequences and on close-ups throughout the film. It has been read as a comment on pornography,[5] as a reflection on regret, guilt, grief and melancholy,[6] and as just another iteration of the road movie.[7] While the idea that *The Brown Bunny* is a critique of pornography is tenuous, with such accounts being over-reliant on highly reductive ideas of what constitutes pornography, it is useful to note the unusual foregrounding of sensuality and sexual fantasy within the process of grieving.

Its original Cannes cut derided as 'unendurably boring',[8] the length of *The Brown Bunny*'s scenes and the inactivity within them draws attention to their length and to the passing of time. Its long average shot length, and narrative sparsity bring it close to the phenomenon of 'slow cinema'. In the disjunction created by the combination of extended shot duration and an apparent lack of audiovisual content, slow cinema 'makes time noticeable in the image and consequently felt by the viewer'.[9] Similarly, *The Brown Bunny* makes time palpable, its passing noticeable. One scene, when Bud visits Daisy's parents, exemplifies this style. A long take from behind Bud's head shows him driving around streets looking for the house; he stops, gets out, and in a static take from the opposite side of the road we see him explain who he is and go into the house. Inside, Bud exchanges a few comments with the elderly couple (the father remains silent throughout) – 'your daughter liked swimming', 'I used to play in the back yard' – and it becomes clear that the couple have no memory of Bud. Without any significant dialogue, Bud announces, 'I have to get going now', and leaves. From the start of his search in the car to leaving the house, this scene is nearly eight minutes long with only eight shots, two of which exceed two minutes in length. Broadly representative of the film's style, this scene can be read as communicating some of the endless, desensitised directionlessness of grief, the numbing experience of seeing the world continue even as the lost person's life does not. It must nonetheless be noted that until the very end of the film, the viewer is unaware that Daisy is dead, and can reasonably assume Bud is mourning the end of their relationship, rather than the end of her life and his role in her death. Importantly, this feeling of grief is resolutely Bud's, a point emphasised by the many shots looking over his shoulder or looking out the windows with him in his van. For an hour before the decisive final sequence, viewers have been locked into Bud's perspective, his sadness and sense of loss.

The film's final scene, a tortured masturbatory reminiscence about Daisy's death, includes significant narrative developments, and a focus on rape and visible sex acts, which bring it into a discussion of transgressive art films. As in *Twentynine Palms*, the denouement comes as a surprise, but the preceding eventlessness cannot be understood without reference to this final scene. Beginning half an hour before the end credits, the final scene occupies nearly a third of *The Brown Bunny*'s running time, contains most of the film's dialogue, and takes place almost entirely in a motel room. Daisy appears, smokes crack cocaine and engages in prolonged discussion with Bud about their relationship. They kiss, lie on the bed, and Bud forcefully encourages Daisy to perform fellatio during which they continue to talk. Towards the end of the scene, we discover in a flashback that Daisy, who it is revealed was also pregnant, was gang-raped at a party while unconscious (witnessed by Bud, who assumed she was cheating on him), and subsequently died. Daisy's presence in the motel was therefore imagined, and part of Bud's process of dealing with guilt and grief. The fact that Daisy is dead, however, comes as a surprise to the viewer, and thus the whole scene plays out as diegetically real rather than solely in Bud's imagination.

The scene is slow with an average shot length of seventeen seconds until the (more quickly edited) flashbacks are shown, emphasising the slow narrative progress towards sex. With the claustrophobia of the room, there is a sense of emotional proximity to the pair, emphasised by the close-up camerawork, which dominates once they start kissing, and the quiet muffled sound which makes it difficult to hear parts of the conversation, especially when Daisy has Bud's penis in her mouth. In terms of the marginal transgressions, Bud's erect penis is made visible but relatively little despite how close the camera is to the fellatio. Often cupped by his hand and Daisy's mouth, ejaculation is not seen (inside Daisy's mouth) and Bud, suddenly coy or ashamed, puts his penis quickly back in his trousers, pushing Daisy away. Moreover, although the fellatio lasts nearly three minutes, this is less than ten per cent of the sequence, which consists predominantly of discussion and clothed kissing. For the entire scene, the camera remains close to the two characters, and the many long takes communicate the progression of their discussion, of their lover's tiff, of the increased eroticism and of their changing attitude towards each other. The fellatio also emphasises process, with a close-up of Bud's crotch beginning ninety seconds before he removes his penis from his underwear. The film shows him removing Daisy's bra and touching her nipples, there are images of Daisy kissing Bud's trousers, and massaging his penis through the material, and close-ups of Bud looking down as Daisy does all this. The scene shows each developmental stage in the scene as a whole.

We can read *The Brown Bunny* as a film about grief, about the trauma of losing one's partner in a brutal and violent way, and about a man's guilt at the role he played in that death. The long, slow, eventless scenes communicate the sense of numbness that comes with grief and depression, the directionlessness that can overwhelm a person. The two short scenes where he invites young women – a shop assistant (whom he kisses) and a sex worker – to ride in his van for a short time as well as the passionate scene of kissing with an apparent stranger might emphasise his contradictory desire for company and for solitude, for physical intimacy despite an emotional disconnection from anyone except his lost partner. This numbness becomes palpable, the very boredom that critics complained about is precisely the communication of that nothingness, the void, the negativity. The final sequence can be read as involving viewers materially, haptically in a sexual fantasy, which is part of how he is coming to terms with his loss: a sad combination of his anger and guilt, together with sexual frustration, becoming a phantasmatic scene of sexual control, where he asserts his dominance over Daisy as a desperate fetishistic attempt to claw back some sense of power over his emotions and her existence. All of this is communicated through the techniques especially of duration (long scenes and takes), but also of proximity (visual and aural close-ups) and visibility (oral penetration), the stylistic hallmarks of transgressive art films. On the face of it: a challenging arthouse film about male grief. This at least is where an analysis of the film's affect and sex scene via a hermeneutic value register would lead us. Before considering the film from a different, less favourable perspective, let us consider *Free Will* through the same hermeneutic value register.

*

In *Free Will*, the narrative also follows the male protagonist, Theo, here the perpetrator and not just an onlooker. Most of the film takes place after Theo is released from prison, having served nine years for several rapes, one of which we see in the opening sequence, and chronicles his attempts to lead a 'normal' life and overcome his desire to rape. He manages to engage in a non-violent sexual relationship with Nettie, but at the same time continues to commit rapes. As the film's title suggests, Theo struggles to work out how much free will he has in his rapist desires, trying to control them with masturbation and long walks, but he eventually commits suicide when he realises his urges cannot be controlled.

Unlike *The Brown Bunny* and its slow progression towards the dramatic finale, *Free Will* follows *Irreversible* and *Battle in Heaven* in placing a challenging and shocking scene right at the beginning of the film. An early sequence in *Free Will* depicts Theo as he stalks and then rapes a woman in a field, an attack that is shown in lengthy and close-up detail. It is shot mostly with long takes from a position accompanying Theo, the rapist. The camera is in a car with him for forty seconds (two shots of thirty and seven seconds) before he jumps out and grabs the cyclist, dragging her over a nearby bank into some scrubland. At the top of a small mound, a ninety-seven-second shot shows her falling down the other side, where he jumps on her, forces her to quieten down and removes her jacket before tying her hands with a bandage. A sixty-second close-up now focuses on him from her perspective as he removes her trousers; the camera tilts down to show him grabbing her breasts and genitals before masturbating through his trousers. We see a close-up of her bloodied face, breasts in shot, quivering with fear. In a seventy-second shot, he continues to masturbate before blindfolding her with another bandage. He pushes her legs up, leaning over her, and masturbates vigorously; the camera watches from roughly her position before moving backwards and being set down on the ground, static, about a metre away from her. He leans over her shouting 'cunt, cunt' and punches her in the face, the shock of which is emphasised by a close-up on her face and subsequent punches, shot from roughly his position. In a sixty-eight-second shot, the image moves back to her perspective looking at him as punches rain down, he moves back, spits on his hand and penetrates her, thrusting vigorously. He suddenly gets up, pulls his trousers up and wanders a short distance away without turning back, at which point the woman escapes. The attack itself, between him jumping out of the car and her escape, lasts around eight minutes, while the sequence as a whole, including the car drive and the subsequent police chase for Theo, must be endured for fourteen.

This long brutal sequence, within a 'relentlessly intense' film,[10] confronts viewers with long takes and close-ups of uncontextualised violence from the start of the film. Over half of the attack is shown in just four shots (of ninety, sixty, seventy and sixty-eight seconds), which include close-ups of the victim's face and body. The process of the attacks is emphasised in the long takes, and in the details of the mechanisms of his assault. He hides his car, he prepares his materials, he ties the woman up, he removes her clothes, he masturbates to gain an erection; there is an aftermath of her escape, and his pursuit. The beating rhythm of Theo's violative thrusts is clearly audible, creating a metronomic effect, emphasising the duration of the attacks, and how the attack is made up of numerous physical violations of the woman's vagina. The length of the scene and of the shots within this long scene highlight the stages of violence in rape and give viewers a hint of the duration. The duration of the long takes is central to this effect, combined with the close-ups of violence, and the visibility of his masturbation. This is not just a contextualising sequence to explain that our protagonist is a rapist but rather, in its engagement with the process of the rape, it is a depiction of the horror and violence of the man's acts. Moreover, when we learn that he is a serial rapist, this opening sequence comes to provide a tense and worrying context to all subsequent interactions with women, not least because the camera adopts Theo's point of view many times during the film.

Given that the film presents Theo's violence as unremittingly awful and appears to condone his decision to commit suicide at the end in order to protect the world from him, the conflation of Theo's gaze with the camera's gaze can be read as a provocation to the spectator. The unpleasantness that viewers might feel at the identification with a rapist gaze alerts us even more strongly to the fact that we are looking, that the film's viewers have been implicated in this way of perceiving women. In his analysis of *Manhunter*, Slavoj Žižek contends that the identification with the gaze of the murderer is particularly disturbing, when it turns out that the murderer is a photo developer looking at the same family snaps as the detective: 'the identification is at the level of the gaze, not on the level of the content. There is something extremely unpleasant and obscene in this experience of our gaze as already the gaze of the other'.[11] Similarly, there is something disturbing about identifying the camera's gaze with that of a rapist. One scene depicts a bar, seen from the street, a gaze which turns out to be Theo's; a close-up reveals that Nettie, his new girlfriend, is in this bar being observed outside by Theo. Again, this highlights the violent potential underlying this gaze, a potential which is immediately actualised because Theo then rapes a woman in an underground car park. In a later scene, when a concerned Nettie is tracking him through a theme park, there are several different gazes: the camera following Nettie, Nettie following Theo, and Theo following women. It becomes clear that the shots of women are from Theo's perspective, and that he is potentially stalking another victim: the film has again adopted a rapist's gaze, analysing whether these women might become victims. In such a reading, the (idealised) viewer is being overtly positioned as a companion, an accomplice even, to Theo's crimes, provoking them to reflect upon their broader complicity in acts of rape.

The film can be read as further emphasising the dynamics of rape and sexual assault, through the distinction made between sex scenes and rape scenes. Not only does it make very clear the difference between sex as pleasure, and rape as power, but also considers how dominance and submission could be integrated into a consensual and pleasurable relationship if Theo wished. In one sex scene, as Nettie leaves the kitchen in their flat, the camera adopts Theo's perspective looking in medium-long shot down the corridor towards her. It subsequently either aligns with Theo's gaze or looks at Theo. He tells Nettie to 'stay there', which she does, and then to 'take your clothes off', which she then also does, unbuttoning her trousers and dropping them to the floor. From a camera position over Nettie's shoulder, Theo stands up to come towards her as they both take off their shirts. They move against the wall kissing; she wraps her legs around him as he penetrates her. They swing round to thrust against the other wall of the corridor, her foot reaching out to steady them. As he ejaculates, he slides slowly down the wall into a sitting position, Nettie also collapsing backwards euphorically. Apart from being remarkably sensuous in the dark close-up shots of skin and contact, this scene is important in a number of ways. Firstly, it demonstrates Theo's capacity for consensual, non-violent sexual contact, and that elements of coercion and game-play – 'take your clothes off' – should not be pathologised in and of themselves; his desire for sexual domination (and perhaps Nettie's desire to be submissive) can be played out in a consensual way. Secondly, in the sex scene's stark difference to the two rape scenes, which are profoundly unerotic, this scene reinforces the sexual, pleasurable qualities of the sex, and the violent nature of the rapes. In the first scene, he struggled to even get an erection and spends very little time penetrating the woman, and much more time tying her up, punching her, and asserting his physical control over her body; the penetration is just another way of exerting physical power and control over her. Afterwards, he jumps up and remains gloomy, staring out into the distance, hurriedly refastening his trousers. By contrast, after the corridor sex, they both stretch out in an orgasmic haze, breathless from the euphoria and follow it up with a bath where they repose, satisfied from their exertions. Recent rape scholars have pointed out that this binary distinction between rape and sex, forged by second-wave feminist scholars, can be unhelpful, by reinforcing a misleading cultural image of rape as mostly committed by strangers and including substantial physical violence: rape instead operates along a scale including many forms of coercion, control and pseudo-consent that make a clear distinction between sex and rape difficult (discussed further below). Nonetheless, the film's indisputable condemnation of Theo's actions, and depiction of rape as harrowing and traumatic for the victim, whilst not pathologising forms of domination/submission in consensual sexual relations is positive, and by including both consensual and non-consensual acts performed by the same person does invite a reflection on sex, rape and power, even if those reflections could be more nuanced.

Free Will does not rehabilitate Theo, nor unhelpfully conflate sex and rape by suggesting that his rapist tendencies can be resolved through good sex: any hope that he might have been 'cured' is brutally quashed when he rapes again not long after the sex scene described above. This disappointment in Theo's failure to overcome his desire to rape places the film within the purview of the 'feel-bad' film, in that 'it creates, and then deadlocks, our desire for catharsis', refusing to allow the spectator any sense of pleasurable resolution to the violence of the earlier images in the film.[12] Like the famous rewind sequence in *Funny Games*, the brutality of the underground rape scene that comes after the sex scene can be read as punishing any spectator who might have expected a happy solution to Theo's problems, who might have hoped that he just needed to meet the 'right woman'.

This reading is further supported by a late scene in which Nettie's desire to rehabilitate Theo is heavily criticised. Nettie meets up with one of Theo's victims in a café, and after a brief conversation, Nettie is confronted in the bathroom where the former victim rapes Nettie with a toilet brush. In this scene, for once, the narrative gaze is entirely brought into Nettie's perspective, and Nettie is brutally punished for her actions even as she is not the perpetrator of the original trauma. In *Free Will*'s world, there is no solution to the trauma of rape, only a perpetuation of its violence, and Nettie is revealed as hopelessly naïve for thinking anything different. Angela Koch reads this scene as showing that any understanding of rape can only come through bodily experience, and therefore remains implicitly out of reach for the film spectator:

> Nettie must rely solely on this ambiguous communication of experience, which is not communicated to her verbally but rather corporeally. Only this ostensibly 'authentic' suffering can for her become the basis for knowledge of the acts perpetrated by her boyfriend Theo.[13]

On the one hand, this fits with the estrangement defence of transgressive imagery, whereby the shock of the film is designed to reorient an idealised spectator's ideas about the film content. On the other hand, it also critiques any film spectator who watches such a film in search of answers to the horror of rape, it critiques the idea that film images of rape will ever contribute meaningfully to debates on real-life rape, and it critiques the fundamental idea that 'understanding' rape is any sort of solution. If the only way to 'understand' rape is to be raped oneself, then how can that possibly be a solution?[14] Although the film does not perhaps explicitly gesture towards a structural critique of rape culture, due to its focus on the individual and the eponymous free will, the analogies between the camera's gaze and Theo's gaze, and the framing of Nettie as misguided therapist does move in the direction of a broader critique of societal attitudes towards rape.

Free Will continually draws connections between the spectator and the rapist, conflating the camera's gaze with his, and thereby inculcating viewers in his crimes, and his way of looking at women. Rather than positioning the spectator as a witness, we can read the spectator as positioned themselves as part of the problem. Like in other transgressive art films, this is communicated to viewers in long, proximate and graphic scenes, which are challenging to watch. In this reading via the hermeneutic register, the disturbing violence and long, repeated visualisation of rape are justified because they aim to have a positive impact on spectators who may subsequently reflect in more complex ways on rape, rape culture and the complicity of ordinary people in the continuation of both. While I am suspicious of any readings that appeal to how an idealised spectator might change the way they see the world, these are the kinds of readings seen frequently in writing on transgressive art films, which extol them as artistic interventions in contemporary social and political issues. Affective imagery communicates the material sensations of sex and violence through shock and haptics, and the visibility of such acts is seen to make visible oppressive power structures, thus potentially altering the outlook and behaviour of viewers.[15] In sum, this is the most positive reading we can make of these films' sexual and gender politics, which tallies with critical and scholarly responses to the film.[16]

*

There is, however, another side to *The Brown Bunny* and *Free Will* if we choose the ethical register rather than the hermeneutic register, if we approach the films from a prescriptive perspective of what kinds of behaviour and images are acceptable or should be shown. From this angle, any affective engagement viewers might feel in Bud's grief and Theo's attempts at restraint poses a number of problems. What is little discussed in commentary on *The Brown Bunny* is that Bud's behaviour towards Daisy is coercive and manipulative, as he convinces her to bare herself outside the covers and perform fellatio when she is reticent to do so. This coercive sexual treatment of Daisy is especially troubling after the revelation that Bud witnessed her rape but did nothing to intervene. Bud pushes Daisy to take off her shirt; she asks to get under the covers, but he ignores her, and he engages in more aggressive bite-like kissing; when she consents to sex on top of the covers, he pulls her head towards his crotch as he undoes his belt. During the fellatio he berates her about previous sexual experiences, and after he has ejaculated, he pushes her away, calling her a whore. After this, when they begin to discuss her rape, he blames her for letting the rapists in, and for taking drugs with them, eliciting an apology from her for being attacked. While this is ultimately presented as a phantasmatic situation and therefore not designed to be realist, sexual violence in arthouse films is frequently disentangled from the complexities of rape, seduction and power, and 'subordinated to political or philosophical purposes . . . reinforc[ing] the hierarchy of masculine imagination over feminine body'.[17] The specificities of Daisy's real-life and fantasy assaults are subsumed into a narrative of male existential crisis.

Bud is here engaging in many of the abusive behaviours that characterise the pseudo-consensual grey zone between consensual mutually desired sex, and rape.[18] This scene exemplifies what Nicola Gavey calls the discursive 'preconditions for rape – women's passive, acquiescing (a)sexuality and men's forthright, urgent pursuit of sexual "release"'[19] given that Daisy more or less does whatever Bud wants, and Bud's desire is a constant whining pressure towards fellatio. Bud's aggressive pursuit of Daisy's acquiescence mobilises a range of misogynistic prejudices about female sexuality: masochism, promiscuity, ever-ready desire to satisfy a man. In line with the pitfalls of an entirely consent-based reading of sex/rape, Daisy also verbally consents to sex, seemingly to placate Bud rather than out of any particular desire for sex, and this limited consent to intercourse on the covers leads immediately to an entirely different form of sex: fellatio. The film's criminal rape may occur elsewhere, but this scene has all the hallmarks of undesired and coercive sex, where cultural norms, normative scripts of heterosex and 'sexual taken-for-granteds'[20] about women as willing respondents to male sexual desire, especially when coupled with the latent threat of physical violence, lead to unwilling and tenuous consent. Bud's grief as well as the spectacular stranger gang-bang rape of Daisy, which ends the film, serve to obfuscate and overshadow the deeply retrogressive sexual politics of this scene.

This is a broader issue with the depiction of rape in transgressive art films in that it is almost always spectacular, extremely physically violent, and performed by complete strangers: the most clear-cut and evident form of rape. In transgressive art films, there is no doubt about rape having taken place, and that it was unmitigatedly terrifying and horrific: rape in transgressive art films is unequivocally about violence rather than sex, about power rather than pleasure.[21] Moreover, in *Irreversible* and *The Brown Bunny*, the victims are later revealed to be pregnant adding potential foeticide to the crimes committed, given the violence accompanying the attacks. The reframing of rape as violence by second-wave feminists was very useful in shifting understanding of sexual violence from the private domestic affairs of individuals to a recognition of its oppressive and regulatory function in patriarchal society. At an extreme, it allows rape to be considered as just another form of assault, little different to being physically beaten. This position was supported by Michel Foucault, because of its move away from seeing rape within a disciplining discourse of sexuality: otherwise sexuality as such, in the body, has a preponderant place, the sexual organ isn't like a hand, hair, or a nose. It therefore has to be protected, surrounded, invested in any case with legislation that isn't that pertaining to the rest of the body.[22]

Rape in films like *The Brown Bunny* and *Free Will* fits with this position; indeed, in *Free Will*, the vaginal penetration is accompanied by verbal abuse, spitting and punching, almost becoming just one part of a multifaceted physical attack. This is a long way from the ambiguous pleasures of the rape victim in *Straw Dogs* or the doubt about the truth of the rape allegations in *Rashomon*. In transgressive art films, there is no doubt that the rape took place, no doubt that it was horrific, no doubt that it was unremittingly traumatic, and no doubt that society should mobilise against such heinous acts. However, just as Foucault's comments are now desperately outdated (in the same conversation he also appears to condone sex with 'a child who doesn't refuse'[23]), so is a perspective on rape that is limited to seeing it as violence, and that only focuses on forced stranger rape combined with other elements of physical violence. In *The Brown Bunny*, this perspective tends to minimise the violence of the phantasmatic 'sex' scene, as the film leaves little space for thinking about rape outside the limited conception of rape as violence alone.

This 'rape as violence not sex' position has been critiqued from a number of angles, especially due to its binaristic division of men/women, nature/culture and especially violence/sex: 'the particular violence of rape is sexual, and . . . the sexuality inherent in it is violent'.[24] As black feminist discussions of the eroticisation of black slaves raped by their owners have long shown, as well as contemporary iterations of this in the hypersexualised framing of black women, which leads to them being seen as 'unrapable', there has never been a clean separation between rape, and erotic or sexual desire.[25] Today, scholarly and popular writing on rape is likely to draw more nuanced connections between these previous dichotomies, with the focus shifting towards more common instances of sexual violence, that do not respond to such easy distinctions. For instance, in Sara Roebuck's widely shared 'A Letter to the Man Who Tried to Rape Me', the list of the rights she asserts in the face of her attacker, and other would-be attackers, is mostly about questions of sex and sexuality.[26] The greater acknowledgement of sex worker perspectives into the debate has also added further nuance to questions of sex, violence, consent and desire. Molly Smith and Juno Mac highlight the changing boundary between sex and rape for sex workers in terms of the services an individual worker agrees to perform: 'forcing a sex worker to (for instance) have sex without a condom constitutes rape *precisely because* the sex worker has *not* sold the right for a client to use her body "as he likes in the time he has purchased it".[27] This is part of a wider debate about the value and meaning of consent in sex, with consent functioning as the amorphous boundary-line between sex and rape, demonstrating that clear-cut claims of violence inherited from second-wave feminists have been overtaken by a range of more nuanced accounts since the 1990s. As Katherine Angel points out, it is important to contextualise consent and desire, which can exist on a huge spectrum as well as being changing and potentially unclear to a person themselves:

> a sexual ethics that is worth its name has to allow for obscurity, for opacity and for not-knowing. We need to start from this very premise – this risky, complex premise: that we shouldn't have to know ourselves in order to be safe from violence.[28]

By contrast, transgressive art films do not allow for obscurity, opacity or not-knowing; their sexual ethics is predicated on the clearest, most palpable communication of sexual violence. In *The Brown Bunny*, this leads to an effacement of the exploitation and coerciveness of the sex scene (signalled by the glaring lack of critical and scholarly discussion of the troubling gender dynamics in this sequence), and in the case of *Free Will*, to a binary dichotomy between rape as violent non-consent, versus sex as sexual (desirable, pleasurable) consent.

Returning to identification and narrative emphasis, in *Free Will* there is a shift in focus from victim trauma to perpetrator trauma, just as Bud's experience dominates in *The Brown Bunny*. In portraying Theo as traumatised by his own actions, much of *Free Will* focuses on the lasting trauma of a perpetrator. This becomes most explicit in a comparison of a second rape scene late in the film with the opening one described previously. The second rape is much shorter than the first: there is a static fifty-second shot of the violation, with the attack itself lasting only eighty-nine seconds and the violence is mainly hidden from view behind a car. After the rape, three shots lasting altogether ninety-seven seconds detail the difficulty Theo has leaving the fob-controlled underground garage where the rape takes place, emphasising his fear of getting caught rather than the comatose woman lying half-naked on the floor. Furthermore, his exit from the garage cuts immediately to an eighty-six-second shot of him crying in his bathroom after having washed incriminating evidence off his visible penis. He sits on the bathroom floor, sobbing into his hands, seemingly traumatised by his own character, his own actions. Thus, while the second rape is disturbing to watch, it is overshadowed, both in its brevity, and in the much longer duration of shots after it, by the practical and psychological concerns of the rapist. Where the visibility of the penis in the rape scenes in *Baise-moi*, *Irreversible* and *Holiday* emphasises the penile violation obscured in most rape scenes, here the visible penis being washed emphasises the rapist's need to hide evidence, even as the presence of blood highlights the violence of the rape. The brutal material aspects of this rape, and the experience of the woman within it, are overshadowed by the perpetrator's anxieties. While the first rape emphasises rape itself, its material, corporeal aspects, the second rape becomes metaphorical, a means by which to explore Theo's existential crisis and his increasing anxiety. In the second rape, it is the perpetrator's trauma of being a rapist that overshadows the victim's trauma of being raped. Similarly to *The Brown Bunny*, although *Free Will* appears to begin with a deep concern for the victims of rape, emphasising their trauma, it is ultimately the perpetrator's trauma that dominates. The basic premise of *Free Will* makes this perhaps unsurprising, but given that the opening sequence gives so much space to the trauma of the victim, that his girlfriend Nettie is so roundly punished for her cackhanded attempts to approach one of Theo's victims, and that the gaze of the spectator is so overtly criticised as overlapping with the rapist's, the effacement of the second on-screen victim's trauma by Theo's is quite striking.

This blurring of the boundaries between victim and perpetrator trauma has much in common with Cathy Caruth's influential account of trauma. Following Sigmund Freud, Caruth argues that a traumatic event is not actually experienced in the original moment.[29] Rather, being too overwhelming for the conscious mind, it is repressed into the unconscious. A second event triggers the person to remember the original event, and thus experience it for the first time. She illustrates this with Freud's retelling of a story from Torquato Tasso's *Jerusalem Delivered* (1581), in which Tancred kills his beloved Clorinda while she is on the battlefield in disguise. Her soul flees to a tree and later, when Tancred angrily lashes out with his sword at this tree, Clorinda's voice floats out, and Tancred experiences the trauma of her death through that voice. He was unable to grieve the first time as he was unaware of Clorinda's death, and so it is only in this second traumatic re-enactment that the initial trauma is made available to Tancred, allowing him to mourn. This is pertinent for thinking about the repression of trauma in terms of psychoanalytic treatment and psychotherapy, but also for thinking about the therapeutic potential of art as a means of giving voice to a trauma, and therefore allowing it to be experienced properly for the first time in its re-presentation.

The central problem with this as a metaphor for the process of dealing with trauma, as Ruth Leys explores in detail, is that Clorinda is the victim, the one who suffered the traumatic event, and yet her murderer (albeit inadvertent) is the one working through his trauma by wounding her again.[30] As Caruth writes:

> The actions of Tancred, wounding his beloved in a battle and then, unknowingly, seemingly by chance, wounding her again, evocatively represent in Freud's text the way that the experience of a trauma repeats itself, exactly and unremittingly, through the unknowing acts of the survivor and against his very will. As Tasso's story dramatizes it, the repetition at the heart of catastrophe—the experience that Freud will call 'traumatic neurosis'—emerges as the unwitting re-enactment of an event that one cannot simply leave behind. . . . Tancred's story thus represents traumatic experience not only as the enigma of a human agent's repeated and unknowing acts but also as the enigma of the otherness of a human voice that cries out from the wound, a voice that witnesses a truth that Tancred himself cannot fully know.[31]

This is not an incidental anecdote that could be brushed off as ill-advised, but rather it opens her book and is integral to Caruth's entire account of trauma:

> The example offered by the poetry of Tasso is indeed, in my interpretation, more than a literary example of a vaster psychoanalytic, or experiential, truth; the poetic story can be read, I will suggest, as a larger parable, both of the unarticulated implications of the theory of trauma in Freud's writings and, beyond that, of the crucial link between literature and theory that the following pages set out to explore.[32]

Although the voice is indeed that of the victim, who is heard for the first time and therefore able in some way to tell her story, we must note that it is her murderer who is framed here as the 'survivor'. Rather than the trauma being the violent death experienced by the victim, it is the killing and loss of the victim that is experienced as traumatic by the perpetrator. Part of Caruth's project is to valorise engagement with trauma art/literature/film as an important part of collectively coming to terms with traumatic events such as the Holocaust; it thus makes sense to focus on listening to the testimony rather than speaking of it. The problem is that in this example, the listener is also the perpetrator, and the trauma of experiencing violence morphs into the trauma of perpetrating or witnessing violence. Caruth reasserts this conflation of different actors within the context of trauma testimony when she claims that 'there's a double survivor situation, but a survivor and a proxy survivor, and it's the meeting of those two that constitutes the witness'.[33] Here the 'proxy survivor', that is, the listener, is co-opted into the role of witness, diminishing the testimony of the actual witness, who in the case of Holocaust survivors, was also a victim of the violence they witnessed. As Leys aptly sums up, the chilling implication of Caruth's reading is that 'not only can Tancred be considered the victim of a trauma but that even the Nazis are not exempt from the same dispensation'.[34] While this story may aptly demonstrate the role of repetition and deferment in the processing of trauma, as well as that of the voice, the shift of focus onto the perpetrator, whilst claiming to emphasise the potential of the victim or witness to benefit from this re-enactment, is deeply worrying. This shift is also precisely what occurs in *Free Will* and *The Brown Bunny*.

At the end of *The Brown Bunny* when we discover that Daisy is a figment of Bud's imagination, a sexual fantasy that is part of Bud's attempt to grieve her loss, we also discover that Bud was instrumental in Daisy's death, and that he feels guilt at his role in it. Bud is implicated in the rape because he walks in on her being raped, and yet assumes that she is cheating on him and so abandons her to her fate. The same images of the rape are played twice from Bud's position peering around the door – one where he sees Daisy alone after the rape and abandons her, one where he runs away whilst the rape is still taking place. The presentation of Bud's exact actions is ambiguous, but in either case, he abandons her and his intervention would likely have saved her life. While Bud is not a rapist, he was a witness who chose to do nothing, preferring to believe in a vision of his girlfriend as promiscuous and hypersexualised (we see repeated images of her bare breasts in this sequence), indulging in adulterous semi-public group sex while intoxicated, rather than considering that the men might be sexually assaulting her. For this reason, I prefer to consider him as an onlooker as well as a witness, because like the third man who watches his friends rape Daisy, Bud effectively participated in the rape by choosing not to intervene, and bears some responsibility for her death, even as the rapists themselves are clearly the main perpetrators. Importantly, even as the victim of this attack is Daisy – it is she who is raped, who is left comatose on the bed after the assault, and who dies as a result – the film returns squarely to Bud as victim of her loss and his guilt, ending not long after the flashback images on a fifty-six-second headshot of him driving.

The film's framing positions Bud as the character trying to deal with a traumatic experience. On the one hand, as a film about the grieving process, this is not a problem; just because his girlfriend was raped does not mean that he avoids grief. On the other hand, when the final sequence turns out to be phantasmatic, and leads onto a traumatic, but potentially therapeutic, reliving of the night of Daisy's death, we can see that the film is less about grief than about re-enacting trauma, and thereby coming to terms with the traumatic experience. Bud's process of working through his grief has several comparisons with that of Tancred in Tasso's poem. Party to his beloved's death, he does not realise in the moment the role that he played in bringing about her demise, and, following Freud's/Caruth's interpretation of this non-experience of her death, is unable to grasp her death as such. Later on, Bud re-enacts a coercive sexual situation just like Tancred slashes at Clorinda's tree (phantasmatic Daisy is unhappy about the sex and is abused throughout as noted above), and it is whilst taking on the role of sexual assaulter that Bud hears her voice (they have a long discussion), which brings about the release of the flashback that has been bottled up and repressed for the first hour of the film.

In other words, I contend that by the end of *The Brown Bunny*, Bud has been positioned as the victim of Daisy's rape. The film is a working through of his trauma at having witnessed her rape, and rather than his witnessing being elevated in order to shed light on her suffering, it minimises and obscures the trauma at the heart of the story. The film not only follows Bud but is dominated by his perspective, with many long shots through the windscreen that look with Bud rather than at him. As Michael Johnston points out, Bud's grasping of Daisy's head in the fellatio sequence also bears some remarkable similarities to his body position while driving. Daisy remains secondary to his controlling of her body, of her memory and her trauma: 'controlling, manipulating, and driving . . . Bud has not left the driver's seat'.[35] What is worse, is not only that he witnessed the event, but that he was in a position to do something about it, and preferred to blame the victim for her assault. The fact that he continues to blame her in his fantasy, points to the semi-coerced fellatio as a perverse form of re-enacted revenge on the victim for having allowed herself to be assaulted, as though to phantasmatically shift the guilt, which he feels so intensely, back onto her. His grief is not just about loss but about his role as an onlooker, a form of perpetrator, in that loss. *The Brown Bunny*'s powerful depiction of grief and loss is undercut by the elision of the female victim's experience in favour of the male onlooker's exposure to the traumatic event and to his own guilt at his involvement.

In a further attempt at recuperation, Cynthia Fuchs considers this effectively to form part of the film's ethics of transgression, punishing the spectator for seeking catharsis in Bud's grief, much like a 'feel-bad film':

> it is his awful, ugly fantasy, vengeful and cheerless, and invites you to dislike Bud (and perhaps Gallo) with a newfound urgency. . . . At the same time, it reaffirms Bud's sadness and sense of responsibility,

> making him again a sort of victim, whether of his own moral tyranny or his love of an indecent woman. This aspect of the film invites judgment, and makes you pay for making it.[36]

Perhaps for an audience in tune with the complex sexual politics of the film, this will be the case, but it is something largely unmentioned in analyses of the film and so it is difficult to see this as a widespread response to the film. Scholars similarly repeat this problematic superiority of male thought over female bodies when reading *Free Will* not as a film about rape, but about contemporary German (male) cultural anxieties. Heidi Schlipphacke, for instance, reads *Free Will* as representing a 'symbolically schizophrenic' German masculinity and Theo as demonstrating the 'split male body [which] mirrors the national German body'.[37] For Schlipphacke the rapes are only interesting inasmuch as they act as metaphors for theorising German male identity, a view of which we should rightly be sceptical: who gets to determine when rape is a metaphor and when it is not?[38] Where the first rape might challenge viewers to ask ourselves why they continue to watch such violence and to perceive rape as about power rather than sex, the second rape's physical elements are lost as they become metaphorical ammunition for Theo's battle between free will and bodily desire. Nonetheless, commentators find ever more acrobatic ways of recuperating the film within a positive ethical framework.

Taken together, this shows that a fundamental part of *The Brown Bunny* and *Free Will* is their resolute focus on the individual such that any sense of the societal structures influencing our understanding of rape fade into the background. Both films have relatively few characters, such that the male perpetrator/onlooker character totally dominates the screen time. Just as *The Brown Bunny* ignores the situation that led to three men feeling able to rape a drunk woman in a semi-public place, in order to emphasise the emotions of a single character, *Free Will*'s title and narrative explicitly guide us towards existential-biological rather than social questions. *Free Will* conforms to Susan Brownmiller's and others' biological argument that men rape because they are men, and that there is little that can be done about it, except, as the film's beginning and end suggest, prison or suicide.[39] Instead of pursuing a societal analysis, *The Brown Bunny* and *Free Will* refocus attention on the individual aberration, which can be dealt with individually. As Angela Davis points out,

> If men rape because they are men – as Susan Brownmiller and other theorists have argued – women will always be forced to regard the police, courts and prisons as their only glimmer of hope. If, on the

> other hand, the incentives for rape are not a natural product of male anatomy or psychology, but are rather social in nature, the prospects for eradicating sexual violence will depend on changes of an entirely different order.[40]

Framing the issues of rape in their narratives as individual, psychological or biological concerns is a distinctly conservative position as it allows society to escape criticism, and for responsibility for rape to be placed on a few 'bad apples'. If those individuals are also reframed as the victims of somebody else's trauma, the responsibility of perpetrators, onlookers and more generally those who enable the system to continue in such a fashion is further reduced.

As with other transgressive art films, this comes down to a fundamental tension in the value registers used for a viewer's analysis. The critical analysis via trauma theory and rape scholarship works on an ethical register, questioning the kinds of images of rape that should exist. The earlier more positive analysis operates on the hermeneutic register, exploring how the films can be interpreted. Analyses of the hermeneutic variety can become increasingly recuperative, faithful as they are to the perceived intentions of the film or filmmakers, where almost any problematic aspect of the film can be reframed within an estrangement defence of a film.

It is also worth noting that *The Brown Bunny*'s incoherences and inconsistencies go beyond this conflict of value registers and are particularly striking. As Daniel Sacco notes, the film plays at the boundaries of numerous different concepts: it 'is structured and presented with the effect of blurring numerous perceived lines delineating various extreme binaries including: life and death (textual); narrative and pornography (artistic); reality and fantasy (ontological); and radicalism and conservatism (political)'.[41] At the same time, there is little resolution to these tensions, with Marc James Léger going as far as to suggest that 'the resultant incoherence of identity becomes a matter of style in his [Gallo's] work'.[42] Just as the politics of the core transgressive art films was difficult to place, an issue that has played out in critical commentary,[43] so is *The Brown Bunny*'s politics a challenge to define. As well as the issues discussed so far, the film combines a radicalism of form and a presentation of vulnerable masculinity, seen in Bud's pleas to women at petrol stations to accompany him in the car for short periods, with a macho controlling vision of masculinity, domestic violence, rape apologism and victim blaming. These confusions coalesce around the figure of Vincent Gallo, almost inseparable from his film as the writer, director, editor, producer and lead actor, who has been described as a queer figure[44] and has been substantially involved with the liberal world of independent arthouse filmmaking,[45] whilst being a self-proclaimed right-wing conservative.[46] Like its director's contradictory profile, *The Brown Bunny* is a touching account of masculine grief, that reasserts a number of highly regressive ideas about sexual and gender politics in the final scenes.

*

Just as in many other depictions of rape in cinema,[47] the men in *The Brown Bunny* and *Free Will* usurp the women, taking centre stage in the narratives despite not being the victim, such that they appear to experience the rape. Indeed, Daisy's subjectivity and that of Theo's victims are all but erased from these films. By dedicating long parts of the films to creating empathy for and identification with Bud's grief, and both Theo and Bud's feelings of guilt, these films cue the spectator to believe that they are watching rape from the 'correct' position 'suggesting that watching a rape and then telling the story of that rape is sufficient to take action against rape', implying in effect, that 'there is nothing left for spectators to do, as long as they are willing to "see" that what they are witnessing *is* rape'.[48] Read thus, the estrangement defence of these films is hugely undermined if the framing of the rape scenes actually facilitates a comfortable position from which to view horrible material, rather than what should be a decidedly uncomfortable viewing position. Incidentally, the notable absence of discussion of rape in criticism of *The Brown Bunny* suggests that this part of the storyline did not make a substantial impact on viewers of the film, as it was overshadowed by the explicitness of the fellatio. This points to a certain scholarly responsibility for the striking lack of reflection this film has encouraged about rape. Both *The Brown Bunny* and *Free Will* ultimately succumb to the same erroneous belief that 'films about social problems help solve these problems'[49] without considering how images of rape are always contributing, in one way or another, to a rape culture.

One seemingly positive element to rape depiction in transgressive art films is the lack of ambiguity about rape: from *Irreversible* to *Baise-moi*, *Romance* and *Trouble Every Day* to *Twentynine Palms* there is no confusion or denial of rape having taken place, there is no questioning of the victim's experience.[50] As viewers we are provided with clear visual evidence of rape mostly through visible genitals, and long takes of the assaults and their aftermath. The same can be said for *Free Will*. At the same time, this reliance on visible evidence contributes to the idea that sexual violence does not exist as such without it, that it cannot become 'real' without it.[51] It demonstrates excessive investment in the value of visual evidence: this relates both to mechanisms for securing legal convictions (incredibly difficult in rape cases), and to a problematic conflation of the 'visible' with the 'real', also a characteristic of much pornography.[52] Relying so substantially on visibility, proximity and duration to make incontrovertibly clear that the rape 'did happen' reduces the discursive issues of rape, its mediation and its cultural ramifications to a reductive ontological question, that has been asked and answered. Films such as *Free Will* exhibit a reductive form of feminism where just the 'ability and desire to *see* the rape, then, become feminist acts', however limited or problematic the visualisation of rape may be.[53]

In both *The Brown Bunny* and *Free Will* durational and material physicality communicate the violence of grief and the suffering of rape victims. Nonetheless, by the end of the film, such suffering is subsumed within the narrative of a male perpetrator's or onlooker's attempts to come to terms with the suffering of their female victims. In this way, any progressive reading of the depiction of grief and perpetrator guilt is undermined by the narrative framing of sexual violence. The conflict between the ethical register, oriented around sexual imagery or depictions of sexual violence, and the defensive recuperations of the hermeneutic register is as visible here as in any other transgressive art film. Detailed exploration of the presentation of sexual assault demonstrates significant similarities with a wide range of troubling images of rape in mainstream cinema, which are compounded by the films' investment in the realist and evidentiary connotations of long, explicit and proximate images of sex and sexual violence.

Ethical and political problems abound when the depiction of rape is set against the overall narrative presentation of the protagonists and their feelings. Close analysis of film form and narrative shows how the films set up a fraught conflict of value registers that is heightened by their political ambiguity and internal incoherences. Reading the films through different value registers leads to quite different evaluations of the films in terms of their sexual and gender politics. A reading undertaken via the hermeneutic register is able to analyse the film as a progressive intervention in debates about the representation of male vulnerability, while a reading via the ethical register tends to see the images of rape as exploitative spectacles that prioritise masculine emotion over physical female suffering. Thinking about the conflict of value registers in terms of narrative also lays some of the groundwork for the more conceptual reflections on witnessing in the following chapter. The kind of troubling political ambiguity seen in these films in relation to highly provocative and challenging imagery is an important factor in the divisive reactions that audiences give to transgressive art films, helping to explain why audiences reach for such different value registers, and why they are so polarised in their evaluations of the films' transgressions.

Notes

1. BBFC, 'A Ma Sœur!'
2. See Krautheim, 'Aspiring to the Void'; Nicodemo, 'Cinematography and Sensorial Assault'; Scott, 'Bearing Witness to the Unbearable'.
3. Wood, 'Against and For *Irreversible*'.
4. See Taylor (*Troubled Everyday*) for a detailed reflection on the everyday, with half a chapter on *Twentynine Palms*, although she does not consider *The Brown Bunny*. Grønstad provides an interesting comparative discussion of 'dedramatized spectacles' in *The Brown Bunny* and *Twentynine Palms* (*Screening the Unwatchable*, 71ff.).
5. Léger, 'Sad Bunny'; Sacco, '"In a Brown Study"'.
6. Battestini, 'The Brown Bunny'; Souza, 'O rosto e a voz'; Sacco, '"In a Brown Study"'.
7. Johnston, 'View from the Road'; Souza, 'O rosto e a voz'.
8. Ebert, 'The Brown Bunny'. Twenty-six minutes was cut from the Cannes version to create the ninety-three-minute general-release cut. All my comments pertain to the final cut of the film.
9. De Luca and Barradas Jorge, *Slow Cinema*, 5; see also Flanagan, 'Towards an Aesthetic of Slow'; Jaffe, *Slow Movies*; Lim, *Tsai Ming-Liang and a Cinema of Slowness*.
10. Schlipphacke, *Fragmented Bodies*, 33.
11. Žižek, *Looking Awry*, 108.
12. Lübecker, *The Feel-Bad Film*, 2.
13. Koch, 'Das ›unsägliche‹ Verbrechen', 193.
14. On exploring the experience and bodies of others whilst articulating their unknowability and unavoidable otherness, and the conceptual problems of trying to 'understand' others, see Silverman, *The Threshold of the Visible World*; Cooper, *Selfless Cinema?*; Kuppers, *The Scar of Visibility*.
15. Although one could argue this is simply part of 'the illusion of being able to solve social problems by going to the movies' (Lukow and Ricci, 'The "Audience" Goes "Public"', 36; in terms of rape, see also Projansky, *Watching Rape*, 117; Horeck, *Public Rape*, 97).
16. For examples of commentary that reads *The Free Will* as forcing reflection through affectively challenging imagery and narrative, see Suchsland, 'Der Freie Wille'; Guillen, 'Review of Der Freie Wille'; Tully, 'Free Will, The'. as well as various comments on 'Letterboxd': https://letterboxd.com/film/the-free-will/ (accessed August 29, 2022). As an example of the polarised reception, see comments on Mubi that range from 'one of the best films this century' to 'misogynistic and disgusting': https://mubi.com/films/the-free-will/ratings (accessed August 29, 2022).
17. Russell, *Rape in Art Cinema*, 6.
18. On the problems of using consent as a marker of rape see West, 'Sex, Law and Consent'; Bailey, 'Sex in a Masculinities World'; Angel, *Tomorrow Sex Will Be Good Again*.
19. Gavey, *Just Sex?*, 3.
20. Gavey, 3.
21. A perspective that has become relatively standard within 'post-feminist' film and television (see Cuklanz and Moorti, 'Television's "New" Feminism').
22. Foucault, *Politics, Philosophy, Culture*, 201–2; see Cahill, *Rethinking Rape*, 143–66 for a detailed discussion of Foucault's and Foucauldian readings of rape.
23. Foucault, *Politics, Philosophy, Culture*, 204.

24 Cahill, *Rethinking Rape*, 9.
25 Davis, 'Rape, Racism and the Capitalist Setting'; Hill Collins, *Black Feminist Thought*; see also Horeck, *Public Rape*, 138ff.
26 'As a human being, I have a right to live my life without my sexuality as a woman being used as justification by men to touch me or sexually benefit from my body. . . . I have the right to have sex if I want to, and that right is identical to that of a man . . . if you are naked with a condom on your penis and I have already said yes but then I change my mind, that does not translate to consent and sex beyond this point is RAPE.' (Roebuck, 'A Letter to the Man Who Tried to Rape Me', 360).
27 Smith and Mac, *Revolting Prostitutes*, 44; see also Grant, *Playing the Whore*, 93 on how issues of desire and consent are articulated differently in sex work than non-commercialised sex.
28 Angel, *Tomorrow Sex Will Be Good Again*, 40.
29 Caruth, *Unclaimed Experience*.
30 Leys, *Trauma*, 292–97.
31 Caruth, *Unclaimed Experience*, 2.
32 Caruth, 3.
33 Caruth and Lifton, 'Interview with Robert Jay Lifton', 174.
34 Leys, *Trauma*, 297.
35 Johnston, 'View from the Road', 9; see also Battestini, 'The Brown Bunny', 4.
36 Fuchs, 'The Brown Bunny'.
37 Schlipphacke, *Fragmented Bodies*, 33–34.
38 Hawkins, *Cutting Edge*, 196.
39 Brownmiller, *Against Our Will*.
40 Davis, 'Rape, Racism and the Capitalist Setting', 39.
41 Sacco, '"In a Brown Study"', 82.
42 Léger, 'Sad Bunny', 86.
43 See Palmer, 'Rites of Passing'; Hawkins, 'Culture Wars', n23; Lübecker, 'Bruno Dumont's *Twentynine Palms*'.
44 Léger, 'Sad Bunny'.
45 Directing the low-budget *Buffalo '66* to much acclaim, and performing starring roles in *Trouble Every Day* and *Essential Killing*, amongst others.
46 Benderson, 'Hating Vincent Gallo'; Léger, 'Sad Bunny', 84; Chaw, 'Gallo's Humor'.
47 Projansky, *Watching Rape*, 21.
48 Projansky, 117.
49 D.B. Jones cited in Horeck, *Public Rape*, 97.
50 Although Emma Wilson's description of the rape in *Romance* as a 'near-rape' suggests this clarity is not universally acknowledged ('Deforming Femininity', 152.).
51 Horeck, *Public Rape*, 101; Koch, *Ir/reversible Bilder*, 36.
52 Williams, *Hard Core*.
53 Projansky, *Watching Rape*, 117.

5

Witnessing

Definitions of the act of rape mostly revolve around the absence of consent, desire, intent, will, agreement, knowledge or awareness, all of which are difficult to prove definitively, given that they are mostly about the state of mind of the victim, and in some cases, the perpetrator, rather than externally verifiable factors. As such, rape is a '"perfect crime for film", dramatiz[ing] questions of subjectivity, storytelling, testimony and interpretation',[1] fuelling an epistemic search and a spectatorial desire to 'understand' that underpins so many film narratives. This chapter, however, is less interested in narrative, and more in how rape is presented formally in transgressive art films, especially given their almost obsessive focus on communicating the 'reality' of violent and sexual diegetic acts through lengthy, clear and proximate images. Transgressive art films frequently place detailed images of rape at the centre of their storylines, in effect creating filmic evidence of the assault, and placing the spectator in the position of witness to the crime. One of the most well-known sequences in all transgressive art films is the rape scene in *Irreversible*, a single, mostly static take, often read as highlighting the viewer's own spectatorship. The witnessing of rape is in many ways a central plank of transgressive art films and the controversy they create.

The main focus of this chapter is long takes of sexual violence, as they draw out questions of realism, politics, censorship, art and scholarly ethics that are pivotal to the impact of, and discourse around, transgressive art films. Using long takes of sexual violence in *The Tribe* and *Holiday* as illustrations, I argue that the ethical issues raised by the visualisation of rape in transgressive art films, and especially the evocation of witnessing in these scenes, are emblematic of the contradictory and contested spectatorial framework set up by these films. Beyond just transgressive art films, these depictions crystallise the irreconcilable ethical tensions at the core of all fictional rape images. On the one hand, rape images exploit suffering as intense affect or metaphorical resonance, on the other hand, they emphasise to a wide audience an unconscionably common yet mostly hidden ordeal that consistently fails to elicit serious political action. By providing visual 'evidence' and clarity, cinematic rape can tap into the central problem of prosecuting actual rapes – the problem of proving that a crime took place – but in doing so makes problematic assumptions about the capacity of images to function as evidence. Examining questions of evidence and truth, this chapter unpicks the ethics and discursive politics of rape imagery to explain why the rape scene is such a recurrent trope in transgressive art films, how it becomes so divisive when shot in long take, and how this fits into the transgressive art film's role as an innovator in the cinema art world.

*

Any examination of how the witnessing of rape might be understood in transgressive art films, demands that we reflect first on what it means to say that a film or film spectator can bear witness. The claim alone that particular stylistic choices evoke a sense of witnessing constitutes the taking of a position with regard to these images that must be unpicked. We can consider film witnessing as predicated on the interconnections of different elements of visual evidence. Firstly, a witness is one who sees an event and thereby provides evidence in the form of eyewitness testimony. Secondly, a photograph or film contains the trace of particular reflections of light passing through the camera lens.[2] Thirdly, films that place the spectator in the position of a witness, or that emphasise the testimonial qualities of their images, highlight these elements of visual evidence through particular stylistic choices associated with realism, the documentary and testimony. In the films discussed here, this is particularly through the use of long takes, minimal or no camera movement, minimal changes to a sparse mise-en-scène and no extra-diegetic sound. If we are to fully grasp the ramifications of bringing these three elements of witnessing together in fictional narrative film more broadly, and transgressive art films in particular, it is important to examine how photos and cinema have become discursively linked to evidence and testimony, and the particular centrality of these concepts in relation to images of rape and sexual assault.

Evidence has long played a dominant role in scholarship on film and photography in terms of 'evidential force',[3] indexicality,[4] recording and revealing,[5] documentary,[6] and theories of cinematic realism.[7] However, as legal scholars and apparatus theorists have argued, the link between photography and evidence has always been discursively produced and cannot be seen as a transparent reflection of processes outside the medium itself.[8] The link between a document and its 'documentary status' is constituted through a nexus of institutions, discursive regimens, and systems of power.⁹ Its evidential force is not:

> a magical 'emanation' but a material product of a material apparatus set to work in specific contexts, by specific forces, for more or less defined purposes ... That a photograph can come to stand as *evidence*, for example, rests not on a natural or existential fact, but on a social, semiotic process ... the emergence of photographic documentation and what Barthes sees as the photograph's 'evidential force' were bound up with new discursive and institutional forms, subject to but also exercising real effects of power, and developing in a complex historical process.[10]

Although we have learned to see photographs as evidence and the location of particular truths, photographs and films play a crucial ideological role in society, 'testing, confirming and constructing a total view of reality'.[11] Indeed, in a legal setting, the epistemic status of evidence is to a large part determined by the identities and beliefs of those who present it, those whom it is seen to represent, and those who are asked to interpret it (lawyers, defendants and jurors/judges).[12] Evidence is not evident: it is produced within precise and circumscribed contexts.

This is also the case for the sense of realism or witnessing that a spectator might experience when watching a film. While visibility, proximity and duration have come to be associated with forms of realism in terms of visible sex acts, a sense of presence or contact, and a shared temporality, these are always bound up with cinematic conventions and audience expectations; they do not inherently signify in a particular way. The meaning of film style, as with all meaning, is bound up with external references and concepts: as Stuart Hall notes, 'things "in themselves" rarely if ever have any one, single, fixed and unchanging meaning. ... we *give them a meaning* [through] ... the frameworks of interpretation which we bring to them'.[13] As such, when fictional films, which by definition have no direct link to their invented narratives, appeal to a testimonial, documentary or evidential mode, it must always be seen within the context of evidence's discursive production. If the emergence of that which can stand as evidence is always bound up in social processes, then the evocation of film witnessing in fictional films is predicated on a double set of discursive processes: first in terms of evidence (testimony and photographic traces), then of an evidential mode via particular filmic conventions.

Images do not, can never, speak for themselves. There can never be an underlying incontrovertible message, a kernel of reality to be extracted from an image: what we 'see' in an image, what an image 'shows' is always filtered through complex interpretative frameworks, that allow us to give meaning to colours, shapes, actions, events. In her discussion of the photos of Rodney King being beaten by police officers, Judith Butler points out how contingent evidence in photography is, how bound up evidence is, with interpretation. Racist interpretative frameworks allowed some to 'see' King as violent even as he was being beaten: 'this is a seeing which is a reading, that is, a contestable construal, but one which nevertheless passes itself off as "seeing," a reading which became for that white community, and for countless others, the same as seeing'.[14] This is the same schema which frames women of colour as submissive, animalistic, hypersexualised and thus 'unrapable'.[15] The interpretative lens does not allow for these rapes to be 'seen' as sexual assault, or even as potential crimes. The police officers' acquittal at trial for using excessive force against King, despite the seemingly evident brutality of their actions, shows that visual media are always being read through interpretative frameworks that depend on the viewer, the context, institutional discourse, and systems of power, rather than being straightforwardly demonstrative of a particular narrative:

> To claim that King's victimization is manifestly true is to assume that one is presenting the case to a set of subjects who know how to see; to think that the video 'speaks for itself' is, of course, for many of us, obviously true. . . . But what the trial and its horrific conclusions teach us is that there is no simple recourse to the visible, to visual evidence, that it still and always calls to be read, that it is already a reading, and that in order to establish the injury on the basis of the visual evidence, an aggressive reading of the evidence is necessary.[16]

This connects with transgressive art film images in that viewers conflate 'reading' with 'seeing', considering the image to be speaking for itself and communicating their interpretation to them, despite their reading always being filtered through the value register through which they choose to interpret the transgressions. While in King's case, there is an actual set of actions and intentions that these readings seek to establish, in the case of fictional images, there is no concrete set of events to which the readings refer back to. However, like in a court of law where conviction and acquittal are mutually exclusive, with transgressive art films these interpretations are also central to mutually exclusive categorisations such as art/not-art, legal/illegal, censored/free-to-distribute.

The question of how to read an image becomes particularly challenging in the context of rape and sexual assault for which the interpretation of the actions is already a fraught issue. Just as the question in police brutality cases is often not specifically about whether a suspect was beaten (as photos of injuries and hospital reports provide ample evidence of this), but whether that violence was justified (self-defence, uncooperative detainee, resisting arrest and so on), so are the motivations of the perpetrator and intentions of the victim central to distinguishing between consensual sex and non-consensual rape.[17] To what extent can we expect images to reveal the motivations and intentions of those involved? As scholarship on images of real-life rapes has shown, those taking photos of sexual assault and those looking at the images later on all engage in an interpretation of the acts or images they are seeing in order to see or not see sexual assault. Alexa Dodge notes in relation to the testimony about images taken of Rehtaeh Parsons in 2011, who was sexually assaulted while unconscious from alcohol, that 'this photo was taken out of excitement, and without recognition that the act being photographed was morally disturbing'.[18] Later viewers of the images 'read' the sexual assault as evidence of the victim being a 'slut' and deserving of humiliation and violation, which led to a discourse and a sustained bullying campaign that ultimately contributed to her suicide two years after the attack.[19] While there were numerous witnesses to the attack, and clear photographic evidence, the shared interpretative frameworks brought to bear by the witnesses and later the police, who chose not to prosecute the attackers, was one that did not allow them to 'see' sexual assault either at the moment of attack or in the images. Despite ample evidence provided by Parsons herself, witnesses, and photos of the attack, that Parsons was too drunk to consent to sex, and that both the attackers and onlookers were well aware of this, the police, and those who watched and shared the rape footage, chose or were unable to 'see' rape, shrugging it off as teenage antics. Debates about rape imagery are therefore more than just arguments over individual moments of violence, but rather are 'struggles over meaning in culture, over who gets to control it and whose interpretation is deemed worthy'.[20] This ideological battle and divisive interpretative struggle further explains why rape imagery remains so common in transgressive art films, predicated as they are upon provocation and a divided public reaction.

In this context, it also becomes clear why progressively minded fiction films would so frequently emphasise witnessing, and the spectator as witness, in their depictions of rape. Where evidence is meagre and real-life witnesses are absent, the film and the spectator can become a witness to fictionalised versions of real-life horrors, creating representation where there is little, and encouraging the public to bear witness to that which generally remains private, or to that which institutions refuse to 'see'. The common view of rape as difficult to prosecute because it comes down to a 'he said, she said' dynamic, implicitly appeals to a fantasy of a third person, a witness who could corroborate the story and tip the balance of evidence in the right direction. Moreover, the visualisation of rape provides 'proof' that it did in fact take place, depicting an idealised situation in which there is no uncertainty about the nature of the events, because they are unambiguously presented to the camera and the film spectator (even as this has been shown above to be more complex than it might seem). In other words, film has the potential to provide precisely the 'aggressive reading of the evidence' that Butler calls for in order to tip the balance of a particular interpretative framing.

Despite all this, interpellating a film witness to rape poses a number of problems. This can appeal unhelpfully to the idea of evidence as a kind of incontrovertible trace of an event, able to transcend discourse and reveal the 'truth'. Such a framing facilitates narrative satisfaction, suggesting that an appeal to the legal system will be successful, because the viewer has seen clear evidence of a crime, even as the justice system is set up in such a way as to inhibit any real chances of prosecutorial success. 'Happy endings' serve to nourish a sense of entertainment and fictional narrative closure, where there is little or none in real life, framing the film as educative, but encouraging an epistemic search that is only resolved by visualising the attack.[21] Moreover, the emphasis placed on the sexuality of rape victims in *Irreversible*, *Holiday*, *The Tribe* and *The Brown Bunny* furthers the idea that rape is part of a film's erotic allure, used to elicit fascination in the spectator and to further shock them by juxtaposing sex scenes with rape scenes.[22] If we also add to this ideas about rape as an art-film trope,[23] an overfocus on the male witness,[24] a continuance of problematic rape scripts that focus on deranged strangers, the woman's silence (as dead or beaten victim), and victim blaming through a focus on the victim's sexuality,[25] there is much to be concerned about in visualisations of rape in general that cannot be resolved by aggressive reading.

The presentation of witnessing in transgressive art films such as *The Tribe*, *Holiday* and *Irreversible* crystallises many of the contradictions and irreconcilable tensions that arise when rape and sexual assault are visualised in fictional films. The position of the film witness – absent from the diegesis but present to its images, brought close to the events through cinematographic techniques but unavoidably distanced from the actual acts – embodies the political and ideological ambiguities of rape imagery. Transgressive art films augment the issues by amplifying the emphasis on visibility/proximity/duration and thereby revealing the problem of evidence, by sexualising the victims and thereby making explicit the erotic allure of sexual assault in arthouse filmmaking, and by excessively underlining the spectator's role as witness and thereby leading to the overemphasis on witnesses in many depictions of rape. They point to how 'seeing' is always mediated by discursive processes such as value registers, whilst also being heavily invested in modes of representation that uncritically elevate the value of evidence. I have argued throughout this book that transgressive art films divide spectators into groups defending mutually exclusive viewpoints, and this manifests itself particularly in the context of long-take sequences of sexual violence.

*

Composed entirely of very long takes, performed entirely in Ukrainian sign language as the characters are all profoundly deaf, and featuring numerous scenes of sex, violence and sexual violence, *The Tribe* provides an excellent example of the use of long takes to evoke a film witness. Following a new arrival, Sergey, at a deaf school, *The Tribe* documents his initiation into, and subsequent relations with, a brutal gang. The film begins and ends with scenes that follow Sergey around the school, viewing him and his surroundings from a position a few metres behind him, positioning the spectator as a witness to his actions.

In the final scene, for instance, after having been assaulted and left for dead by the gang, a single take observes Sergey entering the main building and slowly, metronomically, climbing the stairs to the dormitories. The repetitive heavy steps give the sequence a slow rhythm and a sense of inexorability, while the upturned camera angle necessary to film from below in a stairwell, an angle that lessens as the cameraperson reaches the longer flat sections between each flight of stairs, emphasises the sense of following Sergey, accompanying him and witnessing his actions. This slow unhurried pace is maintained as he walks into a twin room, picks up a bedside cabinet and brings it down forcefully three times on one of the boy's heads. Sergey turns to the other boy and repeats this action. As Sergey leaves the room, the camera follows him as he undertakes the identical manoeuvre on two boys in the adjoining room, completed at the same slow, calculated pace, filmed from the same position in the doorway. At the same pace, Sergey walks back to the stairwell and closes the door behind him, his footsteps reverberating over the end credits.

The same thing is shown in the rape sequence not long before the end of the film, shot in a single take of nearly four minutes. Sergey walks straight into the twin room that his sort-of girlfriend, Anya, shares with her friend. After waking Anya up and thrusting wads of stolen cash at her, the camera turns, positioning itself statically as if on the friend's bed, and shows the process of rape. After undressing himself, Sergey grabs at Anya's breasts, and at her nightie, then pulls off her covers and her pyjama bottoms, then he climbs on top of her, penetrates her, thrusts to ejaculation, dismounts and lies next to her; the static image cuts. The film depicts the process of Anya's attempts to resist, beginning linguistically, then becoming physically cajoling before becoming more aggressively defensive as Sergey becomes violent. During penetration, she hits him repeatedly on his back and after he climaxes, a whimper can be heard and her hands drop as she cries. Over thirty seconds of the scene involves the loud banging of the creaky bed against the wall, emphasising the individual thrusts of violation, the metronomic delineation of rape. The act of witnessing is emphasised not only by the camera following Sergey into the room, but also because the camera is positioned on the bed of her friend. Moreover, the film viewer's helplessness to intervene is mirrored by the friend's profound deafness, which means she sleeps undisturbed through the rape.

This emphasis on the process of rape through a static long take is highly reminiscent of *Irreversible*'s oft-discussed rape scene, as well as scenes of sexual violence in *Holiday*. *Holiday* follows Sascha, the young trophy girlfriend of drug dealer, Michael, on a long holiday in Turkey with his crew. Right from the beginning of the film, long takes are combined with violence. The first scene of violence is a 135-second shot from very close to the protagonist, when she is punished by one of Michael's henchmen for stealing from the package she is transporting. Over a minute elapses before he slaps her suddenly in the face, forces her to take away her hand and then slaps her again, all close to the camera. In another scene, Sascha is comatose on a bed after drinking too much and in a 145-second shot, Michael manipulates her body into various positions, running his hand over her buttocks and legs, spreading her legs before standing and touching himself, then placing her legs and arms behind her as though tied up, and slapping her buttocks. A twenty-eight-second shot follows, showing the reflection in the window of him sitting over her in the previous position, thinking. She wakes up in the next scene naked, suggesting Michael may have raped her in her sleep, although this is not made clear. A later murder scene includes a 105-second shot and there is even a pause of fifteen to twenty seconds between the lethal blows which gives the second one added potency. Given that the film is not solely made up of long takes as in *The Tribe*, viewers are essentially primed to associate the long take with violence in *Holiday*.

This is very pertinent for the film's central rape scene, which begins romantically, sexily even. Its long duration, however, portends violence even before it is shown. The scene begins with Sascha and Michael cuddling on the sofa, shot first from behind (forty-five seconds), then from in front (103 seconds), when he starts strangling her, but then stops. They sit up and he slowly removes his watch, she begins to look scared and tries to get up, he stops her and tries to grab her breasts, she slaps his hand away and stands up to walk off, he grabs her arms and forces her to her knees. The image cuts to the side, to what will be a 225-second take, effectively through a set of French windows, shot from further away than before. Michael pushes her onto the floor on her back, pulls her shorts off, she slaps at him and he slaps her in the face. He pulls out his penis (visible but partially hidden behind her leg), he spits on his hand, rubs some on her vulva and then on his penis, holds her hands down over her head and penetrates her vaginally, he then puts his fingers in her mouth, but she bites him making him shout out, he grabs her head, then sticks his fingers deep into her mouth, and grabs her breasts. Then, still holding her arms he pulls himself up, lifts her head up and orally rapes her, pulling her head back and forth with his hands, we hear choking noises, he starts fingering her vaginally at the same time and slaps her buttocks (at this point the feet of someone coming down the stairs are visible and the slap of their flip-flops audible), his penis comes out and he reinserts it, then he masturbates over her to ejaculation, wiping up the semen with his hand, smearing it on her clothes and in her hair. He puts his penis away, stands over her for a second, touching himself through his shorts, before lying down on the couch, where he puts his watch back on. Sascha remains static, supine on the floor, looking up to see what he's doing; she gets up and goes to collect her shorts, at which point the scene ends. In total, the sequence is over six minutes long.

We can point to numerous similarities between the rape scenes from *Irreversible* and *Holiday*. They are shot in mostly static long takes, the victim has been sexualised throughout the film up to this point, visibility is emphasised in terms of an erect penis (and there is no doubt that the prosthesis does enter her mouth, while the penis in *Irreversible* was actually added in post-production), and the assault was accompanied by significant physical violence. Perhaps the most telling detail about *Irreversible*'s influence on *Holiday* is a brief glimpse of the feet of an unknown witness entering the frame, but retreating on seeing the rape, featuring in both films. Several critics pointed out the ethical indeterminacy of *Holiday*,[26] perhaps as a result of discourse around the problems of the core transgressive art films, and there was greater critical acknowledgement of broader societal discussions about rape culture and #metoo[27] than just individualised spectatorial ethics,[28] which tended to dominate discussions about *Irreversible*.

Commentary on long-take scenes, such as those in *Irreversible*, *The Tribe* and *Holiday* tends to fall into two broad categories: approval for the horrifically drawn-out unpleasantness which throws back at the viewer any voyeuristic pleasure in images of violence and makes them reconsider their position and role as spectator, or denigration of the voyeuristic thrill that the prolonged sequences encourage.[29] This is at the heart of the ambiguous ethics of transgressive art films, where the same provocative shock is read positively (as part of the film's ethical or political project, the negative affect recuperated via a hermeneutic value register) or negatively (as unethical or immoral, via an ethical value register). In the case of *Holiday*, examples of recuperative interpretation include Peter Cox's – '*Holiday* is a film I approve of. Not for how sensational it is, but for how coldly and nihilistically it stares back at us'[30] – and Alexa Dalby's – 'The film leaves the viewer feeling shaken, for the better.'[31] Negative ethical interpretations can be seen in descriptions of *Holiday* as 'morally repugnant, shockingly apathetic and yet strangely alluring'[32] and as 'incredibly out of touch with the current climate, . . . cruel and unforgiving'.[33] Given the many iterations of transgressive art films since the early 2000s, criticism of *Holiday* and *The Tribe* did not reach the peak of attacks levied against *Irreversible* whose rape scene was rejected as akin to pornography or snuff.[34]

Reviews of *Holiday* seemed more uncertain about how to approach the film, with critics unclear about which register to choose for their analysis. For instance, numerous critics framed their analysis as an 'either . . . or . . .' choice, to which they struggled to find a response: 'Is the vile sex scene simple exploitation or absolutely necessary[?]';[35] 'Has *Holiday* anything new to say about rape? Or do scenes like these fetishise sexual violence . . . I'm not sure.'[36] What these reactions to *Holiday* allowed for in 2018, which analysis of *Irreversible* was generally unable to contend with fifteen years previously, is the possibility that the scene could be simultaneously several things at once. Both a problematic eroticised glamorisation of a woman's abused body, and a reminder and reinscription of the material corporeal elements of (sexual) violence.

Commentary on *The Tribe* has tended to focus on the depiction of the deaf community, especially as it pertains to Ukraine and the former Soviet Union.[37] Deaf reviewers and scholars of the deaf community have highlighted numerous reductive references to practices of marginalisation and oppression that were inflicted on the deaf community during the Soviet era. *The Tribe* makes many references to actual political and social problems for the deaf community in Ukraine[38] such as selling postcards on trains, as the gang do at one point, which has been a source of historical shame for the Soviet deaf community as these vendors were thought to be trading off their disability in order to 'shirk honest work' in a factory. The focus on the violence and criminality of the deaf community, and an emphasis on the deaf mafia in the few depictions of the deaf community (see *Land of the Deaf*) also continues a long-standing stereotype linking disability and violence.[39] Bringing these issues around language and stereotypes together, as well as many scenes filmed in long shot (consider the group fight sequence), the characters become distinctly othered (unless you speak sign language, you cannot even discern their names), separate from us, and as Tomas Vollhaber suggests, trapped in their subaltern position.[40] Although an in-depth discussion of this context for an ethics of spectatorship is beyond the scope of this chapter, it points once again to the ambiguous, contradictory and polarising politics of transgressive art films. To take just the lack of subtitling as an example, the film was praised for demonstrating the power of gestural languages,[41] for showing how the deaf community wishes sign language to be understood,[42] and as a welcome move away from the patronising infantilisation of disability in films.[43] However, others heavily criticised it for reverting to harmful stereotypes about the deaf community and for disparagingly comparing sign language to bodily gesture rather than to spoken language, which is a more appropriate linguistic comparison.[44] Here, however, I focus on sexual violence and the evocation of witnessing through long takes with minimal mise-en-scène alterations beyond the scene's primary action.

*

The idea of the film spectator as an absent witness to events in *The Tribe* and *Holiday* can give shape to the contradictory directions in which viewers are pulled when watching transgressive art films, torn between competing interpretative frameworks and mutually exclusive value registers. As Angela Koch notes, 'viewers are the "true" witnesses of the filmic events. They are thereby confronted with various viewing roles'[45] and it is this confrontational forcing of the spectator into a witness role that is most interesting in *Irreversible*, *The Tribe* and *Holiday*. Numerous scholars have read *Irreversible* as evoking empathy for and identification with the characters, especially the victim,[46] but also the perpetrator.[47] However, given how much the act of spectatorship, as well as the presence of almost-witnesses,[48] is emphasised by audiences, the simplest and most important identification is in fact with the camera's gaze, with the position of a witness to the events who does not exist diegetically.

This absent witness has been most compellingly theorised by Roy Brand in an essay on *Elephant*.[49] Brand thinks of the film spectator as an 'ethical witness', meaning someone who is forced to assume the ethical responsibilities of a real-life witness, despite being physically separated from the event. In the context of fictional or re-enacted sequences (rather than, say, footage of real-life atrocities), there are clearly important differences between this form of mediated witnessing, and what Brand calls 'ontological witnessing': being present at a particular event. The 'event' being witnessed is therefore not an event as such, but rather, a means for thinking about real-life manifestations of that event: not a particular rape or rape as a concept, but the numerous actual instances of rape, which our societies must metaphorically bear witness to, the ethical ramifications of which our societies must take responsibility for. As such, 'viewers lose the innocence of not being involved' in a push-and-pull movement, 'as a simultaneously absent and present' party to the diegetic acts.[50] The irreconcilability of this presence and absence is precisely what makes it a good framework for examining the ethical encounter spectators can have with images of rape in transgressive art films.

Duration is the central requirement for this form of spectatorship: when time is experienced 'as duration rather than as a sequence of fragmented happenings', it opens up a space for 'engaging the passage of time [that] is a paradigmatic characteristic of the witness'.[51] Brand argues that this engagement with the temporality of the assault therefore carries ethical weight:

> For many, this engagement means being there at the time and the place of the event. But I would like to claim that it can also mean that the witness is privy to the temporality of the event or to its unfolding in time. The witness is 'there' at the time of the event, though 'being there' does not necessarily mean being at the same place at the same time.[52]

The spectator experiences what Karl Schoonover, after Bazin, calls 'cinepresence', the evocation of which 'has historically altered our conception of presence, expanding its definition to include experiences of delay or dislocation'.[53] This means that certain images can evoke an ethical engagement conventionally considered only to pertain to ontological witnessing: 'the camera's presence at the profilmic event compensates ... for the viewer's absence'.[54] Being physically present is less important than how you look, how you respond, how you (re)think, when viewing the event on screen:

> Being present is not to be taken ontologically (as *being* there) but ethically – as being responsible or at least responsive to the event. . . . Obviously we cannot change the past or determine the future, though we can still see ourselves as answering to their demands. Likewise, we cannot change what we view on screen, but we can see ourselves implicated in some important ways.[55]

In other words, ethical witnessing is not a replacement for ontological witnessing: film spectatorship and real-life witnessing should not be conflated; watching a film can never take on certain elements of witnessing that result from being physically there. However, if we follow Brand in seeing the witness's response to the event as central to the experience of being a witness, long takes can be understood as interpellating the film spectator as ethical witness if they encourage us to reflect on our complicity in, and responsibility for, the events we view. We are clearly not responsible for the immediate act of violence, but we can think about our societal responsibility for the conditions that lead to such events.[56]

In *The Tribe*, the spectator is a witness to the depraved violence to which the gang descends. While many violent scenes are witnessed by other characters (the fight scene outside involving dozens of people, the penultimate scene when Sergey is beaten up), several do not include a diegetic witness: a home abortion sequence, a gang member killed by a reversing lorry he cannot hear, the rape, the murders. These are the elements of this society that are pushed to the margins, ignored and glossed over. In the case of the rape and abortion, these are specifically women's experiences, that societies choose not to bear witness to or 'see', choose to leave to women to negotiate in the shadows. The murders, the accidental death and even the abortion leave traces – blood, bodies, broken cabinets, used equipment – but the suffering of sexual violence leaves no long-term evidence, except for the women's testimony of their own experience, which historically is granted little legal or moral value. In all of these cases, but most especially in the rape scene, we can read the viewer as an interpellated witness stepping in as an ethical witness to this violence, experiencing the duration of the violence, attesting to its horror, potentially recognising the complicity of their spectatorship in the continuance of such acts. Like *Elephant*, *The Tribe* uses long tracking shots from behind the characters to create the sense that the camera is present within the scene, thus creating a witness where none existed before. In this reading, the film becomes a medium for bearing witness to that which could not be witnessed, with the film spectator raised up as an always incomplete mechanism for achieving this. By emphasising the act of looking, draining the image of almost everything apart from the violent acts at its centre, and not providing any character with whom this gaze could be identified, the camera's gaze is framed as a witness's gaze, separate from the gaze of another character or some omniscient observer.

The same can be said of the sexually violent scenes in *Holiday*, situating the viewer as the sole witness to Michael's depravities, not least because one of the characters chooses to run away from potentially witnessing his attack. While *The Tribe*'s very specific context in a Ukrainian deaf community makes larger analogies difficult, *Holiday*'s more representative domestic context highlights the lack of ontological witnesses in most rape cases, despite rape culture making rape common knowledge, and overlooked by those who are best positioned to act against it.⁵⁷ By transposing *Irreversible*'s stranger rape into domestic rape within a family environment, *Holiday* provides an update of the violent long-take rape scenario: *Holiday*'s ideal spectator is not being asked just to witness the horrors of rape, but to recognise the implantation of sexual violence within the power structures of family, and of ostensibly consensual heterosexual relationships, as well as the complicity of all those around who, like the spectator, bear witness but do nothing. The rape takes place in an open-plan sitting room with enormous French windows, in contrast to the dark and secluded tunnel in *Irreversible*. Rape in *Holiday* is visible, open for all to see, and the film tries to confront viewers with the violence of that which they know but choose to turn a blind eye to, interpellating them as an film witness whose response might change their actions in society. Viewers might not be able to help Sascha, but they do have to see her suffering, and potentially reflect on their part in the viewing regime that allows for this to happen to women in the real world.

Like in other recuperative hermeneutic readings in other chapters, the visibility of physical violence is seen as making visible violent systems of oppression and domination. Such a reading suggests that for the ideal spectator, there is potentially much to be gained from the retroactive reassessment of the involuntary, perhaps ethically problematic, reactions they might have had to an image upon seeing it for the first time.⁵⁸ Films like *The Tribe* and *Holiday*, which encourage a retroactive reassessment of our own reactions to an image, can therefore still work towards politically progressive ends. Furthermore, in this reading we should not see a complicity with images as immoral in itself. Our complicity, if acknowledged, might be a productive ethical step in relation to images of rape rather than solely something to be avoided. Even if viewers are provided with a 'sense of explicability' for the failure of the characters to act,⁵⁹ if they are nonetheless also made aware of their own implication in how society views rape more broadly, then they are alerted to their own complicity in acts and images of sexual violence. As Wendy Kozol argues, ethics 'derives as much from reckoning with one's own complicity in structures of oppression as it does in any intentional act to ameliorate those conditions'.⁶⁰ Viewers cannot help fictional characters like Sascha in *Holiday*, or Anya in *The Tribe*, but this does not mean that they cannot ask themselves questions about the nature of rape images, the nature of rape, and how society considers rape. In other words, this would be a film ethics that occurs through rather than despite the spectacle of violence.⁶¹ At the same time, such a reading, by advocating for the ethical value of problematic images of rape, ultimately gives ethical value to the immoral, which opens up tricky questions about how we then value the immoral.

This, at least, is how we can read these long takes of sexual violence if we look for the most positive ethical reading, supposing an ideally receptive spectator, who adjusts their world view by watching arthouse cinema, although an examination of the reviews of *Holiday* does support the fact that this was at least one of the predominant lenses through which the film was interpreted. This reading of the ethical witness returns us to the estrangement defence of transgressive films: the spectator is shocked by their interpellation as a witness into rethinking how they conceptualise the world around them. However, this reading is only one part of what is going on with the film witness. Just as there is an inherent tension between the presence of the camera and the spectator's absence within Brand's notion of the ethical witness, as we shall see, Brand's positive reading of the political potential of this film witness is in inherent contradiction with more negative readings stemming from the very same elements he approves of.

*

Reading the interpellation of the witness through an ethical value register, reveals a different side to this depiction of sexual violence. If we invert Brand's contention that the absence of a diegetic witness is positively compensated by a film witness, we can read the absence or inaction of a diegetic witness as compromised by the film witness. While Brand, and positive analyses of transgressive art films' long-take rape scenes see film spectatorship as being elevated by the spectator's interpellation as absent witness, many scholars of rape imagery see analogies made between the spectator and a witnessing achieved through the visualisation of sexual violence as profoundly problematic.[62] By associating images of crime (presented to the spectator) with narrative moments focused on proof (presented to diegetic characters such as judges, juries or police officers), an ideological link is made between visualisation and proof, which frequently serves both in films and courthouses, to denigrate female experiences of sexual violence.

Emblematic of this is *The Accused*, in which the defendants are only convicted after the male witness's testimony, which is also the moment at which the film spectator is first shown images of the pivotal rape scene, despite the female protagonist having described her assault on several previous occasions. The male forensic capacities are necessary in the authentication of this rape, which, by logical extension, the woman herself cannot confirm by testimony alone, a perspective promoted by the film's representation of the assault. For Alison Young, all depictions of rape suffer from this legalistic desire for proof which rejects a woman's testimony as insufficient for conviction and implicitly doubts the veracity of any allegation of rape.[63] As a woman cannot attest to her own rape under these circumstances, a (male) witness who can corroborate her story therefore has huge power in 'proving' that the rape took place.[64] Even more troublingly, despite being provided with great power in authenticating the act of rape, diegetic witnesses are nonetheless implicitly expurgated of responsibility by the spectator's inability to act. Identifying with a diegetic witness who does not act to help, allows the film spectator, who is unable to help, to condone the diegetic witness's passivity. Young refers to a scene in *Blackrock*, in which a girl is raped and the film spectator watches the protagonist observing the rape and not acting: 'as Tracy [the victim] appeals to "us", we know that "we" cannot do anything to help her. Since we share our viewing position with Jared [the witness], this metonymically excuses his immobility in the face of what he sees.'[65] By conflating the witness's gaze with that of the spectator, judgement of the diegetic witness's inaction is compromised by the spectator's interpellation as film witness.

I have already discussed the issues of visibility, proximity and duration in transgressive art films, especially in rape scenes, pointing out the problematic connections made between visualisation and evidence, between seeing and proving, between representation and ontology. Conceiving of the viewer as a witness raises further issues related to the effects of visualising rape in such long, proximate and visible fashion. While a film may encourage viewers to consider themselves as ethical witnesses, to ask themselves why they watch, why they continue to watch, and what pleasure they gain,[66] there is nonetheless a fundamental exculpation of the spectator, and by extension, of the diegetic witness, from responsibility for the act. Along these lines, viewers may engage with the processive duration of a rape, they may become uncomfortably proximate to the bodies of attackers and victims, they may become an ethical witness to the attack, but these are all undercut by the simple fact that they watch the rape at all: 'looking is never "just looking" . . . a looking that is interested only in the possibilities of justice in the aftermath of injury'.[67] Even if they are encouraged to rethink interpretations of rape through techniques such as duration, they cannot escape the linking of the spectator's inability to act, with a diegetic witness's choice not to act or indeed the camera's non-interventionist documentation of the attack.

Nor can we deny the power of confirmation that the visualising of rape removes from the victim and gives to the film spectator. In scenes that emphasise the reality, the it-is-happening-right-there-ness of the diegetic rape, the images not only underline the value of knowing, seeing, proving that the assault took place, but also the value of the viewer of the event. Without diegetic witnesses, films like *Irreversible*, *Free Will*, *The Tribe* and

Holiday structure their narratives such that, outside the victim and perpetrator, the details of the acts only become known to the film audience. Koch argues that, as well as giving the film viewer great responsibility, images of rape always involve the imaginative translation of the invisible experience of the victim, meaning that, like in the discussion of trauma in the previous chapter, the meaning of the rape is brought out for the first time in its representation on screen.[68] As such, it is not strictly speaking a re-presentation but its own presentation of that which was always invisible, a bringing-to-life that is not just a cultural depiction of a previously existing event, but an event in its own right. Especially when the viewer is explicitly positioned as a witness, they become in fact the primary witness to the events, as there is no diegetic or 'ontological witness' to speak of. As Koch has suggested, this leads to a simultaneous proximity of the viewer to the event and inevitable distancing as the mediation of the attack creates a community of viewers who are always separated from the events, and thereby able more easily to conceive of the diegetic acts as an individual, rather than a societal, problem.[69] In other words, it is possible to analyse the same elements as Brand (long duration, mediated witnessing, detailed presentation of events unavailable to any real-life witness) and come to the exact opposite conclusion to his about the ethical value of the images.

In this case, this appears to come down not only to a different choice of value register (Brand's approach follows a hermeneutic register, Young and Koch choose an ethical register), but also a fundamentally different approach to the ethics of images. While Young puts forward pertinent criticisms of depictions of rape, her scepticism about progressivism in images of rape seems to stem from a fundamental mistrust about images per se. Young picks out depictions of rape that do not visualise the act itself (such as *Kill Bill Vol.1*) as being the only appropriate solution until 'there exists a cinematic ethics as to the depiction of sexual violence – one which would require the invention of a new cinematic grammar'.[70] While her argument about the non-depiction of rape as a workable solution is compelling, it is hard to see how a cinematic grammar or ethics involving the depiction of rape can be developed without attempting (and failing) to produce acceptable depictions of rape. We should therefore separate Young's criticism of how viewers might feel during the film, from Brand's contentions about how they might think about that experience afterwards. The disagreement here is ultimately one about the politics of art and film: between a perspective that sees visual media (and visualisation of the assault in particular) as inappropriate for discussions about rape and sexual assault, and one that sees any subject as fertile ground for filmic exploration, even as such representations may be damaging and ideologically suspect. This point of contention is not specific to these scholars; it is in fact at the heart of the disagreements between viewers of transgressive-art-film images of rape, where they are shown in long, proximate visible detail.

The figure of the film witness is therefore morally ambiguous for possessing a confirmatory power whilst disavowing the film spectator, and the diegetic witness, of responsibility. One synthesising solution to this would be to argue that it is precisely in the problematic nature of this figure that a productive way forward lies: it only works because it does not work. The issues of gun violence in *Elephant*, and of rape and rape imagery in *Irreversible*, *Holiday* and *The Tribe*, are complex societal phenomena that require dialogue, retroactive thought and engagement. Any position that declares itself whole and encompassing automatically sets itself against any other position, whereas a position that is always problematic, and open to critique from numerous perspectives, provokes debate and discussion, and might change the way viewers look at images of violence and sexual violence in the future. Its ethics would arise precisely because it is morally compromised. The spectator will never be able to intervene in the violence of the scene they are watching; they might turn off the film, but this doesn't change the outcome for the fictional images they were watching. The film witness would be inherently compromised but perhaps it provides a way of thinking past the binaries that such scenes so often provoke.

Nikolaj Lübecker's ideas about the potential of certain films to expand concepts such as humanism, the visible world and art are helpful here. Lübecker broadly defines a humanist interpretation of literature and art as focusing on their power as 'a motor for the development of humanist and democratic ways of being together, ... [of] art as a model [for social relations]' before pointing out that the films in his 'feel-bad' corpus 'all communicate in a very different way'.[71] Rather than suggesting that his chosen films do not belong to a humanist tradition of democracy, enlightenment, *Bildung* and understanding, Lübecker argues that they call for a rethinking of 'humanism'. Lübecker therefore coins the term 'humanism XL', which

> takes into account the fact that we cannot fully know ourselves, that the human psyche is a much richer (and also more problematic) field than we may sometimes be inclined to believe when we read about art as an exercise in democracy, empathy, and so on.[72]

This might also be a good way of thinking about the expanded possibilities of interpretation that transgressive art films propose, because in their retrogressive political stances, and provocative, confrontational engagement with the spectator, transgressive art films do not obviously reflect the 'pact of generosity' or 'democratic concern' historically considered as central to humanist art and literature.[73] Expanding the definition of humanism would allow the controversial films discussed here to be humanist, but at the same time would involve including the anti-humanist or the nihilistic within this enlarged definition of the humanist. Ultimately, however, this attempt at synthesis prioritises a hermeneutic approach to transgressive imagery, allowing immoral images into the definition of humanism precisely because the images have already been categorised as artistic, and therefore as worthy of interpretation and exploration. At the limit between mutually exclusive categories such as art and non-art film, between acceptable and unacceptable imagery, a synthetic approach is always doomed to failure.

Another reason for at least a certain reticence in thinking about the film witness is that its particular stylistic qualities conform noticeably to those associated with voyeurism and scopophilia, as theorised in psychoanalytic film theory. Indeed, when describing fetishistic scopophilia in *Morocco*, Laura Mulvey describes 'other witnesses, other spectators watching her [Dietrich] on the screen, their gaze is one with, not standing in for, that of the audience'.[74] Mulvey places great emphasis on the overlapping gazes of the male protagonist and the film spectator, especially in scenes of erotic female spectacle, but more generally in that the masculinised spectator 'projects his look on to that of his like, his screen surrogate, so that the power of the male protagonist as he controls events coincides with the active power of the erotic look, both giving a satisfying sense of omnipotence'.[75] *The Tribe*'s camera and narrative do indeed follow Sergey as he works his way up the hierarchy, pays for sex with Anya, becomes besotted with her and seeks to control her, while the scene in *Holiday* of Michael manipulating Sascha's comatose, nearly naked body on the bed, described earlier, corresponds quite literally to Mulvey's description of fetishistic scopophilia. In this sense, it is entirely logical to see the camera's gaze in these films as voyeuristic, peering in without ostensibly being seen, seeking pleasure in looking, often at the sexualised bodies of attractive young women. Mulvey's psychoanalytic conclusions about what this achieves are quite different to the idea of witnessing I am proposing here, but are also predicated on slightly different stylistic choices even as there are some overlaps. Mulvey focuses substantially on subjective camera shots of which there are few in *Holiday*, and none in *The Tribe*, arguing that the look of the camera is disavowed, and that of the audience denied any force, in order to maintain the illusion of diegetic cohesion, a cornerstone of the classical Hollywood films she is examining.[76] Nonetheless, simply by reframing the spectator's gaze as that of a witness, does not suddenly preclude the evocation of voyeurism, a term used repeatedly in reviews of *Holiday*, and a theoretical touchpoint for some commentators using the ethical register to interpret the film.[77]

If we bring all these readings together, the film witness is analogous to a kind of schizophrenic mode of spectatorship we must adopt when watching transgressive art films, if we are to fully grasp the plurality of different viewing positions such films give rise to. Viewers are jostled back and forth between mutually exclusive perspectives on a film: if we look at it through lens A then we come to ethical conclusion X, but if we choose lens B then conclusion Y, lens C then conclusion Z, a reading supported by the 'either . . . or . . .' interpretations of *Holiday* mentioned earlier. If we prioritise a hermeneutic reading and a positive view of the politics of images, we interpret *Holiday*'s rape scene as a powerful indictment of bystander complicity in rape culture; if we prioritise an ethical register and a suspicion of images, we interpret it as furthering the exploitation of rape imagery in the service of art. In this scenario, conclusions X, Y and Z may be entirely contradictory, which is part of the provocative effect of the films in that they elicit multiple irreconcilable interpretations: viewers will pick a lens, or value register, leading them into conflict with viewers who choose a different value register, and therefore arrive at a completely different ethical conclusion. However, if we are to aggregate the viewing positions, there is no overall consensus, and there will also be viewers, like me, who are unsure of which value register to choose, who are thereby deeply conflicted about how to evaluate the films in ethical terms.

This framework for assessing the viewing positions made possible by transgressive art films is borne out in the concrete answers that respondents gave to Barker et al. as part of their large study into sexual violence in contemporary cinema. In their analysis, Barker et al. divided their participants into 'embracers', 'refusers' and 'ambivalents' suggesting that readings of particular scenes or films were broadly predicated on the viewer's overall decision to embrace, refuse or remain ambivalent about the film. As such the study's results are generally framed in the following terms: 'the more a person embraces [*film X*], the more likely they are to . . .', or 'embracers/refusers/ambivalents tend to . . .' or 'embracers/refusers/ambivalents almost always . . .'. For instance, they write about *Irreversible* that 'to Embracers, the reverse-narrative becomes a meaning in its own right . . . Refusers almost always see the rape scene as excessive',[78] suggesting much like I have so far, that embracers tend to adopt a hermeneutic register interpreting the meaning of images, while refusers mostly adopt an ethical register, judging the rape scene according to how they think that rape should be depicted. Later the authors point out that 'the main prerequisite for embracing this film is about being *willing* to be "made to feel",[79] suggesting that a pre-existing openness to affectively challenging film art also correlates with later conclusions about a particular film. In other words, a viewer's broad convictions about what constitutes film art, and their overall approach to a film, pre-determines many of the ethical conclusions they are likely to draw about the depictions of sex, violence and sexual violence within the film. These early decisions can seem minor (willingness or not to be 'made to feel'), but the bifurcations on the path of analysis at this point often lead to contradictory or even opposite conclusions, because these early decisions about the nature and role of film art, about how to categorise explicit sex, about how to judge images of sexual violence, place a viewer's analysis on one side of an untranscendable boundary between film art/not-art, art/porn, acceptable/not acceptable, free to distribute/censored, legal/illegal. Transgressive art films like *Holiday*, *The Tribe* and *Irreversible* allow for, and encourage, all of these positions to be taken and thereby crystallise all the positive and negative values of rape imagery, as well as provoking significant controversy.

*

Evidence is central to films that place the spectator in the position of a witness. In this context, it has at least three discursive elements – testimony as evidence, images as evidence, film style as evidential mode – which together produce the films' ethical outlook on the diegetic events. In the case of rape imagery, the desire for evidence is simultaneously laudable and concerning, both productive and counter-productive. The emphasis on film witnessing as evidential mode also continues transgressive art films' problematic infatuation with uncovering the 'truth' of the diegetic acts. While analyses of the images of Rodney King or Rehtaeh Parsons involve legitimate searches for intentions, motivations and the details of individual actions, fictional images have no such epistemic anchor point. The myriad possibilities and problems of rape imagery are crystallised in the long takes of sexual violence we see in *Holiday*, *The Tribe* and *Irreversible*. These scenes can be read, on the one hand, as challenging reflections on societal violence, and, on the other hand, as unhelpful exculpations of political and personal inaction, or exploitative depictions of eroticised suffering. Moreover, we can see that these oppositions in viewer reactions derive substantially from their choices of interpretative framework, either of an ethical or hermeneutic value register, or 'willingness to be made to feel'.

Fictional rape is shown to bring together the kinds of provocation and audience division that are emblematic of transgressive art films. The positioning of the viewer as a film witness is particularly conducive to these polarising reactions, and can also be useful for thinking about the ethical framing of rape in other films beyond this corpus. A close analysis of rape sequences demonstrates the importance of looking at film form in terms of visibility, proximity and especially duration, and rape imagery provides a productive case study for applying theories of transgression to controversial images in film.

Notes

1 Horeck, *Public Rape*, 145; citing Higgins, 'Screen/Memory', 307.
2 See Currie ('Visible Traces') on the different kinds of trace photographs might be considered to contain.
3 Barthes, *Camera Lucida*.
4 Bazin, *What Is Cinema?*; on indexicality and the digital image see Rodowick, *The Virtual Life of Film*.
5 Kracauer, *Theory of Film*.
6 Renov, *Theorizing Documentary*; Sobchack, *Carnal Thoughts*; Carroll, 'Fiction, Non-Fiction, and the Film of Presumptive Assertion'; Nichols, *Introduction to Documentary*.
7 For detailed discussions of the history of realism in photography and film studies Aitken, *The Major Realist Film Theorists*; *Cinematic Realism*.
8 Tagg, *Grounds of Dispute*, 143.
9 Tagg, *The Disciplinary Frame*, xxxii.
10 Tagg, *The Burden of Representation*, 3–8.
11 Berger, 'Understanding a Photograph', 21.
12 Gonzales Rose, 'Toward a Critical Race Theory of Evidence'; 'Race, Evidence, and Epistemic Injustice'.
13 Hall, 'Introduction', 3; see also Berger, 'Understanding a Photograph', 20.
14 Butler, 'Endangered/Endangering', 16.
15 Davis, 'Rape, Racism and the Capitalist Setting'; Hill Collins, *Black Feminist Thought*.
16 Butler, 'Endangered/Endangering', 17.
17 See Ferguson, 'Rape and the Rise of the Novel', 88; Horeck, *Public Rape*, 148.
18 Dodge, 'Digitizing Rape Culture', 72.
19 Dodge, 68.
20 Horeck, *Public Rape*, 142.
21 On the rewriting of *The Accused*'s narrative for a 'feel-good' ending that did not happen in the case of the actual trial on which the film was based, see Serisier, 'Speaking Out'.
22 See Riggs and Willoquet, 'Up Against the Looking Glass!' on *The Accused* providing thin justification for showing sexy images of Jodie Foster prior to the rape scene, and ultimately making us 'want to know' the spectacular details of the rape scene.
23 Russell, 'Introduction'.

24 Projansky, *Watching Rape*. On witnessing in male-on-male rape scenes, see Clover, 'Her Body, Himself', 226n34; Coulthard, 'Uncanny Horrors'.
25 For a summary of work on rape myths, rape scripts and rape narratives, see Hogan, 'Anatomy of a Rape'.
26 Lodge, 'Sundance Film Review'; McCarthy, '"Holiday"'; Dang, 'Sydney Film Festival Review'; Bradshaw, 'Holiday Review'.
27 Dalby, 'BFI LFF Review'; Kohn, '"Holiday" Review'; Mirabal, '"Holiday" Review'; Petkova, 'It's a (Wo)Man's World'; Ruimy, '"Holiday" Is an Immensely Impressive Debut'.
28 Kohn, '"Holiday" Review'; Cox, 'Review'; Leeson, 'Cold Hard Cash and Violence'.
29 To my knowledge at the time of writing, there has been no scholarly writing on *Holiday*, hence the focus on critical commentary in the analysis of the reception discourse of the film.
30 Cox, 'Review'.
31 Dalby, 'BFI LFF Review'. Such comments are similar to those received by *Irreversible* (see for instance Brinkema, 'Irréversible').
32 Dang, 'Sydney Film Festival Review'.
33 Leeson, 'Cold Hard Cash and Violence'.
34 Paris, 'Irreversible'. Although this same kind of debate did play out in message board discussions of *Holiday* such as this one on Mubi: https://mubi.com/films/holiday-2018/ratings/18423874 (accessed June 8, 2022).
35 McCarthy, '"Holiday"'.
36 Bradshaw, 'Holiday Review'; see also Lodge, 'Sundance Film Review'; Petkova, 'It's a (Wo)Man's World'.
37 Hynes, 'The Tribe'; Romney, 'Code of Silence'; Shaw, 'Myroslav Slaboshpytskiy'; Zas Marcos, '"La Tribu"'; De Clercq, 'Disability @ the Movies'; Brogna, '*Plemya*'; Czmola and Cezar, 'Myroslav Slaboshpytskiy'; Vollhaber, *Wem gehört die Gebärdensprache?*
38 See Shaw, 'Myroslav Slaboshpytskiy'; Zas Marcos, '"La Tribu"'.
39 Shaw, 'Myroslav Slaboshpytskiy'; De Clercq, 'Disability @ the Movies', 105.
40 Vollhaber, *Wem gehört die Gebärdensprache?*, 290.
41 Brogna, '*Plemya*'.
42 Czmola and Cezar, 'Myroslav Slaboshpytskiy'.
43 Romney, 'Code of Silence', 43.
44 Shaw, 'Myroslav Slaboshpytskiy'; De Clercq, 'Disability @ the Movies'; Vollhaber, *Wem gehört die Gebärdensprache?*
45 Koch, 'Ir/réversible', 154.
46 Brinkema, 'Irréversible'; Keesey, 'Split Identification'; Nicodemo, 'Cinematography and Sensorial Assault'; Scott, 'Bearing Witness to the Unbearable'; von Brincken, 'Das Leid an Der Zeit'.
47 Keesey, 'Split Identification'.
48 The briefly seen witnesses in *Irreversible* and *Holiday* who run away on seeing the attack, and the deaf roommate in *The Tribe*.
49 Brand, 'Witnessing Trauma on Film'.
50 Koch, 'Ir/réversible', 157.
51 Brand, 'Witnessing Trauma on Film', 208.
52 Brand, 208.
53 Schoonover, *Brutal Vision*, 35.

54 Schoonover, 34.
55 Brand, 'Witnessing Trauma on Film', 209; See also Bernstein, 'Bare Life, Bearing Witness' in relation to photography and witnessing.
56 Brand, 'Witnessing Trauma on Film', 211.
57 I follow Buchwald et al. in defining rape culture as 'A complex set of beliefs that encourage male sexual aggression and supports violence against women. . . . A rape culture condones physical and emotional terrorism against women and presents it as the norm. . . . In a rape culture, both men and women assume that sexual violence is a fact of life, as inevitable as death or taxes' (*Transforming a Rape Culture*, xii.).
58 See Silverman, *The Threshold of the Visible World*, 3; see also discussions about long takes in slow cinema as 'a vehicle for introspection, reflection and thinking' in de Luca and Barradas Jorge, *Slow Cinema*, 16.
59 Young, *The Scene of Violence*, 61.
60 Kozol, *Distant Wars Visible*, 15.
61 Kozol, 15.
62 Clover, *Men, Women, and Chain Saws*, 150; Projansky, *Watching Rape*; Horeck, *Public Rape*, 91ff.; Koch, 'Ir/réversible', 143–47; Koch, *Ir/reversible Bilder*, 273; Young, *The Scene of Violence*, 56.
63 Young, *The Scene of Violence*.
64 The overimportance of the (male) witness in rape narratives has been commented on at length, especially in relation to *The Accused*. See Clover, *Men, Women, and Chain Saws*, 150; Projansky, *Watching Rape*, 112–17; Horeck, *Public Rape*, 100–101.
65 Young, *The Scene of Violence*, 61; see also Scott, 'Bearing Witness to the Unbearable', 80–81.
66 The kinds of self-reflective questions that arise repeatedly in audience discussions on *Irreversible*: see https://www.imdb.com/title/tt0290673/reviews (accessed August 31, 2022) and Barker et al., *Audiences and Receptions*.
67 Young, *The Scene of Violence*, 70.
68 Koch, 'Das ›unsägliche‹ Verbrechen', 193–94.
69 Koch, 200.
70 Young, *The Scene of Violence*, 73.
71 Lübecker, *The Feel-Bad Film*, 10.
72 Lübecker, 170.
73 Lübecker, 8–10; referring to ideas from Jean-Paul Sartre and Nicolas Bourriaud.
74 Mulvey, 'Visual Pleasure and Narrative Cinema', 841.
75 Mulvey, 838.
76 Mulvey, 844.
77 See Reviews, 'Holiday'; Bayman, 'Film Review'; Cacoulidis, 'The 59th Thessaloniki International Film Festival'; Freville, 'A Terrifying Probe'; Jameson, 'When Is a Penis Not a Penis?'
78 Barker et al., *Audiences and Receptions*, 8.
79 Barker et al., 151.

6

Limits

Discussion of transgressive art films is often dominated by long lists and detailed descriptions of the violent, erotic and sexually violent acts that populate these films. James Quandt's list is probably the most memorable and most frequently quoted: 'rivers of viscera and spumes of sperm, . . . flesh, nubile or gnarled, . . . penetration, mutilation, and defilement . . . gang rapes, bashings and slashings and blindings, hard-ons and vulvas, cannibalism, sadomasochism and incest, fucking and fisting, sluices of cum and gore'.[1] Violent and sexual acts are the starting point to any discussion of transgressive art films; however, the nature of the acts alone does not help to pinpoint the specificity of transgressive art films. Graphic sex and violence can also be found in other genres, therefore their mere inclusion in these films does not explain their provocative impact and controversial reception. Without contextualisation and theorisation, descriptions of violent and sexual acts do not reveal very much about transgression, extremity, limits, controversy and so on. This chapter can be understood as a kind of theoretical corrective to commentary that overfocuses on diegetic acts.

In what follows, I provide a Bataillean reading of the transgressive acts and their societal context in *Raw* and *In My Skin* in order both to productively engage with diegetic acts in terms of transgression, and to point to the limits of such a reading for thinking about artistic transgressions. Moreover, given that the conflation of different kinds of transgression, and imprecise application of Georges Bataille's theories to images, are two recurring problems in writing on transgressive imagery, this chapter provides an example of how Bataille and transgressive acts can be analysed without falling into these common traps in thinking. My analysis is positioned as a response to previous work on acts in transgressive art films, as well as a rigorous exploration of the potential direct applications of Bataillean thinking to such films, and a demonstration of the limits of this way of framing transgression for understanding the broader socio-cultural phenomenon of the transgressive art film.

Bataille has become a shorthand for fictionalised storylines that contain numerous images of violent or abusive sex in much of the commentary on transgressive art films. Unlike other key theorists of transgression, Bataille's work focuses heavily on sex, violence, death and ritual, and he is therefore a fitting theorist for exploring images of these in film. Nevertheless, as will be made clear through my analysis of *Raw* and *In My Skin*, it is Bataille's work on expenditure and sovereignty that is the most pertinent to transgressive art films. As Tina Kendall suggests, 'if Bataille remains, it is certainly not in the reassuring places we would expect to find him.'[2] Many references to Bataille in analyses of transgressive art films focus mostly on the question of contact and sensation,[3] more generally on the confluence of sex and violence,[4] or on his concept of the 'formless'.[5] While there are often passing references to the idea of expenditure in analyses of individual films,[6] no account has fully probed the value of Bataille's ideas around expenditure, sovereignty, limits and transgression in understanding the eroticised violent acts we see in transgressive art films. In the context of *Raw* and *In My Skin*, as well as other transgressive art films, Bataille's ideas about expenditure and sovereignty can help to explore what it means to engage in limited, marginal transgressions and how their societal role differs from more substantial, egregious and destructive transgressions.

In *Raw* and *In My Skin* these explorations of transgression turn especially around gender roles and the construction of gender. As Dominique Russell has aptly noted, transgressive art films are 'obsessed with sexual difference at all levels'[7] and these two films are no exception. Both films can be considered as female coming-to-consciousness films, with *Raw* more straightforwardly a coming-of-age tale documenting its protagonist's passage into adulthood, while *In My Skin*'s older protagonist is already an adult but becomes conscious of the controlling demands that society places on her body. At the same time, despite many tropes familiar to coming-of-age stories, such as first-time sex (in *Raw*), family drama, and arguments with friends and lovers, neither of these films should be considered in straightforward realist terms. For instance, unlike *Secretary* or *Painful Secrets*, *In My Skin* is not really about self-harm in any conventional sense of the term, nor is its depiction realistic in terms of the actual practices of those who engage in self-harm. From very early on, it is clear that self-harm is a metaphor for something larger, and should not be limited to realistic psychological notions of self-harm, although some scholars have pursued this analysis.[8] A similar argument can be made about *Raw*. *Raw*'s whole setup is unrealistic, while the violence is almost consequence-free, clearly encouraging metaphorical readings, unlike other arthouse cannibal or transformation films like *Let the Right One In* or *When Animals Dream*, which seem partially to pose the question 'what would it mean practically if vampires/werewolves lived among us?'[9] In this sense, we must move beyond the literal representation of self-harm or cannibalism to fully understand these films, even as the widely acknowledged viscerality and discomfort of the images draw viewers into the practical, material mechanics of bodily dismemberment. This is not an easy task, especially given that these films do not offer anything in the way of a clear political message.[10] Just like other transgressive art films, it is unclear precisely how to locate *Raw* and *In My Skin* ethically and politically. Bataille's work on expenditure and sovereignty can facilitate a way of seeing through the violent narratives of *Raw* and *In My Skin* in order to grasp the relevance, and limits, of Bataillean theories in relation to transgression in films.

*

Raw tells the story of a virginal vegetarian, Justine, beginning her university veterinary studies. She experiences, or is subjected to, several initiation rituals, which signal her introduction into different adult worlds. She enters the university community through a series of intense hazing rituals, she explores her burgeoning adult sexuality through two encounters with male students, she learns about her gender identity through the rigid binary system in operation at the school, and, most unusually, she discovers her cannibal desires, an inherited family trait of which she was completely unaware thus far. The cannibalism forms the central core of the film, but it is most instructive to see *Raw* as a depiction of the myriad socialisation processes that frame female development, especially the transition from girlhood to womanhood. These processes are depicted as brutal, repressive and dehumanising, with rape culture, shame, repressed sexuality and behavioural policing as the hallmarks. All of this is shown in substantial detail, with gory close-ups of flesh, numerous shots of sex, explicit detail on pubic-hair waxing, and an affectively gruelling sequence of Justine coughing up long strands of her own matted hair. In some ways, this is a modern-day retelling of German Expressionist films like *Pandora's Box* or *Asphalt*, which present female sexuality as in need of control lest it breaks loose and destroys society.[11] *Raw* depicts in more complex fashion the controls that patriarchal society has developed in order to police and manage women, but still maintains German Expressionism's concern about the volatile and dangerous nature of female sexuality. Like in other transgressive art films, such processes are materialised and affectively transmitted to the spectator, thereby being made visible and feelable. On a narrative level, the film also explores the limits that police gender and sexuality development, and especially how the transgression of those limits is recuperated and transmuted into socially acceptable forms, such as the nuclear family and heteronormative sexual relations. The combination of this feminist critique with the reactionary trope of excessive, out-of-control female sexuality ultimately makes *Raw*'s politics quite ambiguous.[12]

To fully understand *Raw*'s presentation of gender, we must first grasp its depiction and uncomfortable celebration of ritualised excesses, which are heavily foregrounded throughout the film. From the outset, the new students are categorised as an underclass, completely at the will of older students, and forced to undertake arbitrary hazing rituals in order to accede to full membership of the student body. Their rooms are ransacked, they are forced to eat preserved animal organs, they are smeared with paint, they must wear prescribed clothes, and most especially, they must partake in alcohol-fuelled sexually charged parties. Any violation of the rules leads to public humiliation and punishments such as wearing a nappy or *in extremis* having your face cut out of the class photo. This leads to intense sexual, even violent, encounters, a general disregard for the feelings of others, the encouragement of spectacularised violence between students for the viewing pleasure of others, and the humiliation and marginalisation of those who do not fully conform, in this case the protagonist, Justine.

All of this suggests a distinctly Bataillean reading of society, most notably in the separation of the work and leisure spaces, whereby the non-work spaces provide for the nonproductive release of excess energy accumulated within the restrictions of the productive work economy. The students are expected to work hard, with strict discipline in classes; during leisure time, ritualised transgression is encouraged in order to avoid the catastrophic consequences of repressed energy not being released. This framework is also applied to the construction of gender, with the focus being on how Justine's adult gender and sexual identities arise and are constrained by the normative constraints erected by the community. Justine's sister and mother operate as examples of the divergent possibilities within this framework: her sister is an example of catastrophic uncontrolled expenditure, and her mother represents the channelling of excess expenditure into the growth of the system. Reading *Raw* in this way shows that this is a film about limits in the Bataillean sense, about how these limits are central to the construction of society and specifically here to the construction of female identity.

According to Bataille, the global movement of energy 'cannot accumulate limitlessly in the productive forces; eventually, like a river into the sea, it is bound to escape us and be lost to us. ... The problem posed is that of the expenditure of the surplus.'[13] Within any system, excess energy is ordinarily channelled into system growth (production and reproduction), but 'if the system can no longer grow, or if the excess cannot be completely absorbed in its growth, it must necessarily be lost without profit; it must be spent, willingly or not, gloriously or catastrophically'.[14] Productive expenditure takes place in the world of work as we produce all the elements that we need for our lives, as well as the world of reproduction as society produces new life to maintain itself. Economic expansion and population growth function as outlets for excesses of energy that cannot be expended in the maintenance of the system as is. Technological and population growth have allowed for the surplus energy of human systems to dissipate and be returned to the environment.

Bataille argues, however, that it is not possible to expend all of our energy in productive ways, and that in this case it must be 'gloriously' expended in nonproductive ways to avoid a build-up that could explode in catastrophic ways. Bataille considers glorious expenditure to be ritualised forms of excess such as Bakhtinian carnivals, religious festivals, the erection of monuments, potlatches, eroticism, and other forms of squandering and luxury.[15] Within these ritualised, non-work, 'sacred' spaces, conventions and taboos around sex, scarcity, greed or societal roles can be transgressed through eroticism, potlatch and carnival; the rules are broken and the excess is expended. These transgressions are ritualistic in the sense that they are only possible in clearly codified spaces and times. Breaking the rules, or taboos, within these ritualised parameters therefore reenforces the prohibitions within the space of productive work, transcending and completing the taboo.[16] By maintaining these excess expenditures within particular ritualised leisure contexts, nonproductive expenditure is separated from productive expenditure – namely reproduction and work – sheltering the profane world of work from the transgressive limit experiences of the sacred world, especially death and eroticism.[17] This nonproductive expenditure is important because if the surplus energy is not expended through transgressive acts, or these prove to be inadequate, it will explode in the catastrophic expenditure of war:

> If we do not have the force to destroy the surplus energy ourselves, it cannot be used, and, like an unbroken animal that cannot be trained, it is this energy that destroys us; it is we who pay the price of the inevitable explosion.[18]

Limited transgressions of some societal rules (glorious nonproductive expenditure) are necessary in order to maintain the integrity of the system.

As such, within Bataille's thinking there is a repeated veneration of transgression as a necessary release.[19] This has often been misunderstood as a quasi-revolutionary call to arms, leading to Bataillean analyses of transgressive art which appear disappointed that the work is not in fact overturning society.[20] *Raw* does not, however, evoke such veneration. The film's action takes place within an environment which is overtly Bataillean in its depictions of nonproductive expenditure. Complex hazing rituals, riotous sexually charged parties, recreational sport with a focus on the sweaty bodies, promiscuity and sexual experimentation all speak to the excessive expenditure of pent-up energy, colloquially known as 'work hard, play hard'. Apart from the omnipresent white lab coats, the work and play areas are kept separate, with scenes involving a horse running, and later being sedated, almost appearing to be inserted from a different world altogether. It is also notable that each of the sex scenes, whether between Justine and her friend Adrien, or Justine and an unknown paint-covered partygoer, combine eroticism with bloody violence; in each case significant amounts of blood are drawn within what are ostensibly sexual encounters.[21] This evokes Bataille's connection between the inextricable domains of eroticism and violence.[22] In relation to Justine and her family, the idea of excess energy is especially pertinent because of the women's cannibalistic desires, which build up inside them and can only be channelled or expended; they will not dissipate on their own.

Female sexual and cannibalistic desire are constantly conflated in the film, especially in the depiction of Justine's gaze on Adrien, her roommate. When he asks her to tie up his surgical gown, she is seen gazing at the back of his neck, with both her and viewers left uncertain as to whether the hunger is sexual or cannibalistic or both. Later, she watches him playing football shirtless, the camera following him from her point of view in increasing close-up; the violence of her desire is so intense that she takes on the look of an animal about to charge, and begins bleeding from the nose. This link between sexual and cannibalistic desire is made evident firstly in the paint scene when she bites off the lip of her forced suitor after exhibiting signs of sexual arousal. Later in the film when she has sex with Adrien, her reaction to intercourse and increasing arousal is to bite him, flail around as though completely out of control, eventually sinking her teeth into her own arm to draw blood. What she perceived as sexual desire was a desire for flesh, with the film ultimately conflating female sexual desire and destructive murderous desire.

In this sense, female sexuality in *Raw* is dangerous and out of control. Womanhood is conflated with cannibalism and any sexual encounter with the women in this family could be potentially catastrophic (Justine nearly bites her roommate, and her father has the scars from his sexual encounters with her mother). Justine's and her family's sexuality is 'the enduring animality in us [that] forever introduces raw life and nature into the community'; sexual 'prohibitions exist to quell these uprisings and spread oil on the sea of insurgent animal passion and unruliness'.[23] Bataille provides two connected ways of reading the family's different reactions to their cannibal sexuality: first in terms of the denial of (transgressive) eroticism; secondly, as a choice between reproduction, glorious transgression, and catastrophic expenditure.

In a first reading in terms of eroticism, Justine is engaging in erotic encounters and in doing so is encountering the violence of eroticism, and the challenging experience of the extreme limit. Bataille saw two main ways of denying this eroticism – puritanism and libertinism – each of which is practised by one of Justine's relatives. The restriction and control of sexual activity to reproductive functions on the one hand, and the indulgence in animal sexuality on the other, both of which Bataille saw as 'an emanation of the urge for the denial of eroticism'.[24] Justine's mother has pursued the restriction method, somehow controlling her desires and successfully reproducing in the form of her two daughters. Justine's sister, Alexia, pursues an anarchic libertine route, taking sadistic pride in the success of her murderous 'hunts',[25] and also masochistic pleasure in Justine's consumption of Alexia's own finger when it is cut off in an accident. Alexia is out of control, eventually killing and eating Adrien, just after he has had sex with Justine. This latter solution is not countenanced by broader society and Alexia is imprisoned.

In a second reading in terms of (re)production, the mother channels the surplus energy of her sexuality into the growth of the system, namely the reproduction of the species, managing to control her 'enduring animality', while Alexia explodes in the catastrophic expenditure of serial murder. In between these extremes, Justine experiences the glorious, limited transgressions, the nonproductive expenditure of passionate sex, alcohol-fuelled partying, insolence towards her teachers, dancing, and fighting with her sister. This fight sequence, in which the two sisters grapple in front of a crowd of fellow students until the sisters join forces to rebuff the baying spectators, and which includes a graphic shot of Alexia biting a chunk out of Justine's cheek, and them both biting each other's arm, still evokes the limited transgressions that reenforce the taboo on violence. Although this scene is violent, the crowd situates it as a school-type brawl and, given that they are sisters, as a family matter that does not go beyond the family unit; ultimately it brings them together, the crowd dispersing, and likely dismissing it as a sacred spectacle with little impact on the profane world of their studies. When we discover the scars on their father's chest, we realise that Justine is going through a process that her mother and sister both went through before her; all three women experienced the period of glorious transgression at one point. While their mother found the (re)productive route for her surplus sexual energy, Alexia is unable to find adequate means for expending this surplus, and it is unleashed in the violent murders of local drivers in orchestrated car accidents so as to eat their flesh, and the final murder of Adrien. It is notable that when Justine finds Alexia in the morning after the murder, she is almost catatonic, unable to wash herself or stand up, as though recovering after the eruption of the uncontrollable catastrophic, war-like expenditure which was unleashed on the closest target to her. This is not Batailleau transgression because 'transgression is not disorder, but in its interaction with the taboo, obeys its own rules, conscious of but never abolishing limits'.[26] Alexia's actions, by contrast, are disorderly and uncontained, disregarding rather than respecting the validity of society's rules when breaking them.

Regardless of the exact Batailleau reading one follows, at the end, Justine is left with a choice about how to control her desires, because it is not possible to live permanently in the sacred world of glorious transgression. There is no sense that embracing her sexuality is the solution; there is no sense that her actions are liberatory or politically radical. Her slight transgressions of established rules can be tolerated as a Batailleau nonproductive release, but can never be anything more than the sacred transgressions which reinforce the profane taboos: 'transgression should be understood as an irrational indulgence of an instability inherent to the system's in-built failures, not a dialectical means to eradicate social codes once and for all'.[27] Justine is a gloriously transgressive protagonist caught between the opposite poles of her two female family members who embody productive and catastrophic engagements with excess. In *Raw*, female sexuality is represented as a form of energy that builds up, and which must be expended or channelled in order to avoid its otherwise destructive impact on society.

Aside from the cannibal storyline, *Raw*'s narrative is also more broadly concerned with the societal construction of gender. As well as being a film seen almost entirely through the eyes of, or together with, female characters, the narrative is specifically about the protagonist's development as a woman, and how women must negotiate societal norms around sex, violence, identity, behaviour and so on. Justine arrives at university a naïve girl, as yet broadly unaware of sex, desire, adult relationships, peer pressure and community controls. Initiation themes are omnipresent: she eats both animal and human flesh for the first time, loses her virginity, gets drunk and has a hangover. She also quickly conforms to the group's expectations in relation to these, at one point practising her sexy dancing and kissing the mirror while listening to a rap song about sexually voracious girls. Rape culture and male dominance are quickly installed as the dominant outlooks with comments mocking rape victims, and a lorry driver's non-consensual caresses of her roommate, Adrien, coming early in the film. One official hazing ritual involves members of the opposite sex being covered in blue and yellow paint and then locked in a room until they come out green; in Justine's case, the boy takes the commanding role and when she bites off part of his lip, as mentioned earlier, the immediate response of other students is to claim that Justine is crazy rather than wondering what male actions might have led to her attack. Justine partially adopts these attitudes by the end, criticising a murder victim (her roommate) for not having sufficiently defended himself against attack. Although those in charge of the hazing are male, it is frequently women who enforce the rules, with an older female student forcing Justine to wear a nappy for breaking a rule, and her older sister taking a leading role in the enforcement of the initiation rituals, by forcing her to eat meat, initiating her in cannibalism, and managing her eyebrow, armpit and pubic hair.

Conformity is seen as a violent process and the rules of this patriarchal society as even more violent: as Alain-Philippe Durand and Naomi Mandel comment about the 'contemporary extreme', 'violence – often the only stable element – operates as ethos'.[28] This claim also hints at Bataille's idea that 'the domain of eroticism is the domain of violence, of violation',[29] an idea that is roundly adopted in *Raw* (as well as in *In My Skin*) where sex and murder (or sex and self-harm) become inextricable, the erotic and the violent interwoven within the female body. Societal convention is presented as inherently violent. Through gruelling and unpleasant imagery, *Raw* affectively communicates the violent imposition of patriarchal norms, whilst also presenting female sexuality as dangerous. As such, ethically, *Raw* is both progressive and somewhat reactionary.[30] Although it has some echoes, in the metaphor of cannibalistic desire as female sexuality, of feminist theory's critiques of gender and femininity as socially constructed, and of patriarchal society as constructed to police and control women, it also seems to accept the idea that female sexuality is a danger, that it is out of control, and that there can never be a happy equilibrium between the (re)productive and catastrophic ends of the spectrum. Although we never discover Justine's choice at the end, it is clear that her glorious erotic transgressions will have to end one way or another. While on the superficial level of the narrative, this is clear inasmuch as her cannibalistic desires will otherwise lead her to kill people like her sister has done, on a metaphorical level, it suggests that female sexuality can only be tamed from destructiveness through the nuclear family and the channelling of sexual energy into heteronormative reproduction.

This shows multiple links with other transgressive art films such as *Trouble Every Day* and *In My Skin* with their unpleasant affect and exploration of gender through cannibalism and female violence, as well as films such as *Romance*, *Sombre* and *Twentynine Palms*, for their provocative analyses of sexuality and violence. In its depiction of the specificities of transgression and 'glorious' nonproductive expenditure, *Raw* is a reflection on the extent to which transgressive acts are permitted, and how those transgressions end up being policed. It highlights the limits of transgressive acts. A Bataillean reading of the film therefore helps us to think about how limits and transgression function within the diegetic world. However, as should be clear from this discussion of nonproductive expenditure, sex, war, death, ritual and so on, none of these concepts are particularly helpful in grasping what is transgressive about the film itself. The following analysis of *In My Skin*, which also examines the Bataillean concept of sovereignty, draws the same conclusion: inasmuch as the depicted worlds of these films are analogies for our own world, Bataille's theories of transgression are very interesting, but these concepts are not readily applicable to transgressive art films as a socio-cultural phenomenon.

*

In My Skin follows Esther, who works for a marketing company, and lives an ostensibly banal life of corporate work, a steady boyfriend, networking at evening events, and chats with friends. At a work party, Esther accidentally cuts her leg badly and from then on begins to cut herself regularly, slowly receding from her social arenas: boyfriend, friends and eventually society at large. The film is full of long close-ups: grazing along her bare legs while she works, documenting the stages of cutting away a bloodied bandage, visual and aural close-ups of fingernails picking at varnished wood, and of drips of blood on her face.

In My Skin has received quite substantial critical and scholarly interest, particularly in terms of de Van's relation to other French female directors,[31] and as an arthouse body horror film focused on sensation.[32] The twin concerns of gender and horror are made explicit in readings that use psychoanalytic horror theory, with Eugenie Brinkema even suggesting that the film is a reflection on psychoanalytic accounts of cinema, especially on the problematic over-closeness of the feminine to masochism in these theories.[33]

Although de Van resists such readings herself, many commentators have also highlighted the socio-political nature of the film's explorations of the body, especially in terms of gender, social isolation and the female condition in late capitalism.[34] In terms of gender, the self-harm in *In My Skin* has been read metaphorically as an attack on her body's surface, which is the only way to transcribe her inner turmoil.[35] The visible wounds are read as having a metonymic relation to the wounds sustained through engagement with society, a perverse reaction to patriarchal attempts to control her.[36] In a compelling comparison between *Secretary*'s assimilationist (hetero)normative politics, where sadomasochism is tamed within a heteropatriarchal version of marriage, and *In My Skin*'s radically open questioning of normative regulative processes, Brinkema argues that 'Esther may fall into the gap between radically irreconcilable options', evoking in her excessive mutilation new forms of relation, and refusing to allow the excess to be recuperated back into existing romantic, sexual or gender structures.[37]

The context of this evocation of gendered violence is the neoliberal corporate world where Esther works. Many scholars read Esther's violence as turned against herself as a counter-violence to the biopolitical regulations imposed by the neoliberal world. The visceral and violent emotions of her self-harm therefore challenge a system that has 'erected one's own body as a bulwark against societal alienation', aggressively questioning the demands on her body to maintain itself as a fit, productive machine for corporate exploitation.[38] Read in this way, Esther's predicament is not predominantly psychological in nature – demonstrating her inability to cope with the demands of modern life – rather it is a productive choice on her part, an exploration of aspects of the world that had previously eluded her. She does not cut herself because she sees no other way to cope with the world, but because it allows her to counter the alienation from her material body which late-capitalist patriarchy encourages. There is, in *In My Skin*, 'an opposition of the individual body and of the social body, a backlash against the fragmentary corporatisation of humanity'.[39] Alienation – from society, from her body, from her friends – is a central theme and it is in Esther's reconnection with the fleshiness of her body, that *In My Skin* reconsiders the meaning attached to the female body, to self-harm, to agency and to society. In a Marxist reading this is akin to countering the disjunction between labour and value in the commodity fetish, where the product is the human body. In a feminist reading this is a reinstatement of the actual woman in a patriarchal world that reduces women to visual objects for male viewing pleasure. At the same time, it is hard to decipher what political conclusions we might draw beyond a simple critique of the status quo: 'its indictment of office work as a benumbing process and its Foucauldian denunciation of body-formatting, resists straightforward interpretations and historical analogies'.[40] Overall, these hermeneutic readings are very much comparable to those analysed in terms of visibility, proximity and duration in the previous chapters: sexual and violent imagery functions both to address viewers corporeally, and to provide analogies to broader societal questions related to bodies, corporeality, sexuality, sex, gender and violence, thus enabling the transgressive images to be recuperated as part of some form of ethical project, and as part of art cinema.

If, however, continuing the emphasis in this chapter on understanding the transgressiveness of acts, we focus solely on Esther's transgressive acts within the diegetic world, I argue that *In My Skin* can be read as a Bataillean exploration of the consequences of the repression of unproductive expenditure. The catastrophic violence in *In My Skin* is self-harm, as Esther begins to attack herself in ever more destructive ways, leading to an ambiguous ending that suggests death as a likely outcome. Given the lack of outlets for positive evacuation of the desire for unproductive expenditure within Esther's highly controlled corporate lifestyle, violence erupts catastrophically in these unproductive explosions of savage, but emotionally profound, sessions of self-mutilation. Rather than being able to channel eroticism and violence within a carnivalistic period separated from her productive labour environment, these two domains of her life collide with each other leading to 'an irrational attempt to break from the structure of ordinary existence and erotically connect with what exceeds it'.[41] Bataille thought that this form of repression led to war, rather than self-harm, which gives *In My Skin* a distinctly more individualist tone than in Bataille's writings, but the film's critique of corporate capitalism seems clearly linked to Bataille's critique of capitalism's overfocus on productivity.

The centrality of corporate life to the film is made clear from the opening credit sequence, which features photographs of La Défense, the corporate quarter in Paris, from the skyscrapers, to the large stairways and walkways, to the pots of pens and computer screens in the offices. The screen is split in two with these images shown on the left, and colour-inverted, overexposed versions of them on the right, suggesting a disconnect between two ways of viewing this world: the official version, and something disconcerting and sinister. In the middle of this sequence, we encounter the protagonist, Esther, who is already working at home early in the morning as her partner kisses her goodbye, immediately pointing to the intrusion of her work life into her home life. Work's overwhelming presence within her life is further signalled in the next scene, which takes place at a party populated by many of her colleagues, and where she is conscious of trying to secure a position by networking with her superiors. These scenes both overtly point to the corporate sector's exploitative labour practices, evoking Esther's precarious economic position in that she has yet to secure a permanent contract with her current employer. In Bataillean terms, the profane world of work has extended into all parts of Esther's life. Productive expenditure characterises all her actions: from the early morning interactions with her partner and her night-time socialising, to a long take of kissing that is dominated by a discussion about work, her every waking moment is channelled into goals ultimately set by her employer, that are based upon profits and economic growth.

Bataille also notes that the prospect of war and the problems of creating a working class devoted entirely to productive and reproductive expenditure can be attenuated by greater equality, a point that is especially pertinent for *In My Skin* given the increasing inequality brought about by neoliberal economics:

> we will not be able to decrease the risk of war before we have reduced, or begun to reduce, the general disparity of standards of living, that is, the general disequilibrium . . . it is necessary to produce with a view to raising the global standard of living.[42]

As Lübecker notes, Esther's self-harm can be read as the explosion of war on an individual level, a privatised form of catastrophic expenditure, with the film being a broader Bataillean critique of the inequities and atomisation of twenty-first-century neoliberal corporate capitalism: 'late capitalism leaves no space for a *collective* response to the social repression of desire. The social catastrophe has been replaced by a private, bodily catastrophe.'[43]

At the same time, Esther's self-harm can be read not solely in negative terms as the catastrophic expenditure that explodes from the neoliberal worker's totalising focus on (re)production, but as an attempt to achieve Bataillean sovereignty, which eludes her in her current interminably subordinate position. Sovereignty, according to Bataille, is a concept derived from the sovereign position of absolute power occupied by feudal leaders: the sovereign consumes wealth, neither producing nor labouring, and lives a life beyond utility, in complete contrast to the workers, who must reduce their consumption to the necessary.[44] Although this idea has its roots in despotic leaders, sovereignty for Bataille is achievable for anyone through useless consumption, luxury products, eroticism and amusements, because to be sovereign is to exist in the moment, with no regard for anything other than the present time.[45] At the same time, it is not necessarily the rich who attain

Bataillean sovereignty either, given that they tend to be engaged in constant accumulation rather than nonproductive expenditure, although riches certainly allow for the possibility of useless expenditure and non-labour time.[46] Work and even knowledge are never sovereign, they are 'always a servile operation, indefinitely resumed, indefinitely repeated . . . caught up in duration, beyond the present moment', always attached to some idea of utility and productive activity.[47]

Bataille asserts that in capitalism, and in modernity more specifically, the worker is mechanised as a vector of production and accumulation, the profits of which are then reinvested in production. Any nonproductive expenditure or properly sovereign attitude[48] is impossible to attain in the context of productive work and the workers lose their sovereign subjectivity, and the possibility of a life lived without regard for the future:

> Life beyond utility is the domain of sovereignty. . . . The worker turns the bolt in order to obtain this wage. In principle, the wage will enable him to meet his needs. Thus, in no way does he escape the circle of constraint. He works in order to eat, and he eats in order to work. . . . What is sovereign in fact is to enjoy the present time without having anything else in view but this present time.[49]

Bataille argues that thought subordinated to an anticipated result ceases to be sovereign and that it is only in not knowing that 'the ceaseless operation of cognition is dissolved'.[50] In other words, when knowledge is subject to the pursuit of a productive outcome (the anticipated result) as it is in Esther's work domain, her thought is not sovereign. Rather sovereignty is to be found in the rejection of purposive activity, in the refusal to live the present for the sake of the future, and with disregard for death:

> sovereignty is essentially the refusal to accept the limits that the fear of death would have us respect . . . It also calls for the risk of death . . . The sovereign world is the world in which the limit of death is done away with. . . . The sovereign is he who is, as if death were not.[51]

Esther's corporate existence and its tentacular reach into all parts of her life exclude her from sovereignty, but her ecstatic cutting rituals performed outside time, and anathema to her work life, do suggest a form of sovereign release, to the point of disregarding death.

We clearly see the shift into a world of sovereign consumption in a restaurant scene, just after Esther has been promoted at work. As her boss and clients drone on about intercultural differences, advertising ploys and the Japanese markets, Esther's left hand grabs the food on her plate and is nearly stabbed by the fork in her right hand, before her right hand drags her left hand away from the plate. As the camera pans in close-up along her left arm, we see that her left forearm has become severed from her body and lies inert on the table, but no one notices. She stabs at her arm, first with a knife, then her nails and finally a key until blood is drawn. As the violence and her cutting intensifies, close-ups of her eroticised wounds continue to place viewers close to Esther while she inflicts her wounds, leaving her ostensibly unaware dining companions out of the frame. The food on the table is no longer just to feed her but is grabbed and thrown about carelessly, while the knife normally used productively to cut up larger chunks of food is wielded destructively and pointlessly, stabbing at her inert arm, and later drawing blood to no productive end. Most noticeably, although part of her is trying to hide her body's uncontrolled violent impulses, the images viewers see are almost entirely unconcerned with the others at the table, mostly blocking them from view, and including no reactions to what would normally be considered shockingly bizarre behaviour. At this point in the film, Esther is still fighting it, but here we see a disregard for anything but the present moment (she will likely be reprimanded for such behaviour but we never see this). She is moving away from dealing with the bare necessities of sustenance (cavalier use of food) towards pointless destructive violence (nonproductive expenditure).

In a later scene in a hotel, we hear the moans of pleasure/pain as a blood-bespattered Esther bites her arm and uses a knife to cut into her legs while supine on the floor. She wraps her bloody, bitten arm around herself like an embrace before pulling her legs up over her head. A close-up from above shows her face, sometimes obscured by her legs as the camera tries to get too close. She stares greedily at the wounds in her thighs; a cut to the side sees her licking gently at her cuts before we return to the previous shot, as blood drips onto her face. She rubs the blood over her eyes and sucks her fingers to taste it. Her legs obscure her face like the back of a lover's head might when leaning for a kiss, the blood on her face stands in for money-shot semen, her bent posture evokes auto-fellatio, and afterwards she lies immobile on the floor in a post-orgasmic haze. Here, Esther is fully absorbed in the violent eroticism of the moment, savouring the brutal sensations of the knife's incisions and not worrying about the consequences of her actions. Instead of a pornographic utopia, as theorised by Linda Williams,[52] this is a kind of pornographic dystopia, a world separate from ours, temporally as much as conceptually. Much like time appears to pause for sex and music sequences in pornography and the musical, time here is of little concern to Esther, lost as she is in the violent ecstasy of her onanistic cutting. In this moment she is far from the productive pressures of work, of the servile toil of her corporate existence, and in seeking erotic pleasure in non-genital violence even separates herself from any sense of reproduction that penetrative sex could imply.

By the end of the film, this exploration of sovereignty addresses the question of death, which a sovereign person neither fears nor fully contemplates:

> from the viewpoint of the sovereign man, faintheartedness and the fearful representation of death belong to the world of practice, that is, of subordination. In fact, subordination is always rooted in necessity; subordination is always grounded in the alleged need to avoid death.[53]

In subordination, we worry about feeding ourselves, about paying rent, about the consequences of our actions on our future lives. By contrast, sovereignty involves worrying only about the present moment, it involves disregarding one's own physical integrity in the pursuit of useless consumption and pointless expenditure. In the final sequence, all attempts to conform to the profane world of work have been abandoned, as Esther descends into an isolated orgy of self-inflicted violence. The screen splits into multiple images, the camera roaming across sharp instruments, blood-stained clothes and sheets, bits of skin, and a generally chaotic mess. With little natural light and no contextual shots, this scene takes place in complete detachment from the outside world, and with complete disregard for anyone other than herself. A rotating shot zooms in slowly on her face in the final shot, ambiguous as to whether she is alive or dead, a distinction that is ultimately unimportant to a sovereign: 'at the extreme limit of the "possible", everything gives way: the edifice itself of reason – in an instant of insane courage, its majesty is dissipated'.[54] In this sense, Esther's unproductive explorations of her body demonstrate a fundamental disregard for the future, for the productive promises of work, marriage, friends and even life, thereby constituting 'an unreasoned impulse [that gives] a sovereign value to the miraculous, even if the miracle were an unhappy one'.[55]

In *In My Skin*, like in *Raw*, these explorations of nonproductive expenditure and sovereignty are rooted in questions of gender. Esther is not only subordinated as a worker, but specifically as a female worker. The relation of her cutting to femininity is emphasised in a scene at a swimming pool, where three male co-workers try to throw her into the pool fully clothed. As she screams repeatedly, writhing to get away, and grabbing at a chair to hold herself back, it looks much like a sexual assault, while her friend and other male partygoers just look on, unreactive to her shouts for help. Having been dragged across the wet floor, the blood from her wounds seeps into her trousers, making her entire leg look bloody, suggesting to onlookers that she is on her period, which is why the 'attackers' suddenly stop and run away. With the iconography of gang rape and menstruation, her predicament is distinctly feminised. This is made even clearer later in her boyfriend's recriminations, as he complains 'I can't stand looking at that', as though the injuries and attack that she suffered are most problematic because of the visual impact they may have on her male partner, as though she is but a source of visual dis/pleasure for him.

Esther's cutting becomes a rejection of this masculinist control, of the attempts by her boyfriend, her colleagues and her doctor to impose their will on her, especially in visual terms. Indeed, the doctor who initially treats her wounds encourages her to get a skin graft, although he admits it is not medically necessary, its sole rationale being that the leg would not be 'ugly'. Given that film viewers see numerous close-up caressing images of her legs, before and after the accident, as well as those of her friend as she moisturises, the challenge to visual pleasure is targeted at viewers as much as the other male characters. Rejecting such external impositions, Esther seeks to take control of her body and exert corporeal independence: instead of reflecting the desires of the men in her life, her body becomes a productive site of blood as well as her locus of control over her own sexuality and her own desires. Apart from the restaurant scene, her cutting is always away from public spaces – in storerooms, in isolated corridors, in hotel rooms – as much to escape the visual domination of those around her, as it is to secure privacy for her erotic expenditures. The sovereignty that she achieves in these moments is then as much an escape from a patriarchal exploitation of female (re)productive labour, and of women as a product, as it is an escape from the trappings of a neoliberal workplace that precludes anything other than productive labour.

Just like with *Raw*, *In My Skin* allows for a rich Bataillean reading through nonproductive, glorious, and catastrophic expenditure, sovereignty, the profane, the sacred and, above all, transgression. Other transgressive art films also lend themselves to such a reading, especially *Trouble Every Day*, *Romance*, *Twentynine Palms*, *The Tribe*, *Taxidermia* and *The Idiots*. Reading *In My Skin* and *Raw* in this way shows the value of Bataille for understanding the role that sex and violence play within the diegesis.

*

While there is still much to be said about the importance of affective images to the transgressiveness of transgressive art films, the analysis of *Raw* and *In My Skin* has shown that Bataille's theories can be very pertinent to understanding the transgressive acts we see in the films. Beyond Bataille's explicit concerns with expenditure, sovereignty, excess and nonproduction, his concepts allow us to better grasp the films' explorations of gender, even as his own approach to gender is extremely limited. Like other transgressive art films, these films are politically ambiguous, inviting unresolvable contradictory analyses. *Raw* reflects on the social construction of gender, but still centres its narrative on the potentially dangerous and out-of-control nature of female sexuality. *In My Skin* critiques neoliberal patriarchy and its authoritarian biopolitics, but this is undertaken through the pathologising image of a predominantly, or at least stereotypically, female mental health issue: self-harm. The fact that Esther is causing very serious damage to herself, cutting chunks out of her face, and potentially commits suicide at the end of the film, makes it difficult not to see the film as a depiction of a severe mental health breakdown, even as it is so clearly a broader analogy, rather than a straightforwardly realist film.

The aim of this chapter is to demonstrate the value and the limitations of Bataille's theories of transgression for thinking through the images we see in transgressive art films. Bataille's distinction between 'limited transgressions' (which play an important normative role in society) and more substantial transgressions (which are marginalised or punished) plays a key role in my theorisation of artistic transgression. However, his writing on expenditure, sovereignty and eroticism are most relevant to the transgressive acts themselves, rather than to their depictions. The transgressive nature of the acts depicted in the films should not be equated with the films' artistic transgressions in the broader context of the cinema art world, and cannot account for their controversial reception. An exploration of these requires that we move beyond Bataille, and other sociological theories of transgression, to look at artistic transgression, degree and kind of transgression, and the concept of extremity.

Notes

1 Quandt, 'Flesh and Blood'.
2 Kendall, 'Reframing Bataille', 53.
3 Best and Crowley, *The New Pornographies*; Beugnet, *Cinema and Sensation*; Kendall, 'Reframing Bataille'.
4 Angelo, 'Sexual Cartographies'; Featherstone and Johnson, '"Ovo Je Srbija"'; Birks, 'Body Problems'.
5 Beugnet, *Cinema and Sensation*; Chamarette, *Phenomenology and the Future of Film*.
6 Taylor, 'Infection, Postcolonialism and Somatechnics'; Kendall, 'Reframing Bataille'; Lübecker, 'Bruno Dumont's *Twentynine Palms*'; a slightly more in-depth analysis is provided by De Leeuw, '"A Kiss Is the Beginning of Cannibalism"'.

7 Russell, *Rape in Art Cinema*, 8.
8 See Wilson, *Spectatorship, Embodiment and Physicality*. Scholars of self-harm have also used *In My Skin* as an introduction or illustration to certain aspects of their thought, e.g. Le Breton, *La peau et la trace*, 16–17; Failler, 'Narrative Skin Repair', 11.
9 On a basic level, the type of university-level boarding school seen in *Raw* doesn't exist in France (acknowledged by the director as an invention (see Barton-Fumo, 'Pleasures of the Flesh'; Jenkins, 'Julia Ducournau')). The highly regimented, openly violent, and abusive environment almost entirely free of adult presence is closer to *Lord of the Flies* (Golding, 1954) than any real-world university environment.
10 Scholarly work on *In My Skin* frequently repeats that any facile explanations of Esther's self-harm that describe her as a monster, a victim or a deviant should be avoided: see Tarr, 'Director's Cuts', 91; Beugnet and Ezra, 'Traces of the Modern', 35; Palmer, *Brutal Intimacy*, 86; Lübecker, *The Feel-Bad Film*, 134.
11 See Huyssen, *After the Great Divide*, 44–81; Doane, *Femmes Fatales*, 142–62; McCormick, *Gender and Sexuality in Weimar Modernity*, 15–38.
12 This precise tension is noticeable in other transformation films such as *When Animals Dream*, in which the protagonist's puberty changes are visualised as her transformation into a wolf. While the film critiques the community's misogynistic reactions to her burgeoning womanhood, its underlying premise is that her adult female sexuality is a danger.
13 Bataille, *The Accursed Share*, 1:23, 1:69.
14 Bataille, 1:21.
15 Bataille, 1:24ff.
16 Bataille, *Erotism*, 63.
17 Bataille, *Lascaux*, 37; Bataille, *Erotism*, 70.
18 Bataille, *The Accursed Share*, 1:24.
19 Although this can become itself quite extreme, such as when he argues that 'at the elusive extreme limit of my being, I am already dead, and *I* in this growing state of death speak to the living: of death, of the extreme limit' (*The Bataille Reader*, 75 ['The Torment']).
20 See De Leeuw, '"A Kiss Is the Beginning of Cannibalism"', 216–17.
21 And the final shot of her father's scarred chest provides the traces of the violence of her parents' sexual encounters.
22 Bataille, *Erotism*, 16–20.
23 Bataille, *Lascaux*, 37.
24 Richardson, *Georges Bataille*, 104.
25 Alexia runs out in front of cars on a country road, making them swerve and crash and then devours the injured drivers.
26 Richardson, *Georges Bataille*, 102.
27 De Leeuw, '"A Kiss Is the Beginning of Cannibalism"', 226.
28 Durand and Mandel, 'Introduction', 5.
29 Bataille, *Erotism*, 16.
30 Interestingly, Louise Flockhart suggests this is common to female cannibal films: 'ambiguity is built into these texts, and no resolution is offered' ('Gendering the Cannibal in the Postfeminist Era', 71).
31 Palmer, 'Under Your Skin'; *Brutal Intimacy*; Austin, 'Biological Dystopias'; Quinlivan, 'The French Female Butterfly Collector'; Dooley, 'Navigating the Mind/Body Divide'; McGillvray, 'The Feminist Art Horror of the New French Extremity'.

32 Tarr, 'Director's Cuts'; 'Mutilating and Mutilated Bodies'; Angelo, 'Wounded Women'; Chareyron, 'Horror and the Body'; Wilson, *Spectatorship, Embodiment and Physicality*; Lowenstein, 'Feminine Horror'; Coulthard and Birks, 'Desublimating Monstrous Desire'.
33 Brinkema, 'To Cut, to Split, to Touch, to Eat'.
34 Beugnet, *Cinema and Sensation*; Morsch, 'Filmische Erfahrung'; Palmer, *Brutal Intimacy*; Walon, 'Monstrous Embodiments'.
35 Chareyron, 'Horror and the Body', 72.
36 Tarr, 'Director's Cuts', 88; see also Lowenstein, 'Feminine Horror', 472; Azalbert, 'Le corps défendant'.
37 Brinkema, 'To Cut, to Split, to Touch, to Eat', 138.
38 Morsch, 'Filmische Erfahrung', 68–69. see also Beugnet, *Cinema and Sensation*, 161; Le Breton, *La peau et la trace*, 17; Walon, 'Monstrous Embodiments', 43–44; Lowenstein, 'Feminine Horror', 482.
39 Mandelbaum quoted in Palmer, *Brutal Intimacy*, 84–85.
40 Beugnet and Ezra, 'Traces of the Modern', 35; see also Lübecker, *The Feel-Bad Film*, 134.
41 Birks, 'Body Problems', 145; see also Beugnet, *Cinema and Sensation*, 161.
42 Bataille, *The Accursed Share*, 2:188.
43 Lübecker, *The Feel-Bad Film*, 132.
44 Bataille, *The Accursed Share*, 3:198.
45 Bataille, 3:187, 3:199.
46 Bataille, 3:198.
47 Bataille, 3:202–203.
48 Bataille, 3:283.
49 Bataille, 3:198–99.
50 Bataille, 3:208.
51 Bataille, 3:221–22.
52 Williams, *Hard Core*, 160–74.
53 Bataille, *The Accursed Share*, 3:222.
54 Bataille, *The Bataille Reader*, 70 ['The Torment'].
55 Bataille, *The Accursed Share*, 3:209.

7

Genre

Conflict and ambiguity are at the heart of transgressive art films. They are characterised by a playing with boundaries and the marginal transgression of limits, whilst always leaving their exact positioning in relation to such boundaries ambiguous. Understanding the controversy that transgressive art films create requires paying attention to the unresolved tension between legal and cultural conceptions of art as entirely separate from non-art, and high art as entirely separate from low art, despite the obvious influences, connections and commonalities that exist between works of these ostensibly separate categories. One particularly interesting instantiation of this is the question of genre, most notably the genre boundary between art and pornography, with discussions about artistic or pornographic value forming a significant part of scholarly writing on sex in transgressive art films.[1] Given the sexually explicit nature of many of the most controversial scenes in transgressive art films, the question of pornography is highly pertinent when thinking about these scenes.

The central focus here is not on developing exact definitions of art and pornography, but on exploring the consequences of the mutually exclusive nature of these genres. Censorship boards and laws standardly define pornography as illegal or restricted, while art is freely distributed. Despite this ostensibly simple separation, it is clear that each of these genres adopts the mode of the other: Jeff Koons' *Made in Heaven* series was pornographic while still being art (and exhibited as such in museums), while films like *Into the Flesh* and *Ink is my Blood* are artistic while still being pornography (and distributed as such on pornographic streaming sites such as XConfessions).[2] Pornography can be artistic but not art, while art can be pornographic but not pornography, or as Brian McNair puts it, "'art' and 'porn' do not mix, even if there is ample room for creative interplay between the two forms'.[3] All genres are hybrid mixes and therefore there is clearly interplay between pornography and art on an aesthetic, ethical and conceptual level. However, on a legal and institutional level a category must be chosen, and a film is either pornography or not-pornography (what I here call 'art'). Many transgressive art films bridge this unbridgeable gap and therefore provide perfect examples for considering the connections between transgression and genre.

This chapter focuses on type and degree of transgression, specifically in relation to genre. Given the inclusion of standardly pornographic material (visible aroused genitals, penetration, ejaculation) in films not classified as pornography, certain transgressive art films repeatedly transgress the art/porn boundary, even as it remains an important legal and cultural dividing line between two mutually exclusive genres. I explore how genre theory is able to shed light on some of the genre issues provoked by transgressive art films, but is also insufficient to fully explain them. In a sense, this is an attempt to find a rigorous framework for thinking about genre hybridity, the mixing of low/high art, and the relevance of the pornographic to transgressive art cinema. Using *A Hole in My Heart* as a case study, I discuss how the conflict between art and pornography can be found in the form and narrative of transgressive art films, as well as in the commentary on them. By applying ideas about marginal transgression and polarising reception to poststructuralist readings of genre boundaries, I argue that we can grasp the liminal generic positioning of transgressive art films. Films like *A Hole in My Heart* can therefore be understood as part of the untenable genre of 'art-pornography' without dissolving the boundary between its constituent parts.

A huge amount of work has been done on genre in disciplines such as film studies, rhetoric, education, art history, anthropology, linguistics, cognitive psychology, literature, cultural studies and biology, each involving slightly different approaches to questions of classification, taxonomy and definitions. Within film studies, much of this work has revolved around the paradox of genre, called the 'empiricist dilemma'[4] or the 'dilemma of genre history',[5] most comprehensively theorised by Jacques Derrida.[6] The dilemma is that analysis of a genre involves isolating representative examples from which common characteristics are meant to emerge empirically, but the very choice of those examples requires prior awareness of their characteristics: a chicken-and-egg situation. Andrew Tudor suggests two practical means for avoiding this dilemma: either choose *a priori* criteria based on a particular critical purpose (which makes the concept of genre redundant) or work with a common consensus about the films constituting a genre and begin the analysis there (as I did with the core transgressive art films).[7] Much important work has been done on film genre theory, examining genre as inherently hybrid, genre as discourse, genre as speech act, genre as process, genre as ideology and so on. However, to my knowledge, little work on genre theory considers the collision between the inherent hybridity of all genres, and the clearly demarcated genre boundaries arising from censorship and restrictions. In these cases, the stakes of falling on one side of a boundary rather than another are high, even as that boundary is difficult to define. This chapter builds on this work in genre theory to propose a framework that accounts for the phenomenon of art and porn being both mutually exclusive, and mutually influencing, categories.

*

Just as the terms 'transgressive' and 'extreme' have been subject to a wide range of sometimes vague usages in scholarship on transgressive art films, so have 'boundary' and 'limit', central to discussions of genre, been used liberally to describe diverse aspects of transgressive art films.[8] Genre has mainly been mentioned in scholarship on transgressive art films in terms of mixing or appropriation, with many accounts pointing to the commonalities between the films discussed here and body genres, especially pornography and horror, and ascribing a certain hybridity to transgressive art films. However, it is important to note that the inclusion of sex and violence in arthouse films has a long history, even as it is frequently considered as new and transgressive at each iteration.[9] Moreover, this inclusion is sometimes framed in terms of 'usage', 'borrowing' or 'deployment', readings that unhelpfully posit art films as sitting outside genre, or as having a privileged position in relation to genre.[10] The most sophisticated and compelling accounts of hybridity and genre boundaries are from Martine Beugnet, who, after Antonin Artaud, demonstrates how a 'cinema of sensation' participates in both 'the abstract formalism of the "pure" cinema and the derivative commercialism of narrative "psychological" cinema',[11] and from Victoria Best and Martin Crowley, who explore the awkward relationship films like these create with genre norms and literary or intellectual culture.[12] Building on this, I follow work done in a poststructuralist vein on the intrinsic hybridity and impurity of any genre, in order to suggest that if we consider the 'breaching of boundaries and impurity to be features of every text, then any text located as an instance of genre would also, ipso facto, breach generic boundaries and display its excluded otherness. In other words, no genre film is pure'.[13] Rather than seeing transgressive art films as art films first and foremost, which borrow from other non-art genres, we must consider them to be participating in multiple genres simultaneously, without necessarily prioritising any particular genre. In this vein, we must also recognise that their status as art films comes only as a result of particular discourses and conventions, and that they can just as well be approached as pornography that also participates in the genre of art, as many viewers have indeed described them.

The most explicit examination of genre and transgressive art films comes in Mattias Frey's analysis of extreme cinema. He suggests a two-tier 'cluster' definition: firstly, all extreme films must 'explicitly depict and/or primarily thematise sex, violence or sexual violence'. Additionally they must fulfil at least one, but as many as possible, of eight secondary criteria: they must deploy an art-film style; create controversy; play at 'extreme' or 'artsploitation' festivals; be exhibited in arthouse cinemas; be distributed/marketed as art or artsploitation films; be positioned by the filmmakers as intentionally artistic; be discussed by fans as artistic; be awarded the highest classification rating, be banned or left unclassified.[14] Frey notes that most of these secondary criteria are not aesthetic but rather relate to 'institutional, business, functional, artistic, critical, regulatory, and popular discourses'.[15] This is an extremely helpful starting point and, importantly for my discussion here, we can note that his criteria mostly involve a discursive enfolding of explicit sex and violence into the notion of 'art film' by different stakeholders within that world: festivals, cinemas, distributors, fans, critics and viewers (who recognise an 'art-film style'), and the filmmakers themselves.

Frey also usefully encourages scholars to see these films within a set of larger contexts, that go beyond arthouse or festival films, and the discourse of 'high-brow' media artefacts, to consider the multiple other contexts in which sexually explicit scenes circulate. He argues, for instance, that we should look at *The Brown Bunny*, discussed in Chapter 4, with its final fellatio scene between then off-camera couple Vincent Gallo and Chloë Sevigny, in the context of celebrity sex videos by Paris Hilton or Tommy Lee rather than only in relation to other arthouse sex scenes.[16] Many re-edited and recompiled sequences from explicit arthouse films function literally as pornography: 'detached from art cinema culture and contextualised among the short sex clips that make up the majority of online pornography, these films function for the same arousing and masturbatory purposes as any other cheaply produced or amateur offering'.[17] Examining the promotional material for transgressive art films, Frey also points out that, despite the filmmakers claims to the contrary, the films' marketing tends to flirt with softcore imagery and 'downplay or elide the difference between sexual art films and more unambiguously exploitative erotic films'.[18] Thus while censorship boards and scholarly analyses might consider the precise detail of what is visible within particular shots, many viewers, especially those who have not watched the film but only encountered it in adverts, video titles on tube porn sites, short clips shared on social media or racy images in gossip magazines, may well approach the films from quite a different perspective. Frey helpfully shifts the focus away from viewing these films entirely through the lens of art cinema, arguing that in explicit arthouse films, art and pornography

> cannot exist without one another; they are symbiotic in that they depend upon each other for their recognition as supposedly distinctive modes. This is not simply a matter of convergence, the melting of previously rigid formal or medial boundaries, or any postmodern inversions of hierarchies.[19]

As previously mentioned, however, Frey tends to remain within the domain of film history and so does not expand much further on this point in a theoretical vein.

The boundary between the genres of art and pornography is an unusual one. Genre boundaries are normally fluid, changing, porous and open. Ordinarily, when a text troubles generic boundaries, this does not pose too many problems to the genre ostensibly given to the text, and to assert a taxonomy might be a pointless endeavour: for instance, 'it would be absurd to ask whether *Finnegans Wake* [Joyce, 1939] is a prose work or not, or whether it can be called a novel.'[20] As Gérard Genette points out in relation to Arnold Schönberg's atonal work, the introduction of atonality into music had two generic effects: firstly, to create the sub-category of 'atonal music' and secondly, with atonality's acceptance, to expand the previously constituted category of 'music' to include atonal compositions.[21] In the classic transgressive move, the system remained fundamentally unchanged, but adapted and grew to include what was previously considered beyond its boundaries. We see a similar manoeuvre executed when two previously separate categories come together such as prose and poetry, or horror and comedy: a sub-category combining them both ('prose-poetry' or 'horror-comedy') is created, and the broader concepts grow to encompass this development: poetry need no longer be in verse, and horror can be funny as well as scary. Taking a broader perspective, 'the boundaries of a genre dissolve not only to admit new movies, but also to incorporate the surrounding discourses of advertising, marketing, publicity, press and other media reviewing, reporting and gossip, and the "word-of-mouth" opinions of other viewers'.[22] However, a merged sub-category such as 'art-pornography' is not such a simple matter as 'prose-poetry' or 'horror-comedy': the boundaries of art and pornography cannot just 'dissolve', and given the divergent legislation applying to each category, it is far from absurd to ask the question of its genre.

This stems from an ethico-intellectual investment in definitions of art and pornography that is not present in most genre categorisations. Who can exhibit what sexuality where, with whom and in what ways? What are the acceptable links between sexuality, and labour, power, representation, equality, identity or education? Pornography finds itself at the nexus of these political and moral debates, impinging on subjects as wide-ranging as colonialism, capitalism, policing and power, aesthetics, freedom of expression and feminism. As a result, pornography is highly politicised and subject to legislation that mandates different viewing regimes and tax arrangements depending on whether a film is deemed pornographic or not. Entwined with this is also the art-historical idea, derived from long-held Western aversions to emotion in artistic judgement,[23] that base emotions, such as arousal, do not belong to art and, as such, anything described as pornography (frequently defined as material primarily aimed at arousal) cannot be art. The distinction between pornography and not-pornography is morally, legally and intellectually loaded. In this abstract sense, art as a supposed high-cultural, intellectually rigorous and often state-sponsored endeavour is diametrically opposed to pornography as low-cultural, intellectually empty, base, legally restricted and often punitively taxed product.[24]

In practice, delineating the pornographic from the artistic involves far more opinion and preference, contextualisation, ideology and institutionalised guidance than any legal or philosophical definition would suggest, and definitions also shift and mutate over time. This leads most people to undertake unconscious conceptual gymnastics in order to maintain a strong distinction in the absence of any clear external definitional criteria.[25] Writing about a newspaper quiz that took decontextualised stills from pornography and canonical arthouse films, and asked readers to decide whether they were art or pornography, before revealing the answers, Eugenie Brinkema argues that when thinking about art and pornography, we maintain 'that *there is a difference*, while simultaneously enacting and celebrating the invisibility of that difference and the instability of any attempts at classification'.[26] The quiz can only take place if we acknowledge the difficulty of classification, and yet, it asserts the necessity of differentiating. Brinkema suggests that this involves a fetishistic disavowal: I know very well there is a difference, and yet it is very difficult to locate.[27] An inverse disavowal also holds: I know very well that there is no difference, and yet I believe in one nonetheless. This confusion (or delusion) seems particular to the art-pornography generic boundary. Attesting to the complexity of such a genre clash, ostensibly open-minded explorations of the art-pornography divide, such as the light-hearted quiz she mentions, hide 'fundamental anxieties about knowledge, the image and fantasy'.[28] Even as logical dissection quickly reveals the inadequacies of any taxonomical distinction, we want to believe that the two are separable.

As Brinkema's title points out, 'a title does not ask, but demands that you make a choice', we are always asked to choose between art and pornography in our categorisations: but what happens to the denied genre of art-pornography when we are forced to choose? What if we accept that films like *A Hole in My Heart* are pornography, without thereby denying that they are also art? What if we accept that some people consider them art and others pornography, and that neither is categorically right, that neither has a claim to a truthful essence of the film's genre? At the end of her essay, Brinkema declares, 'we need a new theory, a new articulation. A theory that does not choose, but demands that you make and ask. First Question: Art? Porn? Otherwise?'[29] Here I intend to take this 'otherwise' seriously, considering how something can be 'otherwise' without denying our investment in terms such as 'art' and 'porn' in conceiving that 'otherwise'. What if *A Hole in My Heart* were art and/or porn and/or otherwise? This would not only bring greater clarity to considerations of transgressive art films, which wilfully blur the contours of these categories, but also to how we ascribe genre more broadly.

*

Even after the hard-hitting films *Fucking Åmål* and *Lilya 4-ever*, also directed by Lukas Moodysson, *A Hole in My Heart* provoked controversy, dismay and anger, as well as high praise and adulation, on its release.[30] Condemned as 'an ill-considered, at times risible miscalculation'[31] and the worst film of the year,[32] it was also praised as 'yet another proof of Moodysson's fearlessness and his willingness to push forward and break through the boundaries of convention',[33] and favourably compared to '*Salò* reshot for the Big Brother era'.[34] Lukas Moodysson plunged viewers into the sordid world of amateur pornography, making a film that unashamedly revels in what it perceives as the muck of pornography, in order to illuminate the violence and cruelty at the heart of pornography's supposed eroticism. Shot on digital handheld cameras, and detailing the filming of an amateur porn film, it includes sex, vomiting, food fights, sexualised role play with barbies and footage of a labiaplasty. Reactions to the film designated it variously as art, not-art, pornography and not-pornography, thus raising many interesting questions about how to approach it in terms of genre.

A Hole in My Heart is a claustrophobic film in which a father, Richard, brings a man (Geko) and a woman (Tess) into his cramped flat to make a pornographic film, while his son (Erik) hides away in his room. It is rapidly edited and mostly filmed in the apartment on handheld cameras, which emphasises the confinement, as the camera rarely strays from the characters. There are sudden spatial shifts between the rooms, interviews with characters, shots of genital surgery, and whimsical scenes in a field and a supermarket. We see the adult characters' genitals repeatedly in the film (more casually and frequently than in most films screened in cinemas), and there are numerous softcore sequences of sex, including a double penetration, anal sex and female masturbation, as well as pubic hair being shaved, visible naked showering and Geko urinating in a glass. Moreover, there are images of plastic dolls enacting sexual situations, and the somewhat realistic genitalia of a female sex doll being digitally penetrated. Nonetheless, although they are making a porn film, we never see any erect penises or shots of penetration. These images are pornographic inasmuch as a porn film is being made, but do not transgress most censorship guidelines by showing visible aroused genitals, penetration or ejaculation. Finally, we see visible combinations of sex and violence: close-ups of female genital-reconstruction surgery, Geko and Tess masturbating with pieces of meat, a plastic vagina being cut apart, a dildo penetrating a roast chicken, and the genitals and breasts of an image of a naked woman being shot at with a pellet gun. Animate and inanimate sexual objects (human genitals, plastic genitals, sex toys) meet violence and destruction (cutting, stitching, crushing, raping). This eroticised violence transgresses certain censorship conventions, and is therefore mentioned in most critical and scholarly accounts, but these images only constitute a small part of the film; indeed many feature in a single rapidly edited montage. Although scenes are frequently shocking and provocative, only a small minority of images can be considered to step over a line, go beyond the pale or take it 'too far'. For the purposes of this chapter, I will not be discussing the otherwise highly pertinent issues of film form, value registers, gendered socialisation processes or sexual violence in any detail as this has been substantially covered in earlier chapters.

Despite its pornographic elements, *A Hole in My Heart* was widely considered to be art, understood both as not-pornography, and as part of the more restricted genre of art cinema. Regardless of the actual images in the film, it was directed by a celebrated arthouse director, was positioned as an arthouse film in publicity, critical reviews and by the director himself,[35] was passed uncut in most countries, and was screened at Toronto, Gijón and New Zealand international film festivals. From a legal or classificatory perspective, it features no images of visible penetration, a key feature of most pornography, which made it unlikely to be institutionally classified as pornographic. On a discursive level, its controversies and provocations were explained through standard tools of the art world: as shocking us into seeing the truth by destabilising interpretations of conventional images (estrangement defence); as being stylistically similar to acclaimed precursors such as

The Idiots (canonic defence); and as being permitted to adopt different rules to other non-artistic modes of expression (formalist defence).[36] In relation to this third defence, while Moodysson claims that porn actresses are 'stigmatized' and 'abused' both by pornography and commentators, in his art, he claimed to have 'decided not to care if it became exploitative' because art functions differently.[37] Critics and the filmmaker himself have adopted a number of classic positions to cement *A Hole in My Heart*'s status as art.

Nonetheless, we must consider it as at the limit of what is considered as artistic. Looking at Mattias Frey's industrial description of the 'extreme art film', many of his criteria pertain to the status of the film as an 'art film' rather than as 'extreme', but those that do consider its position as extreme are readily applicable to *A Hole in My Heart*: it primarily thematises sex, violence or sexual violence, created controversy and was awarded the highest classification rating in many countries.[38] These are very much interlinked, with images of sexual violence being the main otherwise-legal images that classification boards deal with punitively, and the key issue which reliably creates controversy at film festivals. Films such as *Grotesque* and *Murder-Set-Pieces* contain no more visible sex than *A Hole in My Heart*, and yet were banned in the UK for their alleged eroticisation of sexual violence.[39] While such censorship would not strictly relate to it being pornography, this demonstrates that *A Hole in My Heart*'s depiction of sexual violence in the context of a porn film meant it risked being banned for eroticising sexual violence, placing it at the limits of institutionally tolerated artworks.

Moreover, its pornographic elements – the filming of a porn film, highly sexualised images of food and toys – go marginally beyond the limits of art, and indeed certain critics saw it as artistically defunct, unworthy of artistic status.[40] While it follows in a grand tradition of sexual violence and controversy common to transgressive art films that nonetheless are never doubted in their artistry, the eroticisation of sexual violence and inclusion of pornography, push *A Hole in My Heart* to the limits of art and marginally beyond. The non-artistic elements are not overwhelming but remain in tension with many elements that anchor it within the genre of art: sex does not occupy the majority of the screen time, there is no visible penetration or ejaculation, and there are long scenes of reflective existential dialogue about darkness, worms and family, which have little to do with spectatorial arousal or erotic titillation, and thus conform to the expectations of arthouse cinema even if at the outer limits of those expectations.

From the other perspective, let us consider *A Hole in My Heart* as pornography: firstly, it positions itself thus, chronicling the making of a porn film and being largely composed of images that are diegetically destined to become a porn film.[41] Secondly, *A Hole in My Heart* is gritty, grainy, shaky and coarse: the grainy digital footage, jump-cuts, moments of blurring and candid interviews reference *Big Brother*, but also casting-couch style pornographic videos.[42] The claustrophobic setting, the stark lighting and low-quality sound add to these reality-TV or pornographic conventions. Thirdly, it is pornography in the sense that segments of it are available on porn tube sites, spaces literally devoted to arousing images. Fourthly, by comparing it to the unequivocally pornographic film *Fuck: Sasha Grey* we can see that *A Hole in My Heart*'s scenes of degrading sexual behaviour towards women are less different from popular forms of pornography than one might think.

In *Fuck: Sasha Grey*, a non-narrative compilation of aggressive sex between porn superstar Sasha Grey and multiple partners, several scenes involve masked men, including one coded as rape where Grey plays an asylum resident molested by two orderlies, emitting painful noises throughout. There are numerous scenes of anal sex without lubricant, and of extended deep-throat fellatio and face-fucking, the latter accompanied by choking noises from Grey, and spit flying everywhere. The entire film is replete with abusive, demeaning language directed at Grey, with violent actions accompanying the sex, such as choking, face-grabbing and spanking, and there is a scene that takes place on a toilet. Similarly, in *A Hole in My Heart*, there is a sequence where Tess is aggressively subdued by Geko and Rickard wearing balaclavas, and Geko brandishing a baseball bat; a sequence in which Geko pushes a frankfurter back and forth in Tess's full mouth, saying 'breathe through your nose'; and a disgusting close-up showing washing-up liquid being squirted into Tess's unmoving mouth on the floor, her mouth so full she can barely breathe. Other scenes include an uncomfortable scene of anal sex, a scene where Tess masturbates on the bathroom floor, and a scene where Geko vomits into Tess's mouth. These unpleasant and disturbing sequences are ostensibly intended to demonstrate the 'real' horrors of pornography, to show the violence and domination at the heart of scenes supposedly designed for the viewer's sexual gratification, but comparing these two films, we can see that *A Hole in My Heart*'s scenes are less an interpretation of the symbolic violence inflicted upon women on pornographic film sets, and more a re-enactment of forms of aggressive sex that already exist in certain types of pornography. Indeed, the sausage-stuffing and vomit sequences are also reminiscent of the brutal and deeply problematic sub-category of porn videos ominously named 'facial abuse porn'. Understood thus, the sausage-stuffing scene just replaces the penis that the actress chokes on with a frankfurter, rather than revealing the invisible phallocratic violences of pornography. While these images in *A Hole in My Heart* may be beyond anything one might expect in an arthouse film, they will be readily recognisable to viewers of pornographic films such as *Fuck: Sasha Grey*.

Finally, we can see *A Hole in My Heart*'s visceral scenes of surgery as creating the same kind of affective encounter as many pornographic images. While the film's often disgusting images seem designed to counter conventional assumptions about the arousing or sexual nature of pornographic imagery, the affectively charged close-up images of labiaplasty are no more or less exploitative than images of vaginal sex: as Mariah Larsson rightly asks, 'why should it be acceptable and non-exploitative to show female genitalia in close-up with the intent to shock and disgust but not with the intent to arouse?'[43] If, following Helen Hester's expanded analysis of the pornographic, we understand pornography to be underpinned by 'a desire to witness the human subject suffering or enjoying extreme physical states, and, through the transgression attached to pursuing one's prurient interest in such scenes, to experience at least a ghost of this intensity for oneself',[44] then there is little that separates the spectatorial dynamics of viewing the (albeit anaesthetised) suffering of genital reconstruction surgery, and the enjoyment of sex with those same genitals. Moreover, the director even admits as much, describing his critique of exploitation as itself exploitative and symptomatic of that which he wishes to challenge: 'the film becomes part of what it's talking about. It is a symptom, not a diagnosis.'[45] As such, we can see numerous ways in which *A Hole in My Heart* participates in the genre of pornography; there may not be any visible sex, but there remain significant similarities between Moodysson's film and the very pornographic material it claims to critique.

Despite all this, *A Hole in My Heart* is at, and beyond, the limits of sexual pornography (if not of pornography in a broader understanding of the term), particularly in its evocation of disgust rather than arousal through pornographic imagery. A scene where Tess lies prostrate waiting for Geko's vomit can be read as a disgusting replacement for the money shot where Geko ejaculates vomit rather than semen. It is pornographic in the sense that it presents a direct allegory of the money shot. Instead of the male performer masturbating furiously next to the open-mouthed woman, Geko is furiously stimulating his throat to induce vomiting. Instead of the woman receiving semen, she here receives vomit, but the position of Tess's body lying in wait, and of the male performer being cut out of the frame and barely visible, replicates the framing of this kind of shot in pornography, which tends to emphasise the receiver's face and the ejaculator's genitals. And yet, male and female pleasure are both disrupted as most people will find both the thought of vomiting, and being vomited on, disgusting: a 'more disgusting statement against pornography could not be made. By replacing sperm with vomit, the film defamiliarises what pornography has [often] normalised – the degradation of women'.[46] In the food-fight scene, with her eyes closed, face covered in thick sauces and mouth open, Tess looks like an object of Bukkake, but rather than the evocation of male ejaculatory pleasure, the disgust of mustard and ketchup is emphasised. When the sausage is forced repeatedly into her mouth, she is being instructed on how to submit to an uncomfortable fellatio, but it is ultimately food and not a penis in her mouth. Unmoving on the floor with washing-up liquid sprayed in her mouth, she looks like an abused, rejected sex object, but this could just as well be from a scene of torture. While these acts all make reference to tropes of certain types of pornography, such as face-fucking, deep throat and Bukkake, they emphasise the discomfort for the woman, the violence done to her and her suffering rather than the (sexual) pleasure of the male performer. Moreover, without the contextual framing of the filming of the porn film, many of these images would look like forms of sexualised bullying and harassment rather than being obviously connected to pornography, especially if arousal is part of your definition. It is notable that edited compilations of the film found on porn tube sites do not include these images and focus on the overtly sexual aspects of the film's pornography, especially on actress Sanna Bråding's nakedness in the scene of double penetration, of anal sex and of Tess masturbating on the bathroom floor.[47] Critiquing pornography does not stop *A Hole in My Heart* from being pornography but defamiliarising sexualised or erotic acts and rendering them disgusting places it at least at, and even beyond, the limits of pornography, depending on one's exact definition.[48]

Although the term pornography has certainly expanded far beyond sexual material, and disgust has become an element of many forms of modern pornography,[49] that which is predominantly perceived as disgusting tends to be considered as being at or beyond the boundaries of pornography. As Susanna Paasonen notes about viral video *2 Girls, 1 Cup*, although it was a trailer for a pornographic video, in terms of distribution and most viewers' experiences, it was not generally perceived as pornography: 'what is seen as exceedingly disgusting – like "2 Girls, 1 Cup" – in fact starts to fall outside of pornography proper'.[50] Official institutions also still tend to define pornography as containing arousing or erotic material that is foregrounded or clearly shown, rather than adopting more expansive definitions. As such, while some viewers may find it arousing, *A Hole in My Heart* is more likely to be understood as disgusting, and does not conform to official definitions of (sexual) pornography. At the same time, while pornography need not always show visible penetration or genital contact,[51] the lack of visible penetration or aroused genitals, when combined with the elements of disgust, push it, for many viewers and institutions alike, beyond the boundaries of the pornographic. Moreover, institutionally speaking, *A Hole in My Heart* does not suffer the restrictions imposed upon pornography: being available in most countries on general release, it can be sold on the internet and in ordinary shops.

We can see therefore that *A Hole in My Heart* is both at and just beyond the limits of art, and at and beyond the limits of pornography, according to various definitions that can be put forward of the two genres. There is no correct answer to the question 'art or porn?'; both can be considered correct. And yet at the same time, whichever option one chooses, one must accept that *A Hole in My Heart* is hardly a representative example of either genre. Moreover, given the mutually excluding nature of the art/pornography boundary, viewers, critics and institutions actively exclude the film from the categories of art and pornography. As discussed in previous chapters in relation to value registers, to choose to see the film in one way entails a rejection of other ways of seeing the film, rather than the simpler disagreements seen in debates about art film and horror. As Anne Freadman pithily puts it 'to read "genre" is to read conflict',[52] and this is nowhere clearer than with transgressive art films. This examination of *A Hole in My Heart* ultimately points towards several issues that have not received adequate exploration in genre theory in order to account for untenable hybrids such as 'art-pornography': degree and type of boundary transgression, discussed throughout this book, as well as opinion about genre categories. Transgression is not an issue for most writing on genre, because boundaries are fluid and with 'cluster' definitions like Frey's or family resemblances following Wittgenstein,[53] there is no need for a particular characteristic to be present in a film in order for it to participate in a particular genre. In this final section of the chapter, I examine how genre theory could respond to this unusual situation.

*

I turn especially to a Derridean account of genre because of the affinities between his analysis of words, and the art/pornography border. Many contemporary accounts of film genre tend to gloss over Derrida, ignoring him completely or evoking only briefly his claims that all texts participate in multiple genres and that no text is genreless.[54] However, his focus on destroying yet maintaining oppositions, the divergent receptions of words based on genre, the unavoidability of limits and an emphasis on law seem particularly pertinent to the putative genre of art-pornography, and the boundary between art and pornography at issue here. Broadly speaking, Derrida addresses borders in two ways that are especially relevant to this study: firstly, in judicial terms, the evocation of a border is always a violent event, in which the law is not simply followed but 're-instituted' in such a way that the act of pronouncing the border institutes the laws of its own foundation; in this sense the limit or border is structurally anchored in a limitless void.[55] Secondly, in terms of 'impossibility', such that any demarcation between two concepts always involves contamination, the outside is always included in the inside, the self cannot be conceived without otherness, that which is excluded is always constitutive of the concept itself. In what follows, I address both these approaches to borders in an examination of genre boundaries, suggesting that in relation to genre, transgressive art films and art-pornography can be best read through Derrida with some specific additions and adjustments. I contend that this also addresses a gap in the literature on film genre, that merits further exploration.

Derrida's deconstruction of concepts involves retaining an unresolved tension between undoing and preserving. The unresolved tensions arising from our inability to avoid using terms that are nonetheless untenable are central to Derrida's thinking: 'this undoing yet preserving of the opposition ... is an analogue for Derrida's attitude towards all oppositions'.[56] For instance, in order to 'escape "empiricism" and the "naïve" critiques of experience at the same time' when analysing the concept of 'experience', we must 'exhaust the resources of the concept of experience before attaining and in order to attain, by deconstruction, its ultimate foundation'.[57] This leads him to use concepts 'under erasure', sometimes literally writing the word with a cross through it in order to demonstrate how we should 'use language in terms of a trace-structure, effacing it even as it presents its legibility'.[58] The tension between a word's presence and absence is purposefully unresolved, that tension is part of what writing under erasure is intended to show: 'Derrida's trace is the mark of the absence of a presence, an always already absent presence.'[59] However, no system can ever be entirely understood from within that system: there is always a tension between our empirical understanding of the constitutive elements of a system as self-sustaining and the logical necessity for concepts from outside to underpin the inside's functioning. Derrida demonstrates that in structuralist thought which seeks such systematic logic, 'there has to be a transcendental signified for the difference between signifier and signified to be somewhere absolute and irreducible'.[60] As Gayatri Chakravorty Spivak explains,

> the sign cannot be taken as a homogeneous unit bridging an origin (referent) and an end (meaning), as 'semiology', the study of signs, would have it. The sign must be studied 'under erasure', always already inhabited by the trace of another sign which never appears as such.[61]

Every origin can only ever be a trace of some other sign, 'an originary trace or arche-trace. Yet we know that that concept destroys its name and that, if all begins with the trace, there is above all no originary trace'.[62] Origins are therefore always non-originary, their presence only takes place as an absence. Derrida's critique of structuralism highlights two key notions for an analysis of generic terms – the maintenance of untenable distinctions, and the external mediating role of a generic signifier – which he expands on in his similarly grounded account of the 'law of genre'.[63]

At the beginning of 'The Law of Genre', Derrida presents two contradictory analyses of his opening words, but does not, however, resolve these two interpretations: the phrase 'genres are not to be mixed' can be understood as either constative or illocutionary, and different audiences employing different interpretative schemas will choose one or the other, understanding the same words in ultimately incompatible ways. The genre, or speech genre (Bakhtin), to which the phrase is considered to correspond immediately guides the meaning of the words away from other potential meanings: 'the line or trait that seemed to separate the two bodies of interpretation is affected *straight away* by an essential disruption'.[64] Derrida emphasises that genre is intrinsically about limits, norms and censorship: 'as soon as the word "genre" is sounded... a limit is drawn. And when a limit is established, norms and interdictions are not far behind'.[65] However we may conceive of the links between participants in a genre, the impetus behind our creation of genre is categorisation, and even if these boundaries are blurred or unclear, the idea of a boundary is wedded into the fabric of genre. What constitutes the 'law of genre' is the 'authoritarian summons to a law of "do" or "do not"' and 'the whole enigma of genre springs perhaps most closely from within this limit'.[66]

Traits or marks become of paramount importance in Derrida's account because they are indispensable for the assignation of genre: referencing 'a set of identifiable and codifiable traits to determine whether this or that, such a thing or such an event belongs to this set or that class', a trait, mark or re-mark 'is absolutely necessary for and constitutive of what we call art, poetry, or literature'.[67] A genre label is a possible trait, but it always occupies a position both within and without a film, part of the film which we can point to as a trait of the film, and external to that film as part of the set of codifiable traits which designates that film: it is a paradox, as it must exist outside the film in order to be recognisable within it. Referring to a French publishing custom of naming the genre of a book below the title on the front cover (e.g. Toni Morrison. *Song of Solomon*. Novel.), Derrida suggests that the constituent elements of this appellation do not negate each other but rather remain in unresolved contradiction because the appellation is in a liminal position in relation to the contents of the book. Although it features ostensibly within the title of the book, it is not the title; although it purports to stand outside the book, describing it from without, its 'presence' on and in the book means that it is part of and inside the book:

> This designation is not novelistic; it *does not*, in whole or in part, *take part in* the corpus whose denomination it nonetheless imparts. *Nor is it simply extraneous* to the corpus. But this singular topos places *within and without the work*, along its boundary, an *inclusion and exclusion* with regard to genre in general, as to an identifiable class in general. It *gathers together* the corpus and, at the same time, in the same blinking of an eye, *keeps it from closing*, from identifying itself with itself. This axiom of non-closure or non-fulfilment enfolds within itself the condition for the possibility and the impossibility of taxonomy. This inclusion and this exclusion *do not remain exterior* to one another; they *do not exclude* each other. But *neither are they immanent or identical* to each other.[68]

The genre designation is therefore both inside and outside ('within and without the work'), but it is also neither inside nor outside ('does not . . . take part in' . . . '[not] simply extraneous'). Derrida's law of genre signals inclusion and exclusion, while not approaching the norm or the maximal. Here the limit is both reinforced and broken by the genre designation ('gathers together' . . . 'keeps it from closing') just as transgression breaches a boundary whilst emphasising its existence. At the same time, the two sides of the boundary are neither firmly assimilated nor firmly separated ('do not remain exterior' . . . 'do not exclude' . . . 'neither are they immanent or identical'). This description can readily be applied to the generic designation of *A Hole in My Heart* as art-pornography, a term that does not transcend, negate or destroy the boundary between art and pornography, but nor does it render it any clearer or less blurred. Art-pornography partakes in both sides whilst being excluded from both; it becomes a limit case of both genres and therefore is inside and outside both. The characteristics that Derrida identifies as pertinent to the law of genre in general, through the example of a genre's name, have a particular resonance in the case of 'art-pornography' that other theories of genre cannot provide.

Indeed, when Derrida expounds his ideas through an analysis of *The Madness of the Day [La folie du jour]* (Blanchot, 1973), his description resonates with several of my comments about *A Hole in My Heart*. He begins by describing *The Madness of the Day* as an 'account of an accountless account . . . consisting of a framing edge without content, without modal or generic boundaries'.[69] The negated negation of account in the first phrase speaks to the unresolved nature of the tensions within genre: not only is firm genre negated, but even this negation is uncertain; there is nothing concrete on which the generic designation is anchored. This seems to account for the fact that genre cannot be pinned down, whilst being not only self-evident when used vernacularly, but staunchly defended by audiences. This is reiterated in the phrase 'framing edge without . . . boundaries': we cannot deny that a boundary exists and is important, but at the same time, it does not exist; we can understand the designations but it cannot enclose the participants of that category; it is a limit but it does not limit. While this might well describe any generic descriptor, the negations, denials and unresolved tensions are broadly ignored by most viewers as the stakes of most designations are low (e.g. sci-fi western versus western-influenced sci-fi). Highlighting the contradictions and confrontations in the case of high-stakes generic evaluations (artistic pornography or pornographic art or art-pornography or other?) is, however, important and Derrida's description fits precisely with *A Hole in My Heart*: framed by art and pornography but not contained by them, its participation in each genre negated, only for the reasons for that negation to be themselves negated. Like *The Madness of the Day*, *A Hole in My Heart* demonstrates the contradictions and unresolved tensions inherent to genre labels or traits.

In terms of genre theory, Derrida's account is therefore very persuasive. Not only does it provide ways of accounting for the generic challenges of films like *A Hole in My Heart*, but it responds to many of the key aspects highlighted as integral to a universal theory of genre. It maintains an ahistorical account of genre that allows for changes in generic terms and their meanings over time. It emphasises the institutional role of demarcation that genres play, functioning as 'horizons of expectation' for readers and as 'models of writing' for authors.[70] It foregrounds the intertextual relay function of generic labels, passed on from genre to genre, and film to film without an originary point.[71] Moreover, in connecting linguistic utterances and film genres, it accounts for insights about genre from rhetoric studies especially in relation to Mikhail Bakhtin's concept of speech genres.[72] Derrida's notion of participation also appeals to the notion of family resemblances,[73] and allows for genres to 'be seen as "fuzzy" categories which cannot be defined by necessary and sufficient conditions'.[74] His theory is not designed to consider certain key aspects of film genre, most notably the characteristics of particular genres, but there are elements that still require further reflection, especially in the context of the putative genre of art-pornography.[75] In order to fully account for the specific generic challenges posed by films like *A Hole in My Heart*, we must consider genres as also defined negatively rather than affirmatively and account for diversity within genre designations. As Freadman has noted, 'Derrida's paradox holds for just those genre statements that are made according to the Aristotelian model of genre theory, i.e. class-names asserted positively',[76] but must be pursued further if that positive assertive schema is problematised (as Derrida does elsewhere in his oeuvre).

For Ferdinand de Saussure, meaning arises in opposition rather than being asserted positively: 'concepts are purely differential and defined not by their positive content but negatively by their relations with the other terms of the system'.[77] Like any example of a word, films grouped under a single genre heading may exhibit a certain positive cohesion. They also demonstrate negative cohesion whereby their affinity arises from their not being similar to other films: 'a sermon is defined by its relation to other sermons, even though the kind of thing this is changes over time; but also by the fact that it is *not* a prayer or a eulogy or a political speech'.[78] This is of particular importance when considering 'art' and 'pornography' given that discursively their opposition often works quite simply: viewers may not be able to agree upon a definition of either of the terms positively, but they do tend to accept and defend the idea that art = not porn, and porn = not art.[79] It is not therefore enough to conceive of a genre designation as both inside and outside the boundaries of the genre itself, we must also approach the genre from outside the boundaries coming in. To fully understand the sermon, we must look both at sermons and at not-sermons, and this is especially the case for oppositional genres like art and pornography: to understand art-pornography, we have to consider the unresolved tensions arising in the generic designation of art and/as not-pornography, and simultaneously of pornography and/as not-art.

Furthermore, even if Derrida's claim that texts participate in multiple genres without belonging[80] is applied to *A Hole in My Heart*, it leads us only to the conclusion that the film participates in art and pornography, and does not account for the film's awkward positioning at, and beyond, the edge of these genres, rather than at the centre. Prototype theory demonstrates how terms within a category are not equally demonstrative of a category: as Eleanor Rosch points out, certain 'perceptually salient "natural prototypes"' embody the 'most typical example of the category' while others fit the category less evocatively.[81] Categories should be understood 'in terms of a prototype ... of the category, surrounded by other [terms] of decreasing similarity to the prototype and of decreasing degree of membership'.[82] Elements do not participate equally within a genre; moreover, the limits of a genre are not clear because participation does not follow a binary logic of 'either in or out', but rather occurs along a spectrum of greater or lesser participation in the genre. Formalist work on genre also advanced a comparable claim in their description of 'dominant' elements or examples within a genre.[83] Considering the prototype as the result of a fluid system of relations based on canonisation and reshuffling, whereby non-canonised forms of representation can be taken up to restructure and reanimate older genres,[84] allows us to see genre labels like 'pornography' or 'novel' as centres of gravity for a whole collection of more or less pornographic or novelistic texts. In the case of *A Hole in My Heart*, its weak participation in the genres of 'art' and 'pornography', rather than prototypical presentation, is central to its awkward straddling of the boundary between the genres.

Finally, it is important to note that regardless of how particular words and genre labels function on a theoretical level, the meanings and connotations attached to them are not identical for all users or speakers. By adapting Saussure's totalising idea of *langue* as a single pre-existing system, and reframing it as a layered model of competing systems-in-process, in which each user has a slightly different idea of what each word or concept means, Rick Altman, in his book on film and genre, has argued that we all have slightly different perceptions of individual words and language as a whole. He suggests therefore that 'since everyone's analysis is based on different examples, and thus on different partial knowledge, every word [and genre] must vary slightly when spoken or understood by different users'.[85] In practical terms, this leads to a different array of genre labels depending on the context, with variations between trade, critics' and viewers' generic labels,[86] and with particular genre labels gaining different meanings when used by different groups. Not only does this mean that there will be divergences in how individuals define a genre but also that, in certain cases, there will be irreconcilable oppositions between definitions. While competing definitions of the western are mostly about whether iconography, character archetypes, mode of narrative resolution, location or time period should be prioritised, there is an agreement about the terrain on which the debate is being had, and about prototypical examples: who would argue, for instance, that *Stagecoach* is not a western? However, had Rosch chosen 'sport' as her example category for research into prototypes rather than 'furniture' or 'game', would some people not have argued, not only that bridge or chess are not prototypical, but that they simply are not sports? This same rejection arises in definitions of 'art' and 'pornography', where there are huge fundamental disagreements about the nature of the genre. While it may change the connotations of chess to deny it is a sport, and refuse to place it alongside rugby in a school activities handbook, the immediate practical consequences of being excluded from the genre of 'sport' would be minimal. Genre designation is never entirely anodyne, given how genres reflect but also shape the concerns and values of cinema audiences,[87] but to refuse the label of 'art' to *A Hole in My Heart* would effectively be to call for it to be censored, and for its distribution to be restricted to licensed shops, making its genre designation a much more high-stakes decision than in most cases.

Elaborating on Derrida's analysis of genre by emphasising negative category definitions, greater and lesser participation in genres, and the divergences of individual viewer understandings of genre labels helps us to come to a fuller understanding of how genre operates in the case of art-pornography. Although this analysis makes use of different terms to describe transgressive art films in relation to genre, the connections with the previous chapters are substantial. Thinking of categories in terms of positive and negative cohesion, clusters, family resemblances and so on involves being specific about the type of transgression of a genre boundary. Greater and lesser participation is a rephrasing of the idea of the almost- and marginally transgressive, bringing degree into discussions of genre boundaries. Finally, divergence in understandings of genre labels is connected to the basic idea of value registers: that viewers approach films in disparate ways as a result of preconceived ideas about what constitutes art, or in this case, about what constitutes a particular genre label. This chapter therefore points to the wider theoretical implications of thinking carefully about the transgressions of transgressive art films in terms of film form and reception, and reasserts the deep intertwining of each of the three pillars of this book's overall analysis.

*

The starting point of this chapter was the observation that the boundary between art and pornography is an unusual genre boundary, which poses particular problems for genre theories premised on the idea that genre boundaries are fluid, changing, porous and open. Conventional amalgamations or blurrings of genres do not hold in the case of art-pornography because of legal, ethical and aesthetic arguments that position art and pornography as mutually exclusive. I have suggested that a full examination of art-pornography cannot only take into account the different possible genre classifications of a given film (e.g. *A Hole in My Heart* = art, *A Hole in My*

Heart = porn, *A Hole in my Heart* = otherwise), but must also engage with the multifaceted ways in which a single text interacts with multiple genres in unresolved tension (e.g. some say/deny *A Hole in My Heart* is art, others say/deny it is porn, yet others consider it to be a bit of both, yet others again consider it to be art and porn without it becoming art-porn and so on).

Derrida's 'law of genre' provides a useful framework for this particular genre boundary because it is based upon the idea that genre labels constitute an unresolved paradox. This is helpfully analogous to the contradictory opinions, the fetishistic disavowals, and the discursive inseparability of art and pornography as genres. Nonetheless, Derrida's ideas must be complemented by an awareness of the significant role of degree and variation in designations of art and pornography. Conceiving of genre participation as functioning on a scale from lesser to greater participation also helps to understand art-pornography's liminal position far from the prototypical examples of either genre. Derrida's theory of genre provides a productive way of thinking through how art and pornography can be so fundamentally interlinked whilst at the same time remaining so separate. My analysis focused predominantly on the art-pornography boundary; however, my method of considering genre from multiple angles simultaneously, even when those angles seem contradictory, could also be usefully applied to other boundaries such as low/high culture, art/hardcore horror and progressive/retrogressive.

Notes

1 See MacKenzie, '*Baise-Moi*'; Nettelbeck, 'Self-Constructing Women'; Krzywinska, *Sex and the Cinema*; Bayon, *Le cinéma obscène*; Archer, '*Baise-Moi*'; Larsson, 'Close Your Eyes and Tell Me What You See'; Reifenberger, 'Differenzen im Close-up'; Simonin, 'Problèmes de définition ou définitions du problème?'; Wilson, 'Catherine Breillat and Gustave Courbet'.
2 *Made in Heaven* includes explicit images of penetration including one close-up, but was exhibited in numerous art museums around the world. *Into The Flesh* interweaves re-enactments of the erotic photography of John Kayser with explicit scenes of sex, while *Ink is my Blood* is a collaboration between artist Apollonia St Clair and porn director Erika Lust in which stills from a porn film mutate into ink sketches, where the performers are transformed into fantastical creatures with tails and horns. See a discussion of the distribution of *Ink is my Blood* in Chapter 8.
3 McNair, *Porno? Chic!*, 140.
4 Tudor, 'Genre', 5.
5 Welleck and Warren, *Theory of Literature*, 260.
6 Derrida, 'The Law of Genre'.
7 Tudor, 'Genre', 5.
8 For instance, the limits of narrative form (Chamarette, 'Shadows of Being in *Sombre*',

71), of the real (Wheatley, 'Naked Women, Slaughtered Animals', 101), of performance (Wilson, 'Deforming Femininity', 154), of the possible (Del Río, *The Grace of Destruction*, 5), of visualisation, art and morality (Grønstad, *Screening the Unwatchable*, 40), and of the body and acting (Bordun, *Genre Trouble and Extreme Cinema*, 166, 190).

9. See Austin, *Contemporary French Cinema*; Fisher, 'High Art versus Low Art'; Beugnet, *Cinema and Sensation*; Powrie, 'French Noir to Hyper-Noir'; Frey, *Extreme Cinema*; Hobbs, *Cultivating Extreme Art Cinema*.

10. A prime example of this is the work of Troy Bordun, who argues that 'the avant-garde, documentary, melodrama, pornography, and horror genres play significant roles' in the films, that they 're-order the generic categories of sense-perception', that 'extreme cinema deploys these generic tropes', and that 'they are reorienting and restructuring the notions of genre(s)' (*Genre Trouble and Extreme Cinema*, 1–4). Similarly in an article focused on horror and extremity, Birks and Coulthard discuss how the films 'engage with genre tropes', 'appropriat[e] tropes from the horror film', 'articulate their indebtedness to horror cinema' and 'utiliz[e] horror conventions' ('Desublimating Monstrous Desire', 462–63).

11. Beugnet, *Cinema and Sensation*, 22.

12. Best and Crowley, *The New Pornographies*, 6.

13. Staiger, *Perverse Spectators*, 66; see also 61–76. On Hollywood hybridity see Bordwell et al., *The Classical Hollywood Cinema*, 16–17. On genre as inherently hybrid, see Neale, *Genre and Hollywood*; 'Questions of Genre'; Todorov, 'The Origin of Genres'; Opacki, 'Royal Genres' amongst others.

14. Frey, *Extreme Cinema*, 7–8.

15. Frey, 8.

16. Frey, 204; see also Andrews, *Theorizing Art Cinemas*, 82.

17. Frey, *Extreme Cinema*, 204.

18. Frey, 201–2.

19. Frey, 205. On this idea in relation to Virginie Despentes' fiction writing, see Jordan, '«Dans le mauvais goût pour le mauvais goût»?', 137; Best and Crowley, *The New Pornographies*, 177.

20. Blanchot, *The Space of Literature*, 221n3.

21. Genette, *L'Œuvre de l'art*, 2:207–8.

22. Maltby, *Hollywood Cinema*, 113.

23. A position most notably associated with Kant and Shaftesbury.

24. See McGlynn et al. ('Judging *Destricted*') for a good example of how definitions of art and pornography were central to debates about *Destricted*, a series of explicit artistic shorts directed by, amongst others, Gaspar Noé.

25. On defining art and pornography, see Rea, 'What Is Pornography?'; Maes and Levinson, *Art and Pornography*; Maes, *Pornographic Art and the Aesthetics of Pornography*; Mikkola, *Beyond Speech*; *Pornography*.

26. Brinkema, 'A Title Does Not Ask', 96.

27. Brinkema, 96.

28. Brinkema, 97.

29. Brinkema, 122.

30. Just as with Quandt's disappointment with Bruno Dumont and Claire Denis on the release of *Twentynine Palms* and *Trouble Every Day* (see 'Flesh and Blood'), *A Hole in My Heart* was seen as a juvenile aberration in a promising career.

31 Dargis, 'Pornographers at Work in a Circular World'.
32 Berardinelli, 'Hole in My Heart, A'.
33 Rehlin, 'A Hole in My Heart'.
34 Thomas, 'A Hole in My Heart'. Amateur reviews also reflected this very divergent reaction with reviews on IMDb giving many 9–10/10 scores as well as 1/10, with responses at both ends of the spectrum being equally effusive: https://www.imdb.com/title/tt0381682/reviews (accessed June 19, 2022).
35 Hubner, 'A Taste for Flesh and Blood', 204–6.
36 The taxonomy of defences is drawn from Julius, *Transgressions*, 26ff (see Chapter 1). Examples of estrangement defences are Rehlin, 'A Hole in My Heart'; and Lane, 'Feelings'. Examples of canonic defences are Hoberman, 'A Squalid Swedish Porno Drama Punishes Its Audience'; Dargis, 'Pornographers at Work in a Circular World'; Stevenson, *Scandinavian Blue*, 222.
37 Quoted in Brooks, 'Dirty Business'.
38 See Frey, *Extreme Cinema*, 8.
39 BBFC, '*Murder Set Pieces*'; BBFC, 'Grotesque (Case Study)'.
40 E.g. Berardinelli, 'Hole in My Heart, A'.
41 Unlike Hollywood depictions of porn productions such as *Boogie Nights*, *Zach and Miri make a Porno* or *Sex Tape*, in which very few of the images the viewer sees can reasonably be understood as part of the diegetic porn film filmed by the characters.
42 A common format where performers new to the porn industry are 'interviewed' and then masturbate or have sex with the 'casting agent' on camera.
43 Larsson, 'Close Your Eyes and Tell Me What You See', 149.
44 Hester, *Beyond Explicit*, 122.
45 Quoted in Brooks, 'Dirty Business'.
46 Larsson, 'Close Your Eyes and Tell Me What You See', 149.
47 See for instance https://fr.xhamster.com/videos/sanna-brading-swedish-actress-a-hole-in-my-heart-2818755, https://hotmovs.com/videos/1523263/sanna-brading-a-hole-in-my-heart/ and https://motherless.com/G4377B74/836C3EC (all accessed June 5, 2022).
48 Disgust is a common reaction to scenes from *A Hole in my Heart* (e.g. Berardinelli, 'Hole in My Heart, A'; Rehlin, 'A Hole in My Heart'; Thomas, 'A Hole In My Heart'; JWIN, 'A Hole in My Heart'). Nonetheless, 'facial abuse porn' frequently makes women vomit, showing that vomit is hardly anathema to pornography, although the vomit is generally ejected onto the man's penis rather than into another person's mouth.
49 Sargeant, 'Filth and Sexual Excess'; Jones, 'Horrorporn/Pornhorror'; Paasonen, *Carnal Resonance*, 208; Hester, *Beyond Explicit*, 123.
50 Paasonen, *Carnal Resonance*, 222. Like *A Hole in my Heart*, *2 Girls, 1 Cup* features images of one person vomiting into another's mouth.
51 Award-winning feminist porn films by Jennifer Lyon Bell, for instance, contain almost no images of visible penetration, such as *Headshot* and *Skin.Like.Sun*.
52 Freadman, 'Untitled', 93.
53 Wittgenstein, *Philosophical Investigations*.
54 See Chandler, 'An Introduction to Genre Theory'; Neale, *Genre and Hollywood*; Langford, *Film Genre*; Deleyto, 'Film Genres at the Crossroads'; Dix, *Beginning Film Studies*.
55 See Lawlor, 'Jacques Derrida'.
56 Spivak, 'Translator's Preface', xx.

57 Derrida, *Of Grammatology*, 60.
58 Spivak, 'Translator's Preface', xviii.
59 Spivak, xvii.
60 Derrida, *Of Grammatology*, 20.
61 Spivak, 'Translator's Preface', xxxix.
62 Derrida, *Of Grammatology*, 61.
63 This idea had effectively been addressed in mathematical logic since the 1930s with Kurt Gödel's incompleteness theorems, which, simply put, state that a symbolic logical system can never achieve internal consistency only by means of terms from with the system (see Raatikainen, 'Gödel's Incompleteness Theorems').
64 Derrida, 'The Law of Genre', 57. This also bears a certain resemblance to Todorov's genre reading of the 'fantastic' (*The Fantastic*, 25).
65 Derrida, 'The Law of Genre', 56.
66 Derrida, 56.
67 Derrida, 64.
68 Derrida, 65; my emphasis.
69 Derrida, 73.
70 Todorov, 'The Origin of Genres', 199; see also Jauss, 'Literary History as a Challenge to Literary Theory'; Jameson, *The Political Unconscious*, 92.
71 Lukow and Ricci, 'The "Audience" Goes "Public"', 29; see also Tolson 1996 and Kress 1988 quoted in Chandler, 'An Introduction to Genre Theory', 5.
72 Bakhtin, 'Epic and Novel'; 'The Problem of Speech Genres'; Frow, '"Reproducibles, Rubrics, and Everything You Need"'; Bawarshi, 'The Genre Function'; Miller, 'Genre as Social Action'.
73 Wittgenstein, *Philosophical Investigations*; Jauss, 'Theory of Genres and Medieval Literature'.
74 Neale, 'Questions of Genre', 179; drawing on Todorov, *The Fantastic*; 'The Origin of Genres'; see also Swales, *Genre Analysis*, 45ff.; Fowler, *Kinds of Literature*, 41.
75 While Derrida discusses genre, he does not specifically reflect upon genres such as the novel (his example) or the western (film genre theorists' favourite example). Other absences include questions of the cognitive effects of genre (Grodal, *Moving Pictures*), historically located forms and functions of genre (Buckingham, *Children Talking Television*; Neale, *Genre and Hollywood*; Jameson, 'Magical Narratives'; Todorov, *The Fantastic*; 'The Origin of Genres'), the problems of transferring between disciplines in discussions of genre (Devitt, *Writing Genres*, 163ff.) or indeed how genre theory has had to adapt to technological innovations such as the internet, the widespread use of which appeared only long after his work was published (Manovich, *The Language of New Media*; Folsom, 'Database as Genre'; Olney, 'Predicting Film Genres with Implicit Ideals'; Delaporte, 'La médiation générique').
76 Freadman, 'Le Genre Humain', 363.
77 De Saussure, *Course in General Linguistics*, 117.
78 Frow, *Genre*, 24.
79 For concrete examples of this discourse, see debates around sex in *9 Songs* (Hennigan, 'Michael Winterbottom Interview: *9 Songs*'; Christopher, '*9 Songs*'; Dawson, '*9 Songs* Review'; Johnson, 'Sex, Drugs and Rock and Roll'; Barker, 'On Not Being Porn'), *Baise-moi* (MacKenzie, 'On Watching and Turning Away'; Forrest, 'Disciplining Deviant Women';

Nettelbeck, 'Self-Constructing Women'; Simonin, 'Problèmes de définition ou définitions du problème?'; Archer, '*Baise-Moi*'; Jordan, '«Dans le mauvais goût pour le mauvais goût»?'; Held, 'What Is and Is Not Porn', 20), *Romance* and *Anatomy of Hell* (Gorton, 'The Point of View of Shame'; Wilson, 'Deforming Femininity'; Phillips, 'Catherine Breillat's *Romance*'; Grønstad, 'Abject Desire') and about sex in art films more generally (Krzywinska, *Sex and the Cinema*; Bayon, *Le cinéma obscène*; Reifenberger, 'Differenzen im Close-up').
80 Derrida, 'The Law of Genre', 65.
81 Rosch, 'Natural Categories', 328.
82 Rosch, 'Cognitive Representations of Semantic Categories', 193.
83 See Bakhtin, 'Epic and Novel'; Opacki, 'Royal Genres'.
84 See Neale, 'Questions of Genre', 192-94.
85 Altman, *Film/Genre*, 172.
86 See Maltby, *Hollywood Cinema*; Altman, *Film/Genre*; Gledhill, 'Rethinking Genre'; Neale, *Genre and Hollywood*.
87 See Chandler, 'An Introduction to Genre Theory', 4-9; Neale, 'Questions of Genre', 196-97; Todorov, 'The Origin of Genres', 200; on genre and ideology see Schatz, *Hollywood Genres*; Beebee, *The Ideology of Genre*; on genre as fields of knowledge see Dimock, 'Introduction'.

8
Cinema Art World

Transgressive art films are characterised by their controversial and polarised reception, and the irresolvable tensions at their core. Throughout this book, I have discussed in detail the various ways in which these controversial and ambiguous films gain their status as transgressive art films, for example: by marginally transgressing legal boundaries, by bringing non-art tropes into art cinema and by using viscerally disturbing images of sexual violence. Nevertheless, certain aspects of this process were left unaddressed, left unattributed in the passive voice: boundaries are imposed, films are recuperated, images are legitimised. This chapter moves to a larger scale, shifting the centre of gravity away from the film as text, in order to consider the network of stakeholders that recuperates a film as art, legitimises previously non-art or low-art elements, and condones particular transgressions. The key point here is that the transgressiveness of transgressive art films is produced within, and curated by, a broad network of producers, distributors, exhibitors, festival programmers, funders, trade publications, critics, scholars, film schools, universities, film technicians and filmmakers, who make up the cinema art world.

My main intervention is to argue that transgressive art films are not simply an inevitable by-product of the cinema art world, but a central plank of its need for newness, innovation and renewal, and as such gain wide-ranging institutional support. A transgressive art film is a film that is granted a particular status at the time of its release. It is not just about transgressing, but about being recognised as having transgressed the right boundaries in the right way. In effect, transgressive art films are those that include imagery and structures that were not previously considered to be part of art cinema, but that are incorporated into the domain of film art. This mainly means graphic depictions of sex, violence and sexual violence, which are more conventionally found in non-art genres (such as pornography) and low-art genres (such as horror and exploitation). My use of terms such as 'low art' or 'non-art' in this chapter is meant descriptively, rather than normatively or evaluatively; I do not intend to make any claims as to the value of any particular film. I am particularly interested in investigating the dynamics by which different parts of the cinema art world shift the meaning of art film. It is these dynamics that create transgressive art films, which are low-art and non-art films bestowed with the status of (high-)art film, and therefore temporarily occupying a position both inside and outside art cinema.

A Serbian Film provides a perfect case study of such dynamics. It is a film that uses a variety of transgressive imagery, and displays overt proximity to spectacle horror, exploitation and hardcore horror; however, through the use of arthouse stylistic conventions, and its framing as a national allegory, it was recuperated as an art film. The film chronicles the return of a former porn performer, Miloš, for one final project which turns out to be a snuff film, in which Miloš is coerced through mind-altering drugs to perform all manner of violent sexual acts, to which neither he, nor his victims, consent. It includes a panoply of violence and sexual violence including (fictional) images of rape, murder, sexualised murder, child rape, baby rape, child abuse images, incest, necrophilia and torture. Many of the scenes are highly sexualised, and many of the violent acts are shown in gory detail. In other words, it is a film that could ostensibly have been ignored and thrown on the discard pile with the other numerous examples of torture, rape, and abuse films produced every year.

Nevertheless, *A Serbian Film* was screened at the Cannes Film Festival, exhibited across the world to arthouse audiences, and has been written about in numerous books on art cinema, such as this one. This was in large part due to its framing by the filmmakers, and many industry stakeholders, as an allegory for Serbian history, for Balkan ethnonationalist conflict, and for the contemporary treatment of Serbians by their government. Moreover, it is a well-produced film, with powerful, convincing performances from its actors, a storyline that revolves around the psychological turmoil of its protagonist, and inventive use of editing and mise-en-scène. Many of the scenes of pornography and violence are viewed on small screens as Miloš watches his own performances on a video camera, while computer screens, cameras and video cameras are ubiquitous. Flashbacks and films within films provide a structural mediation whereby few images of violence are presented in the present tense of the diegesis, providing a certain affective distancing from the full horror of the content.[1] It ticks many art-film boxes, and includes a plethora of distancing techniques to isolate viewers in some ways from the otherwise very violent images. As a result, the film was slotted more easily into the category of art cinema, as well as the somewhat reductive lens of world cinema, where successful films are expected to say something about their local condition. This process will be explored in detail, through an examination of the exact mechanisms that legitimised *A Serbian Film*'s savage and disturbing violence, elevating the film to the status of transgressive art film.

This chapter brings together all the ideas about form, reception and theory discussed throughout the book and considers how they are recognised, legitimised and mobilised by the numerous stakeholders that make up the cinema art world. Focusing on film festivals, distribution, and critical/scholarly reception, I point to how the choices to engage with particular sexual and violent films are active legitimisations of non-art or low-art imagery within the world of (high) art cinema. This also highlights the role of criticism and scholarship in recuperating sexual and violent imagery, and points to our ethical and political responsibilities when focusing our attention and research time on specific films. In what follows, I will break down these claims first by considering sociological approaches to cinema as an art world; secondly by exploring the role of newness and transgression in contemporary art, and how this can be applied to cinema; and thirdly by examining three key elements of the cinema art world – festivals, distribution, and critical/scholarly reception. Some of these have already been touched upon in the introduction, but will be examined in greater detail here. Transgressive art films play a central role in breaking new ground for film art, and allowing for its continued renewal and innovation. In order to anchor these claims in concrete illustration, I will use the example of *A Serbian Film* throughout the chapter, giving details of the processes and agents (such as festivals, distributors and scholars) that led to an embrace of this ostensibly low-art film.

*

The basic principle of an 'art world' is that we cannot fully comprehend an individual piece of artwork without taking into account the functioning of art as an institution, that is, without addressing the collective contribution of all the stages and roles that precede, surround, support, follow and make possible the experience of the work of art. Rather than seeing the filmmakers as the producers of the artwork, we can focus on

> the entire set of agents engaged in the field. Among these are the producers of works classified as artistic (great or minor, famous or unknown), critics of all persuasions (who themselves are established within the field), collectors, middlemen, curators, etc., in short, all who have ties with art, who live for art and, to varying degrees, from it.[2]

In the case of the cinema art world, this means that we have to think amongst other things about the materials used in making a film (film itself, cameras, lighting, microphones, set design, costumes), cinema infrastructures (distribution and exhibition networks, cinema buildings, festivals, museums), modes of reception (newspapers, magazines, scholarly journals, amateur fora, blogs), as well as the educational infrastructure required to train people to undertake these jobs and critically analyse the results (film schools, film clubs, university film-studies departments, academic conferences), and the funding required to support these (government grants, festival prizes, scholarships, patronage). A film is only available to watch in a cinema because projectors were designed and bought, a building was renovated with screens and chairs, because programmers sought films from distributors, who had signed contracts at film festivals, who had created a reputation as purveyors of the latest film art. A wider societal discussion about the ethics of a film scene only takes place when festivals and cinemas have screened a film, when newspapers have reviewed it, when participants have gained the analytical tools to engage with it, and have the time and space to devote to it. Sociologists like Pierre Bourdieu, cited above, and Howard Becker argue that instead of seeing art as an individual creative gesture, we must see it as a collective process at the centre of which the artwork can be found: 'we can think of an art world as an established network of cooperative links among participants'.[3] In the context of cinema, while the film itself is the centre of gravity for all that surrounds it, its status as art is maintained only through its material and discursive positioning within a much larger art world.[4]

Scholars of film institutions have repeatedly turned to Bourdieu's work on art and fields of knowledge as useful for understanding the construction and valorisation of knowledge.[5] For Bourdieu, where we view films, who provides them, who recommends them and who we perceive ourselves to be watching them with, have an influence on our understandings of the value and interest of a film, and therefore how we create the hierarchies that separate art films from other films: 'in making distinctions, in constructing categories of meaning and classificatory systems of order, we not only identify benign maps of cultural order but also produce value and hence create some types of objects and not others'.[6] The concept of art is constantly being created, and artworks *qua* art are always social constructions. This means that art is necessarily a kind of game with a vast array of players with different roles, variable levels of power and a 'weak degree of codification' such that 'the rules of the game are being played for in the playing of the game'.[7] Unlike highly codified games such as professional sports, where there is a minimum consensus around a set of explicit rules, art worlds are extremely porous and the very act of making art responds to and can (re)construct the perceived rules of the game.[8] Importantly, this mention of 'making art' refers to all those who participate in the art world system,

> who confront each other in struggles where the imposition of not only a world view but also a vision of the artworld is at stake, and who, through these struggles, participate in the production of the value of the artist and of art.[9]

In the context of (film) art, the production of value, as well as the designation of art and the artist, are intimately connected and neither obviously precedes the other: 'it is through the competition among the agents with vested interests in the game that the field reproduces endlessly the interest in the game and the belief in the value of the stakes'.[10] Given that the work of art can only be constituted as a work of art when apprehended by a viewer, who has already been exposed and trained on other works of art, the process of art-designation is a circular kind of construction that is continually reconstituting itself anew: 'the player, mindful of the game's meaning and having been created for the game because he was created by it, plays the game and by playing it assures its existence'.[11] Bourdieu's point here is that meaning and value in art can only be properly studied via a social history of the subject, in order to identify the precise 'conditions of the establishment of the specific aesthetic disposition' of the field, here art cinema.[12]

One important function of the art world is then the creation of conventions, which allow for the smooth functioning of the system.[13] While the exact form or content of a film will change, there is always a named director, narrative films have a predictable length, films are shot in a limited number of formats, festivals exist to show off new products, friendly reviewers are provided with copies in advance, exhibitors will show the films in the dark to a broadly silent audience and so on. The predictability, with some changes and evolutions, of these and a thousand other aspects of the process of bringing a film to an audience allows for completely unknown texts to circulate easily within the system, for a first-time director with no industry experience to have their film screened on the other side of the world within months of wrapping up shooting. There is no obligation to adhere to the conventions, but if a film does not (for instance, if it is 800 minutes long, shot with an aspect ratio of 2:1 and requires 3D glasses), its makers will struggle to organise the specialised conditions required to distribute, market and exhibit it at scale, which are already in place for a wide-screen-ratio 90-minute film: 'we can understand any work as the product of a choice between conventional ease and success, and unconventional trouble and lack of recognition'.[14] In addition to such practical conventions around programming, projecting, reviewing, distributing and so on, art worlds 'typically devote considerable attention to trying to decide what is and isn't art, what is and isn't their kind of art, and who is and isn't an artist'.[15] In other words, an important aggregate function of the people who make up the art world is to decide upon the conventions that constitute a work of art. This involves both intermedial and intramedial claims: a reflection both on cinema in relation to other arts, and to the specific aesthetics of cinema as an art.[16]

The most important idea to take away from this brief summary is that a large number of people across the cinema art world are involved in bringing any film, including transgressive art films, to a screen where a viewer can watch it. As such, any discussion of how a film becomes connoted as transgressive, or extreme, must account for the role played by all these different agents within the complex multi-stage process of moving from a filmmaker's idea to its being visible on a screen somewhere. While many accounts of transgression focus so closely on the film text and critical reception that it can seem as though artistic transgression arises from a binary duel between transgressive artists and reactionary commentators or policymakers, it is important to see the transgressive art film as curated and discursively framed well in advance of reception, in its passage through the different nodes of the cinema art world network. Given the inherently collaborative process that filmmaking is (in contrast to a novel or an oil painting, the actual construction of which can be more or less undertaken alone), this way of viewing art worlds is especially pertinent for the cinema art world. Thinking about how films come to be legitimised as transgressive art films, or put another way, how non-art and low-art imagery is recuperated within (high) art cinema, therefore involves thinking about the actions of a wide array of people occupying a variety of roles. This can partially be understood by thinking about how the cinema art world identifies and celebrates innovation and originality, which always involve some transgression, in the sense that they break from previous conventions and disrupt previously established limits of the artform.

*

The centrality of newness and innovation, as well as their corollaries reproduction and replication, to definitions of art has long been established with thinkers as varied as Theodor Adorno, Noel Carroll and Page DuBois all positing novelty as an important feature of art.[17] Especially since Modernism, newness as that which exceeds established conventions has become 'a dynamic force in cultural reproduction – it prevents stagnation by breaking the rule'.[18] Newness and transgression in art are very much connected (see Chapter 1), but it is important to note that the new elements do not arise from some extra-cultural space before being incorporated into culture, 'innovation does not consist in the emergence of something previously hidden, but in the fact that the value of something always already seen and known is re-valued'.[19] Mainstream and high-art newness is mostly not a process of discovery or invention, but of the re-articulation of previously de-valued or marginalised ideas in a new context.[20] Indeed, it has been argued that art cinema is conservative precisely because it only alters what comes either from 'commercial' cinema, maintaining its 'commodity-based structures, relations and practices', or seeking inspiration from more radical avant-garde or political filmmaking, which remains nonetheless relegated to a marginal position within the cinema art world.[21] One can debate the validity of this framing for art cinema's newness in general terms, but when it comes to the images of sex and violence that underpin the transgressiveness of transgressive art films, it is quite clear that body genres – mainly horror and pornography – offer a vast array of images to be re-valued and re-purposed within an art cinema framework. Horror scholars have long complained of the double standards applied to negative affect, with sex, disgust and shock in art films read as subversive and challenging, whilst similar images in horror films are dismissed as titillating or juvenile.[22] In essence though, the cinema art world has shown itself to be remarkably flexible in assimilating previously unknown films and providing audiences the means by which to process otherwise unfamiliar texts,[23] consistently re-purposing material from outside its conventional purview, and elevating it to the status of art. For this reason, following David Andrews, it is pertinent to describe one of art cinema's functions as a 'recovery-and-legitimation machine',[24] both in terms of its ability to elevate tropes from commercial films that cinephiles might otherwise mistrust, and especially in relation to the constant inclusion of violent and sexual imagery, which had up until that point belonged to low-art or non-art genres like gory horror and pornography.

If the new, the unfamiliar and the previously de-valued are integral parts of art cinema, it follows logically that the transgressive must also be an integral element of art cinema. By transgression here, I mean narratives, tropes, themes, actors and especially images, that are not part of art cinema at a particular point in time. In order to find the new, art cinema must transgress its own limits in order to keep moving, evolving and innovating. This is in effect the answer to the question: why would an art world systematically designate as art that which it does not consider to function as art?[25] As Leslie Graves has argued, while art does have a function, discourses around art have evolved in such a way that art status can be conferred upon works that 'fail to meet, and even subvert that function'.[26] Read in this way, certain new artworks do not correspond to contemporaneous understandings of art – they transgress – and then in retrospect, they are bequeathed with artistic status. Most participants in an art world are not transgressing the rules in any meaningful way, they are what Becker calls 'integrated professionals' working entirely within the system and using its available materials and procedures to produce art that fits with that art world's understanding of what art is – these are required within an art system as examples of what that system considers to be (functionally) art.[27] By contrast, transgressive art films are made by 'mavericks', who change some of the conventions of their art world, but nonetheless maintain most of its conventions (e.g. duration of work, place of exhibition, instruments/materials used). Ultimately, 'if the contemporary art world does adapt, then artist and work lose their maverick quality, since the conventions of the world now encompass what was once foreign . . . the maverick becomes the conventional'.[28] Conversely if they fail to be integrated, they will be marginalised, dismissed or ignored:

> anyone is free not to play the game according to the rules, if they accept the risk of being excluded: the risk, to be precise, is to be exiled to the margins of art, as are so many of those who claim the status of artist but have not managed either to play by the rules, or to change them to their advantage.[29]

Becker describes this as a 'kind of half-in, half-out relation between maverick artists and conventional art worlds'.[30] In other words, if one looks at evolutions in an art world at a longer scale, one will see smooth changes over decades with slow shifts from one dominant tendency to another. However, if one looks at the scale of the individual work, that slow shift involves numerous 'transgressive' works that challenge the contemporaneous boundaries of the artistic – encompassing both sides of the boundary in a manner I earlier described as extreme – and are only later accepted as part of the new artistic canon. Transgressive art films are not therefore the exception but the rule of art cinema, which is nourished by this train of non-art/low art recuperated as high art.

In relation to contemporary art, this argument has been made in different ways by philosophers of art, and sociologists of art. Graves presents transgression as part of the solution to a long-running dispute between philosophers of art about whether to define art according to its function, or based on the procedures set up by the art world.[31] Artistic transgression appears to discount functional accounts because on the level of the artwork, it involves designating as 'art', work that does not (currently) fulfil the functions of art. However, if one considers the function of the art world more broadly, rather than the individual artwork, then the very procedures that allow for non-art to be designated as 'art' function to maintain a flourishing, constantly renewed art world that will continue to produce non-transgressive works of art: 'art transgression may be relatively common in art history because it constitutes a valuable, and possibly indispensable, causal mechanism in the creation of future non-transgressive art'.[32] In other words, transgressive artworks pave the way for a reassessment of the value of art within an art world, and thus for waves of new artworks that would previously have been dismissed as non-art or low art, but are now appreciated as (high) art. Not all art can be transgressive or anti-functional on an object level – the recuperation of anti-functional artworks has to lay the groundwork for future works that are functional according to the new rules and therefore can provide status, reputation, admiration and acclaim, not just shock and outrage.[33] One example would be the increasing visibility of sex that shocked and created outrage in transgressive art films like *Romance*, *The Idiots*, *The Brown Bunny* or *Baise-moi*, but laid the ground for the admiration of films such as *Blue is the Warmest Colour*, *Love* and *Shame*. Transgressive art films play an important role in preparing the terrain for future non-transgressive films.

In her sociological analysis of contemporary art, and partially following Bourdieu, Nathalie Heinich identifies transgression as a game played by artists, who try to produce work that is optimally transgressive: sufficiently novel to be perceived as going beyond the contemporaneous boundaries of art, but not so far as to be considered 'off-side', outside the rules of the game, too far.[34] Her analysis, just like Graves's, pertains very specifically to contemporary art, and so is not fully analogous to cinema, but her positioning of transgression as central to understanding the development of art worlds is very useful to my discussion of cinema here. Heinich argues that in contemporary art, transgression is no longer a technical matter, but an ontological one: it has become a decisive factor in defining the genre of contemporary art, rather than simply an evaluative criteria of certain works within the genre.[35] Contemporary art is a game of transgression, reaction and integration in which each player in the game (artists, institutions, commentators, audiences) play their role of erecting boundaries, being shocked and outraged, discussing and debating, and ultimately accepting and appreciating the latest novelty as it passes from transgressive to canonic, or rejecting its particular transgressions and consigning it (for now) to invisibility.[36] The game-like nature of this process is made clear when artists who are ignored during their lifetimes are re-evaluated after their deaths, as their transgressions become, at a later date, those which the art world chooses to integrate and celebrate. These boundary transgressions should importantly not be confused with an absence of norms: the exact limits may not be easily definable, but the process of defining which transgressions are acceptable is highly normative.[37] While we should always be wary of any easy aesthetic mapping of tendencies in one artform onto another,[38] I propose that this analysis provides a useful framework for considering transgressive art films' role in the cinema art world.

The most straightforward example is the depiction of sex. I will return to the question of horror later. Sexual imagery and transgression have been linked since the beginning of cinema, with different cinematic institutions weighing in on the acceptability of depictions of sex and sexuality at almost all points in cinema history. Even before the coming together of an idea of 'art cinema' or 'film art' as a coherent and popularly acknowledged concept, and even when many saw cinema strictly as a form of entertainment,[39] there was still a cinema art world that developed a collective idea of what belonged within and without its purview. Regardless of the art-worthiness of many films exhibited publicly for at least the first half-century of cinema's existence, pornography remained separate, and until the softening of laws around pornography and obscenity from the 1950s and 1960s onwards (depending on the country) circulated illegally, being shown mostly in private houses, and therefore remaining distinct from the distribution and exhibition networks of publicly viewable films.[40] Each time a more revealing depiction of flirtation, kissing or sex was included in a film, this was a transgression of the norms around sexual imagery established by the cinema art world that might change the rules or be exiled to the margins. Indeed, more sexually liberal French New Wave films were often marketed in the USA as, or together with, sexploitation and B-genre films, rather than explicitly as art films, as they are now.[41] This was a point where sensuous nudity and eroticised images of (especially female) bodies had not been fully established as part of the art canon in the USA. In the transition from Europe, where the French New Wave's art credentials had been firmly established,[42] to the USA where they had not, there was a frequent marginalisation of these films to the realm of low-art and softcore pornography because of their sexual imagery.[43] It is also important to note that these decisions are not always made unilaterally by censors but could be part of production (adding/removing erotic content), distribution (choosing/refusing to distribute), exhibition (refusal to screen certain content, only screening films in B-run venues, removing certain scenes or even adding erotic inserts depending on the venue) and reception (defending a film as artistic, or denigrating/ignoring a low-art product). Films that shocked and outraged for their sexual content were playing the transgression game, attempting to have their transgressions accepted so that there could be calculated outrage and their integration into the canon. From *The Kiss* to *I'm No Angel*, *The Lovers*, *In the Realm of the Senses*, *Romance* and *The Daughters of Fire*, each of these have integrated elements of sexual explicitness that would not previously have been acceptable within art cinema, always risking being denigrated as pornographic or unworthy of art status, but now being established to a greater or lesser degree as canonic film texts. Their transgressions were recognised as such by the cinema art world, and they were welcomed into the realm of art cinema despite containing imagery that did not correspond to previously held ideas of what constitutes film art.

Regardless of what one may think of transgressive art films, they have been central to the continuing development and renewal of cinema, as evolving ideas and discourses about the nature of film art are oriented in relation to these films, which stand out in a vast field of cinematic images. This integration or recuperation does not signal in itself a particular appreciation for these films by those who work within the cinema art world: the cinema art world is not 'an especially "benevolent" or "tolerant" format. The special permission at work here is a matter of institutional machinery rather than altruism.'[44] Indeed, as we shall see later, these films are frequently disliked by many people involved in cinema, but it is the fact that they are distributed, exhibited and discussed within the framework of the art film that is important, not whether audiences actually like them. As I have demonstrated throughout this book, this also means that films that are recognised as transgressive art films can be ethically and politically rather dubious. Scholars and critics of traditionally low-art genres often lament the unfairness of these mechanisms, suggesting that they show a lack of awareness within the cinema art world of the depths and variety of films within the genres from which art cinema poaches its transgressive tropes,[45] and while this is undoubtedly true, it rather misses the function that the violence or sex is playing within the cinema art world. Incorporating a cannibal film like *Trouble Every Day* into art cinema is not a judgement of the film as the greatest horror film ever, but rather constitutes a shocking inclusion of certain horror tropes (gore, violence, eroticised bloodlust) within a film that is nonetheless recognisably 'arty' in its slow pace, elliptical storyline, muted screenplay, ambiguous characters and philosophical pretensions, to the extent that it is frequently maligned by horror fans for failing to live up to audience expectations of a horror film. Scholars of transgressive art and film also sometimes lament how critics, for want of a means of explaining morally dubious or even indefensible works of art, turn transgression into an aesthetic end in itself, rather than a means to some other political or ethical end.[46] While one might sympathise with complaints about this rather lazy shorthand to avoid detailed discussion of a work's precise transgressions, these critics have in fact inadvertently pointed to the crux of the matter: to be transgressive is to be art. If a film is being widely discussed as a 'transgressive film' (and not just as transgressive in some imprecise way), then it has by definition been incorporated as a transgressive art film by the cinema art world.

I will explain in greater detail what this means using the example of *A Serbian Film*, one of the most contentious general-release art-horror films of recent years because of the sheer amount of sexual violence, gore and child abuse that populates its images. Importantly for my discussion, films must be recuperated through the complex mechanisms of the cinema art world, in order to reframe the non-artistic as worthy of artistic expression, and be recognised as transgressive art films. While some films are retrospectively re-evaluated as art, not having successfully transgressed on their release, many films are legitimised 'from the start, for they were produced to succeed at art cinema's most respected institutions'.[47] In order to fully grasp how particular films are positioned as transgressive, we have to examine the entire process from the initial idea and funding, all the way through to the inclusion on university syllabi, and in academic books like this one. Given the space restrictions, I will focus here on three elements in this process: festivals, distribution, and intellectual reception by critics and scholars.[48] This is not intended to be exhaustive, as it only touches the surface of the different stages, where artistic value can be ascribed, but it provides a clear idea of how to conceptualise the idea of the transgressive art film that is transferable to other parts of the process.

*

Film festivals and festival screenings mostly serve a cultural function, rather than an economic function, allowing for the accrual of symbolic capital rather than necessarily economic capital (although these can be linked). Today the concept of art cinema is mostly linked to film festivals, and therefore any discussion of how film art is defined and how non-art or low art comes to be legitimised as (high) art must contend with festival organisers, programmers and funders.[49] Festivals operate as a key node in the chain of film development, processing new films, reframing them for broader engagement, consumption and discovery,[50] and bringing together many of the key agents within the art cinema network:

> Journalists write in discursive categories such as the scandal film largely because festivals select and exhibit such productions ... In turn, programmers choose them partly because filmmakers create them.... Aspiring filmmakers hope to make their mark with the press attention that extreme cinema has traditionally elicited; festival scouts and subsidy bodies seek or even solicit these films.[51]

While there are good reasons why festivals might engage with transgressive art films, especially commercial ones given the free publicity that a scandal can give,[52] they should primarily be seen as the producers of cultural value, continuing the legacy of their predecessors – film societies and film clubs – by overtly (re)examining, (re)producing and (re)modelling notions of art and artistry. In this context, transgressive art films inevitably play a central role in the identity and programming of film festivals, given how important they are in the continual production of artistic innovation and novelty. While some accounts of film festivals seem to see controversies around 'scandal films' as a fleeting cliché that festivals might perhaps one day grow out of, transgressive art films are actually at the heart of film festivals' claim to authority as tastemakers and cultural arbiters. It is not the festivals that are legitimised by the presence of art films on their programme, rather films become art films partly because they are on the programme.

As scholarly analyses of film festivals have shown, as well as Mattias Frey's interviews of festival organisers, festivals see themselves as establishing and directing world cinema and 'actively *challenging* tastes'.[53] This involves curating non-transgressive films – both films that come with a pre-established pedigree through the reputations of the director, producer or actors, and others that provide new ways of using form and content that has already been established as artistic – and enlarging the purview of art cinema through the inclusion of transgressive art films. The latter category involves actively constructing and reconstructing what is considered to be artistic, and legitimising material that would not otherwise be considered artistic under the guise of novelty, challenge and variety. While individual transgressive films will be chosen for different reasons, festival directors and programmers mostly frame their choices in terms of artistic or aesthetic quality.[54] In other words, if they choose to program a film, it means that they consider it, at that point in time, to be artistic, often adopting the same rhetoric as the filmmakers, who are also trying to frame their challenging images as artistic.[55] While these claims might appear defensive, they are in effect performative utterances, bestowing the status of art upon the films they are defending. Such is the institutional power of the film festival that its representatives are not simply rationalising their programming; instead, their programming is legitimising, as art films, that which was previously marginalised as gore, horror, pornography, trash or other such low-art genres. As Cindy Hing-Yuk Wong observes, 'these are hardly mainstream cinema materials . . . But they were validated at festivals by their screenings, by the awards they received, and by the debates they provoked as not belonging to the mainstream, celebrating the unbounded quality of art.'[56] This process is nothing new, with salacious images of sex and drugs in *L'avventura*, *Blow-up* and *The Lovers* being legitimised in much the same way. Given that newness is integral to any contemporary artform, programmers will always be seeking new material from outside the current notion of art to legitimise as transgressive, and thereby expand the notion of (film) art.

In many cases, the festival programmers describe their most controversial decisions in terms of 'risk',[57] notably the risks of more conservative funders pulling out if associated with sexual or violent content, of censorship boards stepping in to cut or ban particular films, and at the most extreme end, of facing criminal prosecution for screening a film,[58] although commercial or financial risk as a result of film choice is not usually a problem.[59] This being said, it is important not to frame these decisions as a battle between exhibitors and censors, as this positions censors as an arbiter separate from, and superior to, the festival's undertakings. Rather, these complex interactions amongst programmers and with censorship boards are precisely negotiations about what counts as art, what can be recuperated or legitimised, and what remains beyond the pale. A festival's choice to pursue the screening, despite potential negative reactions, is both a recognition of a film's non-art or low-art status, and a decision to frame a film as a transgressive art film. The fact that the decision is considered 'risky' rather than completely unthinkable,[60] demonstrates that the programmers have understood that a film is only marginally rather than maximally transgressive, and that it is a suitable candidate for pushing back the boundaries of art once again. Moreover, the perceived risk changes the further you go into festival season as choices made at the most prestigious festivals, especially Cannes but also Berlin and Venice, have a disproportionate trickle-down impact, with the programming of transgressive films becoming progressively less risky throughout the season, as a consensus develops about the legitimacy of a particular film as a transgressive art film.[61] The aggregate of all these 'risky' choices, cements the status of the previous non-art or low-art film as (high) art, and therefore as a transgressive art film not just in the eyes of a particular festival's programming team, but with sufficient consensus, within the cinema art world as a whole.

Taking a look at the system as a whole, it is also important to note that, while the programmers might present their work as seemingly outside the system of production or censorship, reacting to but not intervening in these processes, their choices and aesthetic dispositions have already been taken into account when the films were being made.[62] Given the importance for future success of being entered into competition at major film festivals, or winning an award, 'certain aesthetic dispositions regarding cinema are continuously confirmed, and thus filmmakers are predisposed to produce films *in* certain traditions and *for* the festival exhibition circuit'.[63] This becomes particularly clear when you consider institutions like the Marché du Film at Cannes, or the European Film Market (EFM) connected to the Berlin Film Festival, which screen films at various stages of production, and therefore are especially open to adapting to the needs of the market and of film festival programmers and juries.[64] In other words, films are produced to succeed according to particular criteria, and given the importance of scandal films for film festivals, it is inevitable that films will be produced precisely with the aim of being controversial. One could argue that concepts of artistic integrity are partially sidelined in this situation, with filmmakers adapting their projects less in relation to their ideas about art, and more in terms of what they think funders and festival juries want.[65] We should, however, see these as one and the same thing: decisions about what to fund, what to include in the festival programme and what to award prizes to, are processes of art-designation, rather than only adjacent to them. Given that scandal and controversy at an art film festival are synonymous with achieving the status of art, and involve much added publicity, not bestowed upon most art films ploughing the already-accepted definitions of art, creating a film that manages to be controversial means that it is operating within the limits of art, even if also partially outside them. In terms of the strategic reasons for doing this, it is worth noting that many filmmakers have capitalised on the name recognition as auteurs, achieved through scandalous films, in order to later pursue less transgressive work. Examples might include Catherine Breillat's turn to period drama and fairy tales with *Bluebeard* and *Sleeping Beauty*, Michael Haneke's Palme d'Or-winning *Amour*, and Gaspar Noé's similar shift to the question of old age in *Vortex*.[66] Their earlier transgressive art films were made to be artistic in a particular way, as transgressive art films show them to be imaginative, innovative, daring mavericks, who then have the name recognition to garner funding for other potentially non-transgressive projects.

While *A Serbian Film* had a rather more tumultuous passage through the film-festival circuit than most transgressive art films, the description above fits well with its integration into art cinema. It was screened at art-film festivals such as Cannes, South by South West Festival (SXSW) and

Raindance Festival (London), and a number of specialist horror and fantasy festivals: Fantasporto (Porto, where it won the Special Jury Prize), Brussels International Fantastic Film Festival, Fantasia Festival (Montreal), Fantaspoa (Porto Alegre), Sitges Film Festival, and prior to censorship interventions, was due to play at FrightFest (London) and the Rio Fantastic Festival. While it may have always been expected to play at horror festivals, the numerous festival inclusions already frame it as a good horror film, and Cannes, SXSW and Raindance gave it artistic credibility by including it in their line-ups. These set the stage for the issues it would face with distributors and exhibitors, with some very keen to collaborate, and others creating problems for the filmmakers. Complete consensus about the film's qualities and value was never likely, but the international recognition by these major art festivals propelled the film from its position as yet another gory sexualised film, to the status of a transgressive art film. Its transformed potential was signalled clearly by its initial inability to find a domestic distributor, perhaps because of a historical aversion towards genre and horror films in Serbia (and in former Yugoslavia),[67] until it had achieved international recognition, and therefore was no longer considered to be solely a generic horror film, but also a work of film art. While distribution has its own dynamics, the prior positioning of films by film festivals is integral to how distributors are then able to market them to a wider audience.

*

Anyone can make a film, but getting films out to the public is a specialist, strategic exercise.[68] Distribution is about visibility and invisibility, what is not distributed cannot be seen or known, it cannot be appreciated or gain renown, it cannot gain the reputation required to be officially transgressive. Many films are made, but only very few have the potential to shape culture, and become a part of our shared cultural imaginary; the circulation or withholding of films by distributors plays a key role therefore in guiding which films are in a position to shape the boundaries of film art.[69] As such, 'distribution is a determinant moment when the economic *and* cultural value of a commodity is produced'.[70] Distributors facilitate the movement of films from producers and film festivals, to exhibitors, and the broader public. In the broadest of definitions, 'intellectual property attorneys, acquisitions executives, festival programmers, television schedulers, web technicians, and marketing assistants all could be identified as part of the distribution business'.[71] They are an integral channel for transmitting to wider audiences any idea of artfulness or transgressiveness accrued in film festival spaces, which although highly mediatised, exhibit films to only a tiny minority of viewers. Distributors prime audiences, critics and institutions through TV, radio, and social media appearances from directors and actors. Strategically chosen reviewers and fan sites are given previews, while retailers and exhibitors are provided with tailored merchandise and marketing materials. DVD covers are designed and video-on-demand (VoD) pages are given images, captions and summaries. Social media campaigns are launched to create hype and expectation. All these impact on how the film is received by audiences.

Distributors construct their audiences in hierarchies in order to transmit the desired message to the desired targets, allowing films to be framed in different ways to different audiences:

> Distribution is the construction of difference; initially in distinguishing producer from audience, buyer from seller, and in a networked world further distinguishing and dividing populations by their temporal and spatial proximity to the economic power and political economy that is increasingly centralized, not at the site of production, but on the terrains of exchange.... Distribution is also the material ground of cultural dominance and political power.[72]

Distributors have a great deal of power in shaping how films are perceived by audiences, but at the same time must negotiate multiple 'layers of constraint', from practical industry, censorship, cinema and their own financial limitations, through to the framing of films by film festivals and critics reporting on them there.[73] Given that any widely released film must inevitably make accommodations in order to be seen, distributors must also deal with tensions between the artistic ambitions of directors and producers, as well as the financial or commercial aims of funders and exhibitors.

In part, distributors do not need to define their transgressive art films as art, as festivals have already done substantial work in legitimising films, the rights for which distributors vie at festival markets.[74] Moreover, there is a sense in which films made to be transgressive at film festivals already prefigure distribution if they wish to be successful beyond a small circle of appreciative viewers. As Becker argues, 'artists produce what the distribution system can and will carry' because that is the only way for artists to succeed within the system.[75] Nonetheless, while prizes and entries into festival competitions might be highlighted as part of the marketing material (especially the bigger festivals), most film viewers do not follow festivals closely and therefore are reliant on distributors and critics (on which more below) to repackage the films and communicate their (artistic) value to the consumer. While distributors undertake a vast array of different tasks, two interconnected elements are of particular interest for transgressive art films: the reputation of the distributor, and the marketing of individual films.

Distributors of art cinema often present themselves in their film choices, and in their rhetoric, both positively in terms of exclusivity, intellectualism and cinephilia, and negatively in terms of non-commercialism. Given that distributors are private companies and generally do not benefit from charity status or government funding like festivals and producers, this can lead to a difficult tightrope to walk for arthouse distributors, who must negotiate between commercial and artistic constraints, in order to bring films they appreciate to market, whilst keeping a viable business going. Within art cinema one can point to distributors like Criterion Collection or Mubi, who have become central to popular access, and therefore to understandings of 'quality film' and 'film art'.[76] As Daniel Herbert notes, this curatorial position can end up having a significant impact on how viewers conceive of art cinema, most clearly in their categorisations, with newer starters in the market often adopting the typologies instituted in well-known distributors' catalogues.[77] It is easy to see then how distribution by a well-known art cinema distributor such as Criterion, Kino or Facets, or inclusion within particular categories that they stock, can be decisive in how viewers encounter a film, which inevitably primes their reaction to it.

As an example of this in the context of art/porn boundaries, the erotic film *Ink Is My Blood* is catalogued both on Mubi and on XConfessions, an adult subscription cinema site. Both sites feature the same description of the film as an exploration of 'artistry and eroticism', but the style and surrounding images and text on each site are otherwise quite distinct. On XConfessions, the film is given tags such as 'oral sex', 'couples' and 'heterosexual', and it is explicitly described as a 'porn movie'. If one scrolls down slightly, stills from the film show scenes of visible masturbation, penetration and nakedness, while subscriber comments declare 'one of the hottest on the site!', 'best porn film' and 'the sex is amazing'.[78] The tags, images and comments all code the film as pornography, albeit artistic and beautiful. By contrast, on Mubi, the tags are 'erotica', 'animation' and 'short', and it is given a national origin ('United States'). If one scrolls down, photos of the director, cinematographer, editor and executive producers are shown. Moreover, given that it was not currently available to view when I looked at it, I was directed instead to watch Agnès Varda's *Salut les Cubains*.[79] The categories here are focused on film form rather than type of sex, the filmmakers are highlighted rather than sexual stills, and the comparison is with Varda, rather than other porn films. The distributor has transformed the film from a porn film with artistic flair, into an erotic art film with a lineage extending to the French New

Wave. Indeed, without prior knowledge of Erika Lust's work, viewers on Mubi would not even know to expect long scenes of visible masturbation, oral sex, penetration and ejaculation, and would likely also interpret such scenes quite differently to those accessing the film on XConfessions. Lust's work has yet to achieve the cultural cachet of explicit art films like *9 Songs*, *Love* or *Nymphomaniac*, but its presentation on Mubi certainly pushes it in that direction. This is nonetheless a good example of how no one part of the art world can unilaterally raise a film, or a kind of film, to the status of transgressive art film. *Ink Is My Blood*'s transgressions may well be recuperated by Mubi, but without the preceding artistic framing by festivals, and the subsequent framing by censorship boards, critics and scholars, there is not the critical consensus across the cinema art world to legitimise these images, and bring them into the space of the art film.

A film's eligibility to be distributed through institutions plugged into the film festival circuit remains necessary to a film's artistic status, even if it is not sufficient alone to bestow such status.[80] Given the borderline and potentially risky nature of transgressive art films, specific distributors step in, who specialise in genre films, exploitation and other traditionally denigrated films, or particular national cinemas, and who are able to bridge the gap between film art, and low art or non-art. Extreme cinema tends to be distributed by a limited cadre of small distributors, such as Tartan Films, Optimum Films, Third Window Films, Invincible Pictures and Artsploitation Films, some of whom do not last very long and are often partially self-financed rather than serious commercially viable entities.[81] Given that these distributors are not solely seen as being in it for the money, and also, by feeding the films to niche audiences, do not have to contend as much with unhappy mainstream audiences, they can develop a sense of 'authenticity', whereby audiences come to associate films with particular distributors, in contrast to bigger films where audiences likely have no idea who distributed them. At the same time, tight margins and uncertain returns make the distribution of extreme films, some of which might attain the status of transgressive art films, an especially risky business,[82] making personal taste and individual distributor predilections about the value of particular kinds of film very important to the success of business decisions. Much like with the question of risk mentioned by film festival programmers, distributors' management of risk is again part of the construction of the transgressive art film. Refusals to distribute films, as happened in the case of *A Serbian Film*,[83] are part of distributors gauging, and judging, the artistic quality of a film, and trying to work out exactly what can be legitimised at that point as art, and what remains too transgressive to be recuperated that year.

Distributors such as Artsploitation and Tartan Films, with their series 'Tartan Asia Extreme', take this further, highlighting the transgressive nature of their catalogue in their very names, which adds the idea of extremity or exploitation to films at the distribution stage, even as it might not have been part of the film's identity at the production stage. Indeed, '"Asia Extreme" is a distribution/marketing term rather than a production category . . . some of the films were released retroactively and categorized as such after the launch of the label'.[84] Tartan were so successful in raising the profile of East Asian cinema in Europe and the USA, that they ultimately provided the framing for several national cinemas – South Korean, Taiwanese, Japanese, Singaporean – even as they distributed an eclectic mix of non-extreme films under the label. Tartan's dominance within East Asian distribution in Europe, and the USA for a period, meant that they effectively imposed a form of 'genrification' on an otherwise heterogeneous group of films.[85] With the festival and critical success of *The Isle* and *Audition*, they were able to present some of their more generic horror films to Western audiences as artistic, substantially through association with their distributor brand.

Beyond the simple choice to distribute a film and associate themselves with it by including it in their catalogue, distributors also decide how the film will be presented in terms of the images, design and descriptions attached to the film in adverts, in reviews, on DVD covers, in trailers and in various other forms of marketing. Here the images, their styling, the title font, the festival logos, the descriptions, named actors/directors/producers all come together to guide potential viewers to read the film in a particular way. Copious blood likely signals horror, a naked couple likely signals erotica, snow or a jungle point to the film's main location, and so on. Inclusion of festival honours, credits for all the main filmmaking roles, or quotations from well-known critics/newspapers likely signal a film's art credentials. In the case of transgressive art films, distributors often seek to emphasise both the non-art and art aspects of these films, recognising their straddling of the boundaries, acknowledging their non-art or low-art qualities to appeal to genre crowds (interested more in horror, violence, and/or sex) as well as their art qualities to attract edgy arthouse audiences. DVD covers and other marketing imagery often combine eroticised imagery of the female leads in a state of undress (see *Baise-moi, Romance, Irreversible, 9 Songs, Clip, Intimacy*) with a quotation from higher-brow outlets such as *The Guardian* or *The New York Times*, and a plot description that focuses on its transgressive nature, thus again highlighting the (high) art and low-art/non-art qualities of the film.

In the case of *A Serbian Film*, one of the DVD covers includes a red-filtered image of the protagonist screaming on a white background, with blood dripping from the edges of the red image, coding the film as gory horror. At the same time, the red image is in the shape of Serbia, the country, emphasising the film's national origins, the title is preceded by 'a film by Srdjan Spasojević' and the full actor/producer/cinematographer/editor details are given at the bottom, suggesting an auteurist art project. Other versions emphasise its censorship, describing it as 'uncut' or listing countries where it has been banned, indicating its transgressive nature. In this way, once again, the film is recuperated as an art film, even as its gory, violent, sexually violent, hardcore-horror connections are also made clear.[86]

*

The third illustrative element of the cinema art world is film scholarship, and other forms of intellectual engagement with cinema. As I have shown in this book, there is a substantial amount of scholarly work that has been done on transgressive art films, especially close reading of the films as texts, but also analysis of actual audiences through surveys and internet fora, detailed discussion of the (often spurious) responses from the tabloid press, and examinations of paracinematic paraphernalia. This is useful scholarship, but as I have noted throughout this book, this research tends to create the sense of a binary debate between embracers and cynics, between progressive scholars and reactionary critics/censors, whilst also focusing on individual films. I have argued forcefully that an analysis of film form is key to thinking about transgressive art films, but if we want to grasp how such formal elements become legitimised at the level of the cinema art world as a whole, we must also move out further, not just to the level of reception, but to a scale that brings discourse, distribution and reception into focus. Zooming out from the scale of individual texts and individual audience responses allows us to see that the precise arguments of critics and scholars do not matter as much as the quantity of their interventions, in the legitimisation of low-art and non-art imagery.

One important point that is often missed in discussions around transgressive art films is that the very fact that substantial discussion is taking place about a film in newspapers, and between scholars, is indicative of a decision having already been made about its artistic qualities. Even if many commentators were very critical of films like *Irreversible*, *A Serbian Film* or *Baise-moi*, every major and many minor newspapers featured reviews of these films, sometimes multiple reviews to allow for a variety of interventions, whilst they took up significant space in specialist film publications. We can see this most explicitly with the oppositional reviews of *Irreversible* in cinephile magazines *Sight and Sound* (UK) and *Positif* (France), which heavily foregrounded the debate, and increased the quantity of reviews with their multiple-page spreads devoted to the film. Despite disliking *A Serbian Film* intensely, *The Guardian, TimeOut, Radio Times, Financial Times* and *Sky Cinema* all ran reviews of it, and these were often given to well-known critics like Peter Bradshaw, Philip French, Nigel Floyd, Nigel Andrews and in the US, Kim Newman, A. O. Scott and Laura Kern, rather than thrown into a compilation piece by a staff writer as is often the case for minor films. Moreover, if we take *The Guardian* as an example of *A Serbian Film*'s reception, it ran at least six separate articles on the film: three reviews, one article on its inclusion in the Raindance Festival 2010, and two news items on its censorship.[87] This contrasts sharply with the dearth of reviews of other violent films censored in the UK at a similar period such as *Murder-Set-Pieces*, *Grotesque* or *Hate Crime*. If there was an article on these films, which there often was not, these films were generally mentioned only in brief articles about censorship or focus groups, and often without even a named author for the article, rather than receiving a proper review.[88]

In effect, the question is not about what reviewers say, 'much more decisive is the sheer *amount* of coverage: the more exposure, whether positive or negative, the more value a film accrues'.[89] This tallies with the mantra that the Cannes Film Festival has adopted in relation to journalists since its inception: the more the better.[90] By virtue of being reported on as films, rather than news stories, the news outlets are signalling that this ostensibly low-art film should be taken seriously; and by receiving an in-depth review, these well-known professional reviewers are bestowing upon the film a credibility that other censored films did not receive. On its own, a single review does not symbolise anything in particular – any reviewer can ultimately end up reviewing any random film – but there are thousands of films produced every year, many of which will never receive a single review, never mind numerous considered reviews from senior reviewers at major newspapers. Moreover, there is always a certain tendency towards groupthink or at least consensus-building amongst reviewers, especially at film festivals, where the number of films to see and judge can be overwhelming. As Marijke de Valck has noted, 'a common fear of film critics is the possibility of missing or not-recognizing a masterpiece, leading to a phenomenon where some critics are influenced by their peers', checking in with each other informally to make sure that their readings are more or less in line with the general consensus.[91] In such a context, the choice to emphasise a particular film does not stem from an individual reviewer's isolated feelings, and there is also a tendency for reviews to converge around the consensus as the festival season progresses. A good example of the changing fortunes of certain films was

Twentynine Palms, which was generally disparaged at earlier festivals for its reliance on long sex scenes and graphic sexual violence, with later reviews becoming progressively more positive as its transgressive art status became cemented by more and more reviewers.[92] Film criticism is another stage in how the cinema art world legitimises non-art and low art as worthy of consideration as (high) art, even if they get just one star out of five. Indeed, even Roger Ebert's infamously vindictive description of *The Brown Bunny* as the worst film in the history of the Cannes Film Festival,[93] was implicitly acknowledging its place in the film-art canon. Even as Ebert thought it a terrible film, he was always saying it was a terrible art film, and thereby acknowledging that this boring blow-job was an artistic blow-job, unlike any of the myriad oral-sex videos one might find on the internet.

Scholars and other film intellectuals support these designations of artistry in a variety of ways. Most visibly, this occurs when members of the film industry come together to protest against the censorship of particular films. When *A Serbian Film* was banned in Brazil, a group of cinephiles, film societies and trade unions campaigned against this perceived impingement on freedom of speech and artistic expression.[94] After the banning of *Baise-moi*, Claire Denis, Catherine Breillat and exhibitor Marin Karmitz engaged in protests outside the cinema and launched a petition, with newspapers writing major features about the scandal, and *Libération* even setting up a web page to document the debates.[95] As horror scholars often lament, no one comes out to defend the marginalisation, dismissal and censorship of films like *The Bunny Game* or *Murder-Set-Pieces*. I contend that there are two reasons that demonstrate the interconnected process of art-designation within the cinema art world. Firstly, it is because they had not been framed as art by the parts of the process preceding the exhibition stage (production, festivals, distribution, marketing). Secondly, it is the very lack of reaction from critics, exhibitors, scholars and other art filmmakers that cements their status as low art or non-art, and prevents its elevation to the domain of art cinema.

Beyond simply the quantity of contributions to discussions about transgressive art films, there is also a role played by a certain politicisation of a film, that is, a reading of a film in political terms thereby assigning it a serious and overt message that mere entertainment would not possess. While this dichotomy between seriousness and entertainment is generally acknowledged to be unhelpful, ascribing a film with a clear political message allows it to fit much more easily within two key parts of art film discourse: auteurism and national specificity.[96] Studies of *A Serbian Film* have shown that it does not lend itself easily to an allegorical reading of recent Serbian history without any contextual knowledge of the film, especially the explanatory preface added to the beginning of the film after issues with censorship boards, distributors and exhibitors, which was not available to the many viewers who sourced it uncut online.[97] However, with the film's title explicitly emphasising the national context, and the director always framing the film in interviews as 'a diary of our own molestation by the Serbian government',[98] a claim repeated by most reviewers, even if just to dispute or ridicule it, directorial intent and country of origin were central to most discussions of *A Serbian Film* in the mainstream press. Although it has long been critiqued, the idea of the director as the auteur of a film remains central to any popular conception of art cinema, just as there has been a long tendency to conflate art cinema and national cinema to the extent that 'representations of locality often ground claims on art film seriousness'.[99] The repeated presentation of Spasojević as a nationalist auteur is therefore a further help in elevating *A Serbian Film* discursively to the status of art, much like critics and scholars have done with Ruggero Deodato, Mario Bava and Dario Argento as Italian horror or *giallo* directors.

Just as critics play a role in applying aesthetic systems to specific art works, so do academic scholars provide the systems that make and justify classifications.[100] In this way, scholars partially function as tastemakers in a comparable way to critics, operating as expert intermediaries between the film product and mass distribution, adding and producing various forms of value.[101] In this case, quantity of inclusion functions just like in newspaper reviews, but on a slower scale. For instance, at the time of writing, I was able to find a total of over twenty-five monographs, academic articles and book chapters that include detailed discussion of *A Serbian Film*, covering a variety of approaches to the film: reception and audience studies,[102] close reading,[103] theoretical analyses,[104] discussions about exhibition and distribution,[105] with several of these explicitly reflecting on the film's status as art,[106] or situating it in the context of other Balkan films already acknowledged as art films.[107] Implicitly, such varied interest, especially in close reading and close theoretical analysis, suggests a richness to the film, normally associated with art cinema. By comparison, horror or porn films not recuperated as artistic tend either to be little studied, examined only within specific journals such as *Horror Studies* or *Porn Studies* rather than more general cultural or film-studies journals, or only included in survey pieces that consider the film in broad cultural terms, rather than necessarily as worthy of closer individual attention. Moreover, the very fact that the film is subject to reception studies reaffirms its artistic rather than low-art/non-art status, as these kinds of studies skew heavily towards canonical films rather than unknown or ignored films[108] when not discussing hugely successful mainstream films and series.[109] Even discussions of censorship often focus on the censorship of films now considered transgressive art films, marginalising those which remain low-art/non-art.[110] This collective attention not only reacts to what has been designated as artistic prior to exhibition but is also part of the art-designation process.

This scholarly interest inevitably then feeds into the curricula and the choices that academics make about what to teach and discuss in lectures. While courses can be taught on all kinds of films, the focus is normally on films and theories that are considered to have value (however that might be defined), which tends to exclude significant emphasis on low art/non-art, as well as on expanding the student's horizons, which does involve unusual, less-known, challenging and transgressive films. Through curricula, degree programmes and even departments, 'universities can preserve and disseminate knowledge of cultural content while simultaneously bestowing legitimacy on that content by its very inclusion'.[111] The valorisation of previously non-art or low-art films therefore both forms and challenges conceptions of which older films might have artistic value, and primes students to be open to recognising particular kinds of images as potentially artistic in the future. This can be highly dependent on a particular researcher's tastes and values. As Laura Hubner notes about her own curriculum choices, following Bourdieu in directly linking class to taste and ascribed value, 'recent cultural and class mobility within Higher Education in the UK has made it possible for those of us who were once young fans of 1970s trash and B-movie horror, for example, to now be teaching in universities'.[112]

Indeed, as Bourdieu has argued, class and education are at the core of how artistic value is ascribed, given that art has no ontological quality, but is inherently phenomenological and sociological:

> Since the work of art only exists as such to the extent that it is perceived, or in other words, deciphered, it goes without saying that the satisfaction attached to this perception – whether it be a matter of purely aesthetic enjoyment or of more indirect gratification, such as the *effect of distinction* – are only accessible to those who are disposed to appropriate them because they *attribute a value to them*, it being understood that they can do this only if they have the means to appropriate them.[113]

We must be taught the skills and given the means in order to be able to evaluate films, to distinguish them in such a way that art as a very concept arises. Explaining, justifying and embracing one ideological paradigm of art over another is precisely where academics and universities play a central role.[114]

Returning to the comparison with critics, academics participate in the construction of conceptual frameworks about the nature of art, the value of particular kinds of films and images, the construction of the canon, as well as the production of 'consumers capable of knowing and recognizing the work of art as such'.[115] This therefore always involves a simultaneous policing, and challenging, of the limits of art, which both reacts to, and produces, particular divisions between high-art and low-art/non-art film, the boundary between which is, by definition, the terrain of the transgressive art film.

*

This discussion of film festivals, distribution, and critical and scholarly reception gives insight into the processes along the cinema pipeline that produce transgressive art films. It demonstrates the myriad ways in which low-art/non-art features are integrated into the domain of art, in a collective process that has no central organising figure. Each agent along the process is able to make their own decisions, and indeed many festivals and cinemas chose not to screen *A Serbian Film*. There is no need, however, for complete consensus across the cinema art world for controversy to arise, there simply needs to be a critical mass of consensus through the right kind of funding, festival screenings, distribution, exhibition and critical/scholarly discussion for a new kind of non-art/low art to be designated as art. As I have shown, actions such as refusal and reversing decisions (such as FrightFest being forced to censor *A Serbian Film*, and therefore reversing their decision to screen it) do not undermine the overall status of a film, but instead contribute to elevating a film to transgressive-art-film status. What undermines a film's potential to attain transgressive art film status is disinterest. It does not matter what value is attached to a sexually explicit or violent film by critics, scholars and programmers; it matters that they engage with it. In doing so they legitimise the film and expand the domain of art film, making it evolve. The films considered transgressive at the time of their release become non-transgressive parts of the canon over time, and find themselves years later in university syllabi, and in books such as this one. Similarly, the filmmakers who find themselves at the centre of a scandal due to the transgressive nature of their film, may go on to create non-transgressive work with their new-found or reasserted artistic status.

Returning to some of the key issues raised at the beginning of the book, this chapter has argued that transgressive art films do not arise organically, nor are they external to the world of art cinema. The language of 'risk' used by festivals, distributors and exhibitors seems to suggest that transgression operates outside the art world's control, and the coordinated outrage of conservative media outlets gives the impression that transgression is surprising and unpredictable. Instead, we should see transgressive art films as actively produced by and for the cinema art world, which requires the disruptive and novel qualities of such films to constantly renew cinema, keeping it innovative, and ensuring that cinema is consistently evolving and changing to avoid stagnation and stultification. While many individuals within the cinema art world may abhor these films, the cinema art world as a whole requires them. This demonstrates that newness and transgression in cinema (as in fine art) are intimately linked. As art worlds have increasingly come to identify newness as central to their existence, there is a need to search beyond the limits of what currently constitutes art in that domain, in order to constantly innovate. In cinema, this is commonly achieved by the elevation of genre tropes related to sex and violence, although a trend such as slow cinema had a similar effect through their use of extremely long takes.

Overall, this chapter reiterates the need to pay close attention to the type and degree of transgression when discussing transgressive or extreme imagery. Films like *A Serbian Film* are almost-transgressive and marginally transgressive in particular ways, which allows them to be recuperated within the domain of art cinema. The choices made by festivals, distributors and exhibitors to 'take the risk' are always positioned in the context of then-current ideas about what constitutes film art. Only films that marginally transgress certain boundaries in certain ways can be elevated to the status of transgressive art films.

Notes

1. See Kimber, 'Transgressive Edge Play' for a detailed discussion of how *A Serbian Film* distances viewers from the violence.
2. Bourdieu, *The Field of Cultural Production*, 261.
3. Becker, *Art Worlds*, 34–35; see also Cubitt, 'Distribution and Media Flows'.
4. Baumann, *Hollywood Highbrow*, 4–15.
5. Hawkins, *Cutting Edge*; Wilinsky, *Sure Seaters*; Wasson, *Museum Movies*; De Valck, *Film Festivals*; Herbert, 'From Art House To Your House'; Frey, *Extreme Cinema*.
6. Wasson, *Museum Movies*, 28.
7. Bourdieu, *The Rules of Art*, 226.
8. Bourdieu, 226.
9. Bourdieu, *The Field of Cultural Production*, 261.
10. Bourdieu, 257.
11. Bourdieu, 257.
12. Bourdieu, 258.
13. Becker, *Art Worlds*, 29.

14 Becker, 34.
15 Becker, 36.
16 Galt and Schoonover, *Global Art Cinema*, 18.
17 Graves, 'Transgressive Traditions', 43ff.; see also Heinich, *Le triple jeu*, 23; 'The Art of Inflicting Suffering', 207; Jenks, *Transgression*, 84; Groys, *On the New*, 103.
18 Jenks, *Transgression*, 7.
19 Groys, *On the New*, 10.
20 This can have quite insidious effects, for instance, in the case of cultural appropriation.
21 Neale, 'Art Cinema as Institution', 37; on transgressive art films and the avant-garde, see Palmer, *Brutal Intimacy*, 57–88, 114–22.
22 See Hawkins, *Cutting Edge*, 6–7; Kermode, 'What Are They Scared Of?' on the exceptional restrictions still placed on *Last House on the Left* in the UK, even in 2002 after films like *Irreversible* and *Sombre* had been passed uncut.
23 Galt and Schoonover, *Global Art Cinema*, 13.
24 Andrews, *Theorizing Art Cinemas*, 87.
25 Cf. Leslie Graves's questions: 'why would our art-designating procedures have come into conflict with the function of art? Why would art-designating procedures that do not respect the function of art have evolved?' ('Transgressive Traditions', 40).
26 Graves, 41.
27 Becker, *Art Worlds*, 228ff.
28 Becker, 244.
29 Heinich, *Le triple jeu*, 56–57.
30 Becker, *Art Worlds*, 246.
31 Graves, 'Transgressive Traditions'.
32 Graves, 46.
33 Graves, 45.
34 Heinich, *Le triple jeu*; 'De la transgression en art contemporain'; 'The Art of Inflicting Suffering', 33.
35 One of Heinich's key interventions was to consider classical, modern and contemporary art as paradigms or genres rather than periodic categorisations. Artistic characteristics such as transgression are then no longer attributable to particular works, but are rather the fundamental defining criteria of a paradigm ('De la transgression en art contemporain', 115–19; 'From Sociology of Culture', 201; *Le paradigme de l'art contemporain*).
36 Heinich, *Le triple jeu*, 53.
37 Heinich, 56.
38 Betz, *Beyond the Subtitle*, 25–26.
39 Wilinsky, *Sure Seaters*; Wasson, *Museum Movies*; Baumann, *Hollywood Highbrow*.
40 Williams, *Hard Core*, 120–52.
41 Lev, *American Films of the '70s*; Frey, *Extreme Cinema*.
42 Neale, 'Art Cinema as Institution'.
43 Andrews, *Theorizing Art Cinemas*, 82–87; Hawkins, *Cutting Edge*, 27–28.
44 Andrews, *Theorizing Art Cinemas*, 87.
45 Jones, 'Hardcore Horror'; Jackson, 'Euro-Snuff'; Andrews, *Theorizing Art Cinemas*.
46 Cashell, *Aftershock*, 100.
47 Andrews, *Theorizing Art Cinemas*, 88.
48 This inevitably leaves out many important aspects of the cinema art world, most notably

censorship, but this has already been covered in detail throughout this book, and by others.
49. Galt and Schoonover, *Global Art Cinema*, 7; Tweedie, *The Age of New Waves*, 23–24; Andrews, *Theorizing Art Cinemas*.
50. Galt and Schoonover, *Global Art Cinema*, 13.
51. Frey, *Extreme Cinema*, 49.
52. For a detailed discussion of the motivations of festival organisers see Frey, 46–68; see also Palmer, *Brutal Intimacy*, 61.
53. Frey, *Extreme Cinema*, 56; see also Schwartz, *It's so French!*; Valck, *Film Festivals*; 'Fostering Art, Adding Value, Cultivating Taste'; Wong, *Film Festivals*.
54. Frey, *Extreme Cinema*, 60–61.
55. Frey, 47.
56. Wong, *Film Festivals*, 90.
57. See interviews in Frey, *Extreme Cinema*, 54–68.
58. After screening *A Serbian Film* at the 2010 Sitges Film Festival in Spain, the festival's director, Ángel Sala, was charged with exhibiting child pornography, although the charges were later dropped (Pape, 'So Scandalous a Prosecutor Took Notice').
59. Rastegar, 'Seeing Differently', 184; Frey, *Extreme Cinema*, 74.
60. As would be the suggestion of programming an amateur orgy compilation from PornHub, for instance.
61. Noah Carey, executive director of the San Francisco International Film Festival noted that 'Interestingly, it does seem that if an extreme film is directed by a big name auteur and/or has played Cannes it will be treated with some respect more so than something that has played at a smaller festival or is low budget' (quoted in Frey, *Extreme Cinema*, 58).
62. Although I am not focusing on censorship in this chapter, in the UK at least, censorship and classification boards are substantially involved in films, especially big-budget productions, at the production and editing stages, so that the studios can be sure to achieve the desired age rating (personal correspondence with David Cooke; see also Pett, 'Access All Areas?').
63. De Valck, 'Fostering Art, Adding Value, Cultivating Taste', 110.
64. For more detail on these film markets see Wong, *Film Festivals*, 136ff.
65. Wong, 157.
66. Interestingly, the marketing for *Vortex* maintains the red, yellow and black colour palette used to market *I Stand Alone*, *Irréversible*, *Love* and *Climax*, apparently aiming to create brand recognition for Noé as an auteur, despite a drastically different subject matter.
67. See Ognjanović, 'Genre Films in Recent Serbian Cinema'; Kapka, 'Understanding *A Serbian Film*', 4.
68. Here I am paraphrasing Cubitt ('Distribution and Media Flows', 200).
69. Becker, *Art Worlds*, 93–95; Lobato, *Shadow Economies of Cinema*, 2.
70. Herbert, 'From Art House To Your House', 4.
71. Perren, 'Rethinking Distribution', 170.
72. Cubitt, 'Distribution and Media Flows', 194.
73. Andrews, *Theorizing Art Cinemas*, 198. Frey notes that distributors have also become completely intertwined with festivals in the figure of the sales agent: 'Increasingly, sales agents perform a role similar to distributors; in addition, their rhetoric often coincides.

... Sales agents often invest at production stage, determine the festivals at which the films play, and broker distributors' acquisition price' (*Extreme Cinema*, 81).

74 Andrews, *Theorizing Art Cinemas*, 78–80.
75 Becker, *Art Worlds*, 129.
76 See Herbert, 'From Art House To Your House'; Hessler, 'Quality You Can't Touch'. They also discuss the interconnection between these two as Criterion Collection was a core part of Mubi's collection from 2007 to 2011.
77 Herbert, 'From Art House To Your House', 9.
78 https://xconfessions.com/film/ink-is-my-blood (accessed June 28, 2022).
79 https://mubi.com/films/ink-is-my-blood (accessed June 28, 2022).
80 Andrews, *Theorizing Art Cinemas*, 76.
81 Frey, *Extreme Cinema*, 76 and 69–93.
82 See quotations from Raymond Murray, chief executive officer of Artsploitation films, in Frey, 76.
83 In interviews, the director Srđan Spasojević reported that there had been difficulties getting the film processed by a German post-production house and that screenings had been cancelled at some film festivals (see Kozina, 'Srpski Film', 157; Kostić, 'Postmoderni Film Strave Kao Balkanski Žanr', 133). See also Frey, *Extreme Cinema*, 72–75 on how Invincible Pictures encountered problems distributing it in North America as many local distributors and exhibition outlets refused to take it.
84 Choi and Wada-Marciano, *Horror to the Extreme*, 5.
85 Shin, 'Art of Branding'.
86 On links to hardcore horror see Aston, *Hardcore Horror Cinema*; Drissel, 'Hardcore Horror'; Jones, 'Hardcore Horror'.
87 Bradshaw, 'A Serbian Film – Review'; Child, 'Raindance Film Festival Announces Controversial Lineup'; French, 'A Serbian Film – Review'; Cox, 'A Serbian Film'; Shoard, 'A Serbian Film Becomes Most Censored Film in 16 Years'; Brooks, 'A Serbian Film Pulled from FrightFest'. Two years later, it was still receiving publicity in relation to the Raindance Festival with an article in *The Independent* on the 2012 festival being introduced by talking about *A Serbian Film* (Steele, 'Observations').
88 See Brown, 'UK Censors Ask Focus Groups to Watch Sexually Violent Films'; Press Association, 'Sadistic Japanese Movie Grotesque Denied Rating by Film Censors'. I couldn't find any reviews for these films in the other newspapers mentioned above.
89 Frey, *Extreme Cinema*, 48.
90 Schwartz, *It's so French!*, 73.
91 De Valck, *Film Festivals*, 156.
92 For a more detailed discussion of *Twentynine Palms*'s festival reception, see De Valck, 155–57.
93 Ebert, 'The Brown Bunny'.
94 See petition at Censura Não, 'Censura Não'; Gomes and Paganotti, 'Censura além da classificação'.
95 See MacKenzie, '*Baise-Moi*', 319–21 who also discusses filmmakers' protests in Canada against different forms of censorship enacted on the film.
96 On auteurism, see Bordwell, 'The Art Cinema as a Mode of Film Practice', 59–60. On nation and auteurism, see Galt and Schoonover, *Global Art Cinema*, vi–x, 4–17.
97 Kapka, 'Understanding *A Serbian Film*'; Smith, 'Serb Your Enthusiasm'.

98 Kohn, '*A Serbian Film* Shocks Midnight Audiences At SXSW'.
99 Galt and Schoonover, *Global Art Cinema*, 7.
100 Becker, *Art Worlds*, 131; Baumann, 'A General Theory of Artistic Legitimation', 58–59.
101 Cubitt, 'Distribution and Media Flows', 205.
102 Gomes and Paganotti, 'Censura além da classificação'; Kapka, 'Understanding *A Serbian Film*'; Weir and Dunne, 'The Connoisseurship of the Condemned'; Kimber, 'Transgressive Edge Play', 117–21; Smith, 'Serb Your Enthusiasm'; Smith, 'Shock Value'.
103 Kozina, 'Srpski Film'; Kendall, 'Affect and the Ethics of Snuff in Extreme Art Cinema'; Batori, 'Newborn-Porn and the Wannabe-Art Film of the Future'; Ognjanović, 'No Escape from the Body'; Drissel, 'Hardcore Horror'; Herron, 'Victim Sells'; Jackson, 'Euro-Snuff'; Jones, 'Hardcore Horror'.
104 Kolarić, 'Odbrana umetnosti u *Srpskom filmu* Srđana Spasojevića'; Kostić, 'Postmoderni Film Strave Kao Balkanski Žanr'; Featherstone and Johnson, '"Ovo Je Srbija"'; Featherstone, 'Coito Ergo Sum'; Kerner and Knapp, *Extreme Cinema*, 61–67; Bonello Rutter Giappone and Tanti, 'Möbius Dick'.
105 Kostić, 'Postmoderni Film Strave Kao Balkanski Žanr'; Kapka, 'Understanding *A Serbian Film*'; Pett, 'Access All Areas?', 185.
106 Kolarić, 'Odbrana umetnosti u *Srpskom filmu* Srđana Spasojevića'; Batori, 'Newborn-Porn and the Wannabe-Art Film of the Future'; Jackson, 'Euro-Snuff'.
107 Kolarić, 'Odbrana umetnosti u *Srpskom filmu* Srđana Spasojevića'; Vidan, 'Spaces of Ideology in South Slavic Films'; Kostić, 'Postmoderni Film Strave Kao Balkanski Žanr'; Ognjanović, 'No Escape from the Body'; Kapka, 'Understanding *A Serbian Film*'; Pająk, 'Early 21st-Century Serbian Exploitation Cinema'. One might also note that two scholars wrote two separate articles each dedicated to *A Serbian Film* (Mark Featherstone and Martin Ian Smith), a notable dedication to the film. I myself also presented preliminary work for this book on *A Serbian Film* at an academic conference, and include some discussion of the film in a book chapter on censorship ('British Film Censorship in the Twenty-First Century').
108 See the following work done on transgressive art films: Barker et al., *Audiences and Receptions*; Barker, '"Typically French"?'; 'Watching Rape'; Weir and Dunne, 'The Connoisseurship of the Condemned'. Work done on single violent or horror films tends towards the formerly transgressive now-canonical such as *The Exorcist* (Smith, 'Researching Memories') and *Clockwork Orange* (Krämer, 'Movies That Make People Sick'), or the overtly art festival film such as *The Act of Killing* and *The Look of Silence* (Kouchakji, 'Activism in Action'.), *City of God* and *Elite Squad* (Gregoli, 'Transnational Reception'.), and it is notable that Janet Staiger's classic text on spectators deals precisely with the 'transgressive' films of the time: *Clockwork Orange*, *Silence of the Lambs*, *Psycho* and *The Texas Chainsaw Massacre* (*Perverse Spectators*.).
109 See *Participations* journal for numerous studies on the most successful Hollywood franchises.
110 See for instance Smith, 'Revulsion and Derision'., which supposedly focuses on the BBFC's censorship of violent films but mostly looks at transgressive art films such as *Antichrist*, *A Serbian Film*, *Irreversible*, *Anatomy of Hell*, *Baise-moi* as well as *Crash*, with *The Human Centipede II* as the main exception. Other censored films like *Murder-Set-Pieces*, *Grotesque*, *Bunny Game* or *Hate Crime* are not considered, all of which had been released before the article's publication. A more considered analysis of revulsion is reserved for transgressive art films.

111 Baumann, 'A General Theory of Artistic Legitimation', 56.
112 Hubner, 'A Taste for Flesh and Blood', 204.
113 Bourdieu, *The Field of Cultural Production*, 227.
114 Galperin, 'Beyond Interests, Ideas, and Technology', 161.
115 Bourdieu, *The Field of Cultural Production*, 37.

Conclusion

The central premise of this book is that transgressive art films are a sociocultural phenomenon. Conceiving of them in them in this way invites many analytical frameworks that help to map out the patterns that matter. My approach, focusing on the analysis of film form, audience responses and the dynamics of the cinema art world offers a framework for understanding the ways in which these films are controversial, how such controversies arise, why these films above all others are controversial and what it means for them to be controversial. The questions of 'how', 'why' and 'in what ways' were explored in the earlier parts of the book, by thinking carefully about the films' formal qualities, how they were received by audiences and how this corresponded to theories of transgression. The later chapters focused mostly on the question of 'what it means' to be a transgressive art film, by exploring and nuancing Bataillean theories of transgression, genre theory, and the cinema art world's processes of recuperation and legitimisation. However disturbing, challenging, politically ambiguous or ethically dubious transgressive art films may be, they help to shed light on many key issues in contemporary cinema, and especially on how societies approach sexual and violent imagery. This cannot be seen specifically as the 'aim' of such films; rather, analysing the actions and reactions of various stakeholders within the cinema art world is revealing about received ideas about art, transgression, aesthetics, ethics, rape, sex and violence.

In this book, I have identified three main pillars for developing an analytical framework capable of discussing transgressive art films in their full complexity: form, reception and theory. Form requires that we think about visibility, proximity and duration, especially in relation to scenes of sex, violence and sexual violence. Visibility refers to the graphic depiction of sex and violence, and how such explicit imagery is often read as making structures of domination visible. Proximity refers to the sense of being brought close to the diegetic acts, whether through close-ups or the evocation of materiality associated with haptic visuality. Duration refers to the prevalence of long takes and long scenes, which create a sense of temporal realism, and emphasise the step-by-step development of depicted acts. Reception means looking at a wide variety of audience responses, from critics and scholars, to audience research and reception studies, surveys, internet fora and blog posts, in order to gain detailed knowledge about how actual audiences responded to particular films or scenes. Building on work done on embracers, ambivalents and refusers, this involved examining audience reactions through value registers, the interpretative frameworks that underpin individual viewers' evaluations of a film. Theory means a nuanced and rigorous discussion about terms such as 'transgression' and 'extremity', and concepts such as the boundary. The most relevant theorist to this discussion is Georges Bataille, but his work focuses on transgressive acts, and is ultimately insufficient to account for artistic transgressions. I have argued that we must take degree and type of transgression into account when analysing artistic transgressions, which also allows for productive reflections on genre theory, and the notion of 'risk' in programming and distribution decisions. Each of these pillars is necessary for understanding transgressive art films as a socio-cultural phenomenon.

If we are to more fully comprehend the phenomenon of transgressive art films, our analysis needs to examine all levels of the cinema art world, from the microscale to macroscale. Details about the visibility of body parts in the frame cannot be grasped without a reflection on broader contextual issues relating to censorship, exhibition, or criticism. Festival programming, distribution choices, or scholarly discourse cannot be properly explored without considering the precise images and aesthetics that are associated with low art or non-art. Judgements of a particular film by an individual cannot be usefully understood without examining the value registers and preconceptions about the nature of art that guide and frame an individual viewer's encounter with the film. More broadly, we must also question the value of analyses predicated substantially on an idealised viewer, that do not account for the very divergent social, cultural, and political contexts that feed into people's interpretations of images, especially those that are provocative and divisive. A film will always be constructing multiple viewer positions and it is important to recognise rather than seek to efface this multiplicity. We cannot separate close analysis from audience studies or industry analyses, and these cannot be undertaken without a coherent theoretical framework, if we really want to understand the mechanisms and role of controversy in contemporary art cinema.

The repeated focus on the ethical and political stakes of scholarly engagement with transgressive art films has highlighted the important role that we as scholars play in the discursive construction of transgressive art films. These stakes are especially significant in relation to images of sexual violence. Writing on transgressive art films featuring rape is often unhelpfully ignorant of the wealth of scholarship that exists on rape and rape imagery, with some scholars even ignoring the ethical stakes of portraying rape on screen, instead focusing on the aesthetics of the film, or reading such violence as metaphorical. Certain commentary has also frequently emphasised the emotional distress of male characters and the spectator, at the expense of the physical and psychological violence inflicted on women. These shortcomings and blind spots highlight the need for greater reflection on the contribution of film scholars to the legitimisation of transgressive art films through our choices of films to analyse and discuss.

In sum, I am suggesting that greater self-reflection on the part of scholars, including myself, is required when engaging with transgressive art films, as we have a role to play in preferentially placing the spotlight on certain films rather than others. We cannot simply see ourselves as responding to already controversial imagery, but must take responsibility for the choices we make in analysing them, and thereby elevating them to artistic status. In other words, given the subject matter, especially the deeply problematic images of sexual violence, choices to research such films cannot simply be framed as disinterested ones. Such choices have ethical and political consequences, regardless of the position one actually takes with regards to a film.

At the beginning of this book, I posed several questions: Why are these films controversial? Why are they described as extreme or as transgressive? What boundaries or limits are they transgressing? What do they and the discourse around them tell us about cinema today? The answers took me into some dark and disturbing places, and it has not always been pleasant to engage again and again with some of the material included in this book. Nonetheless, I hope that readers will appreciate the insights gained from this project, even if they may not be encouraged to seek out and watch all of these transgressive art films.

Filmography

A Hole in My Heart [Ett hål i mitt hjärta]. 2004. Lukas Moodysson.
A New Life [La Vie nouvelle]. 2002. Philippe Grandrieux.
A Serbian Film [Srpski Film]. 2010. Srđan Spasojević.
Anatomy of Hell [Anatomie de l'enfer]. 2004. Catherine Breillat.
Antichrist. 2009. Lars von Trier.
Baise-moi. 2000. Virginie Despentes and Coralie Trinh-Thi.
Battle in Heaven [Batalla en el cielo]. 2005. Carlos Reygadas.
Climax. 2018. Gaspar Noé.
Clip [Klip]. 2012. Maja Miloš.
Enter The Void. 2009. Gaspar Noé.
Fat Girl [A ma sœur!]. 2001. Catherine Breillat.
Free Will [Der Freie Wille]. 2006. Matthias Glasner.
Holiday. 2018. Isabella Eklöf.
I Stand Alone [Seul contre tous]. 1998. Gaspar Noé.
Import/Export. 2007. Ulrich Seidl.
In My Skin [Dans ma peau]. 2002. Marina de Van.
Irreversible [Irréversible]. 2002. Gaspar Noé.
My Mother [Ma mère]. 2004. Christophe Honoré.
Nymphomaniac. 2013. Lars von Trier.
Raw [Grave]. 2016. Julia Ducournau.
Romance. 1999. Catherine Breillat.
See the Sea [Regarde la mer]. 1997. François Ozon.
Sombre. 1999. Philippe Grandrieux.
Taxidermia. 2006. György Pálfi.
The Brown Bunny. 2003. Vincent Gallo.
The Idiots [Idioterne]. 1998. Lars von Trier.
The Piano Teacher [La Pianiste]. 2001. Michael Haneke.
The Tribe [Плем'я]. 2014. Myroslav Slaboshpytskiy.
Trouble Every Day. 2001. Claire Denis.
Twentynine Palms. 2003. Bruno Dumont.
We Fuck Alone. 2006. Gaspar Noé.

*

127 Hours. 2010. Danny Boyle.
2 Girls, 1 Cup [trailer]. 2007. Marco Villanova.

9 Songs. 2001. Michael Winterbottom.
Amélie [Le fabuleux destin d'Amélie Poulain]. 2001. Jean-Pierre Jeunet.
Amour. 2012. Michael Haneke.
Asphalt. 1929. Joe May.
Audition [Odishon]. 1999. Takashi Miike.
Back and Forth. 1969. Michael Snow.
Bad Luck Banging or Loony Porn. 2021. Radu Jude.
Basic Instinct. 1992. Paul Verhoeven.
Big Brother [TV series]. 2000–18. Various.
Blackrock. 1997. Steven Vidler.
Blow-up. 1966. Michelangelo Antonioni.
Blue is the Warmest Colour [La vie d'Adèle: Chapitres 1 et 2]. 2013. Abdellatif Kechiche.
Blue Valentine. 2010. Derek Cianfrance.
Bluebeard [Barbe bleue]. 2009. Catherine Breillat.
Boogie Nights. 1997. Paul Thomas Anderson.
Borat! Cultural Learnings of America for Make Benefit Glorious Nation of Kazakhstan. 2006. Larry Charles.
Born in Flames. 1983. Lizzie Borden.
Buffalo '66. 1998. Vincent Gallo.
Bumfights – Cause for Concern – Volume 1. 2002. Ryen McPherson.
Cannibal Holocaust. 1980. Ruggero Deodato.
City of God [Cidade de Deus]. 2002. Fernando Meirelles and Kátia Lund.
Clockwork Orange. 1971. Stanley Kubrick.
Crash. 1996. David Cronenberg.
Demonlover. 2002. Olivier Assayas.
Destricted [compilation]. 2006. Various.
Diet of Sex. 2014. Borja Brun.
Dog Days [Hundstage]. 2001. Ulrich Seidl.
Elephant. 2003. Gus Van Sant.
Elite Squad [Tropa de Elite]. 2007. José Padilha.
Emmanuelle. 1974. Just Jaeckin.
Family Guy [TV series]. 1999–present. Various.
Fuck: Sasha Grey. 2010. Belladonna.
Funny Games. 1997. Michael Haneke.
Grotesque [Gurotesuku]. 2009. Kôji Shiraishi.
Hate Crime. 2013. James Bressack.
Headshot. 2006. Jennifer Lyon Bell.
Hostel. 2005. Eli Roth.
Hostel: Part II. 2007. Eli Roth.
The Human Centipede (First Sequence). 2009. Tom Six.
The Human Centipede II (Full Sequence). 2011. Tom Six.
I Spit on Your Grave. 2010. Steven Monroe.
I Want Your Love. 2012. Travis Mathews.
I'm No Angel. 1933. Wesley Ruggles.
Ichi the Killer [Koroshiya Ichi]. 2001. Takashi Miike.
In the Cut. 2003. Jane Campion.

In the Realm of the Senses [Ai no korrida]. 1976. Nagisa Oshima.
Ink is my Blood. 2018. Erika Lust.
Inside [À l'intérieur]. 2007. Julien Maury and Alexandre Bustillo.
Intimacy. 2001. Patrice Chéreau.
Into The Flesh. 2018. Montiel.
Jackass [TV series]. 2000–1. Jeff Tremaine.
Japón. 2002. Carlos Reygadas.
Ken Park. 2002. Larry Clark and Edward Lachman.
Kill Bill Vol.1. 2003. Quentin Tarantino.
Kinatay. 2008. Brillante Mendoza.
L'avventura. 1960. Michelangelo Antonioni.
La région centrale. 1971. Michael Snow.
Land of the Deaf [Страна глухих]. 1998. Valeriy Todorovskiy.
Last House on the Left. 1972. Wes Craven.
Last Tango in Paris. 1972. Bernardo Bertolucci.
Leap Year [Año bisiesto]. 2010. Michael Rowe.
Let the Right One In [Låt den rätte komma in]. 2004. Tomas Alfredson.
Lilya 4-ever. 2002. Lukas Moodysson.
Livid [Livide]. 2011. Julien Maury and Alexandre Bustillo.
Lost in the Hood. 2009. Edward James.
Love. 2015. Gaspar Noé.
Manhunter. 1986. Michael Mann.
Martyrs. 2009. Pascal Laugier.
Monster's Ball. 2001. Marc Forster.
Morocco. 1930. Josef von Sternberg.
Murder-Set-Pieces. 2004. Nick Palumbo.
My Daughter's a Cocksucker. 2006. Bobby Rinaldi.
Nanook of the North. 1922. Robert Flaherty.
Oldboy [Oldeuboi]. 2003. Park Chan-wook.
Painful Secrets. 2000. Norma Bailey.
Pandora's Box [Die Büchse der Pandora]. 1929. Georg Wilhelm Pabst.
Psycho. 1960. Alfred Hitchcock.
Q. 2011. Laurent Bouhnik.
Rashomon. 1950. Akira Kurosawa.
Raspberry Reich. 2004. Bruce La Bruce.
Red Road. 2006. Andrea Arnold.
Re-Penetrator. 2004. Doug Sackmann.
Rope. 1948. Alfred Hitchcock.
Russian Ark [Русский ковчег]. 2002. Alexander Sokurov.
Salò, or the 120 Days of Sodom [Salò o le 120 giornate di Sodoma]. 1975. Pier Paolo Pasolini.
Salut les Cubains. 1963. Agnès Varda.
Saw. 2004. James Wan.
Secretary. 2002. Steven Shainberg.
Sex Tape. 2014. Jake Kasdan.
Sexual Chronicles of a French Family [Chroniques sexuelles d'une famille d'aujourd'hui]. 2012. Pascal Arnold and Jean-Marc Barr.

Shame. 2011. Steve McQueen.
Shortbus. 2006. James Cameron Mitchell.
Show Me Love [Fucking Åmål]. 1998. Lukas Moodysson.
Shrek. 2001. Andrew Adamson and Vicky Jenson.
Silence of the Lambs. 1991. Jonathan Demme.
Skin.Like.Sun. 2010. Jennifer Lyon Bell.
Sleeping Beauty [La belle endormie]. 2010. Catherine Breillat.
Stagecoach. 1939. John Ford.
Stranger by the Lake [L'inconnu du lac]. 2013. Alain Guiraudie.
Straw Dogs. 1971. Sam Peckinpah.
Swimming Pool. 2003. François Ozon.
Sympathy for Mr Vengeance [Boksuneun Naui Geot]. 2002. Park Chan-wook.
The Accused. 1988. Jonathan Kaplan.
The Act of Killing. 2012. Joshua Oppenheimer, Christine Cynn and Anonymous.
The Bunny Game. 2011. Adam Rehmeier.
The Daughters of Fire [Las Hijas del Fuego]. 2018. Albertina Carri.
The Exorcist. 1973. William Friedkin.
The Isle [Seom]. 2000. Kim Ki Duk.
The Kiss. 1896. William Heise.
The Life of Jesus [La vie de Jésus]. 1997. Bruno Dumont.
The Look of Silence. 2014. Joshua Oppenheimer.
The Lovers [Les amants]. 1958. Louis Malle.
The Night [La Noche]. 2016. Edgardo Castro.
The Pornographer [Le pornographe]. 2001. Bertrand Bonello.
The Story of Richard O. [L'histoire de Richard O.] 2007. Damien Odoul.
The Texas Chainsaw Massacre. 1974. Tobe Hooper.
The Wayward Cloud [Tiān biān yī duǒ yún]. 2005. Tsai Ming-liang.
Victoria. 2015. Sebastian Schipper.
Vortex. 2021. Gaspar Noé.
When Animals Dream [Når dyrene drømmer]. 2014. Jonas Alexander Arnby.
Zach and Miri Make a Porno. 2008. Kevin Smith.

Bibliography

Aitken, Ian. *Cinematic Realism: Lukacs, Kracauer and Theories of the Filmic Real*. Edinburgh: Edinburgh University Press, 2020.
——, ed. *The Major Realist Film Theorists: A Critical Anthology*. Edinburgh: Edinburgh University Press, 2016.
Aldana Reyes, Xavier. *Body Gothic: Corporeal Transgression in Contemporary Literature and Horror Film*. Gothic Literary Studies. Cardiff: University of Wales Press, 2014.
Altman, Rick. *Film/Genre*. London: BFI Publishing, 1999.
Andrews, David. *Theorizing Art Cinemas: Foreign, Cult, Avant-Garde, And Beyond*. Austin, TX: University of Texas Press, 2014.
Angel, Katherine. *Tomorrow Sex Will Be Good Again: Women and Desire in the Age of Consent*. London; New York: Verso, 2021.
Angelo, Adrienne. 'Sexual Cartographies: Mapping Subjectivity in the Cinema of Catherine Breillat'. *Journal for Cultural Research* 14, no. 1 (January 2010): 43–55. https://doi.org/10.1080/14797580903363082.
——. 'Wounded Women: Marina de Van's Subjective Cinema'. *International Journal of Francophone Studies* 15, no. 2 (December 2012): 215–35. https://doi.org/10.1386/ijfs.15.2.215_1.
Archer, Neil. '*Baise-Moi*: The Art of Going Too Far'. *E-Pisteme* 2, no. 1 (2009): 67–77.
Ardenne, Paul. *Extrême: Esthétiques de La Limite Dépassée*. Paris: Flammarion, 2006.
Aston, James. *Hardcore Horror Cinema In The 21st Century: Production, Marketing And Consumption*. Jefferson, North Carolina: McFarland & Company, Inc, 2018.
Attwood, Feona, and Clarissa Smith. 'Extreme Concern: Regulating "Dangerous Pictures" in the United Kingdom'. *Journal of Law and Society* 37, no. 1 (March 2010): 171–88. https://doi.org/10.1111/j.1467-6478.2010.00500.x.
Austin, Guy. 'Biological Dystopias: The Body in Contemporary French Horror Cinema'. *L'Esprit Créateur* 52, no. 2 (2012): 99–113. https://doi.org/10.1353/esp.2012.0023.
——. *Contemporary French Cinema: An Introduction*. Manchester; New York, NY: Manchester University Press, 1996.
Azalbert, Nicolas. 'Le corps défendant'. *Cahiers du cinéma* 574 (December 2002): 82–83.
Azoury, Philippe. 'Grandrieux sans manières'. *Libération*, 27 November 2002, sec. Cinéma. https://www.liberation.fr/cinema/2002/11/27/grandrieux-sans-manieres_422906/.
Badt, Karin. 'No Slave to Realism: An Interview with Carlos Reygadas'. *Cinéaste* 31, no. 3 (2006): 21–23.
Bailey, Kimberly. 'Sex in a Masculinities World: Gender, Undesired Sex, and Rape'. *The Journal of Gender, Race, and Justice* 21, no. 2 (2018): 281–332.

Bakhtin, Mikhail. 'Epic and Novel: Toward a Methodology for the Study of the Novel'. In *Modern Genre Theory*, edited by David Duff, 68–81. Oxford: New York, NY: Routledge, 2014.

———. *Problems of Dostoevsky's Poetics*. Edited and translated by Caryl Emerson. Theory and History of Literature, v. 8. Minneapolis: University of Minnesota Press, 1984.

———. *Rabelais and His World*. Translated by Helene Iswolsky. Cambridge, MA: MIT Press, 1968.

———. 'The Problem of Speech Genres'. In *Modern Genre Theory*, edited by David Duff, 82–97. Oxford: New York, NY: Routledge, 2014.

Balázs, Béla. 'The Close-Up'. In *Film Theory and Criticism: Introductory Readings*, edited by Leo Braudy and Marshall Cohen, 6th ed., 314–15. New York, NY: Oxford University Press, 2004.

———. 'The Face of Man'. In *Film Theory and Criticism: Introductory Readings*, edited by Leo Braudy and Marshall Cohen, 6th ed., 316–21. New York, NY: Oxford University Press, 2004.

Baqué, Dominique. *Mauvais genres: érotisme, pornographie, art contemporain*. Paris: Regard, 2002.

Barker, Anthony. 'On Not Being Porn: Intimacy and the Sexually Explicit Art Film'. *Text Matters*, no. 3 (November 2013): 186–202. https://doi.org/10.2478/texmat-2013-0034.

Barker, Jennifer. *The Tactile Eye: Touch and the Cinematic Experience*. Berkeley: University of California Press, 2009.

Barker, Martin. '"Typically French"?: Mediating Screened Rape to British Audiences'. In *Rape in Art Cinema*, edited by Dominique Russell, 147–58. New York, NY: Continuum, 2010.

———. 'Watching Rape, Enjoying Watching Rape . . .: How Does a Study of Audience Cha(Lle)Nge Film Studies Approaches?' In *The New Extremism in Cinema: From France to Europe*, edited by Tanya Horeck and Tina Kendall, 105–16. Edinburgh: Edinburgh University Press, 2011.

Barker, Martin, Ernest Mathijs, Jamie Sexton, Kate Egan, Russell Hunter, and Melanie Selfe. *Audiences And Receptions Of Sexual Violence In Contemporary Cinema*. Aberystwyth: University of Wales, 2007.

Barthes, Roland. *Camera Lucida: Reflections on Photography*. Translated by Richard Howard. New York, NY: Farrar, Straus and Giroux, 1981.

Barton-Fumo, Margaret. 'Pleasures of the Flesh'. *Film Comment* 53, no. 2 (April 2017): 42–46.

Bataille, Georges. *Erotism: Death and Sensuality*. Translated by Mary Dalwood. San Francisco, CA: City Lights Books, 1986.

———. *Lascaux: Or, The Birth of Art: Prehistoric Painting*. Translated by Austryn Wainhouse. Lausaane: Skira, 1955.

———. *Literature and Evil*. Translated by Alastair Hamilton. London: Penguin Books, 2012.

———. *The Accursed Share: An Essay on General Economy*. Translated by Robert Hurley. 3 vols. New York, NY: Zone Books, 1991.

———. *The Bataille Reader*. Edited by Fred Botting and Scott Wilson. Blackwell Readers. Oxford; Malden, MA: Blackwell, 1997.

Batori, Anna. 'Newborn-Porn and the Wannabe-Art Film of the Future: Srđan Spasojević's *A Serbian Film* (*Srpski Film*, 2010)'. *East European Film Bulletin* 78 (October 2017).

Battestini, Paul-Marie. 'The Brown Bunny: L'image Mélancolique'. *Chantiers de La Création*, no. 1 (April 2008). https://doi.org/10.4000/lcc.142.

Baudry, Patrick. 'La logique de l'extrême'. *Communications* 61, no. 1 (1996): 11–20. https://doi.org/10.3406/comm.1996.1921.

———. *La pornographie et ses images*. Paris: Armand Colin, 1997.

———. *Le corps extrême: approche sociologique des conduites à risque*. Paris: L'Harmattan, 1991.

Baumann, Shyon. 'A General Theory of Artistic Legitimation: How Art Worlds Are like Social Movements'. *Poetics* 35, no. 1 (February 2007): 47–65. https://doi.org/10.1016/j.poetic.2006.06.001.

———. *Hollywood Highbrow: From Entertainment to Art*. Princeton: Princeton University Press, 2007.

Baumgarten, Marjorie. 'Trouble Every Day'. *Austin Chronicle*, 26 July 2002. https://www.austinchronicle.com/events/film/2002-07-26/trouble-every-day/.

Bawarshi, Anis. 'The Genre Function'. *College English* 62, no. 3 (January 2000): 335. https://doi.org/10.2307/378935.

Bayman, Alasdair. 'Film Review: Holiday'. *CineVue* (blog), 4 August 2019. https://cine-vue.com/2019/08/film-review-holiday.html.

Bayon, Estelle. *Le cinéma obscène*. Paris: L'Harmattan, 2007.

Bazin, André. *What Is Cinema?* Translated by Hugh Gray. 2 vols. Berkeley, CA: University of California Press, 2004.

BBC. 'Cannes Film Sickens Audience', 26 May 2002. http://news.bbc.co.uk/1/hi/entertainment/2008796.stm.

———. 'Director Defends Explicit Movie'. *BBC* (blog), 16 May 2005. http://news.bbc.co.uk/1/hi/entertainment/4550675.stm.

BBFC. 'A Ma Sœur!', 2002. https://www.bbfc.co.uk/release/a-ma-soeur-film-qxnzzxq6vlgtnjk4odmx.

———. 'Annual Report 2001'. London: BBFC, 2001. https://darkroom.bbfc.co.uk/original/47b984bb4e1ee996e4c9fd2cbd84dc04:79d8ee519dbd870316159f2ccaddb59e/bbfc-annual-report-2001.pdf.

———. 'Annual Report 2002'. London: BBFC, 2002. https://darkroom.bbfc.co.uk/original/391d718a1f0e2138ae171c9ff349ff67:86d2056697ae1f50e778c15147c4461e/bbfc-annual-report-2002.pdf.

———. 'Annual Report 2003'. London: BBFC, 2003. https://darkroom.bbfc.co.uk/original/0c4f51a7e2c1dc72774028a3768da0e8:6dedf698a016809df72031ec797359a8/bbfc-annual-report-2003.pdf.

———. 'Annual Report 2004'. London: BBFC, 2004. https://darkroom.bbfc.co.uk/original/da4269d0992d671bd2f13118cd9e0b20:5364b16644c393031a8acf94ddc0553d/bbfc-annual-report-2004.pdf.

———. 'Annual Report 2005'. London: BBFC, 2005. https://darkroom.bbfc.co.uk/original/364556537d0c8eaa5fa462639d23e013:f12a1ec813cf414a2b62785531f8dabd/bbfc-annual-report-2005.pdf.

———. 'Annual Report 2006'. London: BBFC, 2006. https://darkroom.bbfc.co.uk/original/42f65b829d0502d9c24a7df0a69a248e:d93b7daa4f76afee053a05dc9c784b57/bbfc-annual-report-2006.pdf.

———. 'Annual Report 2011'. London: BBFC, 2011. https://darkroom.bbfc.co.uk/original/b928cba4df78199c3f04a42c61d6a120:68a9ccf0b23ebaf301842b7d3dfe5d11/bbfc-annual-report-2011.pdf.

———. 'BBFC Cuts A Serbian Film and Remake of I Spit on Your Grave', 26 August 2010. https://www.bbfc.co.uk/about-us/news/bbfc-cuts-a-serbian-film-and-remake-of-i-spit-on-your-grave.

———. 'Born In Flames', 1983. https://www.bbfc.co.uk/release/born-in-flames-q29sbgvjdglvbjpwwc0zmtq1nta.

———. 'Education – Case Studies – Baise-Moi', 14 August 2020. https://www.bbfc.co.uk/education/case-studies/baise-moi.

———. 'Emmanuelle'. British Board of Film Classification, n.d. https://bbfc.co.uk/case-studies/emmanuelle.

———. 'Grotesque (Case Study)'. British Board of Film Classification, 2009. http://www.bbfc.co.uk/case-studies/grotesque.

———. 'Guidelines 2014–15'. British Board of Film Classification, 2014. http://www.bbfc.co.uk/sites/default/files/attachments/BBFC%20Classification%20Guidelines%202014_5.pdf.

———. 'Guidelines 2019'. British Board of Film Classification, 2019. https://bbfc.co.uk/sites/default/files/attachments/BBFC%20Guidelines_2019.pdf.

———. 'High-Yield Hydroponic Systems'. British Board of Film Classification, 2005. https://www.bbfc.co.uk/release/high-yield-hydroponic-systems-q29sbgvjdglvbjpwwc0zndu wmje.

———. 'Introduction to Indoor Growing'. British Board of Film Classification, 2005. https://www.bbfc.co.uk/release/introduction-to-indoor-growing-q29sbgvjdglvbjpwwc0zndu wmtk.

———. 'Murder Set Pieces'. British Board of Film Classification, 2008. https://www.bbfc.co.uk/releases/murder-set-pieces-1970.

———. 'Mushroom Growing Made Easy'. British Board of Film Classification, 2005. https://www.bbfc.co.uk/release/mushroom-growing-made-easy-q29sbgvjdglvbjpwwc0zndu wnda.

———. 'The Hash Man'. British Board of Film Classification, 2005. https://www.bbfc.co.uk/release/the-hash-man-q29sbgvjdglvbjpwwc0znduwmtq.

Becker, Howard. *Art Worlds*. Berkeley: University of California Press, 1982.

———. *Outsiders: Studies in the Sociology of Deviance*. New York, NY: The Free Press, 1963.

Beebee, Thomas. *The Ideology of Genre: A Comparative Study of Generic Instability*. University Park, PA: Pennsylvania State University Press, 1994.

Belot, Sophie. 'Embracing Sexual Difference in Catherine Breillat's Anatomy of Hell (2003)'. *Women in French Studies* 18, no. 1 (2010): 135–47. https://doi.org/10.1353/wfs.2010.0018.

Benderson, Bruce. 'Hating Vincent Gallo: A Right-Wing Ideologue in Bohemian Clothing'. *Shout Magazine*, July 2002.

Benmiloud, Karim. 'Batalla en el cielo de Carlos Reygadas o la radicalidad de los márgenes'. In *Nationbuilding en el cine mexicano desde la Época de Oro hasta el presente*, edited by Friedhelm Schmidt-Welle and Christian Wehr, 263–74. Madrid, Spain: Iberoamericana Vervuert, 2015.

Berardinelli, James. 'Hole in My Heart, A'. *Reelviews* (blog), 2004. http://www.reelviews.net/reelviews/hole-in-my-heart-a.

Berger, John. 'Understanding a Photograph'. In *Understanding a Photograph*, edited by Geoff Dyer, 17–22. Penguin Modern Classics. London: Penguin Books, 2013.

Bernas, Steven. *La photographie et le sensible: les enjeux du sensible dans la représentation*. Paris: L'Harmattan, 2009.

Bernstein, J.M. 'Bare Life, Bearing Witness: Auschwitz and the Pornography of Horror'. *Parallax* 10, no. 1 (January 2004): 2–16. https://doi.org/10.1080/1353464032000171046.

Best, Victoria, and Martin Crowley. *The New Pornographies: Explicit Sex In Recent French Fiction And Film*. Manchester; New York, NY: Manchester University Press, 2007.

Bétan, Julien. *Extrême!: quand le cinéma dépasse les bornes*. Lyon: Les moutons électriques, 2012.

Betz, Mark. *Beyond the Subtitle: Remapping European Art Cinema*. Minneapolis: University of Minnesota Press, 2009.

Beugnet, Martine. *Cinema and Sensation: French Film and the Art of Transgression*. Edinburgh: Edinburgh University Press, 2007.

———. 'Close-up Vision: Re-Mapping the Body in the Work of Contemporary French Women Filmmakers'. Edited by Gill Rye and Carrie Tarr. *Nottingham French Studies* 45, no. 3 (Autumn 2006): 24–38. https://doi.org/10.3366/nfs.2006-3.003.

———. 'Evil and the Senses: Philippe Grandrieux's *Sombre* and *La Vie Nouvelle*'. *Studies in French Cinema* 5, no. 3 (December 2005): 175–84. https://doi.org/10.1386/sfci.5.3.175/1.

———. 'La forme et l'informe: de la dissolution du corps à l'écran'. In *Images des corps / corps des images au cinéma*, edited by Jérôme Game, 49–71. Lyon: Ecole Normale Supérieure, 2010.

Beugnet, Martine, and Elizabeth Ezra. 'Traces of the Modern: An Alternative History of French Cinema'. *Studies in French Cinema* 10, no. 1 (March 2010): 11–38. https://doi.org/10.1386/sfc.10.1.11/1.

Birks, Chelsea. 'Body Problems: New Extremism, Descartes and Jean-Luc Nancy'. *New Review of Film and Television Studies* 13, no. 2 (2015): 131–48. http://dx.doi.org/10.1080/17400309.2015.1009355.

———. *Limit Cinema: Transgression and the Nonhuman in Contemporary Global Film*. Thinking Cinema. New York: Bloomsbury Academic, 2021.

Blanchot, Maurice. *The Space of Literature*. Translated by Ann Smock. Lincoln, NE: University of Nebraska Press, 1982.

Bonello Rutter Giappone, Krista, and Emanuel Tanti. 'Möbius Dick: The Tragi-Priapic in *A Serbian Film*'. *Lo Specchio Scuro*, 21 February 2022. https://specchioscuro.it/a-serbian-film/.

Bonino, Fabienne. 'La Caméra Haptique de Philippe Grandrieux: «le Surgissement d'un Autre Monde»'. *Entrelacs*, no. 10 (2013). http://entrelacs.revues.org/485.

Bonnaud, Frédéric. 'Review: Battle in Heaven'. *Film Comment* 42, no. 1 (2006): 72.

Booth, Michael. 'It's a Fight, All Right – Just to Watch This'. *The Denver Post*, 19 April 2006. https://www.denverpost.com/2006/04/19/its-a-fight-all-right-just-to-watch-this/.

Bordun, Troy. *Genre Trouble and Extreme Cinema*. New York, NY: Springer Berlin Heidelberg, 2017.

Bordwell, David. 'The Art Cinema as a Mode of Film Practice'. *Film Criticism* 4, no. 1 (1979): 56–64.

Bordwell, David, Janet Staiger, and Kristin Thompson. *The Classical Hollywood Cinema: Film Style & Mode of Production to 1960*. London: Routledge, 1985.

Bourdieu, Pierre. *The Field of Cultural Production: Essays on Art and Literature*. Edited by Randal Johnson. New York: Columbia University Press, 1993.

———. *The Rules of Art: Genesis and Structure of the Literary Field*. Translated by Susan Emanuel. Stanford, CA: Stanford University Press, 1996.

Bradburn, John. 'Nothing Is True. Everything Is Permissible'. *Vertigo Journal*, no. 18 (2008): n.p.

Bradshaw, Peter. 'A Serbian Film – Review'. *The Guardian*, 9 December 2010, sec. Film. https://www.theguardian.com/film/2010/dec/09/a-serbian-film-review.

———. 'Holiday Review – an Unlovely Sojourn around the Twisted Male Psyche'. *The Guardian*, 31 July 2019, sec. Film. http://www.theguardian.com/film/2019/jul/31/holiday-review-an-unlovely-sojourn-around-the-twisted-male-psyche.

Brand, Roy. 'Witnessing Trauma on Film'. In *Media Witnessing: Testimony in the Age of Mass Communication*, edited by Paul Frosh and Amit Pinchevski, 198–215. Basingstoke; New York, NY: Palgrave Macmillan, 2009.

Braziel, Jana Evans, and Kathleen LeBesco, eds. *Bodies out of Bounds: Fatness and Transgression*. Berkeley: University of California Press, 2001.

Brenez, Nicole. 'Entrée (En Matière)'. In *La Vie Nouvelle, Nouvelle Vision: À Propos d'un Film de Philippe Grandrieux*, edited by Nicole Brenez, 11–14. Paris: Scheer, 2005.

———, ed. *La Vie Nouvelle, Nouvelle Vision: À Propos d'un Film de Philippe Grandrieux*. Paris: Scheer, 2005.

Brincken, Jörg von. 'Das Leid an Der Zeit: Gaspar Noés Skandalwerk *Irréversible* Als Zeitbasiertes Filmereignis'. *Medienobservationen* (blog), July 2009. http://www.medienobservationen.lmu.de/artikel/kino/kino_pdf/brincken_irreversible.pdf.

Brinkema, Eugenie. 'A Title Does Not Ask, But Demands That You Make a Choice: On the Otherwise Films of Bruce LaBruce'. *Criticism* 48, no. 1 (2007): 95–126. https://doi.org/10.1353/crt.2007.0016.

———. 'Celluloid Is Sticky: Sex, Death, Materiality, Metaphysics (in Some Films by Catherine Breillat)'. *Women: A Cultural Review* 17, no. 2 (August 2006): 147–70. https://doi.org/10.1080/09574040600795739.

———. '*Irréversible*: A Review'. *Scope*, August 2004.

———. 'Rape and the Rectum: Bersani, Deleuze, Noé'. *Camera Obscura: Feminism, Culture, and Media Studies* 20, no. 1 (2005): 32–57. https://doi.org/10.1215/02705346-20-1_58-33.

———. 'To Cut, to Split, to Touch, to Eat, as of a Body or a Text'. *Angelaki: Journal of the Theoretical Humanities* 14, no. 3 (December 2009): 131–45. https://doi.org/10.1080/09697250903407658.

Brogna, Patricia. '*Plemya*: Regresando a La Tribu'. In *Inclusión, Integración, Diferenciación: La Diversidad Funcional En La Literatura, El Cine y Las Artes Escénicas*, edited by Susanne Hartwig, 233–51. Peter Lang, 2020.

Brooks, Xan. 'A Serbian Film Pulled from FrightFest'. *The Guardian*, 27 August 2010, sec. Film. https://www.theguardian.com/film/2010/aug/27/a-serbian-film-frightfest.

———. 'Dirty Business'. *The Guardian*, 4 January 2005, sec. Film. http://www.theguardian.com/film/2005/jan/04/2.

Brown, Mark. 'UK Censors Ask Focus Groups to Watch Sexually Violent Films'. *The Guardian*, 11 July 2012, sec. Film. https://www.theguardian.com/film/2012/jul/11/censors-focus-sexually-violent-films.

Brown, William. 'Violence in Extreme Cinema and the Ethics of Spectatorship'. *Projections* 7, no. 1 (January 2013). https://doi.org/10.3167/proj.2013.070104.

Brownmiller, Susan. *Against Our Will: Men, Women, and Rape*. New York, NY: Random House, 1975.

Buchwald, Emilie, Pamela R. Fletcher, and Martha Roth, eds. *Transforming a Rape Culture*. Minneapolis, MN: Milkweed Editions, 1995.

Buckingham, David. *Children Talking Television: The Making of Television Literacy*. London: Falmer, 1993.

Burr, Ty. 'Breillat's Graphic "Anatomy" Is Shockingly Theoretical'. *The Boston Globe*. 1 October 2004. https://archive.boston.com/ae/movies/articles/2004/10/01/breillats_graphic_anatomy_is_shockingly_theoretical/.

Butler, Judith. 'Endangered/Endangering: Schematic Racism and White Paranoia'. In *Reading Rodney King/Reading Urban Uprising*, edited by Robert Gooding-Williams, 15–22. New York: Routledge, 1993.

Butterworth, David. 'Twentynine Palms (2003)'. *La Movie Boeuf* (blog), 26 August 2019. https://lamovieboeuf.wordpress.com/2019/08/26/twentynine-palms-2003/.

Cacoulidis, Cleo. 'The 59th Thessaloniki International Film Festival, Greece (Nov. 1–11, 2018)'. *Bright Lights Film Journal* (blog), 14 January 2019. https://brightlightsfilm.com/the-59th-thessaloniki-international-film-festival-greece-nov-1-11-2018/.

Cagle, Robert L. 'The Good, the Bad, and the South Korean: Violence, Morality, and the South Korean Extreme Film'. In *Horror To The Extreme: Changing Boundaries In Asian Cinema*, edited by Jinhee Choi and Mitsuyo Wada-Marciano, 123–43. Hong Kong; London: Hong Kong University Press, 2009.

Cahill, Ann J. *Rethinking Rape*. Ithaca: Cornell University Press, 2001.

Carroll, Noël. 'Fiction, Non-Fiction, and the Film of Presumptive Assertion: A Conceptual Analysis'. In *Philosophy of Film and Motion Pictures an Anthology*, edited by Noël Carroll and Jinhee Choi, 154–71. Malden, MA: Blackwell Pub., 2006.

Caruth, Cathy. *Unclaimed Experience: Trauma, Narrative, and History*. Baltimore, MD: Johns Hopkins University Press, 1996.

Caruth, Cathy, and Robert Jay Lifton. 'Interview with Robert Jay Lifton'. *American Imago* 48, no. 1 (1991): 153–75.

Cashell, Kieran. *Aftershock: The Ethics of Contemporary Transgressive Art*. London: Tauris, 2009.

Censura Não. 'Censura Não'. Censura Não, 2011. https://censuranao.wordpress.com/.

Chamarette, Jenny. *Phenomenology and the Future of Film: Rethinking Subjectivity beyond French Cinema*. Basingstoke: Palgrave Macmillan, 2013.

———. 'Shadows of Being in *Sombre*: Archetypes, Wolf-Men and Bare Life'. In *The New Extremism in Cinema: From France to Europe*, edited by Tanya Horeck and Tina Kendall, 69–81. Edinburgh: Edinburgh University Press, 2011.

Chandler, Daniel. 'An Introduction to Genre Theory', 1997. http://www.aber.ac.uk/media/Documents/intgenre/chandler_genre_theory.pdf.

Chappell, Julie A., and Mallory Young, eds. *Bad Girls and Transgressive Women in Popular Television, Fiction, and Film*. New York, NY: Palgrave Macmillan, 2017.

Chareyron, Romain. 'Horror and the Body: Understanding the Reworking of the Genre in

Marina de Van's *Dans Ma Peau/In My Skin* (2001)'. *Imaginations* 4, no. 1 (August 2013). https://doi.org/10.17742/image.scandal.4-1.9.

Chaw, Walter. 'Gallo's Humor: FFC Interviews Vincent Gallo'. *Film Freak Central* (blog), 3 January 2013. https://www.filmfreakcentral.net/ffc/2013/01/gallos-humor-ffc-interviews-vincent-gallo.html.

Chiesa, Lorenzo. 'Of Bastard Man and Evil Woman, or, the Horror of Sex'. *Film-Philosophy* 16, no. 1 (2012): 199–212. https://doi.org/10.3366/film.2012.0012.

Child, Ben. 'Raindance Film Festival Announces Controversial Lineup'. *The Guardian*, 7 September 2010, sec. Film. https://www.theguardian.com/film/2010/sep/07/raindance-film-festival.

Choi, Eunha. 'Plural Perspectivism: From Flag to Bodies in *Batalla En El Cielo*'. In *Mexican Transnational Cinema and Literature*, edited by Mariacruz Castro Ricalde, Mauricio Díaz Calderón, and James Ramey, 49–67, 2017. https://doi.org/10.3726/b13146.

Choi, Jinhee, and Mitsuyo Wada-Marciano, eds. *Horror To The Extreme: Changing Boundaries In Asian Cinema*. Hong Kong; London: Hong Kong University Press, 2009.

Christopher, James. '9 Songs'. *The Times*, 10 March 2005, sec. Film Reviews.

Citko, Ewa Katarzyna. 'Transcendent Images and *Semina Verbi* in Carlos Reygadas' Films'. *Rocznik Teologii Katolickiej* 20 (2021): 191–212. https://doi.org/10.15290/rtk.2021.20.12.

Clover, Carol J. 'Her Body, Himself: Gender in the Slasher Film'. *Representations*, no. 20 (October 1987): 187–228. https://doi.org/10.2307/2928507.

———. *Men, Women, And Chain Saws: Gender In The Modern Horror Film*. Princeton, NJ: Princeton University Press, 1992.

Cooper, Sarah. *Selfless Cinema?: Ethics and French Documentary*. Research Monographs in French Studies 20. London: Legenda, 2006.

Costa Júnior, Edson Pereira da. 'Apesar Da Noite: A Materialidade Da Figura Humana Em Philippe Grandrieux'. *ARS (São Paulo)* 14, no. 28 (December 2016): 155. https://doi.org/10.11606/issn.2178-0447.ars.2016.122455.

Coulthard, Lisa. 'Desublimating Desire: Courtly Love and Catherine Breillat'. *Journal for Cultural Research* 14, no. 1 (January 2010): 57–69. https://doi.org/10.1080/14797580903363090.

———. 'Uncanny Horrors: Male Rape in Bruno Dumont's Twentynine Palms'. In *Rape in Art Cinema*, edited by Dominique Russell, 171–84. New York, NY: Continuum, 2010.

Coulthard, Lisa, and Chelsea Birks. 'Desublimating Monstrous Desire: The Horror of Gender in New Extremist Cinema'. *Journal of Gender Studies* 25, no. 4 (July 2016): 461–76. https://doi.org/10.1080/09589236.2015.1011100.

———. 'Horrible Sex: The Sexual Relationship In New Extremism'. In *Sex and Storytelling in Modern Cinema: Explicit Sex, Performance and Cinematic Technique*, edited by Lindsay Coleman, 71–94. I. B. Tauris & Co., 2016. https://doi.org/10.5040/9780755694655.

Cox, David. 'A Serbian Film: When Allegory Gets Nasty'. *The Guardian*, 13 December 2010, sec. Film. https://www.theguardian.com/film/filmblog/2010/dec/13/a-serbian-film-allegorical-political.

Cox, Peter. 'Review: Holiday'. *The Lost Highway Hotel* (blog), 29 July 2019. https://thelosthighwayhotel.com/2019/07/29/review-holiday/.

Criminal Justice and Immigration Act, SI 2008/2712 § (2008). http://www.legislation.gov.uk/ukpga/2008/4/pdfs/ukpga_20080004_en.pdf.

Cubitt, Sean. 'Distribution and Media Flows'. *Cultural Politics* 1, no. 2 (1 July 2005): 193–214. https://doi.org/10.2752/174321905778054809.

Cuklanz, Lisa M., and Sujata Moorti. 'Television's "New" Feminism: Prime-Time Representations of Women and Victimization'. *Critical Studies in Media Communication* 23, no. 4 (October 2006): 302–21. https://doi.org/10.1080/07393180600933121.

Currie, Gregory. 'Visible Traces: Documentary and the Contents of Photographs'. In *Philosophy of Film and Motion Pictures: An Anthology*, edited by Noël Carroll and Jinhee Choi, 141–53. Blackwell Philosophy Anthologies. Malden, MA: Blackwell Pub, 2006.

Czmola, Halyne, and Kelly Priscilla Lóddo Cezar. 'Myroslav Slaboshpytskiy: O Cinema Surdo Como Teoria e Prática Criadora'. *Resgate: Revista Interdisciplinar de Cultura* 28 (2020): 1–26.

Dalby, Alexa. 'BFI LFF Review: Holiday (2018)'. *Dog And Wolf* (blog), 31 October 2018. https://www.dogandwolf.com/2018/10/bfi-lff-review-holiday-2018/.

Dang, Harris. 'Sydney Film Festival Review: Holiday (Denmark, 2018) Is an Shocking, Brutal and Unforgettable Experience . . . If You Can Stomach It'. *The AU Review* (blog), 16 June 2018. https://www.theaureview.com/watch/sydney-film-festival-review-holiday-denmark-2018-is-an-shocking-brutal-and-unforgettable-experience-if-you-can-stomach-it/.

Dargis, Manohla. 'Pornographers at Work in a Circular World'. *The New York Times*, April 2005. http://movies2.nytimes.com/2005/04/08/movies/08hole.html?adxnnl=1&adxnnlx=1112914897-Opk4HLZe6K/SQKO4JhXKIA.

Davis, Angela Y. 'Rape, Racism and the Capitalist Setting'. *The Black Scholar* 12, no. 6 (1981): 39–45.

Davis, Nick. 'The View from the Shortbus, or All Those Fucking Movies'. *GLQ: A Journal of Lesbian and Gay Studies* 14, no. 4 (1 January 2008): 623–37. https://doi.org/10.1215/10642684-2008-010.

Dawson, Nick. '9 Songs Review'. *Empire*, 2005. http://www.empireonline.com/movies/9-songs/review/.

De Clercq, Eva. 'Disability @ the Movies: Toward a Disability-Conscious Bioethics'. In *Contemporary Debates in Bioethics: European Perspectives*, edited by Emilian Mihailov, Tenzin Wangmo, Victoria Federiuc, and Bernice Elger, 97–107. De Gruyter Open Poland, 2019. https://doi.org/10.2478/9783110571219-010.

De Leeuw, Ursula. '"A Kiss Is the Beginning of Cannibalism": Julia Ducournau's *Raw* and Bataillean Horror'. *Exchanges: The Interdisciplinary Research Journal* 7, no. 2 (January 2020): 215–28. https://doi.org/10.31273/eirj.v7i2.463.

De Luca, Tiago. 'Carnal Spirituality: The Films of Carlos Reygadas'. *Senses of Cinema* (blog), 11 July 2010. http://sensesofcinema.com/2010/feature-articles/carnal-spirituality-the-films-of-carlos-reygadas-2/.

———. *Realism of the Senses in World Cinema: The Experience of Physical Reality*. London: I. B. Tauris, 2014.

De Saussure, Ferdinand. *Course in General Linguistics*. Translated by Wade Baskin. New York, NY: McGraw-Hill, 1966.

De Valck, Marijke. *Film Festivals: From European Geopolitics to Global Cinephilia*. Amsterdam: Amsterdam University Press, 2007.

———. 'Fostering Art, Adding Value, Cultivating Taste: Film Festivals as Sites of Cultural Legitimization'. In *Film Festivals: History, Theory, Method, Practice*, edited by Marijke De

Valck, Brendan Kredell, and Skadi Loist, 100–116. London: New York, NY: Routledge, 2016.

Dean, Tim. 'The Erotics of Transgression'. In *The Cambridge Companion to Gay and Lesbian Writing*, edited by Hugh Stevens, 65–80. Cambridge Companions to Literature. Cambridge: Cambridge University Press, 2010. https://www.cambridge.org/core/books/cambridge-companion-to-gay-and-lesbian-writing/erotics-of-transgression/31DF1A6E77E49D64AE1D1F94FFE91C4F.

Del Río, Elena. *The Grace of Destruction: A Vital Ethology of Extreme Cinemas*. Thinking Cinema. New York, NY: Bloomsbury Academic, 2016.

Delaporte, Chloé. 'La médiation générique des contenus cinématographiques sur les plateformes de vidéo à la demande'. *Réseaux* 217, no. 5 (2019): 151–84. https://doi.org/10.3917/res.217.0151.

Deleuze, Gilles. *Cinema 1: The Movement-Image*. Translated by Hugh Tomlinson and Barbara Habberjam. Minneapolis: University of Minnesota, 1986.

Deleyto, Celestino. 'Film Genres at the Crossroads: What Genres and Films Do to Each Other'. In *Film Genre Reader IV*, edited by Barry Keith Grant, 218–36. Austin, Tex: University of Texas Press, 2012.

Derrida, Jacques. *Of Grammatology*. Translated by Gayatri Chakravorty Spivak. Baltimore: Johns Hopkins University Press, 1976.

———. 'The Law of Genre'. Translated by Avital Ronell. *Critical Inquiry* 7, no. 1 (1980): 55–81.

Devitt, Amy J. *Writing Genres*. Rhetorical Philosophy and Theory Series. Carbondale: Southern Illinois University Press, 2010.

Di Mattia, Joanna. 'The Devious Conflict: Love and Sex Dissected in Catherine Breillat's *Romance* (1999)'. *Senses of Cinema*, no. 80 (September 2016). https://www.sensesofcinema.com/2016/cteq/romance/.

Dierkes-Thrun, Petra. *Salomé's Modernity: Oscar Wilde and the Aesthetics of Transgression*. Ann Arbor, MI: University of Michigan Press, 2011. https://hdl.handle.net/2027/fulcrum.qn59q4805.

Dimock, Wai Chee. 'Introduction: Genres as Fields of Knowledge'. *PMLA/Publications of the Modern Language Association of America* 122, no. 5 (October 2007): 1377–88. https://doi.org/10.1632/pmla.2007.122.5.1377.

Dix, Andrew. *Beginning Film Studies*. Second edition. Manchester: Manchester University Press, 2016.

Doane, Mary Ann. *Femmes Fatales: Feminism, Film Theory, Psychoanalysis*. New York: Routledge, 1991.

———. 'The Close-up: Scale and Detail in the Cinema'. *Differences: A Journal of Feminist Cultural Studies* 14, no. 3 (2003): 89–111. https://doi.org/10.1215/10407391-14-3-89.

Dodge, Alexa. 'Digitizing Rape Culture: Online Sexual Violence and the Power of the Digital Photograph'. *Crime, Media, Culture: An International Journal* 12, no. 1 (April 2016): 65–82. https://doi.org/10.1177/1741659015601173.

Donnan, Hastings, and Fiona Magowan, eds. *Transgressive Sex: Subversion and Control in Erotic Encounters*. New York: Berghahn Books, 2009.

Dooley, Kath. 'Haptic Visions of Unstable Bodies in the Work of Claire Denis'. *Continuum* 29, no. 3 (May 2015): 434–44. https://doi.org/10.1080/10304312.2015.1025360.

———. 'Navigating the Mind/Body Divide: The Female Cannibal in French Films *Grave* (*Raw*, 2016), *Dans Ma Peau* (*In My Skin*, 2002) and *Trouble Every Day* (2001)'. In *Gender and Contemporary Horror in Film*, edited by Samantha Holland, Robert Shail, and Steven Gerrard, 53–66. Emerald Publishing, 2019. https://doi.org/10.1108/978-1-78769-897-020191005.

Douglas, Mary. *Purity and Danger: An Analysis of Concept of Pollution and Taboo*. London: Ark, 1966.

Downing, Lisa. '*Baise-Moi* or the Ethics of the Desiring Gaze'. Edited by Gill Rye and Carrie Tarr. *Nottingham French Studies* 45, no. 3 (Autumn 2006): 52–65. http://dx.doi.org/10.3366/nfs.2006-3.005.

———. 'French Cinema's New "Sexual Revolution": Postmodern Porn and Troubled Genre'. *French Cultural Studies* 15, no. 3 (October 2004): 265–80. https://doi.org/10.1177/0097155804015003035.

———. 'On the Fantasy of Childlessness as Death in Psychoanalysis and in Roeg's" Don't Look Now" and von Trier's" Antichrist"'. *Lambda Nordica* 16, no. 2–3 (2011): 49–68.

Drissel, Jennifer. 'Hardcore Horror: The Pleasures And Displeasures Of Breaking Cinematic Taboos'. *Messages, Sages and Ages* 5, no. 2 (November 2018): 26–36. https://doi.org/10.5281/zenodo.1552695.

Dumas, Christa, ed. *Genre et Transgression*. Montpellier: Presses universitaires de la Méditerranée, 2015.

Durand, Alain-Philippe, and Naomi Mandel. 'Introduction'. In *Novels of the Contemporary Extreme*, edited by Alain-Philippe Durand and Naomi Mandel, 1–5. Continuum Literary Studies. London; New York: Continuum, 2006.

Durkheim, Emile. *The Rules of Sociological Method and Selected Texts on Sociology and Its Method*. Edited by Steven Lukes. Translated by W. D. Halls. 2nd ed. Basingstoke: Palgrave Macmillan, 2013.

Eagleton, Terry. *Literary Theory: An Introduction*. Oxford: Basil Blackwell, 1983.

Ebert, Roger. 'The Brown Bunny (2004)'. *Rogerebert.Com* (blog), 3 September 2004. http://www.rogerebert.com/reviews/the-brown-bunny-2004.

Edelstein, David. 'Irreversible Errors: Gaspar Noé's Cinematic Rape'. *Slate Movies* (blog), 2003. http://www.slate.com/articles/arts/movies/2003/03/irreversible_errors.html.

Elley, Derek. 'A New Life'. *Variety*, 15 October 2002. https://variety.com/2002/film/reviews/a-new-life-2-1200545470/.

Erensoy, Şirin Fulya. 'Rethinking Pornography within the Context of the New French Extremity: The Case of Baise-Moi'. *CINEJ Cinema Journal* 8, no. 1 (11 March 2020): 60–86. https://doi.org/10.5195/cinej.2020.236.

Evers, Miles M. 'On Transgression'. *International Studies Quarterly* 61, no. 4 (December 2017): 786–94. https://doi.org/10.1093/isq/sqx065.

F., Alex. 'Love Their Movies: Carlos Reygadas'. *Love Their Movies* (blog), 14 May 2009. https://lovetheirmovies.blogspot.com/2009/05/carlos-reygadas.html.

Failler, Angela. 'Narrative Skin Repair: Bearing Witness to Representations of Self-Harm'. *ESC: English Studies in Canada* 34, no. 1 (2009): 11–28. https://doi.org/10.1353/esc.0.0110.

Featherstone, Mark. 'Coito Ergo Sum: Serbian Sadism and Global Capitalism in A Serbian Film'. *Horror Studies* 4, no. 1 (April 2013): 127–41. https://doi.org/10.1386/host.4.1.127_1.

Featherstone, Mark, and Beth Johnson. '"Ovo Je Srbija": The Horror of the National Thing in *A Serbian Film*'. *Journal for Cultural Research* 16, no. 1 (January 2012): 63–79. https://doi.org/10.1080/14797585.2011.633837.

Felperin, Leslie. 'Reviews: *Irreversible*'. *Sight and Sound* 13, no. 3 (2003): 46–48.

Ferguson, Frances. 'Rape and the Rise of the Novel'. *Representations* 20 (October 1987): 88–112. https://doi.org/10.2307/2928503.

Firobri. 'Anapola Mushkadiz: "No Tengo Tabúes Sexuales" / 17 de Octubre de 2007'. *La Cronica de Hoy*, 18 October 2007. https://web.archive.org/web/20071018021634/http://www.cronica.com.mx/nota.php?id_nota=206825.

Fisher, John. 'High Art versus Low Art'. In *The Routledge Companion to Aesthetics*, edited by Berys Nigel Gaut and Dominic Lopes, 409–22. Routledge Philosophy Companions. London; New York: Routledge, Taylor & Francis Group, 2001.

Flanagan, Matthew. 'Towards an Aesthetic of Slow in Contemporary Cinema'. *16:9* 6, no. 29 (November 2008). http://www.16-9.dk/2008-11/side11_inenglish.htm.

Flockhart, Louise. 'Gendering the Cannibal in the Postfeminist Era'. In *Gender and Contemporary Horror in Film*, edited by Samantha Holland, Robert Shail, and Steven Gerrard, 67–81. Emerald Publishing Limited, 2019. https://www.emerald.com/insight/content/doi/10.1108/978-1-78769-897-020191006/full/html.

Foley, Matt, Neil McRobert, and Aspasia Stephanou. 'Introduction'. In *Transgression and Its Limits*, edited by Matt Foley, Neil McRobert, and Aspasia Stephanou. Newcastle upon Tyne, UK: Cambridge Scholars Publishing, 2012.

———, eds. *Transgression and Its Limits*. Newcastle upon Tyne, UK: Cambridge Scholars Publishing, 2012.

Folsom, Ed. 'Database as Genre: The Epic Transformation of Archives'. *PMLA/Publications of the Modern Language Association of America* 122, no. 5 (October 2007): 1571–79. https://doi.org/10.1632/pmla.2007.122.5.1571.

Forrest, Amy E. 'Disciplining Deviant Women: The Critical Reception of *Baise-Moi*'. *Gender Forum*, no. 46 (2013). http://www.genderforum.org/issues/gender-and-contemporary-film/disciplining-deviant-women-the-critical-reception-of-baise-moi.

Foucault, Michel. *Politics, Philosophy, Culture: Interviews and Other Writings 1977–1984*. Edited by Lawrence D. Kritzman. Translated by Alan Sheridan. New York, NY: Routledge, 1990.

———. 'Preface to Transgression'. In *Language, Counter-Memory, Practice: Selected Essays and Interviews*, translated by Donald F. Bouchard, 29–52. Ithaca, NY: Cornell University Press, 1977.

Fowler, Alastair. *Kinds of Literature: An Introduction to the Theory of Genres and Modes*. Oxford: Clarendon, 1982.

Freadman, Anne. 'Le Genre Humain (a Classification)'. *Australian Journal of French Studies* 23 (1986): 309–75.

———. 'Untitled: (On Genre)'. *Cultural Studies* 2, no. 1 (January 1988): 67–99. https://doi.org/10.1080/09502388800490041.

French, Philip. 'A Serbian Film – Review'. *The Observer*, 12 December 2010, sec. Film. https://www.theguardian.com/film/2010/dec/12/a-serbian-film-review.

———. 'Romance'. *The Guardian*, 10 October 1999. https://www.theguardian.com/film/News_Story/Critic_Review/Observer_review/0,,90612,00.html.

Freville, Bob. 'A Terrifying Probe into the Consequences of Female Naïveté: Isabella Eklöf's

Holiday'. *Silent Motorist Media* (blog), 19 February 2019. https://silentmotoristmedia
.wordpress.com/2019/02/19/a-terrifying-probe-into-the-consequences-of-female-na
ivete-isabella-eklofs-holiday/.
Frey, Mattias. *Extreme Cinema: The Transgressive Rhetoric of Today's Art Film Culture*.
London: Rutgers University Press, 2016.
Frodon, Jean-Michel. 'A l'horizon des corps'. *Cahiers du cinéma*, October 2005.
Frow, John. *Genre*. The New Critical Idiom. London; New York: Routledge, 2006.
———. '"Reproducibles, Rubrics, and Everything You Need": Genre Theory Today'. *PMLA/ Publications of the Modern Language Association of America* 122, no. 5 (October 2007): 1626–34. https://doi.org/10.1632/pmla.2007.122.5.1626.
Fuchs, Cynthia. 'The Brown Bunny (2003)'. *PopMatters* (blog), 17 September 2004. https://www.popmatters.com/brown-bunny-2496225817.html.
Galperin, Hernan. 'Beyond Interests, Ideas, and Technology: An Institutional Approach to Communication and Information Policy'. *The Information Society* 20, no. 3 (July 2004): 159–68. https://doi.org/10.1080/01972240490456818.
Galt, Rosalind, and Karl Schoonover, eds. *Global Art Cinema: New Theories and Histories*. New York: Oxford University Press, 2010.
Gavey, Nicola. *Just Sex? The Cultural Scaffolding of Rape*. Second edition. Women and Psychology. Abingdon, Oxon; New York, NY: Routledge, 2019.
Genette, Gérard. *L'Œuvre de l'art*. Vol. 2. 2 vols. Collection Poétique. Paris: Editions du Seuil, 1997.
Gingrich, Plexico. 'Irreversible'. *Ruthless Reviews* (blog), 13 March 2006. http://www.ruth
lessreviews.com/1377/irreversible/.
Gledhill, Christine. 'Rethinking Genre'. In *Reinventing Film Studies*, edited by Christine Gledhill and Linda Williams, 221–43. London; New York, NY: Arnold; Oxford University Press, 2000.
Goddard, Michael. 'Eastern Extreme: The Presentation of Eastern Europe as a Site of Monstrosity in *La Vie Nouvelle* and *Import/Export*'. In *The New Extremism in Cinema: From France to Europe*, edited by Tanya Horeck and Tina Kendall, 82–92. Edinburgh: Edinburgh University Press, 2011.
Gomes, Mayra Rodrigues, and Ivan Paganotti. 'Censura além da classificação: a recepção brasileira de A Serbian film'. *Significação: revista de cultura audiovisual* 39, no. 38 (2012): 278–301.
Gonzales Rose, Jasmine B. 'Race, Evidence, and Epistemic Injustice'. In *Philosophical Foundations of Evidence Law*, edited by Christian Dahlman, Alex Stein, and Giovanni Tuzet, 380–94. New York: Oxford University Press, 2021.
———. 'Toward a Critical Race Theory of Evidence'. *Minnesota Law Review* 101 (2017): 2243–2311.
Gorton, Kristyn. '"The Point of View of Shame": Re-Viewing Female Desire in Catherine Breillat's *Romance* (1999) and *Anatomy of Hell* (2004)'. *Studies in European Cinema* 4, no. 2 (August 2007): 111–24. https://doi.org/10.1386/seci.4.2.111_1.
Gournelos, Ted, and David J. Gunkel, eds. *Transgression 2.0: Media, Culture, and the Politics of a Digital Age*. New York, NY: Continuum, 2012.
Granados, Blanca. '¿Quién diablos es Carlos Reygadas?' *Animal Político* (blog), 24 November 2012. https://www.animalpolitico.com/2012/11/quien-diablos-es-car
los-reygadas/.

Grandrieux, Philippe. Au commencement était la nuit. Interview by Nicolas Renaud, Steve Rioux, and Nicolas Rutigliano, 14 October 1999. http://www.horschamp.qc.ca/Emulsions/grandrieux.html.

Grant, Melissa Gira. *Playing the Whore: The Work of Sex Work*. London: Verso, 2014.

Graves, Leslie. 'Transgressive Traditions and Art Definitions'. *The Journal of Aesthetics and Art Criticism* 56, no. 1 (1998): 39–48. https://doi.org/10.2307/431946.

Gregoli, Roberta. 'Transnational Reception of *City of God* and *Elite Squad*'. *Participations: Journal of Audience and Reception Studies* 8, no. 2 (November 2011): 350–74.

Grodal, Torben. 'Antichrist, Explicit Sex, Anxiety, and Care'. In *Sex and Storytelling in Modern Cinema: Explicit Sex, Performance and Cinematic Technique*, edited by Lindsay Coleman, 179–94. I. B. Tauris & Co. Ltd, 2016. http://www.bloomsburycollections.com/book/sex-and-storytelling-in-modern-cinema-explicit-sex-performance-and-cinematic-technique.

———. *Moving Pictures: A New Theory of Film Genres, Feelings, and Cognition*. Oxford: New York, NY: Oxford University Press, 1999.

Grønstad, Asbjørn. 'Abject Desire: *Anatomie de l'enfer* and the Unwatchable'. *Studies in French Cinema* 6, no. 3 (9 February 2007): 161–69. https://doi.org/10.1386/sfci.6.3.161_1.

———. 'On the Unwatchable'. In *The New Extremism in Cinema: From France to Europe*, edited by Tanya Horeck and Tina Kendall, 192–205. Edinburgh: Edinburgh University Press, 2011.

———. *Screening the Unwatchable: Spaces of Negation in Post-Millennial Art Cinema*. New York, NY: Palgrave Macmillan, 2012.

———. 'Slow Cinema and the Ethics of Duration'. In *Slow Cinema*, edited by Tiago de Luca and Nuno Barradas Jorge, 273–84. Edinburgh: Edinburgh University Press, 2016.

Groys, Boris. *On the New*. Brooklyn: Verso, 2014.

Guest, Haden. 'Darkness Visible'. *Film Comment* 46, no. 6 (2010): 42–45.

Guillen, Michael. 'Review of Der Freie Wille / The Free Will'. *Screen Anarchy* (blog), 25 January 2007. https://screenanarchy.com/2007/01/2007-berlin-beyondreview-of-der-freie-wille-the-free-will.html.

Gwynne, Joel, ed. *Transgression in Anglo-American Cinema: Gender, Sex and the Deviant Body*. London; New York: Wallflower Press, 2016.

Hainge, Greg. 'A Full Face Bright Red Money Shot: Incision, Wounding and Film Spectatorship in Marina de Van's *Dans Ma Peau*'. *Continuum* 26, no. 4 (August 2012): 565–77. https://doi.org/10.1080/10304312.2012.698036.

———. '*Le Corps Concret*: Of Bodily and Filmic Material Excess in Philippe Grandrieux's Cinema'. *Australian Journal of French Studies* 44, no. 2 (2007): 153–71. http://dx.doi.org/10.3828/AJFS.44.2.153.

———. '*L'Invention Du Troisième Peuple*: The Utopian Vision of Philippe Grandrieux's Dystopias'. In *Nowhere Is Perfect: French and Francophone Utopias/Dystopias*, edited by John West-Sooby, 228–39. Newark, DE: University of Delaware Press, 2008.

———. *Philippe Grandrieux: Sonic Cinema*. Ex:Centrics. New York; London: Bloomsbury Academic, 2017.

Hall, Stuart. 'Encoding/Decoding'. In *Media and Cultural Studies: Keyworks*, edited by Meenakshi Gigi Durham and Douglas Kellner, 163–73. Malden, MA: Blackwell, 2006.

———. 'Introduction'. In *Representation: Cultural Representations and Signifying Practices*, edited by Stuart Hall, 1–11. London: Sage; Open University, 1997.
Hallam, Lindsay Anne. *Screening the Marquis de Sade: Pleasure, Pain and the Transgressive Body in Film*. Jefferson, N.C: McFarland, 2012.
Hawkins, Joan. 'Culture Wars: Some New Trends in Art Horror'. *Jump Cut* 51 (Spring 2009). http://www.ejumpcut.org/archive/jc51.2009/artHorror/.
———. *Cutting Edge: Art-Horror and the Horrific Avant-Garde*. Minneapolis, MN: University of Minnesota Press, 2000.
Heinich, Nathalie. 'De la transgression en art contemporain'. In *Paradoxes de la transgression*, edited by Michel Hastings, Loïc Nicolas, and Cédric Passard, 111–24. Paris: CNRS éditions, 2012.
———. 'From Sociology of Culture to Sociology of Artistic Producers: How to Become a Contemporary Artist'. In *Routledge International Handbook of the Sociology of Art and Culture*, edited by Laurie Hanquinet and Mike Savage, 199–206. London: Routledge, 2016.
———. *Le paradigme de l'art contemporain: Structures d'une révolution artistique*. Paris: Gallimard, 2014.
———. *Le triple jeu de l'art contemporain: Sociologie des arts plastiques*. Paris: Les Editions de Minuit, 1998.
———. 'The Art of Inflicting Suffering: Animals and Spectators in the Crucible of Contemporary Art'. In *Suffering, Art, and Aesthetics*, edited by Ratiba Hadj-Moussa and Michael Nijhawan, 207–23. New York: Palgrave Macmillan US, 2014.
Held, Jacob. 'What Is and Is Not Porn: Sex, Narrative, and *Baise-Moi*'. In *Sex and Storytelling in Modern Cinema: Explicit Sex, Performance and Cinematic Technique*, edited by Lindsay Coleman, 25–48. I. B. Tauris & Co. Ltd, 2016. http://www.bloomsburycollections.com/book/sex-and-storytelling-in-modern-cinema-explicit-sex-performance-and-cinematic-technique.
Hemmens, Alastair, and Russell Williams, eds. *Autour de l'extrême littéraire*. Newcastle upon Tyne: Cambridge Scholars Publishing, 2012.
Hennigan, Adrian. 'Michael Winterbottom Interview: *9 Songs*'. *BBC* (blog), 3 March 2005. http://www.bbc.co.uk/films/2005/03/03/michael_winterbottom_9_songs_interview.shtml.
Herbert, Daniel. 'From Art House To Your House: The Distribution Of Quality Cinema On Home Video'. *Revue Canadienne d'Études Cinématographiques / Canadian Journal of Film Studies* 20, no. 2 (2011): 2–18. https://doi.org/10.3138/cjfs.20.2.2.
Herron, Adam. '"Victim Sells": The Commercial Context of Snuff Fiction and *Serbian Film*'. *Film Matters* 9, no. 3 (December 2018): 28–41. https://doi.org/10.1386/fm.9.3.28_1.
Hessler, Jennifer. 'Quality You Can't Touch: Mubi Social, Platform Politics, and the Online Distribution of Art Cinema'. *The Velvet Light Trap* 82, no. 1 (2018): 3–17.
Hester, Helen. *Beyond Explicit: Pornography and the Displacement of Sex*. Albany, NY: State University of New York Press, 2014.
Hickin, Daniel. 'Censorship, Reception and the Films of Gaspar Noé: The Emergence of New Extremism in Britain'. In *The New Extremism in Cinema: From France to Europe*, edited by Tanya Horeck and Tina Kendall, 117–29. Edinburgh: Edinburgh University Press, 2011.
Higgins, Charlotte. '"I Am the Only Normal Director"'. *The Guardian*, 22 August 2005.

http://www.theguardian.com/film/2005/aug/22/edinburghfilmfestival2005.edinburghfilmfestival.

Higgins, Lynn A. 'Screen/Memory: Rape and Its Alibis in *Last Year at Marienbad*'. In *Rape and Representation*, edited by Lynn A. Higgins and Brenda R. Silver, 303–21. Gender and Culture. New York: Columbia University Press, 1991. http://www.neugraphic.com/marienbad/marienbad-text8.html.

Hill Collins, Patricia. *Black Feminist Thought: Knowledge, Consciousness, and the Politics of Empowerment*, 2000.

Hobbs, Simon. *Cultivating Extreme Art Cinema: Text, Paratext and Home Video Culture*. Edinburgh: Edinburgh University Press, 2018.

Hoberman, J. 'A Squalid Swedish Porno Drama Punishes Its Audience'. *The Village Voice*, 29 March 2005. https://www.villagevoice.com/2005/03/29/a-squalid-swedish-porno-drama-punishes-its-audience/.

——. 'Carlos Reygadas'. *Artforum*, February 2006. https://www.artforum.com/print/200602/carlos-reygadas-10267.

Hogan, Jackie. 'Anatomy of a Rape: Sexual Violence and Secondary Victimization Scripts in U.S. Film and Television, 1959–2019'. *Crime, Media, Culture* 18, no. 2 (2021): 203–22. https://doi.org/10.1177/17416590211000388.

Holden, Stephen. 'FILM REVIEW; Erotic Horror With Enough Gore to Distress Dracula'. *The New York Times*, 1 March 2002, sec. Movies. https://www.nytimes.com/2002/03/01/movies/film-review-erotic-horror-with-enough-gore-to-distress-dracula.html.

Horeck, Tanya. *Public Rape: Representing Violation in Fiction and Film*. Sussex Studies in Culture and Communication. London: Routledge, 2004.

——. 'Shame and the Sisters: Catherine Breillat's *À Ma Sœur!* (*Fat Girl*)'. In *Rape in Art Cinema*, edited by Dominique Russell, 195–209. New York, NY: Continuum, 2010.

Horeck, Tanya, and Tina Kendall, eds. *The New Extremism in Cinema: From France to Europe*. Edinburgh: Edinburgh University Press, 2011.

——. 'The New Extremisms: Rethinking Extreme Cinema'. *Cinephile* 8, no. 2 (2012): 7–9.

Hubner, Laura. 'A Taste for Flesh and Blood? Shifting Classifications of Contemporary European Cinema'. In *Valuing Films: Shifting Perceptions of Worth*, edited by Laura Hubner, 198–214. London: Palgrave Macmillan UK, 2011.

Huyssen, Andreas. *After the Great Divide: Modernism, Mass Culture, Postmodernism*. Bloomington, IN: Indiana University Press, 1986.

Hynes, Eric. 'The Tribe'. *Film Comment*, June 2015, 73.

Jackman, Myles. 'The Following Content Is Not Acceptable'. *Myles Jackman Blog* (blog), 2014. http://mylesjackman.com/index.php/my-blog/106-the-following-content-is-not-acceptable.

Jackson, Neil. 'Euro-Snuff: *A Serbian Film* for the Family'. In *New Blood: Critical Approaches to Contemporary Horror*, edited by Eddie Falvey, Jonathan Wroot, and Joe Hickinbottom, 247–63. Horror Studies. Cardiff: University of Wales Press, 2020.

Jaffe, Ira. *Slow Movies: Countering the Cinema of Action*. New York, NY; London: Wallflower Press, 2014.

Jameson, Fredric. 'Magical Narratives: On the Dialectical Use of Genre Criticism'. In *Modern Genre Theory*, edited by David Duff, 167–92. Oxford: New York, NY: Routledge, 2014.

——. *The Political Unconscious: Narrative as a Socially Symbolic Act*. London: Routledge, 1983.

Jameson, Martin. 'When Is A Penis Not A Penis?' *NinjaMarmoset* (blog), 6 August 2019. https://ninjamarmoset.com/2019/08/06/when-is-a-penis-not-a-penis/.
Jauss, Hans Robert. 'Literary History as a Challenge to Literary Theory'. *New Literary History* 2, no. 1 (1970): 7. https://doi.org/10.2307/468585.
———. 'Theory of Genres and Medieval Literature'. In *Modern Genre Theory*, edited by David Duff, 127–47. Oxford: New York, NY: Routledge, 2014.
Jean, Grégori. 'Le Porno et la grâce'. In *La sexualité en images: regards croisés sur l'érotisation des corps*, edited by Bertrand Cochard and Grégori Jean, 11–32. Paris: Hermann, 2018.
Jenkins, David. 'Julia Ducournau: "The Way Losing Your Virginity Is Portrayed in Most Movies Is Very Outdated"'. *Little White Lies*, 2 April 2017. https://lwlies.com/interviews/julia-ducournau-raw/.
Jenks, Chris. *Transgression*. London: Routledge, 2003.
Johnson, Beth. 'Sex, Drugs and Rock and Roll: Analysing Aesthetics, Performance and Pleasure in *9 Songs*'. In *Sex and Storytelling in Modern Cinema: Explicit Sex, Performance and Cinematic Technique*, edited by Lindsay Coleman, 137–58. London; New York, NY: I. B. Tauris, 2016.
Johnson, G. Allen. '"Battle in Heaven"'. SFGATE, 31 March 2006. https://www.sfgate.com/movies/article/FILM-CLIPS-Opening-today-2520640.php.
Johnston, Michael. 'View from the Road: Vincent Gallo's *The Brown Bunny*'. *Mise-En-Scène: The Journal of Film and Visual Narration* 1, no. 1 (Winter 2016). https://journals.sfu.ca/msq/index.php/msq/article/view/6.
Jones, Steve. '"Extreme" Porn? The Implications of a Label'. *Porn Studies* 3, no. 3 (July 2016): 295–307. https://doi.org/10.1080/23268743.2016.1196011.
———. 'Hardcore Horror: Challenging the Discourses of "Extremity"'. In *New Blood: Critical Approaches to Contemporary Horror*, edited by Eddie Falvey, Jonathan Wroot, and Joe Hickinbottom, 35–51. Horror Studies. Cardiff: University of Wales Press, 2020.
———. 'Horrorporn/Pornhorror: The Problematic Communities and Contexts of Online Shock Imagery'. In *Porn.Com: Making Sense of Online Pornography*, 123–37. New York, NY: Peter Lang, 2010.
———. *Torture Porn: Popular Horror after Saw*. Houndmills, Basingstoke: Palgrave Macmillan, 2013.
Jordan, Shirley. '«Dans le mauvais goût pour le mauvais goût»? Pornographie, violence et sexualité féminine dans la fiction de Virginie Despentes'. In *Nouvelles écrivaines: nouvelles voix?*, edited by Nathalie Morello and Catherine Rodgers, 121–39. Amsterdam: Rodopi, 2002.
Jorgensen, Kristine, and Faltin Karlsen, eds. *Transgression in Games and Play*. Cambridge, MA: The MIT Press, 2018.
Joyard, Olivier. 'Sexe: La Prochaine Frontière Du Cinéma'. *Cahiers Du Cinéma* 574 (October 2002): 10–12.
Julius, Anthony. *Transgressions: The Offences of Art*. London: Thames & Hudson, 2002.
JWIN. 'A Hole in My Heart'. *Time Out London* (blog), 2005. https://www.timeout.com/london/film/a-hole-in-my-heart.
Kang, Taran. *Transgression and the Aesthetics of Evil*. Toronto; Buffalo: University of Toronto Press, 2022.
Kapka, Alexandra. 'Understanding *A Serbian Film*: The Effects of Censorship and File-Sharing on Critical Reception and Perceptions of Serbian National Identity in the UK'.

Frames Cinema Journal, no. 6 (December 2014). https://framescinemajournal.com/article/understanding-a-serbian-film-the-effects-of-censorship-and-file-sharing-on-critical-reception-and-perceptions-of-serbian-national-identity-in-the-uk/.

Keeling, Stanley. *Time and Duration: A Philosophical Study*. Edited by Gerald Rochelle. Lewiston, NY: E. Mellen Press, 1991.

Keesey, Douglas. 'Split Identification: Representations of Rape in Gaspar Noé's *Irréversible* and Catherine Breillat's *A Ma Sœur!/Fat Girl*'. *Studies in European Cinema* 7, no. 2 (December 2010): 95–107. https://doi.org/10.1386/seci.7.2.95_1.

Kendall, Tina. 'Affect and the Ethics of Snuff in Extreme Art Cinema'. In *Snuff: Real Death and Screen Media*, edited by Neil Jackson, Shaun Kimber, Johnny Walker, and Thomas Joseph Watson, 257–75. New York: Bloomsbury Academic, 2016.

———. 'Reframing Bataille: On Tacky Spectatorship in the New European Extremism'. In *The New Extremism in Cinema: From France to Europe*, edited by Tanya Horeck and Tina Kendall, 43–54. Edinburgh: Edinburgh University Press, 2011.

Kenny, Oliver. 'Breaking Conventions? Political Ideology of Films With Explicit Sex'. *Open Screens* 5, no. 1 (July 2022): 1–21. https://doi.org/10.16995/OS.8008.

———. 'British Film Censorship in the Twenty-First Century'. In *The Palgrave Handbook of Violence in Film and Media*, edited by Steve Choe, 143–68. Cham, Switzerland: Palgrave Macmillan, 2022.

———. 'Eroticism, Pornography, Love: The Discursive Politics of Reactionary French Scholarship on Sexual Imagery'. *Studies in Arts and Humanities* 5, no. 2 (December 2019): 30–50. https://doi.org/10.18193/sah.v5i2.174.

Kermode, Mark. 'Mark Kermode on Censorship: What Are They Scared Of?' *The Independent*, June 2002. https://www.independent.co.uk/arts-entertainment/films/features/mark-kermode-on-censorship-what-are-they-scared-of-180943.html.

Kermode, Mark, and Nick James. 'Horror Movie'. *Sight and Sound* 13, no. 2 (2003): 20–22.

Kerner, Aaron, and Jonathan Knapp. *Extreme Cinema: Affective Strategies in Transnational Media*. Edinburgh: Edinburgh University Press, 2016.

Kimber, Shaun. 'Transgressive Edge Play and *Srpski Film/A Serbian Film*'. *Horror Studies* 5, no. 1 (April 2014): 107–25. https://doi.org/10.1386/host.5.1.107_1.

Kipnis, Laura. *Bound and Gagged: Pornography and the Politics of Fantasy in America*. Durham, NC: Duke University Press, 1999.

Koch, Angela. 'Das >unsägliche< Verbrechen. Überlegungen zur Tabuisierung von sexueller Gewalt im Spielfilm'. In *Geschlecht Als Tabu: Orte, Dynamiken und Funktionen der de/Thematisierung Von Geschlecht.*, edited by Ute Frietsch, Konstanze Hanitzsch, Jennifer John, and Beatrice Michaelis, 187–202. Bielefeld: Transcript Verlag, 2008.

———. 'Ir/réversible – die audiovisuelle Codierung von sexueller Gewalt im Film'. In *Sex/ismus und Medien*, edited by Kerstin Knopf and Monika Schneikart, 139–64. Herbolzheim: Centaurus, 2007.

———. *Ir/reversible Bilder: zur Visualisierung und Medialisierung von sexueller Gewalt*. Berlin: Vorwerk 8, 2015.

Kohn, Eric. '*A Serbian Film* Shocks Midnight Audiences At SXSW'. *The Wall Street Journal* (blog), 15 March 2010. http://blogs.wsj.com/speakeasy/2010/03/15/a-serbian-film-shocks-midnight-audiences-at-sxsw/.

———. '"Holiday" Review: Devastating Danish Drama Has the Most Unsettling Rape Scene Since "Irreversible" — Sundance 2018'. *IndieWire* (blog), 26 January 2018. https://

www.indiewire.com/2018/01/holiday-review-isabella-eklof-rape-sundance-2018-120 1921797/.

Kolarić, Vladimir. 'Odbrana umetnosti u *Srpskom filmu* Srđana Spasojevića'. *Kultura* 127 (2010): 82–101.

Kostić, Toni. 'Postmoderni Film Strave Kao Balkanski Žanr: Srpski Film Srđana Spasojevića'. *Hrvatski Filmski Ljetopis* 69 (2012): 133–43.

Kouchakji, Kristi. 'Activism in Action: Screening *The Act of Killing* and *The Look of Silence* in the West'. *Participations: Journal of Audience and Reception Studies* 15, no. 1 (May 2018): 427–38.

Kozina, Mario. 'Srpski Film (Srđan Spasojević, 2010)'. *Hrvatski Filmski Ljetopis* 64 (2010): 156–59.

Kozol, Wendy. *Distant Wars Visible: The Ambivalence of Witnessing*. Minneapolis, MN: University of Minnesota Press, 2014.

Kracauer, Siegfried. *Theory of Film: The Redemption of Physical Reality*. Princeton: Princeton University Press, 1960.

Krämer, Peter. '"Movies That Make People Sick": Audience Responses to Stanley Kubrick's *A Clockwork Orange* in 1971/72'. *Participations: Journal of Audience and Reception Studies* 8, no. 2 (November 2011): 416–30.

Krautheim, Graeme. 'Aspiring to the Void: The Collapse of Genre and Erasure of Body in Gaspar Noé's *Irreversible*'. *Cinephile* 4 (2008): 13–17.

Krzywinska, Tanya. *Sex and the Cinema*. London: Wallflower, 2006.

Kuhn, Annette, and Guy Westwell. *Oxford Dictionary of Film Studies*. 1st ed. Oxford Paperback Reference. Oxford: Oxford University Press, 2012.

Kuppers, Petra. *The Scar of Visibility: Medical Performances and Contemporary Art*. Minneapolis, MN: University of Minnesota Press, 2007.

Ladegaard, Jakob. 'Spatial Affects: Body and Space in Philippe Grandrieux's *La Vie Nouvelle*'. In *Exploring Text and Emotions*, edited by Lars Sætre, Patrizia Lombardo, and Julien Zanetta, 151–76. Aarhus, Denmark: Aarhus University Press, 2014.

Lahr-Vivaz, Elena. *Mexican Melodrama: Film and Nation from the Golden Age to the New Wave*. Tucson, AZ: The University of Arizona Press, 2016.

Lane, Anthony. 'Feelings'. *The New Yorker*, 11 April 2005. http://www.newyorker.com/magazine/2005/04/11/feelings.

Langford, Barry. *Film Genre: Hollywood and Beyond*. Edinburgh: Edinburgh University Press, 2005.

Larsson, Mariah. '"Close Your Eyes and Tell Me What You See": Sex and Politics in Lukas Moodysson's Films'. In *The New Extremism in Cinema: From France to Europe*, edited by Tanya Horeck and Tina Kendall, 142–53. Edinburgh: Edinburgh University Press, 2011.

Lastens, Emeric de. 'D'une Histoire Naturelle Du Mal'. In *La Vie Nouvelle, Nouvelle Vision: À Propos d'un Film de Philippe Grandrieux*, edited by Nicole Brenez, 35–40. Paris: Scheer, 2005.

Lawlor, Leonard. 'Jacques Derrida'. In *The Stanford Encyclopedia of Philosophy*, edited by Edward N. Zalta, Winter 2021. Metaphysics Research Lab, Stanford University, 2021. https://plato.stanford.edu/archives/win2021/entries/derrida/.

Le Breton, David. *La peau et la trace*. Paris: Editions Métailié, 2003. https://doi.org/10.3917/meta.breto.2003.01.

Leeson, Chloe. 'Cold Hard Cash and Violence – Holiday (Film Review)'. *VultureHound Magazine* (blog), 12 February 2019. https://vulturehound.co.uk/2019/02/cold-hard-cash-and-violence-holiday-film-review/.

Léger, Marc James. 'Sad Bunny: Vincent Gallo and The Melancholia of Gender'. *Revue Canadienne d'Études Cinématographiques / Canadian Journal of Film Studies* 16, no. 2 (2007): 82–98. https://doi.org/10.3138/cjfs.16.2.82.

Lehnen, Jeremy. 'Sex, Silence And Social Disintegration: *Batalla En El Cielo*'. *Cine y . . .: Journal of Interdisciplinary Studies on Film in Spanish* 4, no. 1 (2014): 1–12.

Lev, Peter. *American Films of the '70s Conflicting Visions*. Austin, TX: University of Texas Press, 2010.

Levit, Donald. 'The Race Is Not to the Swift'. *Reel Talk Movie Reviews* (blog), n.d. http://www.reeltalkreviews.com/browse/viewitem.asp?type=review&id=5269.

Levy, Emanuel. 'Twentynine Palms (Aka 29 Palms): Bruno Dumont's Violent Art Film'. *EmanuelLevy.Com* (blog), 15 June 2011. https://emanuellevy.com/review/twentynine-palms/.

Lewis, Justin. *The Ideological Octopus: An Exploration of Television and Its Audience*. London: Routledge, 1991.

Leys, Ruth. *Trauma: A Genealogy*. Chicago: University of Chicago Press, 2000.

Lim, Song Hwee. *Tsai Ming-Liang and a Cinema of Slowness*. Honolulu: University of Hawai'i Press, 2014.

Lobato, Ramon. *Shadow Economies of Cinema: Mapping Informal Film Distribution*. Cultural Histories of Cinema. London: Palgrave Macmillan [on behalf of the] BFI, 2012.

Lockwood, John, and William Smith. *Chambers/Murray Latin-English Dictionary*. Edinburgh; London: Chambers & Murray, 1976.

Lodge, Guy. 'Sundance Film Review: "Holiday"'. *Variety* (blog), 31 January 2018. https://variety.com/2018/film/reviews/holiday-review-1202681429/.

Lowenstein, Adam. 'Feminine Horror: The Embodied Surrealism of *In My Skin*'. In *The Dread of Difference: Gender and the Horror Film*, edited by Barry Keith Grant, 2nd ed., 470–87. Austin, TX: University of Texas Press, 2015.

Lübecker, Nikolaj. 'Bruno Dumont's *Twentynine Palms*: The Avant-Garde as Tragedy?' *Studies in French Cinema* 11, no. 3 (2011): 235–47. https://doi.org/10.1386/sfc.11.3.235.

———. *The Feel-Bad Film*. Edinburgh: Edinburgh University Press, 2015.

Luca, Tiago de, and Nuno Barradas Jorge, eds. *Slow Cinema*. Edinburgh: Edinburgh University Press, 2016.

Lucca, Violet. 'Internal Affair'. *Film Comment* 49, no. 3 (2013): 16–16.

Lugan, Camille. 'Mangeuses d'hommes'. *Avoir à Lire* (blog), 9 December 2016. https://www.avoir-alire.com/trouble-every-day-la-critique-du-film.

Lukes, Steven. 'Introduction'. In *The Rules of Sociological Method and Selected Texts on Sociology and Its Method*, by Emile Durkheim, xi–xxxv. edited by Steven Lukes, translated by W. D. Halls, 2nd ed. Basingstoke: Palgrave Macmillan, 2013.

Lukow, Gregory, and Steven Ricci. 'The "Audience" Goes "Public": Intertextuality, Genre, and the Responsibilities of Film Literacy'. *On Film*, no. 12 (1984): 29–36.

Lury, Karen. 'Closeup: Documentary Aesthetics'. *Screen* 44, no. 1 (2003): 101–5. https://doi.org/10.1093/screen/44.1.101.

MacKenzie, Scott. 'Baise-Moi, Feminist Cinemas and the Censorship Controversy'. *Screen* 43, no. 3 (2002): 315–24. https://doi.org/10.1093/screen/43.3.315.

———. 'On Watching and Turning Away: Ono's "Rape", "Cinéma Direct" Aesthetics and the Geneology of "Cinéma Brut"'. In *Rape in Art Cinema*, edited by Dominique Russell, 159–70. New York, NY: Continuum, 2010.

Maes, Hans, ed. *Pornographic Art and the Aesthetics of Pornography*, 2013.

Maes, Hans, and Jerrold Levinson, eds. *Art and Pornography: Philosophical Essays*. Oxford: Oxford University Press, 2012.

Maltby, Richard. *Hollywood Cinema: An Introduction*. Oxford: Blackwell, 1996.

Manovich, Lev. *The Language of New Media*. Cambridge, MA: MIT Press, 2001.

Marks, Laura U. *The Skin Of The Film: Intercultural Cinema, Embodiment, And The Senses*. Durham, NC: Duke University Press, 2000.

———. *Touch: Sensuous Theory and Multisensory Media*. Minneapolis, MN: University of Minnesota Press, 2002.

Martin, Adrian. 'A Magic Identification with Forms: Philippe Grandrieux in the Night of Artaud'. *Image [&] Narrative* 17, no. 5 (2016): 30–40.

———. 'Dance Girl Dance: Philippe Grandrieux's *La Vie Nouvelle* (*The New Life*, 2002)'. *Kinoeye* 4, no. 3 (July 2004). http://www.kinoeye.org/04/03/martin03.php.

Marzano, Michela. *La pornographie, ou, L'épuisement du désir*. Paris: Hachette Littératures, 2007.

Mauss, Marcel. *The Gift: The Form and Reason for Exchange in Archaic Societies*. Translated by W. D. Halls. Routledge Classics. London: Routledge, 2002.

McCarthy, Todd. '"Holiday": Film Review | Sundance 2018'. *The Hollywood Reporter* (blog), 25 January 2018. https://www.hollywoodreporter.com/movies/movie-reviews/holiday-review-1078574/.

McCormick, Richard W. *Gender and Sexuality in Weimar Modernity: Film, Literature, and 'New Objectivity'*. New York, NY: Palgrave, 2001.

McGillvray, Maddi. 'The Feminist Art Horror of the New French Extremity'. In *Women Make Horror*, edited by Alison Peirse, 122–32. Rutgers University Press, 2021. https://www.degruyter.com/document/doi/10.36019/9781978805156-010/html.

McGlynn, Clare, Erika Rackley, and Ian Ward. 'Judging *Destricted*'. *King's Law Journal* 20, no. 1 (February 2009): 53–67. https://doi.org/10.1080/09615768.2009.11427720.

McMahon, Laura. *Cinema and Contact: The Withdrawal of Touch in Nancy, Bresson, Duras and Denis*. Legenda Moving Image 2. London: Modern Humanities Research Association and Maney Publishing, 2012.

McNair, Brian. *Porno? Chic!: How Pornography Changed the World and Made It a Better Place*. Routledge, 2013.

Mikkola, Mari, ed. *Beyond Speech: Pornography and Analytic Feminist Philosophy*. New York: Oxford University Press, 2017.

———. *Pornography: A Philosophical Introduction*. New York: Oxford University Press, 2019.

Miller, Carolyn R. 'Genre as Social Action'. *Quarterly Journal of Speech* 70, no. 2 (May 1984). 151–67. https://doi.org/10.1080/00335638409383686.

Mirabal, Marisa. '"Holiday" Review: Director Isabella Eklöf Addresses the Stigmatization of Sexual Assault Through a Highly Stylized Lens'. *Slash Film* (blog), 26 September 2018. https://www.slashfilm.com/holiday-review-fantastic-fest/.

Morsch, Thomas. 'Der Körperdiskurs des Films, *Audition* und die ästhetische Moderne'.

In *Wort und Fleisch: Kino zwischen Text und Körper*, edited by Sabine Nessel, Winfried Pauleit, Christine Rüffert, Karl-Heinz Schmid, and Alfred Tews, 10–26. Berlin: Bertz + Fischer, 2008.

———. 'Filmische Erfahrung im Spannungsfeld zwischen Körper, Sinnlichkeit und Ästhetik'. *montage AV. Zeitschrift für Theorie und Geschichte audiovisueller Kommunikation* 19, no. 1 (2010): 55–77. https://doi.org/10.25969/MEDIAREP/336.

———. *Medienästhetik des Films: verkörperte Wahrnehmung und ästhetische Erfahrung im Kino*. Munich: Wilhelm Fink, 2011.

Mortensen, Torill Elvira, and Kristine Jorgensen. *The Paradox of Transgression in Games*. New York: Routledge, 2020.

Mtshali, Marya T., and Breanne Fahs. 'Catherine Breillat's *Romance* and *Anatomy of Hell*: Subjectivity and the Gendering of Sexuality'. *Women: A Cultural Review* 25, no. 2 (April 2014): 160–75. https://doi.org/10.1080/09574042.2014.944415.

Mulvey, Laura. 'Visual Pleasure and Narrative Cinema'. In *Film Theory and Criticism: Introductory Readings*, edited by Leo Braudy and Marshall Cohen, 833–44. New York, NY: Oxford University Press, 1999.

Münsterberg, Hugo. 'The Photoplay: A Psychological Study'. Project Gutenberg, 16 March 2005. http://www.gutenberg.org/files/15383/15383-h/15383-h.htm.

Nancy, Jean-Luc. 'Icon Fury: Claire Denis's "Trouble Every Day"'. *Film-Philosophy* 12, no. 1 (2008): 1–9. https://doi.org/10.3366/film.2008.0002.

Neale, Steve. 'Art Cinema as Institution'. *Screen* 22, no. 1 (May 1981): 11–40. https://doi.org/10.1093/screen/22.1.11.

———. *Genre and Hollywood*. London; New York, NY: Routledge, 2000.

———. 'Questions of Genre'. In *Film Genre Reader IV*, edited by Barry Keith Grant, 178–202. Austin, Texas: University of Texas Press, 2012.

Nettelbeck, Colin. 'Self-Constructing Women: Beyond the Shock of "Baise-Moi" and "A Ma Sœur!"' *Fulgor: Flinders University Languages Group Online Review* 1, no. 3 (2003): 58–68.

Nichols, Bill. *Introduction to Documentary*. 2nd ed. Bloomington, IN: Indiana University Press, 2010.

Nicodemo, Timothy. 'Cinematography and Sensorial Assault in Gaspar Noé's "Irreversible"'. *Cinephile* 8, no. 2 (2012): 33–39.

Ogien, Albert. 'Les Limites Du Tolérable'. In *Paradoxes de La Transgression*, edited by Michel Hastings, Loïc Nicolas, and Cédric Passard, 49–66. Paris: CNRS éditions, 2012.

Ognjanović, Dejan. 'Genre Films in Recent Serbian Cinema'. *KinoKultura* (blog), 2009. https://www.kinokultura.com/specials/8/ognjanovic.shtml.

———. 'No Escape from the Body: Bleak Landscapes of Serbian Horror Film'. *Humanistika* 1 (April 2017): 49–66.

Olney, Andrew McGregor. 'Predicting Film Genres with Implicit Ideals'. *Frontiers in Psychology* 3 (2013). https://doi.org/10.3389/fpsyg.2012.00565.

Opacki, Ireneusz. 'Royal Genres'. In *Modern Genre Theory*, edited by David Duff, 118–26. Oxford; New York, NY: Routledge, 2014.

Ordóñez, Samanta. 'Carlos Reygadas' *Batalla En El Cielo/Battle in Heaven* (2005): Disarticulating the Brown Male Body from Myths of Mexican Masculinity'. *Studies in Spanish & Latin-American Cinemas* 14, no. 1 (March 2017): 77–94. https://doi.org/10.1386/slac.14.1.77_1.

Oxen, Nicolas. 'Das Sensorische Bild: Instabile Wahrnehmungsrelationen Im Kino von Philippe Grandrieux'. In *Medienanthropologische Szenen*, edited by Christiane Voss, Katerina Krtilova, and Lorenz Engell, 183–203. Leiden, The Netherlands: Brill | Fink, 2019. https://doi.org/10.30965/9783770561971_013.

Paasonen, Susanna. *Carnal Resonance: Affect and Online Pornography*. Cambridge, MA.: MIT Press, 2011.

Pająk, Patrycjusz. 'Early 21st-Century Serbian Exploitation Cinema'. *Images. The International Journal of European Film, Performing Arts and Audiovisual Communication* 23, no. 32 (December 2018). https://doi.org/10.14746/i.2018.32.07.

Palmer, Tim. *Brutal Intimacy: Analyzing Contemporary French Cinema*. Wesleyan Film. Middletown, CT: Wesleyan University Press, 2011.

———. *Irreversible*. Controversies. London; New York, NY: Palgrave Macmillan, 2015.

———. 'Rites of Passing: Conceptual Nihilism in Jean-Paul Civeyrac's "Des Filles En Noir"'. *Cinephile* 8, no. 2 (2002): 11–17.

———. 'Style and Sensation in the Contemporary French Cinema of the Body'. *Journal of Film and Video* 58, no. 3 (Autumn 2006): 22–32.

———. 'Under Your Skin: Marina de Van and the Contemporary French Cinéma Du Corps'. *Studies in French Cinema* 6, no. 3 (2007): 171–81. https://doi.org/10.1386/sfci.6.3.171_1.

Pape, Eric. 'So Scandalous a Prosecutor Took Notice'. *The New York Times*, 12 May 2011, sec. Movies. https://www.nytimes.com/2011/05/15/movies/in-spain-serbian-film-raises-questions-of-artistic-license.html.

Papenburg, Bettina, and Marta Zarzycka, eds. *Carnal Aesthetics: Transgressive Imagery and Feminist Politics*. International Library of Visual Culture 3. London: I. B. Tauris, 2013.

Paris, Barry. '"Irreversible" Gives New Meaning to Sick and Repulsive'. *Pittsburgh Post-Gazette*. 11 April 2003.

Paz, Mariano. 'Las leyes del deseo: sexualidad, anomia y nación en el cine de Carlos Reygadas'. *Bulletin of Spanish Studies* 92, no. 7 (August 2015): 1063–77. https://doi.org/10.1080/14753820.2015.1041326.

Perren, Alisa. 'Rethinking Distribution for the Future of Media Industry Studies'. *Cinema Journal* 52, no. 3 (2013): 165–71. https://doi.org/10.1353/CJ.2013.0017.

Peskoller, Helga. *Extrem*. Vienna: Böhlau, 2001.

Petkova, Savina. 'It's a (Wo)Man's World: Close-Up on Isabella Eklöf's "Holiday"'. *Mubi* (blog), 18 June 2019. https://mubi.com/notebook/posts/it-s-a-wo-man-s-world-close-up-on-isabella-eklof-s-holiday.

Petley, Julian. '*Cannibal Holocaust* and the Pornography of Death'. In *The Spectacle of the Real: From Hollywood to 'reality' TV and Beyond*, edited by Geoff King, 173–86. Bristol, UK; Portland, OR: Intellect, 2005.

———. *Film and Video Censorship in Contemporary Britain*. Edinburgh: Edinburgh University Press, 2011.

———. 'The Censor and the State in Britain'. In *Silencing Cinema: Film Censorship around the World*, edited by Daniël Biltereyst and Roel Vande Winkel, 149–65. Global Cinema Series. New York, NY: Palgrave Macmillan, 2013.

Petrenko, Dmitrii. 'Philippe Grandrieux's Transversal Cinema: Affect, Gesture, Touch'. *The Journal of V.N.Karazin Kharkiv National University. Series: Theory of Culture and*

Philosophy of Science, no. 61 (2020). https://doi.org/10.26565/2306-6687-2020-61-01.

Pett, Emma. 'A New Media Landscape? The BBFC, Extreme Cinema as Cult, and Technological Change'. *New Review of Film and Television Studies* 13, no. 1 (January 2015): 83–99. https://doi.org/10.1080/17400309.2014.982910.

———. 'Access All Areas? Anglo-American Film Censorship and Cult Cinema in the Digital Era'. In *The Routledge Companion to Cult Cinema*, edited by Jamie Sexton and Ernest Mathijs, 180–89. London; New York, NY: Routledge, Taylor & Francis Group, 2020.

Philippe, Fabien. 'La Vie Nouvelle de Philippe Grandrieux'. *Ciné-Bulles* 21, no. 4 (2003): 54–55.

Phillips, John. 'Catherine Breillat's *Romance*: Hard Core and the Female Gaze'. *Studies in French Cinema* 1, no. 3 (2001): 133–40. https://doi.org/10.1386/sfci.1.3.133.

Powrie, Phil. 'French Noir to Hyper-Noir'. In *European Film Noir*, edited by Andrew Spicer, 55–83. Manchester: Manchester University Press, 2007.

Prédal, René. *Le jeune cinéma français*. Paris: Armand Colin, 2005.

Press Association. 'Sadistic Japanese Movie Grotesque Denied Rating by Film Censors'. *The Guardian*, 19 August 2009, sec. Film. https://www.theguardian.com/film/2009/aug/19/japanese-film-grotesque-censors.

Projansky, Sarah. *Watching Rape: Film and Television in Postfeminist Culture*. New York: New York University Press, 2001.

Quandt, James. 'Flesh and Blood: Sex and Violence in Recent French Cinema'. *ArtForum*, February 2004.

Quinlivan, Davina. 'The French Female Butterfly Collector: Hadžihalilović, Denis, de Van and the *Cinéma Du Corps*'. *Studies in European Cinema* 10, no. 1 (March 2013): 35–44. https://doi.org/10.1386/seci.10.1.35_1.

Raatikainen, Panu. 'Gödel's Incompleteness Theorems'. In *The Stanford Encyclopedia of Philosophy*, edited by Edward N. Zalta, Spring 2022. Metaphysics Research Lab, Stanford University, 2022. https://plato.stanford.edu/archives/spr2022/entries/goedel-incompleteness/.

Rastegar, Roya. 'Seeing Differently: The Curatorial Potential of Film Festival Programming'. In *Film Festivals: History, Theory, Method, Practice*, edited by Marijke de Valck, Brendan Kredell, and Skadi Loist, 181–95. London; New York, NY: Routledge, 2016.

Rea, Michael. 'What Is Pornography?' *Noûs* 35, no. 1 (2001): 118–45.

Rehlin, Gunnar. 'A Hole in My Heart'. *Variety* (blog), 9 September 2004. https://variety.com/2004/film/markets-festivals/a-hole-in-my-heart-1200531223/.

Reichert, Jeff. 'Head Trip: Carlos Reygadas's "Battle in Heaven"'. *IndieWire* (blog), 13 February 2006. https://www.indiewire.com/2006/02/head-trip-carlos-reygadass-battle-in-heaven-77169/.

Reifenberger, Julia. 'Differenzen im Close-up: Pornografische Geschlechterkämpfe im narrativen Spielfilm'. In *Global Bodies: Mediale Repräsentationen des Körpers*, edited by Ivo Ritzer and Marcus Stiglegger, 145–59. Medien/Kultur 5. Berlin: Bertz + Fischer, 2012.

Renov, Michael, ed. *Theorizing Documentary*. AFI Film Readers. New York, NY: Routledge, 1993.

Resmini, Mauro. 'Reframing the New French Extremity: Cinema, Theory, Mediation'. *Camera Obscura: Feminism, Culture, and Media Studies* 30, no. 3 90 (2015): 161–87. https://doi.org/10.1215/02705346-3160685.

Reviews, B. S. 'Holiday (Sundance 2018) Movie Review: Vacation's All I Ever Wanted'. *Medium* (blog), 11 February 2018. https://medium.com/@BSReviews/holiday-sundance-2018-movie-review-vacations-all-i-ever-wanted-9f619b6f646e.
Richardson, Michael. *Georges Bataille*. London; New York, NY: Routledge, 1994.
Richardson, Niall. *Transgressive Bodies: Representations in Film and Popular Culture*. Oxford, UK: Routledge, 2016.
Riggs, Larry, and Paula Willoquet. 'Up Against the Looking Glass! Heterosexual Rape as Homosexual Epiphany in *The Accused*'. *Literature/Film Quarterly* 17, no. 4 (1989): 214–23.
Rodowick, David. *The Virtual Life of Film*. Cambridge, MA: Harvard University Press, 2007.
Roebuck, Sara. 'A Letter to the Man Who Tried to Rape Me'. In *Burn It down! Feminist Manifestos for the Revolution*, edited by Breanne Fahs, 353–62. London; New York: Verso, 2020.
Romney, Jonathan. 'Battle in Heaven (18)'. *The Independent*, 29 October 2005, sec. Culture. https://www.independent.co.uk/arts-entertainment/films/reviews/battle-in-heaven-18-322939.html.
———. 'Code of Silence'. *Sight and Sound*, no. June (2015): 42–43.
———. 'Le Sex and Violence'. *The Independent*, 10 October 2011. http://www.independent.co.uk/arts-entertainment/films/features/le-sex-and-violence-546083.html.
Rondeau, Corinne. '*Sombre*, la surface et la chair. A propos d'un film de Philippe Grandrieux'. In *Cinéma et inconscient*, edited by Murielle Gagnebin, 74–87. Seyssel: Champ Vallon, 2001.
Rosch, Eleanor. 'Cognitive Representations of Semantic Categories'. *Journal of Experimental Psychology: General* 104, no. 3 (1975): 192–233. https://doi.org/10.1037/0096-3445.104.3.192.
———. 'Natural Categories'. *Cognitive Psychology* 4, no. 3 (May 1973): 328–50. https://doi.org/10.1016/0010-0285(73)90017-0.
Rosenbaum, Jonathan. 'Problèmes d'accès: Sur les traces de quelque films et cinéastes «de festival»'. Translated by Jean-Luc Mengus. *Trafic* 30 (Summer 1999): 54–70.
Rouyer, Philippe. '"Irréversible": Bonheur Perdu'. *Positif*, August 2002, 497–98.
Ruimy, Jordan. '"Holiday" Is an Immensely Impressive Debut [Review]'. *World of Reel* (blog), 12 February 2019. https://www.worldofreel.com/blog/2019/2/holiday-is-an-immensely-impressive-debut-review.
Russell, Dominique. 'Introduction: Why Rape?' In *Rape in Art Cinema*, edited by Dominique Russell, 1–12. New York, NY: Continuum, 2010.
———, ed. *Rape in Art Cinema*. New York, NY: Continuum, 2010.
Sacco, Daniel. '"In a Brown Study": Vincent Gallo's Muddied Waters'. *New Review of Film and Television Studies* 15, no. 1 (January 2017): 81–94. https://doi.org/10.1080/17400309.2017.1265426.
Saporosi, Lucas. 'Corporeidad, distanciamientos y el concepto de praxis en la estética de Carlos Reygadas'. In *IX Jornadas de Sociología*. Universidad de Buenos Aires, 2011. https://cdsa.aacademica.org/000-034/466.
Sargeant, Jack. 'Filth and Sexual Excess: Some Brief Reflections on Popular Scatology'. *M/C Journal* 9, no. 5 (2006). http://www.journal.media-culture.org.au/0610/03-sargeant.php.

Saunders, Tristram Fane. 'Box-Office Gross: 10 Movies That Made Audiences Sick'. The Telegraph, 7 July 2016. http://www.telegraph.co.uk/films/2016/07/07/box-office-gross-movies-that-made-audiences-sick/.

Schatz, Thomas. *Hollywood Genres: Formulas, Filmmaking, and the Studio System*. New York, NY: Random House, 1981.

Schlesinger, Philip, R. Emerson Dobash, Russell Dobash, and C. Kay Weaver, eds. *Women Viewing Violence*. London: British Film Institute, 1992.

'Schlipphacke, Heidi. 'Fragmented Bodies: Masculinity and Nation in Contemporary German Cinema'. In *Mysterious Skin: Male Bodies in Contemporary Cinema*, edited by Santiago Fouz-Hernández, 27–41. London: Tauris, 2009.

Scholz, Sebastian, and Hanna Surma. 'Exceeding the Limits of Representation: Screen and / as Skin in Claire Denis's "Trouble Every Day" (2001)'. *Studies in French Cinema* 8, no. 1 (January 2008): 5–16. https://doi.org/10.1386/sfc.8.1.5_1.

Schoonover, Karl. *Brutal Vision: The Neorealist Body in Postwar Italian Cinema*. Minneapolis: University of Minnesota Press, 2012.

Schwartz, Vanessa. *It's so French!: Hollywood, Paris and the Making of Cosmopolitan Film Culture*. Chicago, IL; London, UK: University of Chicago Press, 2007.

Scott, Kathleen. 'Bearing Witness to the Unbearable: Ethics and the Phallic Gaze in *Irréversible*'. In *Sensational Pleasures in Cinema, Literature and Visual Culture: The Phallic Eye*, edited by Gilad Padva and Nurit Bukhyaits, 74–87. Basingstoke: Palgrave Macmillan, 2014.

Selfe, Melanie. '"Incredibly French"?: Nation as an Interpretive Context for Extreme Cinema'. In *Je t'aime . . . Moi Non plus: Franco-British Cinematic Relations*, edited by Lucy Mazdon and Catherine Wheatley, 153–67. New York: Berghahn Books, 2010.

Serisier, Tanya. 'Speaking out, and Beginning to Be Heard: Feminism, Survivor Narratives and Representations of Rape in the 1980s'. *Continuum* 32, no. 1 (January 2018): 52–61. https://doi.org/10.1080/10304312.2018.1404675.

Shaw, Claire. 'Myroslav Slaboshpytskiy: *The Tribe* (*Plemya*, 2014)'. *KinoKultura*, 2015. http://www.kinokultura.com/2015/48r-plemya-CS.shtml.

Shin, Chi-Yun. 'Art of Branding: Tartan "Asia Extreme" Films'. *Jump Cut: A Review of Contemporary Media* 50 (Spring 2008). https://www.ejumpcut.org/archive/jc50.2008/TartanDist/2.html.

Shoard, Catherine. 'A Serbian Film Becomes Most Censored Film in 16 Years'. *The Guardian*, 26 November 2010, sec. Film. https://www.theguardian.com/film/2010/nov/26/serbian-film-most-censored.

Silverman, Kaja. *The Threshold of the Visible World*. New York, NY: Routledge, 1996.

Silverman, Maxim. *Facing Postmodernity: Contemporary French Thought On Culture And Society*. London; New York, NY: Routledge, 1999.

Simmel, Georg. 'The Metaphysics of Death'. Translated by Ulrich Teucher and Thomas Kemple. *Theory, Culture and Society* 24, no. 7–8 (2007): 72–77.

Simonin, Damien. 'Problèmes de définition ou définitions du problème? La «pornographie» dans «l'affaire Baise-moi»'. *Genre, sexualité et société*, no. 14 (December 2015). https://doi.org/10.4000/gss.3672.

Smith, Clarissa. 'Breathing New Life into Old Fears: Extreme Pornography and the Wider Politics of Snuff'. In *Snuff: Real Death and Screen Media*, edited by Neil Jackson, Shaun Kimber, Johnny Walker, and Thomas Joseph Watson, 81–104. New York: Bloomsbury Academic, 2016.

Smith, Martin Ian. 'Researching Memories of *The Exorcist*: An Introduction to Grounded Audience Studies'. *Participations: Journal of Audience and Reception Studies* 16, no. 1 (May 2019): 844–64.
——. 'Revulsion and Derision: *Antichrist*, *The Human Centipede II* and the British Press'. *Film International* (blog), 13 January 2015. http://filmint.nu/revulsion-and-derision-antichrist-the-human-centipede-ii-and-the-british-press/.
——. 'Serb Your Enthusiasm: Anti-Fandom and *A Serbian Film*'. *Participations: Journal of Audience and Reception Studies* 15, no. 2 (December 2018): 115–34.
——. 'Shock Value: Audiences on the Censorship of *A Serbian Film*'. *Journal of British Cinema and Television* 16, no. 2 (April 2019): 191–212. https://doi.org/10.3366/jbctv.2019.0468.
Smith, Molly, and Juno Mac. *Revolting Prostitutes: The Fight for Sex Workers' Rights*. London; New York: Verso, 2018.
Smith, Neil. 'Claire Denis: Trouble Every Day'. bbc.co.uk, 28 October 2014. http://www.bbc.co.uk/films/2002/12/24/claire_denis_trouble_every_day_interview.shtml.
Smith, Paul Julian. 'Battle in Heaven'. *Sight and Sound*, November 2005.
Sobchack, Vivian. *Carnal Thoughts: Embodiment and Moving Image Culture*. London: University of California Press, 2004.
——. *The Address Of The Eye: A Phenomenology Of Film Experience*. Princeton, NJ: Princeton University Press, 1992.
Souza, Gustavo. 'O rosto e a voz como inscrições do sofrimento em dois *road movies*'. *Significação: Revista de Cultura Audiovisual* 43, no. 46 (December 2016): 69–84. https://doi.org/10.11606/issn.2316-7114.sig.2016.114479.
Spivak, Gayatri Chakravorty. 'Translator's Preface'. In *Of Grammatology*, by Jacques Derrida, ix–xc. translated by Gayatri Chakravorty Spivak. Baltimore: John Hopkins University Press, 1976.
Staiger, Janet. *Perverse Spectators: The Practices of Film Reception*. New York: New York University Press, 2000.
Stallybrass, Peter, and Allon White. *The Politics and Poetics of Transgression*. London: Methuen, 1986.
Stanners, David. 'New Life'. *Eye For Film* (blog), August 2003. https://www.eyeforfilm.co.uk/review/new-life-film-review-by-david-stanners.
Steele, Francesca. 'Observations: Still Lighting up the Screen'. *The Independent*, 13 September 2012, sec. Culture. https://www.independent.co.uk/arts-entertainment/films/news/observations-still-lighting-up-the-screen-8134917.html.
Stevenson, Jack. *Scandinavian Blue: The Erotic Cinema of Sweden and Denmark in the 1960s and 1970s*. Jefferson, NC: McFarland & Co, 2010.
Stiglegger, Marcus. 'Haptische Bilder: Das performative Körperkino von Philippe Grandrieux'. In *Global Bodies: Mediale Repräsentationen des Körpers*, edited by Ivo Ritzer and Marcus Stiglegger, 42–54. Berlin: Bertz + Fischer, 2012.
Suchsland, Rüdiger. 'Der Freie Wille'. *Artechock* (blog), 2006. https://www.artechock.de/film/text/kritik/f/frwill.htm.
Swales, John M. *Genre Analysis: English in Academic and Research Settings*. The Cambridge Applied Linguistics Series. Cambridge; New York, NY: Cambridge University Press, 1990.
Szurmuk, Mónica. 'Batalla En El Cielo'. *Nuevo Mundo Mundos Nuevos*, 24 January 2006. https://doi.org/10.4000/nuevomundo.1400.

Tagg, John. *Grounds of Dispute: Art History, Cultural Politics and the Discursive Field*. Basingstoke: Macmillan, 1992.

——. *The Burden of Representation: Essays on Photographies and Histories*. Basingstoke: Palgrave Macmillan, 1988.

——. *The Disciplinary Frame: Photographic Truths and the Capture of Meaning*. Minneapolis: University of Minnesota Press, 2009.

Tait, Sue. 'Pornographies of Violence? Internet Spectatorship on Body Horror'. *Critical Studies in Media Communication* 25, no. 1 (2008): 91–111. https://doi.org/10.1080/15295030701851148.

Tarr, Carrie. 'Director's Cuts: The Aesthetics of Self-Harming in Marina de Van's *Dans Ma Peau*'. Edited by Gill Rye and Carrie Tarr. *Nottingham French Studies* 45, no. 3 (Autumn 2006): 78–91.

——. 'Mutilating and Mutilated Bodies: Women's Takes on "Extreme" French Cinema'. In *Visions of Struggle in Women's Filmmaking in the Mediterranean*, edited by Flavia Laviosa, 1st ed., 63–80. New York, NY: Palgrave Macmillan, 2010.

Taylor, Alison. *Troubled Everyday: The Aesthetics of Violence and the Everyday in European Art Cinema*. Edinburgh: Edinburgh University Press, 2017.

Taylor, Kate. 'Infection, Postcolonialism and Somatechnics in Claire Denis's *Trouble Every Day* (2002)'. *Studies in French Cinema* 7, no. 1 (February 2007): 19–29. https://doi.org/10.1386/sfci.7.1.19_1.

Tesson, Charles. 'Souverain Poncif: *A Ma Sœur!* De Catherine Breillat'. *Cahiers Du Cinéma* 555 (March 2001): 81–82.

Thomas, William. 'A Hole In My Heart'. *Empire* (blog), 2004. https://www.empireonline.com/movies/hole-heart/review/.

Todorov, Tzvetan. *The Fantastic: A Structural Approach to a Literary Genre*. Cornell University Press, 1975.

——. 'The Origin of Genres'. In *Modern Genre Theory*, edited by David Duff, 193–209. Oxford: New York, NY: Routledge, 2014.

Tompkins, Cynthia. *Experimental Latin American Cinema: History and Aesthetics*. Austin, TX: University of Texas Press, 2013.

Tudor, Andrew. 'Genre'. In *Film Genre Reader IV*, edited by Barry Keith Grant, 3–11. Austin, Tex: University of Texas Press, 2012.

Tully, Michael. 'Free Will, The'. *Hammer to Nail* (blog), 7 July 2008. https://www.hammertonail.com/reviews/drama/the-free-will-film-review/.

Turan, Kenneth. 'Uneasy Bedfellows in Hard-Core "Romance"'. *Los Angeles Times*, 1 October 1999. https://www.latimes.com/archives/la-xpm-1999-oct-01-ca-17450-story.html.

Tweedie, James. *The Age of New Waves: Art Cinema and the Staging of Globalization*. New York: Oxford University Press, 2013.

Valens, Grégory. '*Irréversible*: Irresponsible'. *Positif*, August 2002, 497–98.

Vidan, Aida. 'Spaces of Ideology in South Slavic Films'. *Studies in Eastern European Cinema* 2, no. 2 (July 2011): 173–92. https://doi.org/10.1386/seec.2.2.173_1.

Vollhaber, Tomas. *Wem gehört die Gebärdensprache? Kulturwissenschaftliche Essays zu einer Sprache des Körpers*. Bielefeld: Transcript Verlag, 2021.

Walker, Alexander. 'No Real Bite'. *Evening Standard*, 10 April 2012, sec. Culture. https://www.standard.co.uk/culture/film/no-real-bite-7428363.html.

Walon, Sophie. 'Monstrous Embodiments of Post-Modern Capitalism and Corporatism in the Cinema of the "New French Extremity"'. In *Monstrous Reflections*, edited by Petra Rehling and Elsa Bouet, 39–49. Freeland: Inter-Disciplinary Press, 2014.

Walton, Saige. *Cinema's Baroque Flesh: Film, Phenomenology and the Art of Entanglement*. Amsterdam: Amsterdam University Press, 2016.

Wasson, Haidee. *Museum Movies: The Museum of Modern Art and the Birth of Art Cinema*. Berkeley: University of California Press, 2005.

Watkins, Raymond. 'Robert Bresson's Heirs: Bruno Dumont, Philippe Grandrieux, and French Cinema of Sensation'. *Quarterly Review of Film and Video* 33, no. 8 (November 2016): 761–76. https://doi.org/10.1080/10509208.2016.1191895.

Weir, Kenneth, and Stephen Dunne. 'The Connoisseurship of the Condemned: *A Serbian Film*, *The Human Centipede 2* and the Appreciation of the Abhorrent'. *Participations: Journal of Audience and Reception Studies* 11, no. 2 (November 2014): 78–99.

Welleck, René, and Austin Warren. *Theory of Literature*. New York, NY: Harcourt, Brace and Company, 1942.

West, Robin. 'Sex, Law and Consent'. *Georgetown Law Faculty Working Papers* 71 (2008). https://scholarship.law.georgetown.edu/fwps_papers/71.

Wheatley, Catherine. 'Contested Interactions: Watching Catherine Breillat's Scenes of Sexual Violence'. *Journal for Cultural Research* 14, no. 1 (January 2010): 27–41. https://doi.org/10.1080/14797580903363066.

———. 'Naked Women, Slaughtered Animals: Ulrich Seidl and the Limits of the Real'. In *The New Extremism in Cinema: From France to Europe*, edited by Tanya Horeck and Tina Kendall, 93–101. Edinburgh: Edinburgh University Press, 2011.

Wilinsky, Barbara. *Sure Seaters: The Emergence of Art House Cinema*. Minneapolis: University of Minnesota Press, 2001.

Williams, James S. 'His Life to Film: The Extreme Art of Jacques Nolot'. *Studies in French Cinema* 9, no. 2 (May 2009): 177–90. https://doi.org/10.1386/sfc.9.2.177_1.

Williams, Linda. 'Film Bodies: Gender, Genre, and Excess'. *Film Quarterly* 44, no. 4 (Summer 1991): 2–13.

———. *Hard Core: Power, Pleasure, and the 'Frenzy of the Visible'*. Expanded edition. Berkeley, CA: University of California Press, 1999.

———. 'Hard-Core Art Film: The Contemporary Realm of the Senses'. *Quaderns Portàtils*, no. 13 (2007): 1–20.

———. *Screening Sex*. Durham, NC: Duke University Press, 2008.

Wilson, Alexa. 'How Does the Use of Haptic Visuality in Gaspar Noe's Film *Irreversible* Affect the Film's Representation of Sexual Violence?' *TransArt: Alexa Wilson* (blog), 2012. http://www.transart.org/wilsona/files/2012/06/Research-Irreversible-essay.pdf.

Wilson, Emma. 'Catherine Breillat and Gustave Courbet's "The Origin of the World" ['L'Origine Du Monde'] (1866)'. In *Embodied Encounters: New Approaches to Psychoanalysis and Cinema*, edited by Agnieszka Piotrowska, 11–21. London; New York, NY: Routledge, 2015.

———. 'Deforming Femininity: Catherine Breillat's *Romance*'. In *France on Film: Reflections on Popular French Cinema*, edited by Lucy Mazdon, 145–57. London: Wallflower, 2001.

Wilson, Laura. *Spectatorship, Embodiment and Physicality in the Contemporary Mutilation Film*. Basingstoke; New York, NY: Palgrave Macmillan, 2015.

Wittgenstein, Ludwig. *Philosophical Investigations*. Translated by G. E. M. Anscombe. 3rd ed. Cambridge, MA: Blackwell, 1986.

Wong, Cindy Hing-Yuk. *Film Festivals: Culture, People, and Power on the Global Screen*. New Brunswick, NJ: Rutgers University Press, 2011.

Wood, Robin. 'Against and For *Irreversible*'. *Film International* (blog), April 2011. http://filmint.nu/?p=1475.

Woodend, Dorothy. 'Not Your Usual Sex Movie'. *The Tyee* (blog), 28 April 2006. https://thetyee.ca/Entertainment/2006/04/28/UsualSexMovie/.

Young, Alison. *The Scene of Violence: Cinema, Crime, Affect*. New York, NY: Routledge, 2009.

Young, Damon. '*Visage/Con*: Catherine Breillat and the Antinomies of Sex'. *Qui Parle* 24, no. 2 (2016): 45–74. https://doi.org/10.5250/quiparle.24.2.0045.

Zas Marcos, Mónica. '"La Tribu", denuncia y violencia en lenguaje de signos'. *El Diario*, 7 May 2016, sec. Cine. https://www.eldiario.es/cultura/cine/tribu-denuncia-mafia-sordera-lenguaje-sordomudos_1_4012830.html.

Žižek, Slavoj. *Looking Awry*. Cambridge, MA: October Books, 1997.

——. *The Plague of Fantasies*. London; New York, NY: Verso, 1997.

Zolkos, Magdalena. 'Violent Affects: Nature and the Feminine in Lars von Trier's *Antichrist*'. *Parrhesia* 13 (2011): 177–89.

Index

Note: This index is arranged in word-by-word order. The letter n following a page number indicates a note.

9 Songs, 20n, 38–9, 56n, 226, 227

Accused, The, 80, 84, 153, 160n, 160n, 162n
Altman, Rick, 201
ambiguities, 112, 149, 183
   of bodies, 37
   and conflict, 183
   and ethics, 148
   in female cannibal films, 181n
   and imagery, 99
   and morality, 156
   and outcomes, 174, 178
   political, 102, 136, 166, 180
   and rape, 118, 124, 127, 131, 135, 144
Anatomy of Hell
   close-ups in, 71, 72–3, 74, 77
   and duration, 78
   as pornography, 9, 56n
   reception of, 60
   and visibility, 64, 65, 68
Andrews, David, 214
Angel, Katherine, 128
Antichrist, 56n, 68, 93
Ardenne, Paul, 37, 38
art
   Bourdieu on, 232
   conventions of, 213
   definitions of, 188, 211–12
   erotic, 49, 52
   and film, 155–6, 211
   humanist interpretations of, 156, 157
   newness in, 213–15

   and pornography, 2, 9, 12, 95–6, 183, 200, 203
   and transgression, 30, 32–6, 38, 215–17
art cinema
   and film festivals, 219
   newness in, 214
   post-millennial, 13
   and the transgressive, 214–15
   see also transgressive art films
art world
   definitions, 20n, 210
   and newness, 213–14
   see also cinema art world
Artsploitation (distributors), 226, 227
audiences
   distributors and, 224
   divisions, 84, 112
   reaction to films, 1, 2, 4, 5, 6, 14, 22, 46–7, 48, 49–53, 84
   and value register, 136
   see also viewers
Audition, 227
Australia: censorship, 57n, 59, 85n
auteurism, 23, 27, 222, 230, 231

BBFC
   appeals committee, 44–5
   and *Baise-moi*, 67–8
   reports, 14, 43
   and visibility, 61
Baise-moi, 56n
   audience response to, 14, 22
   censorship of, 43, 44, 59, 62, 67–8, 230

Baise-moi (*cont.*)
  close-ups in, 71
  critics and, 59
  as extreme cinema, 22
  murder in, 67
  plot, 67
  reception of, 46, 59, 60
  and visibility, 64, 66–7, 68
Bakhtin, Mikhail, 25, 28, 29
Baqué, Dominique, 62
Barker, Martin et al., 5, 14–15, 70
  on *Baise-moi*, 67
  on *Irreversible*, 69, 82–3, 158–9
Basic Instinct, 39
Bataille, Georges
  and economics, 175
  and energy, 166–8
  on eroticism, 169, 171, 180
  on expenditure, 164
  and gender, 179–80
  and repression, 174
  on sovereignty, 164, 175–6
  and transgression, 8, 25, 28–9, 30, 31, 32, 37, 163, 164, 180, 241
Battle in Heaven, 91–100
  critics and, 95
  gender in, 96, 99
  haptic visuality in, 95
  murder in, 146
  production ethics of, 98–9
  racial issues in, 92, 97, 99
  reception of, 95–100
  sexual imagery in, 90–5, 96–8, 99
  social class in, 92, 99
  storyline, 91, 98
  symbolism in, 92
  transgressions in, 76
  value registers in, 68, 93, 94–5, 98
Baudelaire, Charles, 33
Baudry, Patrick, 37
Baumann, Shyon, 56n
Bazin, André, 81
Becker, Howard, 2, 25, 27, 28, 211, 215, 224
Berlin Film Festival, 221; *see also* European Film Market (EFM)

Best, Victoria, 185
Bétan, Julien, 11
Beugnet, Martine, 12, 69, 74, 106, 110, 185
Blackrock, 154
Blanchot, Maurice: *The Madness of the Day* [*La folie du jour*], 198–9
blasphemy, 41, 56n
Blue is the Warmest Colour, 56n
Blue Valentine, 39
Bordun, Tony, 12
Born in Flames, 39
boundaries, 8, 9, 12
  art and pornography, 196
  artistic, 35, 46
  distributors and, 225
  and duration, 84
  and genres, 183, 185, 187, 195, 202, 203
  sex workers and, 127–8
  transgression of, 25, 27, 28, 29, 35, 39, 51
  and visibility, 62
Bourdieu, Pierre, 2, 211–12, 232
Brand, Roy, 149–50, 155
Breillat, Catherine, 70, 74, 222, 230
Brenez, Nicole, 108, 110, 111
Brinkema, Eugenie, 83, 172, 173, 188–9
British Board of Film Censors *see* BBFC
Brown Bunny, The
  as an arthouse film, 120
  critics, 120
  duration, 118–19
  Ebert on, 230
  ethical perspective, 125, 132–3, 136
  female victim, 136
  haptic visuality, 120
  male dominance, 135
  male identity, 133
  politics of, 134–5
  as pornography, 117–18
  rape imagery, 117, 126, 127, 131, 135
  sex scene, 128, 186
  storyline, 117
  trauma, 116–17, 119, 131–2
  value register, 134, 136
Bunny Game, The, 43
Butler, Judith, 142, 144

Canada
  censorship, 59
  Fantasia Festival (Montreal), 223
Cannes Film Festival, 221, 222, 223, 229; see also Marché du Film (Cannes)
cannibalism, 4, 46, 68
  female cannibal films, 181n
  see also Raw; Trouble Every Day
Carey, Noah, 236n
carnival, 29–30
Caruth, Cathy, 129, 130–1
censorship, 2, 4, 39, 191, 232, 236n
  categories, 40–5, 53, 61
  and film festivals, 221
  of New Wave films, 217–18
  and reviews, 229, 230
  of speech, 61
  and visibility, 61, 64, 65, 70
Chamarette, Jenny, 75, 110, 111
child abuse
  censorship of, 41
  Foucault on, 127
  in Serbian Film, A, 209, 219
Choi, Euhna, 98
cinema art world, 208–34
  definitions, 211
  film distribution, 223–8
  film festivals and screenings, 219–23
  film scholarship, 228–33
  functions, 212–13
  newness, 214
  sex in, 217–18
cinema du corps, 12
cinema of sensation, 12, 185
close-ups, 4, 63, 65, 71, 73; see also proximity
Cox, Peter, 148
crime, 26
  blasphemy as, 56n
  images of, 41, 153
  and proof, 153
  witnesses of, 139, 140, 144
Criterion Collection (distributors), 225
critics, 34, 65–6, 218–19, 233
  and censorship, 46
  and consensus, 229, 230
  and ethics, 110
  and exaggeration, 40
  and film classification, 23, 231–2
  and film form, 112
  and proximity, 71
  and scholarship, 228
  and value registers, 49, 52
  and visibility, 61, 62
  see also reviewers
Crowley, Martin, 185

Dalby, Alexa, 148
Darwin, Charles, 26
Davis, Angela, 133–4
Deleuze, Gilles, 73
Denis, Claire, 230
Derrida, Jacques, 195–200
  on Blanchot's *The Madness of the Day*, 198–9
  deconstruction of concepts, 196
  on genre, 184, 197–200, 203
directors
  as artists, 27
  as auteurs, 222, 230, 231
  and distributors, 224
  and film festivals, 212, 220
  transgressions, 55n
distributors, 223–8
  and audiences, 224
  and boundaries, 225, 226
  as curators, 225
  and film festivals, 236n
  and film presentation, 227–8
Doane, Mary Ann, 73
Dodge, Alexa, 143
Douglas, Mary, 25, 26, 28
Downing, Lisa, 12
Durand, Alain-Philippe, 171
duration, 78–84, 240–1
  boundaries of, 84
  definition of, 4–5
  ethical and political consequences of, 78–9
  long takes, 83, 84
  processive, 81–2
  and rape scenes, 78, 160

duration (*cont.*)
   and realism, 78, 80, 81, 84
   and sex scenes, 78, 94–5, 105
   and slow cinema, 83
   unitary, 81–2
   witnesses and, 150
Durkheim, Emile, 25–6, 28

Eagleton, Terry, 30
East Asian cinema, 6, 227
Ebert, Roger, 230
Edelstein, David, 83
Elephant, 149–50, 156
Emmanuelle, 33
erotic: definition, 62
eroticism
   and art, 49, 52
   Bataille on, 169, 171
   and pornography, 76, 95–6, 189, 194–5
   power dynamics of, 111
   and ritual, 167
   and sexuality, 31, 91, 93–4, 95, 217, 225, 227
   and violence, 39, 41, 46, 52, 77, 83, 89, 101–2, 107, 109, 127, 144–5, 159, 168, 169, 171, 177–8, 179, 190, 191
   and witnesses, 157
ethics, 210–11
ambiguous, 148
   in *Battle in Heaven*, 98–9
   in *Brown Bunny, The*, 125
   derivation of, 152
   and discourse, 241–2
   in *Free Will*, 125
   in *New Life, A*, 100–2, 104–5, 106–7, 108–9
   sexual, 128
   and sexual imagery, 97
   and sexual violence, 84, 110
   and slow cinema, 83
   and witnesses, 149–51
   see also morality; value registers: ethical; visibility: ethico-political readings of
European Film Market (EFM), 222

Evers, Miles, 27, 28
extreme cinema, 36–7
   Asia Extreme, 227
   contexts, 186
   criteria, 186
   definition, 12
   distributors, 226, 227
   high art, 52
   non-art/low art, 8–9, 12, 36–7, 42, 45, 46
   responses to, 5–6, 50, 51
   studies, 14–15
extremism, 12, 37
'new extremism', 12–13
extremity, 11–13, 25
   and censorship, 42, 43, 44–5
   and duration, 81
   extremus/exter function, 37
   interpretations of, 6
   meaning of, 8–9
   'New French', 12, 76
   and pornography, 45

Fantasia Festival (Montreal), 223
Fantasporto Festival (Porto), 223
fantasy, 132
   film festivals, 223
   pornography, 64, 65, 188
   and reality, 134
   sexual, 118, 120, 131
   witnesses and, 143
Fat Girl, 68, 116
Felperin, Leslie, 83
feminism, 166
   black, 127
feminist film theory, 76–7
   in *Free Will*, 136
   on gender and femininity, 171
   and patriarchy, 173
   and pornography, 188
   reductive, 136
   second-wave, 123, 126, 128
film festivals, 219–23
   and aesthetics, 222
   and censorship, 233
   and risk, 221, 234

and taste, 220–1
see also Cannes Film Festival
film studies, 184, 232
films
   classification, 231–2
   conventions, 212–13
   form, 2, 3, 13, 100, 112, 136, 225, 228, 240
   politicisation, 230–1
   scholarship, 228–33; *see also* film studies
   style, 141
Finnegans Wake see James Joyce
Flockhart, Louise, 181n
Foucault, Michel
   on sexuality, 31, 126–7
   on transgression, 25, 30–1
France
Cannes Film Festival, 221, 222, 223, 229
   censorship, 59, 85n
   Marché du Film (Cannes), 222
   'New French Extremity', 76
   New Wave films, 217–18
   reviews, 228
   see also Cannes Film Festival
Freadman, Anne, 195, 200
Free Will, 120–5
   critiques, 124
   duration, 120–1, 128–9
   ethical perspective, 125, 136
   female victim, 136
   gender politics, 125
   haptic visuality, 125
   male identity, 133, 135
   proximity, 121
   rape scenes, 120, 122, 123–4, 125, 126, 127, 128–9, 135, 136
   sex scenes, 122–3
   trauma, 116–17, 128–9
   value register, 134, 136
   viewer as accomplice, 122, 124–5
   witnesses, 154–5
Freud, Sigmund, 129
Frey, Mattias, 5, 14–15, 50, 51, 95, 186–7, 236n
FrightFest, 223, 233

Fuchs, Cynthia, 132–3
Fuck: Sasha Grey, 192

Galilei, Galileo, 26
Gallo, Vincent, 134–5
Gavey, Nicola, 126
gender
   in *Battle in Heaven*, 96, 99
   and ethics, 242
   and masochism, 172
   in *In My Skin*, 164
   in *Raw*, 164, 165–6, 168–9, 170–2, 180
   see also feminism; masculinity; women
Genette, Gérard, 187
genres, 183–203
   boundaries, 12, 183, 185, 187, 195, 202, 203
   Derrida on, 184, 197–200, 203
   labels, 201
   and prototype theory, 200–1
   studies, 184
German Expressionist films, 165
Germany
Berlin Film Festival, 221
   censorship, 57n, 85n
   male identity, 133
   pornography, 38
   Serbian Film, A, 237n
Gogh, Vincent van, 33
Grandrieux, Philippe, 75, 100, 108
Graves, Leslie, 35, 214–16
Grønstad, Asbjørn, 12–13, 69, 83
Grotesque, 43, 191, 229
Groys, Boris, 34
Guardian, The (newspaper), 227, 229

Hainge, Greg, 108, 109–10, 111
Hall, Stuart, 47, 141
Haneke, Michael, 222
haptic visuality, 73–5, 240
   in *Battle in Heaven*, 95
   in *Brown Bunny, The*, 120
   in *Free Will*, 125
   in *New Life, A*, 101
   and optical visuality, 74–5
Hate Crime, 229

Hawkins, Joan, 110
Heinich, Nathalie, 6, 33, 47–8, 216–17
Herbert, Daniel, 225
Hester, Helen, 193
Hobbs, Simon, 12
Hole in my Heart, A
  allegory in, 193
  as art, 190
  critics and, 189, 191, 195
  as extreme cinema, 191
  genre labelling of, 198, 199, 201, 202–3
  as pornography, 189–95
  storyline, 189–90
  surgery scenes, 193
Holiday, 18, 52
  Critics, 147, 148, 153
  murder, 146
  rape scene, 146–8, 151–2, 156, 158, 159
  voyeurism, 158
  witnesses, 149, 155, 157
Horeck, Tanya, 12–13, 77
horror
  and maximalism, 38
  psychoanalytic horror theory, 172
horror films
  distribution, 227
  festivals, 223, 233
  newness, 214
  studies, 231
  see also Hostel; Saw; Serbian Film, A
Hostel, 43, 57n
Hostel: Part II, 57n
Hubner, Laura, 232
Human Centipede II, The, 43
humanism, 156–7

I Spit on your Grave, 62, 80
In My Skin, 172–9
  alienation, 173–4
  boundaries, 52
  censorship, 43
  gender roles, 164
  proximity, 172
  self-harm, 164, 171, 172, 173, 174, 175, 176–8, 180

  setting, 174
  sovereignty, 175, 176–7, 179
  storyline, 172, 174–5
  violence, 108
  visibility, 68
Ink is my Blood, 183, 225, 226
Into the Flesh, 183
Irreversible
  censorship, 44
  duration, 78, 79–80, 82–3
  explicitness, 59
  as extreme cinema, 22
  innovation, 34
  murder, 62, 83
  physical aggression, 43
  as pornography, 62
  proximity, 71, 75–6
  rape, 116, 139, 147–8, 156, 159
  reception, 14, 46, 60
  reviews, 228–9
  visibility, 64, 65, 68
  witnesses, 149, 154–5
Isle, The, 227

Jenks, Chris, 25, 33
Jerusalem Delivered, 146
Johnston, Michael, 132
Joyard, Olivier, 103, 110
Joyce, James, 187
Julius, Anthony, 34, 36

Karmitz, Marin, 230
Keeling, Stanley, 81–2
Kendall, Tina, 12–13, 164
Kerner, Aaron, 11
King, Rodney, 142
Kipnis, Laura, 34
Kiss, The, 33, 218
Knapp, Jonathan, 11
Koch, Angela, 124, 149, 155
Kojève, Alexandre, 25
Koons, Jeff, 52, 183
Kozol, Wendy, 152

Lahr-Vivaz, Elena, 96, 97
Larsson, Mariah, 193

Léger, Marc James, 134
Leys, Ruth, 129–30, 131
Libération (French newspaper), 230
Lübecker, Nikolaj, 98, 156, 175
Lust, Erika, 226
Luca, Tiago de, 97

Mac, Juno, 127–8
McMahon, Laura, 63–4
McNair, Brian, 183
magazines, 1, 228, 231
Mandel, Naomi, 171
Manhunter, 122
Marché du Film (Cannes), 222
Marks, Laura, 73, 74
Martin, Adrian, 107–8, 109, 111
Marzano, Michela, 62
masculinity
    and grief, 135
    and imagination, 77, 109, 125–6
    schizophrenic, 133
    and spectatorship, 70
    vulnerable, 134
Mauss, Marcel, 31
Mexico, 92, 97
Monster's Ball, 39
Moodysson, Lukas, 189, 191, 193
morality, 108, 156; *see also* ethics
Morocco, 157
Morsch, Thomas, 69, 75, 110
Mubi (distributors), 225–6
Mulvey, Laura, 76–7, 157
murder
    in *Baise-moi*, 67
    in *Battle in Heaven*, 146
    and boundaries, 42
    filming of, 41–2
    in *Holiday*, 146
    in *Irreversible*, 62, 83
    in *Jerusalem Delivered*, 146
    in *Raw*, 169, 170, 171
    in *Sombre*, 75
    in *Tribe, The*, 151
    in *Twentynine Palms*, 79
    visibility of, 62, 65, 67
Murder-Set-Pieces, 191, 229

music
    atonal, 187
    and crowd scenes, 107
    heavy metal, 65
    non-diegetic, 78
    and time, 82, 94, 177

Nanook of the North, 81
New Life, A, 100–12
    aesthetic qualities, 102, 107, 111
    critics, 100–1, 106–11
    ethics, 100–2, 104, 106–7, 108–9
    gender politics, 102
    haptic visuality, 101
    morality, 108
    rape scene, 116
    sexual violence, 101, 102–3, 104–5
    storyline, 101
    value registers, 101, 111–12
New Wave films, 217–18
New Zealand, 59, 190
Noé, Gaspar, 34, 80, 222
nudity
    in art, 52
    and eroticism, 52
    in film, 33, 217
    and illegality, 41
    and pornography, 44

obscenity
    laws of, 41
    literature and, 49
onlookers, 117; *see also* witnesses
optical visuality, 74–5
Ordóñez, Samanta, 96, 97, 99

Palmer, Tim, 12, 83
Parsons, Rehtaeh, 143
Parsons, Talcott, 53n
Peacock, Michael, 11, 12
Peskoller, Helga, 37
Pett, Emma, 44
photography, 140–2, 143
pornography
    amateur, 42, 83

pornography (*cont.*)
   and art, 9, 12, 51–2, 95–6, 183, 196, 200, 203
   arthouse films as, 74, 83, 95–6, 186–9
   and censorship, 42, 44–5, 61
   definitions of, 38–9, 62, 183–4, 193, 194–5
   and disgust, 193, 194, 195
   distributors and, 225–6
   and duration, 83
   and dystopias, 177
   and eroticism, 76, 95–6, 189, 194–5
   exhibiting of, 217–18
   'facial abuse porn', 192–3, 194
   fantasy, 64, 65, 188
   and feminism, 188
   and feminist films, 205n
   hardcore, 44, 61, 93
   horror, 65, 66
   and the law, 38–9
   literature and, 49
   and maximalism, 38
   politicisation of, 188
   and proximity, 77
   softcore, 44, 93, 190, 217
   studies of, 231
   and violence, 192
   and visibility, 38, 40, 61–2, 70
prototype theory, 200–1
proximity, 4–5, 40, 59, 71–8, 240
   definition, 4
   and female bodies, 76–7
   and pornography, 77
   and rape scenes, 77–8, 160
   and sexual imagery, 71, 74, 76, 93, 95, 98, 105
   viewers and, 71
   see also close-ups

Quandt, James, 12, 13, 76, 163

race
   in *Battle in Heaven*, 92, 97, 99
   and evidence, 142
   and rape, 127
Raindance Festival (London), 223, 229

rape
   and ambiguity, 118, 124, 127, 131, 135, 144
   definitions of, 139
   interpretation of, 143
   as metaphor, 133
   and race, 127
   reasons for, 133–4
   and sex compared, 123, 127–8
   and value registers, 136
   victims' experience of, 135
   as violence, 127
   witnesses to, 144–5, 150, 151–2, 153–5
rape culture, 124, 125, 135, 171
rape imagery
   audience reactions to, 84
   in *Brown Bunny, The*, 117, 126, 127, 131, 135
   contradictions of, 103
   critiques of, 109
   and duration, 80, 82–3, 105
   ethical tensions of, 140–1
   explicitness of, 33, 59
   in *Free Will*, 120, 122, 123–4, 125, 126, 127, 128–9, 135, 136
   interpretation of, 52, 143
   in *New Life*, 116
   and proximity, 77–8
   and trauma, 116, 119, 123, 124
   in *Tribe, The*, 145–6, 156, 159
   in *Twentynine Palms*, 116
   and value registers, 6–7
   viewing of, 135, 145–8, 159, 160
   witnesses to, 158
rape trials, 77, 136, 143–4
Raw
   cannibalism, 164, 165, 168–9, 171–2
   energy, 168, 170
   eroticism, 169, 171–2
   gender roles, 164, 165–6, 168–9, 170–2, 180
   murder, 169, 170, 171
   storyline, 164, 166
   violence, 165–6
Re-Penetrator, 65
realism, 78, 81, 84, 141

reviewers, 229, 230, 231–2; *see also* critics
reviews, 228–9
Reygadas, Carlos, 99
del Río, Elena, 11
Roebuck, Sara, 127
Romance, 22
  close-ups in, 71–2, 74, 77
  critics and, 89
  duration in, 78
  explicitness of, 59, 218
  extremeness of, 22
  as pornography, 9, 38–9, 56n
  and visibility, 64, 65, 68
Rosch, Eleanor, 200–1
Russell, Dominique, 109, 164

Sacco, Daniel, 134
Sala, Ángel, 236n
sales agents, 236n
Salut les Cubains, 225–6
de Saussure, Ferdinand, 200
Saw, 43
scandal films, 220, 222
Schlesinger, Philip et al., 83
Schlipphacke, Heidi, 133
Schönberg, Arnold, 187
Schoonover, Karl, 150
scopophilia, 157
self-harm *see In My Skin*
Serbian Film, A, 209–10
  as allegory, 230–1
  censorship of, 230, 233
  distribution of, 226
  festival showings, 222–3
  presentation of, 227–8
  reviews of, 229, 231
  transgressiveness of, 234
  and value registers, 58n
  and visibility, 68
sex
  and censorship, 41–2
  and explicitness, 33
  images of, 1, 2, 3–4, 39–40, 70, 90–4, 217–18; and proximity, 71, 74, 76, 93, 95; and visibility, 64, 95
  and pornography, 9, 38, 39, 61

  and rape, 123, 127–8
  see also violence: sexual
sex workers, 127–8
sexuality
  and eroticism, 31, 91, 93–4, 95, 217, 225, 227
  Foucault on, 31, 126–7
Simmel, Georg, 37
slow cinema, 83, 234
Smith, Clarissa, 58n
Smith, Molly, 127–8
social class
  in *Battle in Heaven*, 92, 99
  and behaviour, 27
  and education, 232
Sombre
  criticism of, 89, 100
  duration in, 78
  murder in, 75
  proximity in, 71, 75
  reception of, 59–60
sovereignty, 164, 175–6
  in *In My Skin*, 175, 176–7, 179
Spain
  censorship, 57n
Sitges Film Festival, 223, 236n
Spasojević, Srdjan, 228, 231, 237n
Spivak, Gayatri Chakravorty, 196–7
stereotypes
  and disability, 149
  and mental health, 180
Sternberg, Josef von, 76
Stiglegger, Marcus, 75, 110

taboos, 28–30, 35, 167, 169, 170
Tartan Films (distributors), 226, 227
Tasso, Torquato: *Jerusalem Delivered*, 129–30
Taylor, Alison, 12
torture films, 43, 57n
transgressions, 22–4
  artistic, 27, 28, 30, 32–4, 38, 53, 215–17; distinctions, 36; and newness, 33–4
  Bataille on, 8, 25, 28–9, 30, 31, 32, 37
  and boundaries, 25, 27, 28, 29, 35, 39, 46, 51

transgressions (*cont.*)
  and censorship, 39; categories, 40–5, 47
  contexts of, 28, 33
  Foucault on, 25, 30–1
  and genres, 195
  and identity, 27
  limited, 28–31
  and 'New French Extremity', 76
  and politics, 27, 28
  and pollution, 26
  and sex scenes, 76
  and taboos, 29, 30
and theory, 8–9, 241
  and visibility, 62–3, 65–6
transgressive art films, 234
  as art cinema, 215, 230, 233
  and consensus, 5
  defining, 1, 3, 11, 13, 208
  form of, 3–4
  future of, 216
  legitimisation of, 3, 10, 16, 112, 213, 219–21, 224, 230, 233
  non-art/low art, 6, 47, 53, 61, 62, 70, 85, 157, 191, 208–9, 213, 214, 215, 230
  reception of, 5–8
  role of, 10, 218
  stakeholders, 208
trauma
  in *Brown Bunny, The*, 116–17, 119, 131–2
  experience of, 129–31
  and rape imagery, 116, 119, 123, 124
Tribe, The, 18
  murder, 151
  rape sequence, 145–6, 156, 159
  sign language, 145, 149
  witnesses, 145, 149, 151, 154–5, 157
Trouble Every Day
  close-ups, 71, 77
  duration, 78
  as extreme cinema, 22
  reception, 60, 218
  visibility, 63–4, 66, 68
Twentynine Palms
  close-ups, 71, 77
  denouement, 118
  duration, 78, 79, 83
  murder, 79
  narrative strands, 98
  rape, 116
  reception, 60, 230
  visibility, 68

United Kingdom
  blasphemy, 56n
  censorship, 40–5, 191, 229, 236n; *see also* BBFC
  film reviews, 228, 229
  film studies, 232
  obscenity laws, 41
  pornography: definition, 38
  Raindance Festival, 223, 229
United States
  censorship, 42–3, 217–18
  East Asian cinema, 227
  film reviews, 227, 229
  South by South West Festival (SXSW), 222

Valck, Marijke de, 229
value registers, 47–50, 51–2, 89–90, 111–12, 144
  aesthetic, 6, 48–9, 49–50, 52, 90
  ethical, 6, 7–8, 48, 49–50, 52, 78, 96, 97, 101–2, 103–4, 107, 125, 134, 136, 155, 158–9
  and genres, 202
  hermeneutic, 48, 50, 52, 90, 96–7, 104, 107, 108, 110, 125, 134, 136, 155, 158
  sociology of values, 58n
  see also duration; proximity; visibility
Van, Marina de, 172, 173
Varda, Agnes, 225
Venice Film Festival, 221
viewers
  as accomplices, 122, 124–5
  and duration, 82
  experience of, 12–15
  and proximity, 71, 73–4
  and rape scenes, 135
  reception of films, 1, 5, 69, 186

and visibility, 66
as witnesses, 149, 152, 153, 154, 156, 157–60
see also audiences
violence, 163
  aesthetics of, 108
  audiences' reactions to, 5
  censorship of, 43
  and conformity, 171
  and disability, 149
  and eroticism, 41, 46, 52, 63–4, 77, 83, 89, 101–2, 107, 109, 127, 144–5, 159, 168, 169, 171, 177–8, 179, 190, 191
  evidence of, 142–3
  gendered, 43, 173
  images of, 1, 2, 3, 4, 39–40
  and proximity, 40, 71
  sexual, 51, 101; audiences, 14; censorship, 45, 62, 191; duration, 79; as empowerment, 109; ethics, 110, 155; and gender politics, 125–6; interpretation, 110; and proximity, 105; and value registers, 6–7; and visibility, 63–4, 65, 66–7, 102–3, 151
  witnesses, 143, 145, 151, 153
  women and, 43, 67, 173, 192, 193, 194
  see also self-harm
visibility, 4–5, 59, 60–71, 240
  and boundaries, 62
  and censorship, 61, 64, 70
  denigration of, 62
  ethico-political readings of, 68–70
  and 'new French extremity', 12
  and pornography, 38, 61–2
  and rape scenes, 160
  and sex scenes, 9, 64, 95, 102–3

and transgressions, 62–3, 65–6
viewers and, 66
visuality *see* haptic visuality; optical visuality
Vollhaber, Tomas, 149
Vortex, 222
voyeurism, 41, 77, 79, 82, 83, 147–8, 157, 158

Webster, Kevin, 41, 42
West, Mae, 33
When Animals Dream, 181n
witnesses, 140, 145, 149
  of crime, 139, 140, 144
  and duration, 150
  and eroticism, 157
  and ethics, 149–51
  and fantasy, 143
  of sexual violence, 143, 153
  of rape, 144–5, 150, 151–2, 153–5, 158
  as viewers, 152, 153, 154, 156, 157–60
  women as, 151
women
  and evidence, 142
  male domination of, 101
  and sexuality, 113n, 126
  and violence, 43, 67, 173, 192, 193, 194
  as witnesses, 151
  see also feminism; feminist film theory
Wong, Cindy Hing-Yuk, 221
Wood, Robin, 116

XConfessions (adult subscription cinema site), 225

Young, Alison, 153, 155

Žižek, Slavoj, 122

EU representative:
Easy Access System Europe
Mustamäe tee 50, 10621 Tallinn, Estonia
Gpsr.requests@easproject.com